COLLISION
OF POWER

COLLISION OF POWER

TRUMP, BEZOS,

and

THE WASHINGTON POST

MARTIN BARON

FLATIRON
BOOKS
NEW YORK

www.flatironbooks.com

Library of Congress Cataloging-in-Publication Data

Names: Baron, Martin, 1954– author.
Title: Collision of power : Trump, Bezos, and The Washington Post / Martin Baron.
Description: First edition. | New York : Flatiron Books, 2023. | Includes bibliographical references and index.
Identifiers: LCCN 2023006383 | ISBN 9781250844200 (hardcover) | ISBN 9781250844217 (ebook)
Subjects: LCSH: Baron, Martin, 1954– | Journalists—United States—Biography | Newspaper editors—United States—Biography. | Trump, Donald, 1946– —Press coverage. | Presidents—Press coverage—United States—History—21st century. | Washington Post (Washington, D.C. : 1974)—History. | United States—Politics and government—2017–2021.
Classification: LCC PN4874.R3265 A3 2023 | DDC 070.4/1092 [B]—dc23/eng/20230526
LC record available at https://lccn.loc.gov/2023006383

First Edition: 2023

10 9 8 7 6 5 4 3 2 1

In memory of my parents,
Howard and Rebecca Baron

CONTENTS

Contents

COLLISION
OF POWER

PROLOGUE

The White House, June 15, 2017

The dinner with President Trump was to be kept confidential. He wouldn't talk about it. We wouldn't either. Our reporting staff was to be kept in the dark, and to this day the meeting has never been reported. No one in the newsroom ever suggested to me they were aware of it. Reporters who had dug up many secrets about the Trump White House somehow missed this one.

The black SUV with tinted windows carrying Jeff Bezos, owner of *The Washington Post,* would be allowed onto the White House grounds at 6:50 p.m.—waved in through a wrought-iron vehicle entrance gate—so that he could enter without being observed. On that clear June evening in 2017, with temperatures in the low eighties, *The Post*'s publisher, Fred Ryan, its editorial page editor, Fred Hiatt, and I as the executive editor who oversaw news coverage would walk up to a gate at the northeast corner of the White House grounds, avoiding the Northwest Gate, where we would almost certainly be spotted by journalists entering and exiting.

This was not a dinner I was looking forward to. I had not met Trump, even though our reporters had spent many hours with him. Except for natural curiosity, I didn't feel a need to. I could assess him on what he said and did. And what good could come from spending time with him that evening? Surely he would see dinner as a favor and expect something in return. And surely he would conclude from our visit as a group that Bezos had a hand in news coverage.

Although Ryan had proposed the meeting to the White House, he sought to allay my concerns about how Trump would interpret it. He assured me that he had made one thing clear: The White House should not expect this get-together to influence coverage. And yet why else would the White House agree to have us over for dinner if Trump felt he had nothing to gain?

Ryan was taken with the idea of getting together face-to-face: Leadership of the dominant news organization in the nation's capital should meet with the new leader of the country. Ryan had even broached the idea of holding the meeting at his own home. Not likely. And sure enough the White House said no.

Trump would not be coming to us. We would go to him, five months into his position as the most powerful person on the planet. If word leaked out and there were press inquiries about the presence of *The Post*'s owner, Bezos suggested just saying he "was invited" rather than, as a prewritten statement worded it, that it was appropriate for him to attend.

We must have been an odd-looking group: Bezos, the impressively fit Amazon founder who was among the richest people in the world, recognizable anywhere for his bald head, short stature, booming laugh, and radiant intensity; Ryan, an alumnus of the Reagan administration who was a head taller than my own five feet eleven inches, with his graying blond hair and a giant glistening smile; Hiatt, a thirty-six-year *Post* veteran and former foreign correspondent with an earnest and bookish look; and me, still a relative newcomer to *The Post*, with a trimmed gray beard, woolly head of hair, and what was invariably described as my dour and taciturn demeanor.

We were politely welcomed by Trump, First Lady Melania Trump, and son-in-law Jared Kushner. Ivanka Trump had planned to be with us but instead attended the annual Congressional Baseball Game, where thousands prayed for Representative Steve Scalise of Louisiana, who had been shot and severely injured the previous day during a practice game in Alexandria, Virginia. The shooter was a Trump hater.

Although Trump had visited MedStar Washington Hospital Center, where Scalise was in critical condition, he appeared at the game only on a big screen. "By playing tonight," he declared, "you are showing the world that we will not be intimidated by threats, acts of violence, or assaults on our democracy. The game will go on . . . I know you all will be playing extra hard tonight for Steve."

Ivanka's place setting was removed from the table in the Blue Room—an egg-shaped reception room with blue and gold accents and a lavish chandelier—suggesting a last-minute decision on her part to attend the game (where media took particular note of her more formal wear). I wondered why Trump himself had opted to be with us rather than at the game. A strong supporter of his was in the hospital receiving blood transfusions and undergoing surgeries. A bullet had entered Scalise's hip, the hospital reported, traveling "across his pelvis, fracturing bones, injuring internal organs, and causing severe bleeding." His survival was in doubt. The baseball game provided a rare opportunity for bipartisanship. The president could have seized on the moment.

Trump's press secretary at the time, Sean Spicer, later cited security reasons for Trump's absence from the game. Maybe so, but the president's image could not have been enhanced if, at such a fraught moment, the public knew he chose to spend his time with the very sorts of media people whom he called the "lowest form of life." Away from the memorial, Trump would pass the evening with us—crowing about his election victory, mocking his rivals and even some in his own orbit, boasting already of imagined accomplishments, calculating how he could win yet again in four years, and describing *The Washington Post* as the worst of all media outlets. As we dined on cheese soufflé, pan-roasted Dover sole, and chocolate cream tart, he went on to disparage other media outlets—*The New*

York Times came in just behind us in his ranking at the time—whose journalists he had labeled for months as scum and garbage.

As our visit commenced, at seven p.m. *The Post* published a report that was likely to secure our No. 1 spot for a while: Special Counsel Robert S. Mueller III was inquiring into Kushner's business dealings in Russia, part of his investigation into that country's interference in the 2016 election. The story landed on top of a previous one by *The Post* that revealed Kushner had met secretly with Russian ambassador Sergey Kislyak and had proposed that a Russian diplomatic post be used to provide a secure communications line between Trump officials and the Kremlin. *The Post* had reported as well that Kushner met later with Sergey Gorkov, head of a Russian-owned development bank.

Jamie Gorelick, one of Kushner's lawyers who was also a director of Amazon, had previously called me to push back against the idea that her client was the "focus" or "subject" of an investigation. Kushner, for his part, was bristling at the attention, both from investigators and the press. He had called and emailed my boss, Ryan, fretting over what headlines might say and labeling as "jackasses" the national security reporters who were digging into his Russia contacts. He followed up with a series of agitated emails, even copying in Bezos ("Looping in Jamie who can vouch on this with Jeff since she knows him well," read one), while declining to speak directly to the reporters involved and steadfastly avoiding communication directly with me. In a meeting later that week with White House correspondents Philip Rucker and Ashley Parker as well as national editor Steven Ginsberg, he had pounded a table in fury, wailing about the good life he and Ivanka had left behind in New York and the potential injury to his reputation. As *The Post*'s journalists made their exit, Kushner patted Steven on the back, declaring, "Well, that was therapeutic."

Also annoyed was Trump, who at our White House dinner derided what he had been hearing about our story on the special counsel and his son-in-law, suggesting incorrectly that it alleged money laundering. "He's a good kid," he said of Kushner, who at the time was thirty-six and a father of three.

As we were about to take our seats, twenty-eight-year-old Trump aide Hope Hicks handed Kushner her phone. Our alert had just gone out, reaching millions of mobile devices, no doubt including hers. "Very Shakespearean," she whispered to Kushner. "Dining with your enemies."

Hiatt whispered back, "We're not your enemies."

But Trump, his family, and his team had affixed us on their enemies list, and nothing was going to change anyone's mind. We had been neither servile nor sycophantic toward Trump, and we weren't going to be. Our job was to report aggressively on the president and to hold his administration, like all others, to account. In the mind of the president and those in his orbit, that most fundamental journalistic obligation made us the opposition.

There was political benefit to Trump in going further. We would not just be his enemy. We would be the country's enemy; in his telling, we would be traitors. Less than a month into his presidency, Trump had denounced the press as "the enemy of the American People" on Twitter. It was an ominous echo of the phrase invoked by Joseph Stalin, Mao Zedong, and Hitler's propagandist Joseph Goebbels and deployed for the purpose of repression and murder.

Trump could not have cared less about the history of such incendiary language or how it might incite physical attacks on journalists.

And it was clear from that moment, if it had not been earlier, that he saw all of us at that table as his foes—not just me as the one who directed news reporting, not just Fred Hiatt as the one who separately oversaw editorials, but also Fred Ryan, who was our superior as publisher, and Jeff Bezos. Perhaps most especially Bezos because he owned *The Post* and, in Trump's mind, was pulling the strings—or could pull them if he wished.

At our dinner, though, Trump sought to be charming. It was a superficial charm, entirely without warmth or authenticity. He did almost all the talking. We scarcely said a word, and I said the least out of discomfort at being there and seeking to avoid any direct confrontation with him over coverage in front of Bezos and Ryan. Anything I said could set him off. Since I didn't see any good that could come out of the meeting, perhaps at least I could avoid the bad. Why risk fireworks between us?

We had agreed to keep this meeting off the record. And yet Trump has by now said publicly largely everything he said then in private. What's more, we were exploiting an administration policy *The Post* itself had editorially condemned: Trump's refusal to follow President Obama's practice of releasing voluminous records on who visited the White House.

In an April 2017 editorial titled "The Secret Presidency," *The Post* declared that "Trump's decision to claw the White House logs back into the shadows follows several other moves that show contempt for the public." We were now party to one of those secrets. Trump's public statements since render moot the confidentiality accorded his comments. And to continue maintaining the secrecy of the meeting itself would be an act of persistent hypocrisy.

With the passing of years, nothing said at the meeting will still shock. Trump's rhetoric became only more inflammatory. His self-aggrandizement became only more routine. His belittlement of senior members of his administration became a signature of his presidency.

At the dinner, he let loose on a long list of perceived enemies and slights: The chief executive of Macy's was a "coward" for pulling Trump products from store shelves in reaction to Trump's remarks portraying Mexican immigrants as rapists; he would have been picketed by only "20 Mexicans. Who cares?" He had better relations with foreign leaders than Obama, who was lazy and never called them. Obama left disasters around the world for him to solve. Obama was hesitant to allow the military to kill people in Afghanistan; he told the military to just do it, don't ask for permission. Egypt needed a rough guy like President Abdel Fattah el-Sisi; otherwise, the country would be a disaster. And, foreshadowing Trump's remarks revealed in a book by Barak Ravid released almost a year after he departed the White House, the president said he was surprised to find that the Palestinians want a peace deal more than the Israelis. Fresh from visiting several weeks earlier with Palestinian Authority president Mahmoud Abbas in Bethlehem and Israeli prime minister Benjamin Netanyahu in Jerusalem, Trump took note of the billions of dollars in aid the United States provided Israel and acknowledged asking early on whether it couldn't be leveraged to pressure Israel to make peace. "I was told 'there's no connection,'" he said. He was incredulous. "No connection?"

Attorney General Jeff Sessions, fired FBI director James Comey, former deputy attorney general Andrew McCabe, and special counsel Robert Mueller were slammed for reasons that are now familiar. Defense Secretary Jim Mattis was "the best." (He'd later call him "the most overrated general.") Trump went on at length about how devastating nuclear weapons could be, how the entire South would be demolished if Miami were hit, how Amazon would be turned to "shit" if Seattle were targeted. By his accounting, Russia's nuclear weapons were all new and worked well—"not like ours, but we're going to fix that." And there was no real harm in being friends with Vladimir Putin, the Russian president. No one really knew for sure, he said, whether Russia was behind the election interference in 2016.

He promised to soon deliver a better health-care plan, a big tax cut, and a major infrastructure plan. (One of three turned out to be true.)

As Trump meandered from one subject to the next, Jared sat straight, impassive, and almost entirely uncommunicative. (So, we had that in common.) Melania was the same, only briefly interjecting to offer a thought about the investigation into Russian interference in the election: "There is no proof it was Russia."

Two themes stayed with me from that dinner. First, Trump would govern primarily to retain the support of his base. He pulled a sheet of paper from his jacket pocket. The statistic "47%" appeared above his photo. "This is the latest Rasmussen poll. I can win with that." The message was clear. That level of support, if he held key states, was all he needed to secure a second term. What other voters thought of him, he seemed to say, would not matter.

Second, his list of grievances appeared limitless. Atop them all was the press, and atop the press was *The Post*. We were awful, he said repeatedly. We treated him unfairly. And with every such utterance, he would poke me in the shoulder with his left elbow.

The physical jabs were annoying but harmless. Yet they were a hint of hard punches to come. Trump would move to disrupt and damage Amazon. Four days after Christmas that year, he called for the Postal Service to charge Amazon "MUCH MORE" for package deliveries, claiming Amazon's rates were a rip-off of American taxpayers. He later intervened to obstruct Amazon in its pursuit of a $10 billion cloud computing contract from the Defense Department. Bezos was to be punished for not reining in *The Post*.

This book will recount the years of my editorship of *The Washington Post*, a news organization that has performed a singular role in American history as it demanded truth, honesty, transparency, and accountability from powerful individuals, particularly those entrusted to govern the country. Over the decades, it faced vilification and retribution for doing work that was central to its mission. That was true as well in my eight-plus years as its top editor, with an unremittingly weighty responsibility for all of its news coverage. I joined *The Post* at a moment of crisis, when its commercial viability was in doubt and its capacity to measure up to its journalistic heritage imperiled. In short order, I would be swept into a unique confluence of events: the takeover of *The Post* by Jeff Bezos, a technology titan who had radically changed the way Americans shop and would soon set the paper on a course of transformation, restoration, and growth; and the assumption of the presidency by Donald Trump, who would upend the political system and govern with a mix of populism, nativism, and fantastical thinking that defied verifiable facts.

Taking shape was a collision of power: The occupant of the White House, the world's most powerful person, aiming to bring *The Post* to submission through ceaseless public attacks on our journalists and unrelenting pressure on our organization's owner; *The Post*'s owner, with ample power of his own as one of the world's richest humans, seeking to avoid open confrontation with Trump but unwilling to succumb to his censure and coercion; and *The Washington Post*, famous for its role in felling a prior president, aggressively revealing the administration's unsavory secrets, persistent lies, flagrant constitutional sabotage, and pattern of incitement.

My personal experience will be a part of the story. I led a storied newsroom in its journalism and in its arduous journey toward a sustainable business model when newspapers were on a seeming death march. But this is not strictly my memoir. I was a participant in these events but also a witness and an observer during tumultuous years when politics, technology, and media would meet head-on in a critical, historic test of strength and will. The story of that collision continues to unfold, with enduring consequences for a free press, democracy, and the future of the country.

With no delay and without pause during his four years as president, Trump and his team would go after *The Post* and everyone else in the media who didn't bend to his wishes. In December 2019, Kushner would lean on Ryan to withdraw support for me and our Russia investigation. Kushner suggested *The Post* issue an apology and there be a "reckoning of some sort"—as he advised that he himself had made a huge mistake in once standing by a former editor of *The New York Observer* and one of its stories when he owned the publication. "Standing by my editor at that time was my biggest regret in the 10 years I owned the newspaper," he wrote in the email to Ryan. Kushner's intent was clear to me. "He aims to get me fired," I told Ryan.

Trump tweeted against *Post* reporters Ashley Parker and Philip Rucker by name, calling them "nasty lightweight reporters" who "shouldn't be allowed on the grounds of the White House because their reporting is so DISGUSTING & FAKE," subjecting them to even more harassment and threats. Trump had tweeted incessantly to vilify *The Post* and the press overall, and even to dehumanize us. And he piled on by saying "the Fake Washington Post" should register as a "lobbyist" for Amazon.

Over many decades as a journalist and as the top editor of three news organizations, I had never witnessed such a raw abuse of power. The mainstream press had always seen its role as keeping watch on those who had the means, motive, and might to profoundly influence the lives of ordinary people, above all politicians and policymakers. When the First Amendment was crafted, that's what the founders of this country had in mind. If Trump even understood that elemental idea of American democracy, he gave it no weight. His objective was to bring us to heel.

A few times during that dinner, Trump—for all the shots he had taken during the campaign at Bezos's company—would mention that Melania was a big Amazon shopper, prompting Bezos to joke at one point: "Consider me your personal customer service rep." Trump's concern, of course, wasn't Amazon's delivery. He wanted Bezos to deliver him from *The Post*'s coverage.

The effort began gently and politely but the pace quickened the next day. Kushner called Ryan in the morning to get his read on how the dinner went. After Fred offered thanks for the generosity and graciousness with their time, Kushner inquired whether *The Post*'s coverage would now improve as a result. Fred diplomatically rebuffed him with a reminder that there were to be no expectations about coverage. "It's not a dial we have to turn one way to make it better and another way to make it worse," he said.

Trump would be the one to call Bezos's mobile phone that same morning at eight a.m., urging him to get *The Post* to be "more fair to me."

"I don't know if you get involved in the newsroom, but I'm sure you do to some degree," Trump said. Bezos said he didn't and then delivered some lines he was prepared to make at the dinner itself if Trump had leaned on him then: "It's really not appropriate to . . . I'd feel really bad about it my whole life if I did."

The call ended without bullying about Amazon but with an invitation for Bezos to seek a favor. "If there's anything I can do for you," Trump said.

Three days later, the bullying began. Giants of the technology sector gathered at the White House for a meeting of the American Technology Council, created by a Trump executive order a month earlier. Trump briefly pulled Bezos aside to complain bitterly about *The Post*'s coverage. The dinner, he said, was apparently a wasted two and a half hours.

In truth, it was. The White House get-together and its aftermath, however, also offered some welcome reassurance. We had an owner who would neither be courted nor clobbered into submission by President Donald Trump. We would need that. And we would need him for another mission as well: to save *The Post* from fiscal failure and its inevitable end result, journalistic irrelevance.

1

"TAKE THE GIFT"

Washington, D.C., was deep into its swampy summer weather when the publisher of *The Washington Post* asked if I could make myself available for drinks. She proposed five p.m. at Loews Madison Hotel, diagonally across 15th Street NW from our drab but imposing headquarters, a landmark that acquired a certain glamour after the Academy Award–winning movie *All the President's Men* celebrated the newspaper's Watergate investigation that brought an end to the presidency of Richard M. Nixon.

Late afternoon is no time to be ducking out of a newsroom, with stories piling up on deadline. Reading journalism, not sipping cocktails, was how I was supposed to be spending my time. But when the boss calls, you go. And the timing of the invitation suggested a surprise might be in the works. As a veteran of endless upheaval in my profession, I had learned to sense when to expect the unexpected.

Katharine Weymouth was the fifth member of the Graham newspaper family to hold the title of *Washington Post* publisher. When named to the position in 2008, she followed in the path of the widely revered family patriarch Don Graham, her uncle and CEO of *The Post's* parent company, who was now also her boss; her grandmother Katharine Graham, famed for her role in overseeing the paper through Watergate and the Pentagon Papers; her grandfather Phil Graham, who helped persuade Democratic presidential nominee

John F. Kennedy to select Lyndon B. Johnson as his running mate in 1960; and her great-grandfather Eugene Meyer, who bought *The Post* at a bankruptcy sale in 1933.

Smart and tough with a cutting wit, Katharine was as direct a person as I knew. Though she had grown up in a life of privilege in Manhattan's Upper East Side, she was devoid of pretense and bullshit. A graduate of Harvard College who got her law degree at Stanford, she worked as a litigator at a top-tier Washington firm before joining the newspaper her family controlled, first as a lawyer and later as the head of advertising. Katharine would be a different sort of publisher. She was divorced and a single mom, managing a household of three kids, and she was now preoccupied with a daughter who had fallen while horseback riding and undergone more than a dozen surgeries to her left arm. Even so, she welcomed casual get-togethers at her unpretentious home in the Chevy Chase neighborhood of Washington.

I had been at *The Post* for only seven months, but our relationship was easing into a comfortable groove. To my surprise, she trusted me implicitly from the start, almost to an unsettling degree. The day I began in the newsroom, she was on vacation, anticipating that I could make my debut in *The Post*'s culture entirely on my own. Helping to shore up my relationship with the news staff, she cut me slack on first-year budget constraints. When I appeared exhausted months into the job, she insisted I take time off for my physical and mental well-being. Our meetings were conversational and crisp, without a list of agenda items. We both preferred plain talk, informality, and brevity.

On July 30, 2013, Katharine got straight to business: *The Washington Post* was going to be sold. The buyer would be Jeff Bezos, the megabillionaire founder of Amazon. It would be announced after the weekend, on Monday.

The Graham family had held dominion over *The Post* for eighty years, and in two months they would relinquish control. One hundred percent of a famed news organization would be entirely in the hands of one of the planet's richest people. The buyer's home was 2,300 miles away, near Seattle. And, of particular interest to hired hands like me, the internet shopping behemoth he ran was fast acquiring notoriety for high-pressure working conditions.

There was another reason for me to be wary. Amazon also sold cloud computing services to the U.S. government, most notably the CIA. That happened to be one of many intelligence agencies that were livid over *The Post*'s publication less than two months earlier of the government's most highly classified documents, leaked by Edward Snowden, that revealed unprecedented surveillance of individuals' digital communications. *The Post* had assumed giant risks in publishing those documents. There was no shortage of officials who felt we had aided and abetted treason. What would become of such stories with Bezos in charge?

Katharine explained the sale plainly: *The Post* was in a bind. It couldn't find its way out. Revenues would continue to slide as print advertising vanished in the internet era, online ad rates would wilt, and getting people to pay for digital subscriptions was more something to pray for than something to count on. Costs would continue to be cut. Our news coverage, continuing to atrophy, would become unrecognizable to anyone with memories of *The Post*'s proud record of ambitious journalism. We were in the same fix as every other American newspaper except *The New York Times* and *The Wall Street Journal*. The company had run dry of ideas for salvaging itself. CEO Don Graham had looked for someone who might figure things out, and Bezos had the very qualities we might need: brains, tech savvy, and money.

Katharine was struggling to keep *The Post* profitable. Don had decreed she must, even as he pressed her to spare the newsroom from major budget cuts. At the same time, she had to find new revenue from digital advertising, which sold for pennies. "I often felt like the miller girl in Rumpelstiltskin," she later told Bezos in a memo summarizing our financial condition, "being asked to spin gold out of straw—the straw being our digital business—only I could not find the little man to magically do it for me."

I had a good feel for what she was going through. I arrived at *The Post* that January from *The Boston Globe*, where I had been the top editor for more than eleven years. Near-death financial losses were still fresh in mind. Over time I had to slash the number of *Globe* journalists by 40 percent. Bureaus in Berlin, Bogotá, and Jerusalem were closed, ending a proud legacy of foreign coverage since the 1970s. Losses by 2009, in the midst of the Great Recession, were so catastrophic that *The Globe*'s owner, the New York Times Company, threatened to shut the paper down unless thirteen unions immediately agreed to massive sacrifices in compensation.

When the unions ultimately yielded after bitter protests, the Times Company seized the moment by putting a "For Sale" sign on *The Globe*. Months later, apparently dissatisfied with the bids, it took *The Globe* off the market. Within two years, word was out that the Times Company was again earnestly shopping *The Globe* to the monied class of Boston and anyone else who might be interested. The controlling family of the New York Times Company saw *The Globe* as a dead weight on *The Times*' grander ambitions. No doubt it was.

The Times Company addressed rumors of a sale in its customary rote, nonresponsive manner: It could "neither confirm nor deny" them. But intentions were unmistakable when Vice Chairman Michael Golden told me in a private lunch that the "flesh, blood, and bone" of the New York Times Company was *The New York Times* itself. It stung to hear it stated so bluntly, and yet Golden was telling me what I already knew. The paper once so coveted by the Times Company that it shelled out $1.1 billion to purchase it in 1993 was now a burden best rid of, if even for a pittance.

Prospective buyers were no mystery. One possibility was a private equity firm that was likely to slice staffing by a third or more. A previous bidder had already confided its view that investing in quality journalism was a fool's errand. Another possibility was a local power broker, putting our journalistic independence at risk. The top editor was often the first casualty of a sale. Time to leave, I figured.

I was already one of two finalists for a job outside daily journalism when Katharine called in late 2012 to inquire whether I might be interested in leading *The Post*. Relations with her editor of four years, Marcus Brauchli, the former top editor of *The Wall Street Journal*, had suffered from budget pressures and a breakdown of communication and trust, rupturing in part over disclosure of *Post* plans to allow lobbyists and association executives to pay large sums to attend off-the-record "salons" with Obama administration officials, members of Congress, and the paper's journalists at Katharine's Washington home. That was a perceived breach of ethics guardrails for journalists.

Katharine's overture intrigued me. Perhaps the homestretch of my career could be at *The Post*, in a newsroom that occupied an exalted position in American journalistic history. While *The Globe* could never have been the heart and soul of an outfit named the New York Times Company, I felt confident that *The Washington Post* held that treasured position in an enterprise called the Washington Post Company. No matter how rocky the future, I couldn't imagine *The Post* being sold. Not by the Graham family. There were few certainties in journalism any longer, but that had to be one of them. *The Post* and the Grahams were ostensibly inseparable. Don loved *The Post*, spending almost his entire adult life there after a brief stint as a Washington policeman—he could identify just about everyone by name—and the people at *The Post* loved him back.

Now, seven months after I was hired as *The Post*'s executive editor, Don was selling it out from under me. Katharine swore me to secrecy and instructed me to call Don later that evening. He wanted to talk. After dinner at the Blue Duck Tavern in Washington, D.C.'s

West End neighborhood with Sally Quinn, wife of legendary *Post* editor Ben Bradlee—where I offered no hint of the momentous events about to unfold—I called Don. It was getting late, about nine p.m., but he invited me to swing by his brick Dupont Circle town house.

Don was gracious, as always, promptly apologizing for selling *The Post* just as I had started there. He volunteered that he had been shopping *The Post* even before my arrival. "That's okay, I understand," I told Don, assuring him that I wasn't naive about the way business works. Don twice repeated his apology, I repeated my answer. An exasperated Don said, "Would you let me apologize?"

In truth, I wasn't upset. I had my worries, not least for my own career, but I took the sale as a sign of hope. It was the only one I knew of. As much as I admired Don and what he and his family had accomplished in building *The Post* into one of America's most distinguished and fearless newspapers, no one had a plan other than managing decline. Sale of *The Post* was a reckoning with the facts. I found that refreshing and overdue. It was only after my retirement that I reconstructed how the Graham family came to part ways with *The Post*, asking its top executives to recollect conversations and key details that had yet to be published.

When Katharine was named publisher in 2008 in the midst of a punishing recession, Don had told her at a board meeting, "Kath, I'm counting on you to save the newspaper." But by July 2012, her assessment of *The Post*'s prospects over the long term was grim. Katharine's own president, Stephen Hills, had emphasized to her a year earlier in a memo that a sale should be considered for a wide variety of reasons: Business trends were becoming only more disturbing, internal differences over strategy were great, and the parent company's stock would be pummeled if it made further big investments in *The Post*. At a meeting in Fort Lauderdale of the company's

Kaplan Education unit, she stressed to Don how keeping *The Post* profitable was at odds with his desire to maintain a newsroom of robust resources and a paper he could be proud of.

"You would tell me if you thought we should sell it," Don occasionally remarked to Katharine. It was a line she had long dismissed as fanciful. It was unthinkable that he would sell the paper that was the object of his passion. But the unthinkable was quickly becoming top of mind.

By the summer, Katharine could see only limited options for *The Post* in the years ahead: Make drastic cuts in its newsroom that might ensure profitability over the long run but severely damage coverage and the paper's reputation. Or make gradual cuts year after year, hoping that new business ventures would bring in more money than they had so far. Or sell *The Post*, striving to find an owner who believed in the paper's mission, had deep pockets and possibly better ideas.

With Don's permission, she conferred in June with Warren Buffett, the famed investor who was his close and constant adviser, in a private room in Washington, D.C.'s Jefferson Hotel. "Am I missing some thing? Is there something else?" she asked. Her analysis struck Buffett as spot-on, but he added: "Your uncle will never sell." So he advised her to concentrate on the two distasteful options that remained.

In October 2012, Katharine and Don met for lunch at the Bombay Club, a high-end Indian restaurant less than two blocks from the White House. Sitting far from other diners to ensure privacy, Katharine told him, "I've been publisher of *The Post* five years. Every one of those years, I had to cut expenses and lay off people when it was bad for the newspaper. And I've done my best to look at the next five years. I think they're going to be like the last five years."

The conversation continued on a bench in Lafayette Square, the seven-acre park that fronts the White House. Katharine stopped short of calling for *The Post* to be sold, but she recommended that the parent company's board of directors consider identifying a potential owner who would be committed to the paper's mission and could be a good steward as her great-grandfather Eugene Meyer had become when he bought *The Post* in 1933. Although members of the family had presided over the company ever since, its shares were publicly traded and the board of directors would have to approve a sale. "Maybe we should start to think about whether someone out there would be a better owner," Katharine told Don. There was also a more pointed message, as Katharine remembers it: "If you want me to cut the shit out of the newsroom, I want to know you have my back because I'm going to be eaten alive."

Only days later, in November, a board meeting of the parent company was scheduled. While on a walk shortly before the meeting, Don suggested to Katharine that the idea of finding a different owner for *The Post* be discussed when directors convened for dinner at Washington's Ritz-Carlton hotel. When Don asked the waiters to leave the room, she brought it up. There was no PowerPoint, only a conversation. In a series of sharp questions, Katharine was asked how much *The Post* might lose in the next recession. Hundreds of millions of dollars, she answered. Before heading to bed, board members authorized Don to explore whether the right kind of buyer could be found.

Under its ownership, the Graham family had displayed a "quasi-religious dedication to *The Post*," as Don put it to me. But with the board's assent, he embarked on a course that showed how even such fervor has limits. He contacted investment banker Nancy Peretsman of Allen & Co., who had worked closely with *The Post* in the past, confident that she would safeguard the secrecy of a search for a suitable buyer. "I was petrified of a leak," Don said. "We didn't want to auction *The Post* to the highest bidder," a process that could put it in the hands of someone with political aims.

Among those contacted were David Rubenstein, the Washington, D.C., philanthropist who had earned riches in private equity. He took a pass, as he would periodically remind me when we happened upon each other in D.C. Another was Pierre Omidyar, the founder of eBay, who was keenly interested. Negotiations with Omidyar started in the spring and continued through summer. When I sent questions his way more recently, he dispatched a representative to tell me it allowed him to "think more concretely about what might be possible with an outlet he respected greatly and, more importantly, one that he felt played a critical role in our democracy." Katharine recalls Omidyar writing "a moving letter" that she summarized as "I'm going to take care of your baby if you give it to me." He doesn't recall writing anything but "certainly believes he did relay those intentions at some point." Still, Omidyar offered only $150 million, far less than the asking price.

Don identified Bezos as a prospective purchaser. They had known each other in a cursory way as far back as 1995. Bezos knew technology inside and out. He was obviously successful in running a company. And then there were his bottomless pockets, allowing him to pay for *The Post* and invest even more in its future. Don told me there were other reasons he liked the idea of Bezos as owner: "Jeff's a reader." And he kept his politics to himself. "I didn't know what his politics were . . . I was not about to sell to someone who bought it to tell the president what to do."

Bezos has said he was "startled" when Peretsman called. "I said, 'Nancy, you know, why me? Why are you calling me? I don't know anything about the newspaper business.'" For months Bezos never called back, never manifested a bit of interest. Suddenly Don received an email from Bezos saying he'd like to talk, if Don was still interested. He had thought things through. He had done his research. The two met over lunch in Sun Valley, Idaho, where Allen & Co. held its annual media conference for one week in July. Bezos paid a visit to Don at his lodging.

Don quizzed Bezos on whether his interest in *The Post* had to do with political motives, warning that if it did, it would "blow up in his face." Bezos responded, "It's the furthest thing from my mind."

At a follow-up Sun Valley lunch, Bezos shook hands with Don on a deal to acquire *The Post* for the $250 million he was seeking, and within a couple of weeks a three-person team that handled Bezos's personal investments was in Don's Dupont Circle town house reviewing detailed financials with *The Post*'s publisher and president as well as a senior financial executive of the parent company. The Bezos team's primary concern could not have been a surprise, given Amazon's business history: *The Post* had a unionized workforce. How big a problem would that be?

When, in July, Katharine told me that a deal was struck and an announcement was imminent, I thought it had to be good for *The Post*. We were starved for unconventional thinking and long-term investment. If anyone could help us, surely Bezos could. I figured he would aim for growing, not shrinking, our way to profitability. I wasn't as confident, though, that the deal would be good for me. I'm a realist if nothing else. If Bezos wanted to signal quickly that things were going to change, he might just send me packing.

The immediate mandate was to keep the sale secret while also getting a story written in advance and preparing key editors to publish it online at the right time. Press releases and the letters Don and Katharine would address to *Post* employees had yet to be written.

Don suggested that perhaps I should write the news story of the sale myself. I demurred. This historic transaction should be covered as any other news would be. A reporter would have to be assigned. Paul Farhi, the media reporter, was the natural choice.

Paul was startled when I reached him on Saturday as he and his wife, Lisa, were wrapping up a vacation at a resort in Punta Cana, Dominican Republic, planning a return home later that day. Why would I be calling him? Why now? What I conveyed wasn't helpful. I told him nothing, except to be at his phone at 9:30 Sunday morning for a story of major significance. At dinner that night, Paul and Lisa discussed what the story might be about. "Maybe the paper is going to be sold," she said. Ridiculous, he responded.

I broke the news to the twenty-five-year *Post* veteran the next morning, with instructions to prepare a story that I would personally edit via email to avoid anyone stumbling across a copy in our computer system. The story would be kept under embargo until 4:30 Monday afternoon, when Don and Katharine would jointly announce the sale to staff.

On Sunday afternoon an Amazon staffer connected Paul with Bezos, who spoke for fifteen minutes or so. "He was very friendly and chatty and didn't duck or avoid anything I asked him," Paul later told me. One word stuck out to Paul: "Runway." Bezos said he wanted to give *The Post* the "runway" to grow and become profitable again. "I remember being a bit skeptical about that," Paul said. "It sounded like standard corporate PR to me—positive but extremely vague, with no real commitment or identifiable goal. As it turned out, there was an enormous amount of significance in that one word!"

Paul stayed up most of the night to write, sending me a final version that included my edits before he headed into the office at noon Monday. As Paul drove in, a good friend of his called on his cell phone. Paul told him a big story was coming. "Let me guess," he said. "*The Post* is going to be sold." He rattled off three would-be buyers, ending with "Amazon."

"I practically had a heart attack on the Whitehurst Freeway! The next few hours went by agonizingly slowly. I just knew—knew!—the story was going to leak at any second. It was like those movies in which the main character hears every single tick of the clock."

Word had, in fact, begun to seep out. Don had told his senior staff by midafternoon, and Katharine had told hers. A couple of journalists dropped into my office to signal they knew what was up. But word had not spread widely. At 4:15 p.m., Katharine sent an email to the entire newsroom to meet fifteen minutes later in the auditorium on the first floor. As staff speculated about what might be happening, features editor David Malitz said to Paul, "Whatever this is, it sounds like you're going to have to write a story about it." Replied Paul: "I already have, David."

Employees began to weep as Don told them his family's eight decades of stewardship would end in less than two months. "*The Post* could have survived under the company's ownership and been profitable for the foreseeable future," Don told them. "But we wanted to do more than survive. I'm not saying this guarantees success, but it gives us a much greater chance of success."

In a letter to staff, Don wrote, "The point of our ownership has always been that it was supposed to be good for *The Post*. As the newspaper business continued to bring up questions to which we have no answers, Katharine and I began to ask ourselves if our small public company was still the best home for the newspaper."

Bezos issued a requisite but reassuring statement of his own, declaring that journalism "plays a critical role in a free society." *The Post*, he said, "will continue to follow the truth wherever it leads."

Bezos did not join Don and Katharine for the meeting with employees. Understandably, that was the Graham family's day, not his. We did, however, count on hearing from him in person immediately afterward about an acquisition that was likely to have a profound impact on our careers and arguably on all of journalism. As a week passed with no sight or sound of him, *Post* journalists naturally began to question why. The news staff grew agitated that Bezos had not yet showed up to speak directly to them and other employees, and in particular they expressed worry that I had yet to hear from him. I was worried, and annoyed, myself.

"The vacuum of information is causing some anxiety already and could get worse," I emailed Katharine. Meeting with the most senior newsroom leaders "would demonstrate some genuine interest in the journalism, allow us to share what we do, and permit us to communicate his general thoughts to others."

Bezos was said to be hesitant about injecting himself into *The Post* before he actually owned it. Don promised to urge Bezos to visit *The Post* as soon as he could, assuring me that "when the deal closes, you'll see plenty of him and you'll like each other." Two hours later, Bezos emailed Katharine and me that he was working on the "schedule surgery" that would enable a visit in the weeks ahead. "I'd especially like to sit down with the newsroom and take questions in an unhurried way," he said. And he dispatched a follow-up note that he had heard from "everyone" that I was doing an excellent job. If that was intended as a sedative for an apprehensive editor, it worked.

I had made no public remarks about the Bezos acquisition. But in early August, I was scheduled to travel to Bogotá, Colombia, to give a lecture at the Universidad del Rosario. With the shocking news of Bezos's purchase, the country's media were suddenly in frenzied pursuit of interviews. Without consultation, my host in Colombia took the liberty of committing me to a battery of interviews with radio stations, newspapers, and magazines, starting early in the morning on the day after my arrival. Although still knowing nothing about Bezos's plans or thoughts, I couldn't reasonably hold off on commenting any longer. My first public remarks about Bezos were in Spanish, and entirely unnoticed in the United States. I did my best to answer questions to which I had no definitive answers.

"The acquisition is not a crisis, definitely not," I told the country's leading magazine, *Semana*. "For us at *The Post*, it's an opportunity to go on the offensive." Asked what guarantees I had that *The Post* would maintain its independence, I said there were two: "The first, all of us who work in *The Post* newsroom fiercely protect our independence and journalistic integrity. And second: the readers will hold any owner accountable because the heart of the brand '*The Washington Post*' is precisely its independence and journalistic integrity."

A month after the sale was announced, just after Labor Day, employees would hear from Bezos in person. He entered *The Post*'s headquarters a few blocks from the White House and spent two days of serial meetings with hundreds of key employees in every department.

My first meeting with Bezos was over lunch on September 3 in a ninth-floor private dining room of the parent company, where I was joined by managing editors Kevin Merida and Emilio Garcia-Ruiz. Kevin oversaw our reporting staff and their direct editors. Emilio ran digital and other operations. Bezos's manner was genial even as he posed penetrating questions that focused primarily on innovation. During a visit to the newsroom, he participated in a decades-old tradition by striking a musical steel triangle, amplified by a microphone system to every department, that summoned editors to the afternoon news conference where Page One was conceived. That day he would observe the front-page decision-making process with visibly intense concentration. When deputy national editor Anne Kornblut explained that two stories about Syria didn't conflict with each other as they certainly appeared to, Bezos found the quandary amusing. At least one of those stories had to be right. "You know you can't be wrong!" he joked.

Bezos wanted his visit with the entire newsroom to be his last stop before heading home to Seattle. Newsroom employees were invited to a question-and-answer session on September 4 in the windowless, cavernous, and thoroughly charmless "community room" that served as the anteroom to *The Post*'s auditorium. At least six hundred people attended. The front row was packed with the oldest veterans and retirees, giving our newsroom a geriatric look. Even though most were *Post* luminaries, that couldn't have been a good first impression.

With the microphone consistently failing—an embarrassingly poor and ill-timed showing of our technological capabilities—Bezos parried questions from twenty journalists, offering an early outline of his thinking with a mix of gravity, directness, and breezy humor. As I look back on a transcript of his recorded remarks, they stand out as an uncannily accurate preview of how he would run his new possession.

There were sweeping statements of philosophy. On nostalgia: "The death knell for any enterprise is to glorify the past, no matter how good it was." On focus: "We shouldn't put ourselves at the center. We shouldn't put advertisers at the center. We should put readers in the center." On growth: "You can be profitable and shrinking. And that's a survival strategy, but it ultimately leads to irrelevance, at best. And at worst, it leads to extinction." On the lone genius (presumably addressing how he was perceived): "The myth of the lone genius who comes up with these ideas, sends them down, is just that: a myth. The reality is that great ideas, great strategies emerge."

There were clues to upcoming strategies and tactics. On buying a subscription: "Should it be as easy to buy a subscription to *The Washington Post* as it is to buy diapers on Amazon? I think it should." On the internet: "We need to also figure out how to use the gifts that the internet gives us at the same time we are acknowledging that there are many things the internet has disrupted in this business." On youth: "If your customer base ages along with you, then you're Woolworth's." On reconstituting the best attributes of a newspaper into digital form: "How do we rebundle? How do we get a package in the online world? . . . If you're reading the tablet edition of *The Post*, does that have the same feel of this beautifully edited paper package we have been honing for decades? I'm very optimistic that we'll find something readers love and engage with that we can charge for." On getting readers nationwide: "There are only a few newspapers that really have even the possibility of being national, and that's because of the rightly earned reputation that *The Washington Post* has, and because of its geographic location here [in D.C.] in probably the most important country in the world."

There was advice on competitors we could learn from: "What's successful at the *Huffington Post*? How can we learn from that? How can we be inspired by that? What's successful at *Business Insider*? How can we be inspired by that? What can we learn from it?"

There were hints of his mindset: "I'm genetically optimistic." "I'm stubborn on vision, flexible on details." And hints on his own ideology in relation to *The Post*'s editorials: "I don't self-identify with any political party. I am very issues-focused. I do have things I care about. And some of those things are known, like gay marriage . . . I think [the editorial page of] the paper is very focused on freedom and . . . so it ends up lining up with quite a few of my ideas anyway, such as they are. And . . . I don't feel the need to have an opinion on every issue."

Well before Bezos bought *The Post*, it had become a running joke among journalists who covered Amazon that the company would say "no comment" to any inquiry. He was asked how he could own a newspaper when Amazon routinely stiff-armed the press. "I've always thought that the most powerful minds in the world can hold powerful inconsistencies," he said to laughter. "And I really don't see any problem with that . . . My view is, you always have the right to ask, but the subject always has the right not to answer."

As for how *The Post* could be expected to cover Amazon, which was fast acquiring dominant influence in retailing and cloud computing: "Feel free to cover Amazon any way you want. Feel free to cover Jeff Bezos any way you want."

There was advice for the journalism. "Number one rule, don't be boring." Subsequent events in Washington made that counsel perhaps the easiest to follow.

Even famed Watergate reporter Bob Woodward directed a question at Bezos. "How and why did you decide to buy *The Post*?"

"Hardball," cracked one staffer sarcastically, alluding to Bob's reputation as a tough investigator.

Bezos's explanation is one I've heard at least a dozen times by now: He had to go through "three gates," answering three questions. First, was *The Washington Post* an important institution? That was answered quickly. Yes, of course. Second, does it have a future? "Because even if it is an important institution, if it's hopeless—well, I would feel sorry for you guys, but I wouldn't want to join you." He thought about it, and ended up optimistic. Third, did he have anything to contribute, especially from the opposite coast? That took the longest time to answer, Bezos said, and he concluded he could provide "runway"—investment for the long term that would allow time for experiments to play out.

The explanation struck me then as overly mechanical and most likely incomplete. Over the years, I expected to unearth some agenda that Bezos had been unwilling to own up to. I've come to believe, however, that Bezos's answer was genuine. Cynics will scoff, something I can appreciate as a journalist who is preternaturally skeptical. And a man of his riches and power deserves to be doubted. But everything I've heard and seen tells me that Bezos honestly believes in an essential role for journalism in a democracy, even if for good reason he has become the searing target of it. Acquiring *The Post* for a price of only $250 million, not a heavy burden for a man who was then worth $25 billion (and now is a centibillionaire), would allow him to revive an institution that was freighted with historic significance.

Bezos never interfered in *The Post*'s journalism during my seven-plus years under his ownership, even when its coverage of Amazon put the company in an unfavorable light. For all the speculation that Bezos would use *The Post* to exercise influence, I never saw any evidence he had or would. I got the sense that Bezos relished the challenge of turning around *The Post*. Business, as far as I can tell, is his favorite sport. And *The Post* presented a unique property. "There is nothing else like it," one member of his small team handling personal investments finally told me when I pressed him on what Bezos saw in *The Post*.

The Post, in Bezos's view, could remake itself into a paper of nationwide, even worldwide, reach unlike any other local newspaper company. It was based in the nation's capital, an ideal setting for a national media outlet. Its name was also a natural for a publication with grander aspirations. It had a heritage going back even before Watergate of "shining a light in dark corners," as Bezos liked to say, that had cemented its identity among Americans nationwide, even those who had never once read it. And now, he told us, the internet was giving us a "gift": We could distribute our journalism digitally, meaning at low cost throughout the country and the world. With *The Post* having suffered all the pain of the internet, Bezos instructed us, "Take the gift."

Bezos was long on ambition. He began to speak of attracting ten million digital subscribers to *The Post*, eventually one hundred million. Asked during one of his early September meetings with the senior editorial staff what he thought the market might be for *The Post*, he responded, "The English-speaking world."

While Bezos could envision rewards that eluded others, he also knew full well the risks. Escalating commercial perils for news organizations like *The Post* were the reason it was put on the market in the first place. He himself wondered whether his strategy for *The Post*—shifting from relatively few subscribers paying a lot for print subscriptions to lots of subscribers paying fairly little for digital subscriptions—would actually work. That, not a *Post* union, was his real worry.

There were other, arguably more menacing dangers for Bezos, too. By the time he struck a deal with Don Graham, he had at least some idea, however inchoate, of what might await him. Before the Sun Valley handshake with Bezos that sealed the deal, Don had issued a concluding, and prophetic, warning to Bezos. "If you own *The Post*, and *The Post* under you makes somebody really mad, they will try to hurt you," Don told Bezos.

"You mean they might come after Amazon?" Bezos asked.

"Absolutely."

Don had in mind the hazard of a vengeful China, he later told me. But the threat to Bezos would be closer to home, from a vindictive president in his own country.

2

TOP SECRETS

I first set foot in *The Post*'s newsroom on November 16, 2012. Publisher Katharine Weymouth was to introduce me to the staff that I would lead in six weeks as executive editor. A full two months earlier, I had accepted the position and was asked to keep the news to myself.

The time seemed right for me to leave *The Boston Globe*. I had been the top editor there for eleven-plus years, and I was proud of what we had accomplished together. Among them were six Pulitzer Prizes. One was for public service, an investigation of the Catholic Church's cover-up of sexual abuse by clergy in the Archdiocese of Boston and beyond. We had taken on what was arguably the most powerful institution in New England. Evidence over time revealed that the Church worldwide was concealing thousands of abuse cases. A historic reckoning with its betrayal of parishioners and principles continues today.

The Globe's staff had delivered revelatory investigations of other powerful institutions in Boston as well. The state's probation department practiced rampant patronage in hiring and promotion. The market grip of its largest hospital system was so tight that it drove up health-care costs. Debt collectors' abusive behavior was facilitated by the complicity of courts. But for all its investigative chops, high ambitions, and dazzling coverage of the arts, sports, local news, and national affairs, *The Globe* gave the appearance at the time of surviving on borrowed time.

With losses in 2009 piling up and the parent New York Times Company demanding severe cuts in union members' wages and benefits, the environment in our office on Boston's Morrissey Boulevard had become poisonous. No year to date in my professional life had been worse. A newspaper, founded in 1872 and with a glorious history, might close on my watch. What a legacy that would be.

The Globe ultimately returned to a measure of stability, but 2009 served as a warning of what was ahead for local papers like ours. We could cover our regions well, but we were stuck with the same outlook: less revenue, fewer staff, heavier demands. It wore me down. I had been dealing with crushing financial pressures since 2000, when I was the top editor at *The Miami Herald*, where the parent Knight Ridder Inc. demanded cuts month after month. As far as I could tell, there would be no end to budget worries. And there was no satisfying readers who were understandably agitated at finding less to read.

The Post suffered the same debilitating economics. But this was a newspaper with a distinct allure: It had changed the course of American history. Its groundbreaking Watergate work offered inspiration to journalism students like myself in the 1970s. For decades it was a beacon for no-holds-barred investigations and lyrical narrative writing. If I was offered the job by Katharine after a round of interviews with senior *Post* executives, there was only one right answer: an enthusiastic yes.

The company's governing hierarchy had some doubts about me, I've learned since, and Katharine had to overcome them. CEO Don Graham and the board of directors feared I might be "too print" (too much in the traditional newspaper mold) and "too *New York Times*" (overly marinated in an archrival's culture that was seen as imperious and arrogant). Katharine proved persuasive, first by describing me as the superior journalist she needed and then by downplaying my tenure at *The Times*. Reinspecting my résumé, she assured directors that I "was there only 5 minutes." No matter that it had been thirty-eight months—not counting my tenure at its corporate little sister, *The Boston Globe*—it was brief enough to escape the taint of having worked at one of the world's great news organizations.

The Post was the third newsroom I had been asked to head up, and once again I had been selected from outside existing ranks. Maybe only twenty journalists at *The Post* knew me personally, leaving 560 who didn't. There was good cause to wonder whether this stranger to their newsroom would fare any better than his predecessor.

The exit of Marcus Brauchli, previously the top editor at *The Wall Street Journal*, after only four years in the job was described by *New York Times* media columnist David Carr as "akin to switching drivers just as the car is sputtering to a stop." *The Post*, in Carr's diagnosis, was on the brink of a breakdown. His catalog of defects was a lengthy one: declining print and digital advertising, a pinched strategy of being "for and about Washington" that was "underwhelming," a franchise on political coverage that had been allowed "to disperse to other news outlets," and leadership by a publisher "struggling to get a grasp on a huge job at a company whose journalism has at times altered the course of a nation." *The Post*, he wrote, "now finds itself sharing a destiny with struggling regional newspapers."

Carr offered a faint note of hope for *The Post*, but even that could not have been more grudging: "It is not what it once was but it isn't nothing either."

In mid-November, standing before the staff at the "hub," the nerve center of *The Post*'s newsroom, I felt an empathy for Katharine that Carr couldn't muster. The Great Recession and technology had demolished the financial underpinnings of most news organizations. Recovery was no slam-dunk. And yet I could appreciate the depth of the staff's frustration. I had felt it myself.

The anxiety in *The Post* newsroom that day was unmistakable. It seemed wise to keep my remarks to only a few minutes. There would be less to pick at, as journalists tend to do. I first paid tribute to

The Post's "defining role in American journalism," and then I took note of the disquiet in the room. Journalists were losing their jobs. We would have to be realists about the economics. We needed to adapt. I did not offer a "plan." I didn't have one. I had to learn the place. Nor could I make any promises. There was no pretending that all would be fine.

When I wrapped up, education reporter Valerie Strauss posed the question that everyone wanted answered. Would there be more staff cutbacks? I wasn't reassuring. "The resources we have," I said, "will be dependent on the revenues of the company. That's as true of *The Washington Post* as it is true of *The Boston Globe*. People will know where the resources are headed when they look at the revenues. It can't be otherwise. No institution can spend more money than it has."

With that, Katharine called an abrupt end to question time. I had left no room for interpretation of what was ahead. I anticipated the direct question, and Valerie tells me she appreciated the straightforward answer. But the session didn't go over well with *The Post's* own media critic. Erik Wemple wrote sneeringly that my remarks were "depressing," depicting me as a management stooge. "More like a publisher justifying staff reductions," he wrote, "than an editor taking over a great journalistic property."

I wasn't there to tell people what they wanted to hear. Our business was in trouble. It was way past time to be honest with ourselves about where things stood and what needed to be done. Journalists persisted in mourning what used to be. I had grown weary of that—and with those who felt our travails were a problem for the "business side" to figure out, as if the future were completely out of the newsroom's hands. A news staff that based its work in reality once and for all needed to face its own reality. Sentimentalism didn't help. I wasn't the sentimental type anyway.

At *The Post*, I found a staff that was proud of the newspaper's heritage and yet no less despondent over its condition, hopeful that the place could be turned around but short on confidence that it would be. Memos I solicited from newsroom leaders told me a lot.

"*The Post* can be a difficult place to come into from the outside," one influential journalist wrote me. "It is a room of great achievement and strong friendships, but it is also a culture that has traveled in just a few years from overly self-satisfied to deeply uncertain and anxious, and that exacerbates the difficulty of making serious and meaningful change at a time when that is crucial." He recommended "fast moves that might help address the malaise and doom that is too much with us right now." And he concluded: "I cannot emphasize enough how hungry this place is for some sign of interest, direction and passion."

Another wrote of halting progress in adapting to the digital world. "All but one newsroom department editor lacks enough understanding of digital to properly plan and execute digital coverage of a news event. And almost all digital people lack enough understanding of journalism to be able to properly execute any coverage at all."

A third lamented the failure to break more big stories. "We do analysis extremely well . . . But we should value scoops more than we do, and especially the kinds of scoops that leave readers with their jaws hanging open."

My practice in other newsrooms, in Boston and Miami, had been to spend the first few weeks taking stock of the place, understanding how it worked, who did what, the strengths, the weaknesses. Only a couple of weeks into my arrival in Washington, I came to an assessment: I was stunned that we struggled almost every day to identify stories good enough to put on the front page of the printed paper. We were settling for Page One stories that were undeserving. Some departments went days without proposing anything for the front page. This was *The Washington Post*? I could scarcely believe it. Every department needed to have at least several stories worthy of the front page every day; we only needed five or six to fill it. We needed more of what we called "enterprise" work—investigations, narratives, profiles, and analyses that go deeper than the day's news and demonstrate initiative on our part. And at *The Post*, with its history and mission, "accountability work"—investigations—had to take priority.

Above all, I thought, we needed to break a big story. Nothing energizes a newsroom more. At times it can involve scandal, other times tragedy. There is a wide range. Regardless, the finest journalists find purpose in rising to the task of covering the most consequential events. I had witnessed that again and again.

Big stories seemed to erupt shortly after I became a publication's new top editor. When I began heading up *The Miami Herald* in January 2000, the paper was already aggressively covering the case of Elián González. The boy had been picked up at sea clinging to an inner tube, after his mother and eleven others who had fled Cuba drowned three miles off the Florida coast. Elián became the center of a fierce custody dispute, with Miami relatives and the Cuban exile community demanding he remain in the United States so he could enjoy the freedoms they had sought in escaping the regime of Fidel Castro. The Cuban government and his father, as the remaining parent, insisted on having him returned to his home in Cárdenas, a port town seventy-two miles east of Havana on the island's north coast. The story quickly flared into a furious national debate over Elián's fate. His future was finally sealed by the Clinton administration when it launched an April raid to seize him from a Miami home and deliver him to his father, then waiting in Washington, D.C. *The Herald*'s breaking-news coverage earned it a Pulitzer.

Then, in November 2000, less than a year after I had become editor in Miami, the identity of the next president hinged on results in Florida, where the official count showed Republican George W. Bush prevailing by a mere 537 votes over Democrat Al Gore. The Supreme Court, in a 5–4 vote that understandably infuriates Democrats to this day, called a halt to a statewide recount, handing Bush the presidency by only one more electoral vote than required for victory. We would embark on a monthslong recount ourselves, relying on Florida's expansive public records law to review every ballot in the state's sixty-seven counties. We even went so far as to hire a major accounting firm to do its own independent count. (Many Democrats still refuse to acknowledge the result: Bush almost certainly won, under the most common vote-counting standards.)

On September 11, 2001, six weeks after I became editor of *The Boston Globe*, nineteen terrorists seized four planes to carry out suicide attacks that ended in the deaths of nearly three thousand people. One hit the Pentagon. A second crashed into a field in Pennsylvania. And the two others flew into the twin towers of the World Trade Center, causing both to collapse in rubble. Those two planes flew out of Boston's Logan Airport.

Four months later, in January 2002, *The Globe* broke the story of the cover-up of serial sexual abuse by clergy within the Boston Archdiocese—inspiring the 2015 movie *Spotlight*, which won the Academy Award for Best Picture and affirmed what I consider journalists' paramount mission: exposing wrongdoing by society's most powerful. My role in launching that investigation was portrayed by Liev Schreiber, who afforded me a lasting image as humorless, laconic, and yet resolute.

Each of these stories seized the world's attention. In every instance, the news staffs were animated by the immensity of the events and rose to the difficult, often emotionally wrenching challenges that come with coverage. Events of colossal scale bring newsrooms together. Strong performance lifts morale, reinforcing a collective sense of purpose.

I had no expectation that this pattern would repeat itself at *The Post*, and yet it did, starting May 22, 2013. Barton Gellman, a former reporter for *The Post*, one of its most distinguished, furtively walked into our headquarters that day with a story that would put us in receipt of the nation's most closely held intelligence secrets. The entire national security hierarchy would soon train its fury on *The Post*, accusing us of placing the country at greater risk of terrorist attack. We judged the massive trove of classified documents differently: The leaked information was a window on an American surveillance regime of breathtaking scope that jeopardized citizens' personal privacy, all without public debate.

In an instant, coverage in *The Post* leaped to the forefront of the nation's news agenda. All the eulogies for *The Post*, with their ritual lamentations about its squandered influence, were suddenly rendered null and void. There had been no story like this for *The Post* since the Watergate investigation and publication, following *The New York Times*, of the Pentagon Papers, the voluminous classified history of the Vietnam War that revealed a pattern of failure and deceit at the highest levels of government.

When Bart walked into our office, he was returning to his professional home of twenty-one years where he had been a correspondent covering the Middle East, diplomacy, and national security. A member of the Pulitzer Prize–winning team that covered the 9/11 attacks, in 2008 he won the prize again with colleague Jo Becker for a penetrating series on Dick Cheney, revealing the vice president's frequently hidden but routinely decisive influence on national policy. Having also written his master's thesis on "Secrecy, Security, and the Right to Know" and having taught at Princeton on "Secrecy, Accountability and the National Security State," Bart was steeped in the sensitivities surrounding the press when it gets its hands on classified documents. No documents previously in his possession were more delicate than those he was bringing us now.

Bart had first taken his story proposal to *Time* magazine, where he was writing on contract, and yet his conversation with *Time*'s outside lawyer left him in despair that the revelations could ever see the light of day at that publication. He thought of going to *The New York Times* but worried about navigating an unfamiliar newsroom while working on a story so sensitive. Former colleagues advised him to return to *The Post*, where he would still be seen as "part of the institution." And now he was back.

Bart had left *The Post* in February 2010, disaffected with my predecessor. He could not be sure I would be receptive to a story that carried risks exceeding anything either of us had ever confronted. Though he was returning to his longtime professional home, he and I had never met. Bart only knew of me through what he later described as *The Boston Globe*'s "gutsy" investigation of the Catholic Church. So he entered *The Post*'s headquarters with a measure of hope but also abundant uncertainty.

Much was at stake for *The Post*, as Bart well knew. Publishing a fragment of the tens of thousands of these most highly classified documents carried the possibility that all of us would face prosecution under the Espionage Act of 1917 or under a related statute that specifically cited publication about a "cryptographic system" or "communication intelligence activities." The very institution of *The Washington Post* could be vulnerable to crushing fines. While the Department of Justice had never criminally pursued journalists for publishing classified information before, it was not inconceivable, given the sensitivity of what would soon be in our possession, that the government might now choose to make an exception. And then there was the reputational risk. Inevitably, *The Post* would be accused of a traitorous act.

Bart first met in a seventh-floor conference room with managing editor Kevin Merida, national editor Cameron Barr, and investigations editor Jeff Leen, whom Bart had first solicited for an introduction to me. Also attending was a trio of lawyers, Jay Kennedy and Jim McLaughlin of *The Post*, and Kevin Baine, powerhouse attorney with *The Post*'s longtime outside counsel, Williams & Connolly. No question, we needed the lawyers.

The next morning the group reconvened for a meeting where I would serve as the primary audience and ultimate decision-maker. There were none of the pleasantries that typically accompany a first-time introduction. Bart wrote years later that I "projected authority without overt display." Bart himself was genial enough but carried the mien of someone bearing a heavy burden, and he was more circumspect than any reporter I'd ever worked with. He began with an unusual demand: All cell phones had to be left outside the room or the batteries removed because they could be turned on and their microphones activated remotely. I was among those who had never heard of such a thing. In the days ahead, he would insist upon a series of precautionary measures that, even for a newsroom practiced in dealing with confidential sources, was unprecedented in rigor, stealth, and sophistication.

In his book *Dark Mirror* on this investigation and the "American surveillance state," Bart recalled his lengthy list of requirements:

> *When working with the source material, the* Post *team would need dedicated computers with freshly wiped, encrypted hard drives. Networking hardware should be physically removed from those machines, cutting them off from the internet and newsroom production systems. Baron would have to find us a windowless room with a high-security lock, reinforced door, and a heavy safe bolted to the floor. Decryption key files, stored on memory cards, would never be in the same room except when in use . . . Once these precautions were in place, access to the classified material would require four credentials: door key, safe combination, digital key card, and passphrases. We would divide the credentials among team members. No one but me would have all of them.*

He wasn't finished. He would need a researcher, and it would have to be *The Post*'s incomparable Julie Tate. Whenever we were prepared to assign other reporters to the story in the future, he could effectively exercise a veto. And an acclaimed maker of provocative documentaries, Laura Poitras, whom the leaker had first contacted, must have a byline. Laura had enlisted Bart to report on the documents. I had yet to meet her.

The intelligence documents that would be so securely protected came from a source first known as Verax and later revealed to be Edward Snowden, a National Security Agency contractor who was already a fugitive by the time Bart first called us together. Bart didn't give us the source's name then but he outlined the initial story by showing us an NSA slide presentation that bore Top Secret classifications: "sensitive compartmented information," "special intelligence," and others.

The program displayed on his computer screen was called PRISM. The NSA was tapping into accounts at the nation's most prominent internet companies, whose services were familiar to just about everyone with a computer: Google, Facebook, Apple, Yahoo, Hotmail, AOL, Skype, and a smaller outfit none of us had ever heard of. The NSA was able to gather more than "metadata"—sender and recipient, time and date, for example. It could vacuum up the content of communications, whether text or images. For intelligence purposes, it was a gold mine.

The NSA wasn't legally authorized to harvest information on just anyone—targets had to be considered most likely foreign—but many thousands of Americans' internet accounts were being swept up by the NSA's surveillance system and into its data bank. By April 5, 2013, 117,675 accounts were already under active surveillance, and the number was rapidly ascending.

"Could there be that many terrorists, spies, and foreign government targets with Hotmail or Yahoo accounts?" Bart would later write in his book. "What definition of 'terrorist,' the top target category, would result in numbers like that?" In fact, despite the targeting of terrorists, many Americans' internet activities were subject to observation by the NSA.

Bart explained to us how the NSA previously had been required to obtain individual warrants from the FISA (Foreign Intelligence Surveillance Act) court to search each account. Now, after Congress passed the Protect America Act and the FISA Amendments Act, and after the Department of Justice obtained a secret interpretation of the law, the NSA could tap into an unlimited number of accounts. The court would approve the rules governing how accounts were selected for surveillance and the methods for "minimizing" how much was collected about Americans. It would no longer review each and every search, and the Justice Department was trusted to self-report whenever it violated any rules.

None of this was journalistic territory I had previously traveled. None of my experiences had prepared me to deal with classified material, not to mention the most secret in the U.S. government. While I had overseen local news organizations in Boston and Miami, and stories that would rise to national and international prominence, national security itself was well outside my orbit.

I felt the immense weight of a decision on moving ahead with the reporting that could lead to publication. No reasonable person who had observed the attacks of 9/11 could be unmindful or desensitized to the threat of terrorism. The worst attack on the United States since Pearl Harbor had left an enduring impression on me, as it had on most Americans. In Boston, we had covered, one after the next, the funerals of the passengers, pilots, and crew on the planes hijacked from Logan Airport that served as missiles to demolish the World Trade Center and murder the innocents within. We chronicled as well the heartrending human loss in lower Manhattan, Pennsylvania, and the Pentagon in northern Virginia. I sat in the pews of Trinitarian Congregational Church in Concord, Massachusetts, for the memorial service of Alexander Filipov, who had served there as a deacon and was the father of *The Boston Globe's* Moscow correspondent, David Filipov. The electrical engineer, Boy Scout leader, Little League baseball coach, and avid sailor was killed on American Airlines Flight 11, which was steered on a deadly course toward the World Trade Center's North Tower.

"Every time I see that grainy image of AA11 exploding against the tower," David wrote in *The Boston Globe* on the tenth anniversary, "every time I see the thick plumes streaming from the skyscrapers like giant, malevolent balloons, I am watching my dad's violent death. I do not know how many times I have to see it, but I know I have seen it hundreds of times. And there does not seem to be a way to avoid seeing it, or hearing about it." That image is burned into my memory as well. It was impossible to be cavalier about national security.

And yet I was sensitive as well to every individual's right to privacy, and the necessity of it, and how privacy protections distinguished the United States from many countries, safeguarding citizens from a government that might have every incentive to pry into their lives while rationalizing away reasons not to. I've always been wary of the overwhelming power of government. Without adequate protections, it easily can be abused—if not immediately, then someday—by malicious actors. It was not hard to imagine then, even less so today after how Donald Trump sought to weaponize his presidential authorities, that an administration would exploit law enforcement and intelligence agencies to target its perceived political and media enemies and accrue power.

A constitutional principle of the United States is that government power needs to be constrained. The potential for abuse may seem like a gauzy hypothetical, but hypotheticals often become real. The nation's founders, thankfully, were hardwired to think about eventualities.

A thoroughly intrusive government surveillance system, as revealed in the documents that Bart was showing us on his air-gapped laptop, suggested that the NSA had secretly shed its previous constraints. American citizens would remain in the dark about its activities unless we published what we knew. And so, with plenty of thought but no delay, I said, "Okay, I want the story." We were willing to publish.

Because my decision could put the entire *Washington Post* at risk,

I was obligated to tell my publisher, Katharine Weymouth. She, in turn, told CEO Don Graham. Neither of them sought to block me. More recently, Katharine told me, "I trusted your judgment completely on how to handle it." Similarly, Don said of Katharine and me, "My reaction, as I remember it, was that I trusted you and trusted her"—and "trusted Bart, whom I had known a long time."

That was a lot of trust being spread around, particularly toward me, an employee for a mere five months at *The Post*. To many Americans, especially those in the intelligence community, it is unimaginable that a decision of such import should be made by someone in my position. And yet the First Amendment of the Constitution generally bars prior restraint on the press. The responsibility landed in my lap, and there was no evading it.

As prompt as my decision was in our morning meeting, I spent the night turning over the arguments for and against publication. There was still time to reverse myself. A good portion of my evening was devoted to reading the Espionage Act of 1917, underlining provisions that spelled out fines and prison terms, imagining the possibility that an indignant Justice Department might feel motivated to bring a case against *The Post*, my colleagues, and myself. What was I getting us—and the country, no less—into?

Still, I kept returning to the worrisome prospect of a government exploiting enormous powers as citizens were left clueless about a widening ring of surveillance. What would be my own culpability if that came to pass? I went into the office the next morning confident of the decision I had made.

Our first story went online on June 6, disclosing the PRISM program to explosive effect. The NSA was furious that one of its most powerful tools was now public, alerting likely targets to run for cover from the agency's surveillance. Major tech companies were aghast at the appearance that they had swung open the doors to government spying on the public. In truth, the exaggerated language of an NSA PowerPoint left the impression, reflected in *The Post*'s initial story online, that the NSA had tapped more easily and widely into tech companies' communications pipelines than turned out to be the case. But the public's outrage at an incursion on their privacy did not abate even as we gained greater clarity about the NSA's more limited, but still far-reaching, surveillance practices.

Before year's end, Bart and *The Post*'s national security staff, aided immensely by the expertise of technologist Ashkan Soltani, published dozens of stories on government surveillance, going well beyond the PRISM documents that Bart initially displayed for us upon his return to the newsroom. With each one, the breadth and brazenness of the NSA's efforts became more astonishing. The NSA was breaking into the main communications links that connected Google and Yahoo data centers around the world. Millions of email address books globally were snatched and stored. Nearly five billion records a day were being compiled on the location of cell phones around the world.

Glenn Greenwald, then working with Britain's *Guardian* newspaper, had broken the first story about NSA surveillance when he reported on June 5 that it was collecting the telephone records of millions of Verizon's American customers. Snowden also had provided him with tens of thousands of NSA documents. Mining the vast repository, he and his colleagues were publishing jaw-dropping stories one after the next. Our news organizations were competing fiercely with each other, worrying over what the other would unearth first in files that were unintelligible to any layperson. We both posed an unprecedented challenge to the nation's intelligence fortress.

American intelligence agencies were aghast at the breach of security and enraged over our willingness to publish their most closely guarded secrets. *The Post*'s practice was to seek their comment and to invite them to provide context and cautions. At times there were details they asked us to withhold, and sometimes we would, inevitably when lives of agents might be endangered or essential listening posts could be disabled. After the first set of stories, *The Post*'s principal reporters set out to establish a protocol for dealing with the intelligence agencies. With many disclosures to come, a system for communicating with the various spy services was needed.

A communications officer for the director of national intelligence arranged for Bart and Greg Miller, an experienced intelligence reporter who was also plowing through the documents, to meet with representatives of every spy agency. The setting was a conference room off the main lobby at agency headquarters in Liberty Crossing, Virginia, a complex that had all the grandeur of an ordinary office park.

"As we came into the room," Greg told me in describing the scene years later, "it was clear that the setup was unlike anything I'd ever encountered. Normally, you come in, the reporters are on one side of the table, the experts on the other, and there is some symmetry or balance to the arrangement. In this case, Bart and I were positioned at the front of the room, I want to say on risers, slightly above floor level, looking out at a roomful of intel officials. Their hostility was palpable. The whole power dynamic was upside down. Usually, we're the ones in the dark trying to extract answers from people who own the info. Now we were the ones with the info, and they were the ones looking for answers."

The questions from the intelligence officials were soaked in grievance: What are you going to do next? What gives you the right to do that? "Incredulity" is how Greg described the reaction to me. "There was eye-rolling at our answers . . . I tried to say that we were determined to handle this information responsibly, that we intended to give affected agencies ample opportunity to comment or provide guidance before we published, but that we felt that there were many stories of legitimate, if not paramount, public interest in these files. And we were going to pursue them. More eye rolls."

Still, both sides needed a standardized means of speaking with each other. We at *The Post* felt obligated to convey what we anticipated publishing. Intelligence agencies could then make comments or raise objections. A system was set up. And yet for all the worries over Snowden walking off with the government's intelligence treasures, subsequent communication was remarkably lax. "We were talking about extraordinary classified information with officials who were dismayed that we would publish any of it," Greg recalled, "and yet we were conversing over ordinary phone lines routinely."

In August, I caught a flavor of officials' wrath myself. We were on the cusp of publishing details from a 178-page summary of the $52.6 billion secret budget for classified and covert operations—commonly known as the "black budget." A communications officer speaking for the director of national intelligence, James Clapper, said there were deep concerns over what we would reveal. Clapper wanted to meet with me in person.

Accompanied by Kevin Merida, managing editor for news, and Cameron Barr, then our national editor with long experience in coverage of intelligence matters, I walked from our headquarters to the Executive Office Building, adjacent to the White House. Built in the late 1800s in French Second Empire–style architecture, the building features walls that are four feet thick, ceilings eighteen feet high, and vast granite spiral staircases. Along with the White House, Capitol, and Treasury buildings, the EOB stands as a formidable symbol of government authority. There is nothing subtle about it.

Neither was anything subtle about our meeting there with Clapper and Shawn Turner, his agency's communications director. Regularly described as a gruff and dour former lieutenant general in the Air Force, Clapper lived up to expectations. A "kind of menacing visage" is how Kevin recalled his look. "He seemed to want to make us feel guilty if not traitorous for publishing." Clapper spelled out four subject categories that he didn't want us to touch in our story. In my estimation, they were extraordinarily broad, covering a good share of what we intended to report. When I asked Clapper if he could be more specific, I was met with a growl and an emphatic bark. "I just was!" While we removed a couple of details from our story, including one regarding North Korea and another involving Pakistan, the story remained intact.

Intelligence officials were unsparing in their criticism of *The Post* and *The Guardian*, portraying the damage from disclosures as severe and irreversible. American lives, they said, had been put at risk. NSA director Keith Alexander testified over the summer that "grave harm has already been done." Months later, he would make the preposterously false accusation that the press was "selling" classified documents. "We ought to come up with a way of stopping it," he told a Defense Department blog. "I don't know how to do that. That's more of the courts and the policymakers, but from my perspective it's wrong to allow this to go on."

During testimony early the following year, Clapper suggested that the press were Snowden's "accomplices" and called for the "return of the remaining stolen documents that have not yet been exposed to prevent even more damage to U.S. security." The language of intelligence officials betrayed their view that, although we hadn't been prosecuted, perhaps we should be.

And yet by December, a powerful counterforce had emerged. The country's biggest technology companies would no longer stand for the surveillance status quo. Taken aback by *The Post*'s disclosures about how the NSA had penetrated tech firms' communications links, Microsoft, Google, Facebook, Apple, LinkedIn, Yahoo, AOL, and Twitter drafted a forceful letter calling upon the Senate to place sharper limits on government snooping and fortify privacy protections for individuals. "We understand that governments have a duty to protect their citizens," they wrote. "But this summer's revelations highlighted the urgent need to reform government surveillance practices worldwide. The balance in many countries has tipped too far in favor of the state and away from the rights of the individual—rights that are enshrined in our Constitution. This undermines the free-doms we all cherish."

Just over a month later, President Obama spoke at the Justice Department to address the issue. In a wide-ranging speech, he ac-knowledged everyone's point of view—and also seemed to take ev-eryone's side. Even as he defended the methods and motives of the NSA, he proposed some reforms. Obama said that "in our rush to respond to a very real and novel set of threats, the risk of government overreach—the possibility that we lose some of our core liberties in pursuit of security—also became more pronounced." And, he added, "all too often new authorities were instituted without adequate public debate."

On the day that Obama gave that speech—January 17, 2014—I, too, was immersed in the subject of national security. The context was different but the NSA disclosures were very much on my mind. The Jeff Bezos era was only a few months old, and the new owner was just beginning to get acquainted with what he had bought, including its news operations. That was the occasion for his second visit to *The Post*. He had set aside two days for a full-scale orientation. No time was wasted, every hour earmarked for meetings with executives in virtually every department. That Friday, a half hour at noontime had been reserved, at his request, to address how we handled the most sensitive stories about national security. I would attend, along with our lawyers and Katharine Weymouth.

I couldn't help but be anxious. We had spent months revealing intelligence secrets based on tens of thousands of documents leaked to us by Snowden. National security officials were apoplectic. If they had their way, we would have been barred from publishing and per-haps even criminally charged. Why was this on the schedule? What was Bezos's real agenda? Would he obstruct such reporting in the future? Was he fearful of the impact on Amazon's cloud computing contracts with the government, including the CIA?

Bezos never mentioned Snowden, and I certainly wasn't going to raise the subject. I was naturally curious about what he thought about *The Post*'s ongoing work. But what possible good could come of bringing it up? I wasn't going to invite his involvement in our coverage. Still, there was no mistaking the backdrop to this conversation. Government surveillance had been the biggest story in the country for almost seven months. And Bezos himself, in his first meeting with newsroom staff in September 2013, made a telltale nod to national security as an area of particular sensitivity.

"There will come a time here—because it comes, it's happened already, it's happened recently—where the administration or somebody else says, look, if you publish this, there is going to be national security ramifications. And those . . . I'm going to, since I'm recognizing my T-ball status, I'm going to consult with people who actually have dealt with these issues before. But I'm very comfortable we have a team of professionals who can help guide us through those complicated situations." I dwelled on his words: "it's happened already, it's happened recently." Obviously, he was referring to *The Post*'s publication of the Snowden leaks.

When the January meeting got underway, Bezos's question was straightforward: What were our standards for publication of national security matters? We explained them. He suggested they should be codified in some form. He wanted reassurance that we didn't publish solely because it was "cool" that we had obtained secret material.

The legal department, consulting with me, later returned with a summary of our existing practices, noting that *The Post* had a long history of breaking news in the realm of national security, from the Pentagon Papers in 1971, to the existence of secret CIA prisons in 2005, to the latest disclosures about the NSA's practices. What was presented was long-standing policy: There must be a substantial public interest in such disclosures. We would withhold details if they fell outside the scope of public interest. We would always inform the government of what we intended to publish and allow officials to express concerns, and we would take objections seriously into account. We would be particularly careful in posting classified documents online. Confidential sources would be protected, classified material safeguarded. Bezos seemed satisfied.

I never shared this conversation with others on the staff for fear of unduly alarming them. They would be predisposed to assume the worst about Bezos's intentions. Instead, I would wait and see what happened. None of our standards for publication, after all, had been altered. I wouldn't rein in our reporting either. I hadn't been asked to.

We never stopped publishing classified material when there was a strong rationale rooted in public interest. Although the Trump administration would target *The Post* from the very start, Bezos never asked us to hold back. I was relieved.

National security is the most delicate area of coverage for any news organization, with potential to put at risk the entire enterprise, not to mention the country itself. So, I felt that Bezos's question about our standards was entirely appropriate. He owned the place, after all. He was entitled to know our principles and practices, just as Katharine Weymouth and Don Graham needed to be informed of our intention to publish stories on the Snowden documents. His questions posed no problem in my mind. Repudiation of our answers would have been a problem. Bezos had, from my perspective, passed an important test.

Still, in all the years that followed that January 2014 meeting on national security coverage, we never published anything as highly charged as the stories on NSA intelligence activities. Stories like those don't come along often. But they can land at any moment. If it happens again, Bezos will be challenged on his convictions. Inevitably, it seems, he will hear competing voices.

In late 2020, an appointment at Amazon drew more attention

than usual for announcements of that sort, largely because Snowden made sure of it. Keith Alexander, the NSA director who had overseen its surveillance activities, would become a member of Amazon's board. Alexander had called for government and the courts to block *The Washington Post* and others from publishing intelligence secrets contained in the documents Snowden provided. And as Bart Gellman disclosed in his book, Alexander advocated conducting a raid to seize his notes and files. Now, as an Amazon board member, he would be closer than ever to the company's founder and executive chairman, Jeff Bezos.

If Snowden-variety leaks occur again, it is hard to imagine that Alexander will temper his views, even though he is out of government. He can share them directly with Bezos. Would he be among the people Bezos might hear from—"people who actually have dealt with these issues before"? On the other side will be *The Washington Post*, seeking faithful allegiance to the same principles that guided publication of classified information, not just in the year that Bezos acquired *The Post* but for decades before and every year since.

With the NSA investigation, there was a revised assessment of *The Post* within our organization and outside it: *The Post* had its "swagger" back. The impact of the surveillance investigation on the newsroom's mood and *The Post*'s national image was immediate and profound. Once again, we were seen as doing groundbreaking and important work. We had challenged power with a vigor reminiscent of *The Post*'s golden years.

3

REGIME CHANGE

We arrived at Jeff Bezos's residential compound in Medina, Washington, the final weekend of October 2013 on a cool and classically overcast morning for the Seattle area. Met by security at the gated entrance, we were escorted downslope toward Lake Washington, along a pathway set among lush gardens, bypassing the 29,000-square-foot home of *The Post*'s new owner, to a wing of a 4,500-square-foot boathouse. For our purposes at least, a portion had been transformed into a conference room. A screen was set up for presentations, side tables for snacks and, later, a healthy light lunch.

Brainstorming a business strategy for the Bezos era would now begin. We would need to extract ourselves from financial quicksand and find a way to grow. Absent success, *The Post* would be a fragile institution, handicapped in everything we did, especially if we needed to take on the U.S. government or a president as *The Post* had famously done over decades.

Only weeks after Bezos closed on his purchase, we would now find out what he really thought about *The Post*, maybe even what he thought of us and our ideas. We were eager to listen, nervous about what we'd hear.

Bezos kicked off the meeting in an upbeat, welcoming mood. By the look of him, he was enthusiastic about getting started. He pointed out some stray equipment that had no perceptible purpose for boating or the business that brought us there. They were pieces, Bezos said, for the "10,000-year clock" he was building in a hollowed-out mountain on his land in Texas, intended as a symbol of long-term thinking. I was tempted to ask whether he'd give us that kind of "runway" to fix things at *The Post*, but this was no foolin' around time.

Four of us took our seats: Katharine as publisher, president Steve Hills, chief technology officer Shailesh Prakash, and me. Uninvited, and back at headquarters, was the head of advertising, typically a power player in the natural universe of newspaper owners. Bezos had said emphatically to staff that readers and not advertisers deserved our overriding attention. The group's composition suggested he really meant it. If he had any concerns that a senior *Post* executive might be feeling excluded and hurt—and he was—Bezos didn't show it. Tenderhearted he was not.

Bezos's mind was fixated on two things. One was our journalism, remastering it for the digital era and ensuring that it captivated readers. The other was leading-edge technology, giving us the tools that would determine our own destiny. I was expected to deliver in the first category, Shailesh in the second.

Only two years into his tenure at *The Post* as its technology chief, Shailesh was considered a prized asset. With a computer science degree from the Indian Institute of Technology Bombay, a master's from Clemson, and an MBA from Georgia State, he had previously held key engineering positions at Netscape, Microsoft, and Sears. Because he still maintained a residence with his family in Chicago at the time, while occupying a small apartment in Washington, D.C., for regular commutes to headquarters, *Post* executives fretted that he was susceptible to being lured elsewhere. (Within a few years, Bezos would put him on the advisory board for his space company, Blue Origin. He wouldn't leave *The Post* until 2022.)

Steve, as *The Post*'s president for eleven years, functioned as the chief operations officer. He was a trusted confidant of Katharine's, so much so that he was widely regarded up and down the organization as her "Svengali," a depiction they both detested as an irritating and inaccurate caricature. Trim, silver-haired, and sharply analytical, Steve had the classic attributes of a business consultant. Educated at Yale and Harvard, where he got his MBA, he performed granular inspections on our financial performance. It was not a pretty sight. As the bearer of bad news—and with his hunt for efficiencies, evangelizing for radical reinvention, and fondness for bubble charts—he was, of course, suspect in the eyes of many in the newsroom, where there was scant tolerance for any of that.

Weeks before our meeting in Seattle, Bezos sent us a "grab bag" of "starter ideas and questions," as he put it. We labored over them. "In one sentence, what's our mission or vision?" Bezos asked first. "Most read? Most influential? Most subscribed to? Most riveting? Own the morning's first coffee?"

The pointed (and leading) questions continued. "A small number of subscribers paying a lot? Or a large number paying a little? I lean to the latter." "What are the possibilities for actions we can take immediately that would create wow in the short term?" "Double down on investigative reporting? How?" "Double down on exciting columnists?" "Brag (tastefully but overtly and forcefully) about our efforts, expenses and successes, and risk-taking. Readers won't know otherwise. How do we organize to do so daily?" "Broaden local stories so they appeal nationally. How?" And, in a nod to the coming presidential election that was about to take off, with unimagined consequences for *The Post*, Bezos, and everyone else: "Dominate 2016. How?"

With Bezos's queries came the refreshing scent of new investment. It was a thrilling shift in tone from what we had all become wearily accustomed to. Yet my business colleagues felt a responsibility to let Bezos know, if he didn't already, what exactly he had bought. For *The Post*'s publisher and president, that was Agenda Item No. 1 in the boathouse that October morning.

Steve had prepared a memo intended as a "clear-eyed" statement of our financial plight. Worded guardedly so as not to sound alarmist or defeatist, the memo nonetheless delivered a grim message: There was a "wide gap" between "current state" and "desired state," between "current trends" and "ultimate sustainability."

"Today," it continued, "we are primarily a local business that is dependent on print and on advertising. Our belief about the future is that we must face some 'brutal truths': print profits will decline, advertising on all platforms will be threatened, and it will be hard to create scale for local digital products." In ten years, *The Post* already had lost almost half of the revenue from its physical newspaper above the cost of print and distribution, and it was projected to lose an equal sum in the next ten to fifteen years. That left little to pay the costs of a newsroom or anything else. And when Americans were asked which websites "come to mind," *The Post* fell humiliatingly far down the list.

While the memo contained an upbeat note here or there—"the prospect of investing materially in our business is very exciting to us"—it was impossible to read Steve's memo in that boathouse without fearing Bezos had just berthed a sinking ship. We all wondered whether Bezos grasped just how bad things were. As we sat in silence, he studied the memo's six pages, then rose without a word to leave our table. "Are you coming back?" Steve cracked. No response. Bezos picked up a beverage, returned, sat down, paused as if for dramatic effect, and looked directly at Steve. "I don't scare that easily," he said. "You're right, we need to grow. So how are we going to do that?"

By the time our meetings that weekend concluded, all of us on *The Post* team had our marching orders. The mood was one of encouragement. Bezos was deeply engaged, asked penetrating questions, and seemed prepared to invest in an emerging strategy. He was a model of hospitality, too, inviting the four of us to his home for Sunday breakfast. Then-wife MacKenzie and their four kids were cheerfully making pancakes. Katharine came bearing bags of company swag, including *The Washington Post Cookbook* with "Readers' Favorite Recipes" for one son who had a starring role in the Bezos kitchen.

After we feasted at a long communal table, Bezos walked us to a van waiting at the front gate. Shailesh quickly organized a group photo. That evening he emailed it to what would now be known as the "Pancakes" group. "At least we all started out smiling," he wrote. It was a quip, but it captured the peculiar blend of optimism and unease every one of us was feeling.

I couldn't help but be hopeful about the fresh thinking Bezos brought. He saw light at the end of the tunnel that was imperceptible to the rest of us. We had coalesced around an ambitious, and principled, business mission: become Americans' first choice for what to read—by being honest, riveting, and comprehensive. Coverage of politics and government, central to *The Post*'s identity, was destined to get more resources; investigations, too. We'd likely be able to invest in a broad set of new blogs, pursuing readers nationally and going after a younger audience. We would hire "star" contributors who would cause people to say "Wow, *The Post* is back." We would "brag" more about our achievements. A new, visually appealing tablet app would get priority attention. Technology would have to be top-notch, giving us the tools to do what we needed when we wanted. And Bezos was going to spend to make it all happen.

Still, I found my stomach tightening on the flight back to D.C. Some of Bezos's ideas for a digitally oriented newsroom would send a jolt through our staff. I puzzled over how to execute on Bezos's aspirations without igniting open revolt. Once back home, I composed an email to managing editors Kevin Merida and Emilio Garcia-Ruiz that struck an awkward balance: Things were looking up. But there would be "lots of work to do," I wrote with studied understatement, and "perhaps some cultural adjustment in the newsroom required."

Soon I would tell Kevin and Emilio exactly what I was getting at. We would now be expected to rewrite the stories of other news outlets without always re-reporting them, just as the ascendant digital news sites *Business Insider* and *Huffington Post* were doing.

Bezos had mentioned both outfits at his first town hall with news staff, suggesting we find lessons in their success. His own familiarity with *Business Insider*'s practices was obvious. He was an early investor in the company, and in the months that followed our boathouse meeting he aimed to inject some of its DNA into our bloodstream. On January 17, 2014, on Bezos's invitation, *Business Insider* founder Henry Blodget paid a visit to *The Post*. After joining the "Pancakes" team for a quick lunch, he met with senior newsroom editors in the auditorium to school us in his internet-era brand of fast-turnaround, aggregated journalism. Editors listened warily. Bezos sat attentively toward the front.

The Blodget method—known as "aggregation"—was going to be a hard sell in a newsroom like *The Post*'s. Traditional journalists made up the vast bulk of the staff. Among the old guard, aggregators were held in especially low esteem. They did little, if any, original reporting. They were quickly reusing our stories and everybody else's, cherry-picking the most seductive elements, all without being saddled with the hard work and burdensome expense of original reporting. It was commercial genius—a bargain-basement way to profit off the work of others. And it was incredibly annoying: Readers drawn into their digital gillnets rightfully should have been ours.

Accomplished journalists at *The Post* would not be inspired by outlets whose behavior was, to their thinking, parasitic. Yet now Bezos anticipated us doing exactly as they did, with an early-morning "wake-up report" as the centerpiece of such an effort. Overnight reporters, as he conceived it, would rapidly rewrite other people's work into stories with crisp and clever headlines. Unless there were special circumstances—huge news, where our failure to provide on-the-ground reporting would be glaring and embarrassing—we'd rely on aggregation to let readers know what was happening around the country. Considering the esteemed organizations we regarded as our rivals—chief among them *The New York Times* and *The Wall Street Journal*—this was going to look as if Bezos's ambition for us was to swim with the bottom feeders.

The overnight team also was to be Exhibit 1 in a wider application of metrics to *Post* journalists. Bezos envisioned aggregated stories being turned around in fifteen minutes. Performance would be measured to keep reporters on pace. I was horrified. The metric was so unpalatable and unworkable—what journalist of *Post*-level quality would work overnight under such arduous, unsatisfying conditions?—that I had to come up with another way. I privately plotted how we might meet Bezos halfway: set up an overnight team, write stories that were at least partially aggregated (but with significant original reporting) and carried snappy headlines. We then committed to boosting our online readership with a team that came to be called "Morning Mix," working from about ten p.m. to six a.m. Early results were excellent, journalistically and commercially. Traffic soared. I congratulated myself on having avoided a draconian metric that would drive the staff mad, in every sense of the word. Celebration was premature, however. Bezos never forgot his fifteen-minute metric as I hoped he would. Nine months later, a new publisher, Fred Ryan, brought it up in our weekly one-on-one meeting. I flatly refused to implement it.

It wasn't just speed that Bezos wanted to measure. Customer satisfaction with our online journalism was on the list, too. Was our journalism, as he liked to put it, "riveting"? Metrics were fast becoming a big part of my professional life. Shailesh Prakash's engineers immediately went to work developing metrics to continually assess how well our writing, headlines, photos, and story selection appealed to readers in comparison with our competitors. Over time, this metric consistently scored us ahead of major competitors. I had no idea whether satisfaction was being measured accurately or not. But no matter. Mission accomplished, as far as I was concerned.

Bezos wasn't doctrinaire about metrics: Investigative reporting got a reprieve. Bezos's perspective on that was thoughtful and nuanced. "Some things," he told employees at a town hall in early 2016, "are so hard to measure that you . . . really can't measure them, and you have to use gut feel and intuition. And there are other things that are elevated above metrics that are principles that you care so much about that even if the metrics told you to do the opposite, you'd still do what your principles say to do."

He went on: "With our deepest mission . . . I imagine metrics could lead us to a place that was against some of our principles: We would say, oh, you know these big, long, six-month investigative stories don't pay off. They just don't pencil out. So let's stop doing them. I wouldn't believe that study . . . And I think that 20 years from now we would regret believing that study. So principles trump metrics."

One minute I was heartened by statements like that. On other occasions, when I felt metrics were misapplied, I was indignant. Within months of our first meeting at Bezos's home, I was fighting what I considered an abomination. Word came that he was insisting on an analysis of our staffing: Which employees had a "direct" impact on the product? Which ones had an "indirect" impact? The goal, as communicated to me at the time, was to keep the number of "indirect" employees as low as possible: less managerial bureaucracy, more resources directed toward the customer.

Bezos's hypothesis was that, in a newsroom setting, reporters were "direct," editors "indirect." Using that yardstick, a document was submitted for my review that situated every newsroom employee into one of those two categories. It was a horror show, a complete misreading of how quality journalism is practiced. Editors are essential to directing and coordinating coverage, and ensuring that it meets our quality standards. It was also a misunderstanding of who gets the title "editor"—a term that can be applied to staffers who manage a website, develop graphics, select photos, copy-edit stories, and conduct polls as well as "assignment editors" who work seamlessly with reporters throughout the day and at times are called upon to do significant rewriting.

Ultimately, and grudgingly, I classified 11 percent of our newsroom employees as "indirect"—by far the lowest of any department at *The Post*. Even then, I felt the number was too high. I told publisher Katharine Weymouth that if Bezos rejected the figure, I was prepared to argue with him personally. "I consider it an obligation," I said.

"If he wants to have that discussion, we can have it," I wrote in an email. "It might be an occasion to explain to him what editors do . . . I think he views editors as nonessential."

I never heard back from Katharine or Bezos. I assumed the direct/indirect analysis had met a well-deserved death. Not so. By November 2015 the head of our human resources department informed me that quarterly reports were being sent to Bezos's staff. And getting approval for more editors proved a constant, exasperating struggle, even as hundreds of additional reporters were added.

To avoid setting off alarms up the line, my deputies and I would strip the word "editor" from proposed new positions whenever possible. "Analyst" or "strategist" were among the limited set of workarounds. But none of that was a solution to the strain felt by editors whose workload had exploded over time. Some editors, exhausted, chose to go elsewhere. One talented and ferociously hardworking *Post* veteran, in 2021, seeking a more family-friendly environment found it with an employer not normally known for it: Amazon, which was building a new second headquarters in Virginia, just across the Potomac River.

Since that early metrics dustup, I've learned that Bezos at some point took my strenuous objections to heart. Initially, he imagined that reporters could mostly self-edit, except on the most highly sensitive investigative and national security stories where editing by others would be imperative. Although he wasn't about to forswear the direct/indirect metric—a rising proportion of managers was seen as a sign of deteriorating corporate health—I'm told he came to better appreciate how integral editors were to a well-functioning newsroom. They were, in fact, doing direct customer work. None of that conversion on Bezos's part was apparent to me during my time at *The Post*. But finally, after my retirement, *The Post* played catch-up, announcing in September 2021 that it would be hiring forty-one editors. My successor had achieved what I couldn't. The astounding number betrayed just how far we'd fallen behind.

For all the fretting over metrics and the like, the meeting at Bezos's home has to be judged a huge success. The new initiatives we settled upon dramatically expanded our readership, catapulting *The Post* to traffic numbers that would rival those of *The New York Times*, whose staff and budget were far greater than ours.

One breakaway triumph was the overnight team that Bezos wanted us to set up, and it was accomplished without the oppressive fifteen-minute meter he had in mind. The "Morning Mix" team would post stories by daybreak—or immediately, if warranted by news. A *Post* veteran who has since gone elsewhere, Fred Barbash, returned as its founding editor. He arrived with two useful attributes: One was deep and varied journalistic experience, bringing the sound judgment we needed when other senior editors were asleep. The other: He was an insomniac.

Nervous that Morning Mix would come under assault from traditionalists, I made myself a layer of protection. Fred would report directly to me: Anyone who interfered with the team's work would have to contend with the executive editor. It also meant Morning Mix reporters would not be diverted to purportedly more important endeavors, often late-night work that daytime reporters wanted to delegate to others. I wasn't going to allow a Bezos-inspired initiative to be smothered in the cradle.

Every member of the small Morning Mix team—a good number hired from struggling local alternative weeklies—turned out one or two supremely readable articles per night. Many were the product of entirely original reporting. Others were a blend that included rewriting. The aim was always to deliver a distinct, enticing story angle. "Second-day stories today" was Fred's apt synthesis. In short order, a handful of young journalists were turning out a dispropor-tionate number of our most-read stories, often getting to topics well before our competitors: "How BBC Star Jimmy Savile Allegedly Got Away with Abusing 500 Children and Sex with Dead Bodies." "The Real King Tut Revealed: Weak, Infirm and Not Much to Look At." "How the Bandidos Became One of the World's Most Feared Biker Gangs." Many of the hires for Morning Mix later became star writers in other roles.

A huge advantage of Bezos's ownership was that he had his eye on the long run. He often spoke of what might be in "twenty years." When I first heard that timeline, I was startled. News executives I'd dealt with routinely spoke, at best, of next year—and, at worst, next quarter.

Bezos also made decisions at a speed that was unprecedented in my experience. He personally owned 100 percent of the com-pany. He didn't need to consult anyone. Whatever he spent came directly out of his bank account. In preparing the newsroom budget for 2014, the first full year of Bezos's ownership, managing editors Merida and Garcia-Ruiz joined me in calling upon newsroom per-sonnel to come up with ideas we'd ask Bezos to fund. "Welcome to the dream factory!" we'd say as they entered my office with their bulging wish lists. Many of those dreams quickly came true almost overnight. Bezos's commitment to invest was real. The era of cease-less cutbacks had come to a halt.

By May 2014, we were adding fifty new positions in the newsroom as we kicked off a series of initiatives, with a heavy weighting against more editors and toward more reporters and other frontline positions. We launched "Post Everything," a venture for quick-reflex commentary from experts and also ordinary citizens narrating the most telling experiences of their lives. A breaking-news desk was added to instantly jump on fast-developing stories. Data-visualization specialists were hired, along with extra designers, social-media experts, and frontline staff for the website.

Bezos outlined a strategy that ran along two tracks: First, we urgently needed more readers overall. Only a tiny percentage of the American public had ever read *The Post*. If they were ever going to subscribe, they had to get to know us and really like us. For that, we needed to capitalize on the powerful distribution channels of Facebook and Google to make our journalism visible. But we couldn't put our fate entirely in the hands of the tech giants.

Google and Facebook were offering the public a free, all-you-can-eat news buffet. We would have to persuade people to pay for the full menu of what we had to offer—"the bundle," as Bezos called it, just as people used to pay for an entire newspaper for all it published. The ultimate goal was to entice readers, lots of them, to pony up for a subscription. Bezos was bitingly dismissive of the idea that information should be available for free. That's how it had been at *The Post* before we timorously introduced digital subscriptions in the summer of 2013. "I'd like my car to be free. I'd like my house to be free" was his sarcastic retort. Steadily we reduced the number of free articles people could read before being required to subscribe. Years later Bezos would joke about what to tell readers who griped about having to pay: "Sorry for the misunderstanding for 20 years. We gave away content for free. Sorry. Our bad."

With Bezos's money, we launched an array of new blogs—on food, internet culture, the military, sports statistics, science, popular culture, and more—and buttressed existing blogs on politics and world affairs. We recruited journalists who had grown up in the internet age. They could not have cared less if their stories were published in a physical paper. They cared a lot, however, about the number of online readers, assiduously cultivating them on social media and by polishing headlines for maximum attention. They wrote with a stronger voice and an informal, highly accessible style, no matter how complex the subject. The digital era called for breaking free, in many instances, of newspaper-writing conventions—simulating instead a conversation with friends or relatives. The internet was a distinct medium from print, requiring new approaches to communicating with the public, just as the arrival of radio and television once did.

Meanwhile, *The Post*'s engineering staff, highly skilled and now beefed up, was making fast strides in giving us cutting-edge technology. Our site and mobile apps loaded at accelerated speed, a high priority for Bezos. In coming years, we acquired new tools that allowed us to design our site for optimal performance and to manage a workflow made infinitely more complex by the introduction of an array of new digital products. One, dubbed "Bandito," allowed simultaneous testing online of several different headlines and images for a single story. Whichever attracted the most readers remained as the survivor on our site, without human involvement. We also devised a schedule for publishing on our digital platforms that synchronized with the public's known rhythms for online reading. Reporters received automated reminders of their upcoming deadlines. *The Post*'s engineers designed it to contain an image of me, and named it "MartyBot." As early as February 2015, *Fast Company* magazine listed *The Post* at No. 1 on its list of the "most innovative" media companies in the world.

Given that Bezos had to run the far bigger Amazon, *Post* staff wondered how much time he spent even thinking about us. Bezos said we occupied a lot of his "shower time." From what I could tell, he packed a lot into those showers. "Please," he once told employees, "do not confuse my scarce physical presence with the amount of mental presence I have here." Bezos was, in fact, heavily involved in *The Post*'s strategies and tactics, holding one-hour teleconferences every two weeks with senior executives and key staffers who were implementing initiatives that were on the day's agenda. "I've done my homework," he'd typically say at the start of our meetings. "Should we go to questions?" Almost always he had read and absorbed every memo to the slightest detail. No time was spent on presentations.

When Bezos's purchase of *The Post* was announced, I had read that he hated PowerPoints and had banned them at Amazon. In a 2004 memo, he had called for up to six-page memos because "the narrative structure of a good memo forces better thought and better understanding." PowerPoints, on the other hand, "somehow give permission to gloss over ideas, flatten out any sense of relative importance, and ignore the interconnectedness of ideas." I despised them, too, and was eagerly awaiting a prohibition at *The Post*, if only to witness the dread of business colleagues addicted to their benumbing features. A ban took longer than I expected and hoped, but eventually it happened in an instant. Agitated over one staffer's inability to explain a slide in July 2015, Bezos brusquely interjected. "The more bullet items there are, the less intelligible it is." Memos from then on were to be "narratively structured" with "nouns, verbs, and sentences." That way, he said, "it'll be easy for you to understand what's being proposed."

By then, Fred Ryan was publisher, and Bezos's exasperation led him not only to enforce the call for narrative memos but to also demand rehearsals for our meetings with him. "We have UX, CX, and now we have JX," he said, referring to user experience, customer experience, and now Jeff's experience. Bezos's mandate against PowerPoints, however, was an incomplete victory from my perspective. When he wasn't present, thick PowerPoint decks were circulated with abandon, Bezos's wisdom be damned.

No item was too small for Bezos to discuss, and nothing on our website was too small to test. When one memo mentioned we were experimenting with a different color for the "Subscribe" button to see if it elicited a better response, he waxed enthusiastic: Often what seemed like a trivial matter proved not to be. And designs that work best aren't always the prettiest. "Artists against sales," he said of designers who emphasized aesthetics over results.

Development of a new tablet app became an immediate priority for Bezos. It was his biggest bet at creating what he called the digital "bundle." The idea was to create a visually appealing app that readers would be willing to pay for. It would feature what he saw as the best qualities of a physical newspaper, which he identified with exceptional discernment and concision: clear hierarchy; navigation signals that were easy and intuitive; and, unlike internet sites, finite content, giving readers the satisfaction of completion. In January 2014, he dedicated a full four hours to thinking through the new app with engineers, designers, newsroom leaders, and the heads of advertising, research, and circulation. Everyone was invited to suggest radical ideas. Yet when one participant suggested an app that would no longer carry "The Washington Post" name, Bezos instantly dismissed the idea: The value was in the brand. That's what he had just shelled out $250 million to buy.

Bezos advised against incessantly trying to fix problems that seemed to defy solution. It was human nature to play Mr. Fix-It, he noted, but our time would be better spent looking for "positive surprises"—things that were succeeding in spite of our inattention. At one daylong update, he set aside the report on email newsletters, coming back to it at the meeting's end as the "big takeaway." It was what he most wanted to discuss. Readers were signing up for newsletters in ever greater numbers, even though we had scarcely given them a second thought and our offerings at the time were a mess. That was where we should focus, he said. A major (and mostly successful) initiative on newsletters was born.

Bezos had his share of bizarre notions. As technology chief

Shailesh Prakash in 2016 disclosed to *Fortune* magazine, early on he had tossed out the idea of a game-like feature that would allow a reader who disliked an article to pay to remove its vowels (with other readers paying to restore the vowels if they liked it). The media universe couldn't contain its hilarity. One outlet suggested Bezos was getting "a little punchy." Shailesh apologized to Bezos for subjecting him to ridicule; the anecdote was only intended as an example of our brainstorming. "God no!" Bezos responded. "I'm highly amused by it . . . And I hope folks at *The Post* will follow my lead here and come up with some crazy ideas. We can edit them, and in and amongst them will be good ones." The "disemvoweling" idea—as Bezos called it—went nowhere, of course. As Shailesh told *Fortune*'s reporter, "Marty wasn't very keen."

In other ways, we did break the mold. Early in Bezos's tenure, *The Post* didn't have the budget to reconstruct a traditional network of national reporters working out of bureaus around the country. Nor did Bezos seem to think that was necessary or cost-effective when we could aggregate other news outlets' work. But if we were to be a true national news organization, we needed to genuinely compete with outlets like *The New York Times* and Associated Press that had reporters situated all over the place. So, in June 2015, *The Post* announced the Washington Post Talent Network, which sought to capitalize on the growing reservoir of skilled journalists around the country (and world) who had been laid off, retired (sometimes prematurely), or were now engaged in other endeavors. The idea was to create a network of journalists we could use only as needed, paying them by the piece as freelancers. They would be our eyes and ears for stories everywhere, and we could deploy them instantly when major news broke far from home base.

Deputy national editor Anne Kornblut developed the idea while on a fellowship at Stanford University. Having just read *The Second Machine Age* by MIT professors Erik Brynjolfsson and Andrew McAfee, I advised her to see if she could create a journalistic version of TaskRabbit (freelance labor for everyday tasks) and Amazon's Mechanical Turk (a crowd-sourcing site for on-demand business tasks). When we invited journalists to apply for acceptance into the network, a thousand did in the first week alone. The talent network quickly grew to several thousand around the world. Bezos proclaimed himself a "huge fan" of the idea, funding it immediately. When we needed more money to sustain and expand the Talent Network, Bezos instantly and avidly approved. "Will *Washington Post*'s Talent Network Become the Uber of Freelancing?" asked one news site. In a way, it did. Overnight, it dramatically expanded the journalistic reach of *The Post* at a bargain-basement price.

Early in Bezos's ownership, we'd have quarterly meetings for a top-to-bottom review of pretty much everything. A mid-April 2014 meeting in Seattle, held in a conference room at Amazon headquarters, lasted more than six hours. Spirits were high, and Bezos came across as satisfied with the pace of progress. Finally, the marathon work session was over. At 7:30 p.m. we gathered in a private room at Canlis, a New American restaurant that won praise a year earlier from *The New York Times* as Seattle's "fanciest, finest restaurant for more than 60 years." Our day in Seattle had been one of light rain and fifty-degree weather. But as we finished cocktails and were seated for dinner, sunlight made a fleeting appearance. A double-rainbow traced a brilliant arc over Lake Union. We rushed to take photos. It was a good omen. We all agreed on that.

For at least one of us, though, it sent a false signal. The months that followed saw relations fray between Katharine Weymouth and one of Bezos's close advisers, as she later recalled to me. Katharine argued vehemently against Bezos's plans to freeze defined-benefit pension plans for employees and eliminate future retirement medical benefits. Hit hard were employees hired before 2009. The company had stopped offering those benefits to employees brought on board since—a turn away from more magnanimous benefits that well preceded Bezos.

Post executives knew the pension maneuver would set off a firestorm among employees, especially since the pension plan was overfunded to the tune of $50 million. Sure enough, it did. When the company's plans were announced in late September, an informational picket line organized by an employee union formed outside *The Post*'s headquarters. "Shame on Bezo$," declared one sign. Bezos's team also sent instructions to cut retirement pay and reduce contributions to employees' 401(k) plans. The company would implement a separate plan that would give employees a lump sum or annuity upon retirement.

The Post's intentions fit into a nationwide pattern of companies eliminating pensions, saddling employees with more responsibility for their own retirement. It also fed into fears about Bezos, whose antipathy toward unions has played in rancorous battles over labor organizing at Amazon warehouses.

By Katharine's account, the pension issue put her at odds with *The Post*'s new owner: She sent a long email arguing that a pension freeze was a mistake. Paul Dauber, a lawyer and key figure in Bezos's private-investment firm, got back to her. "We don't want a lot of people sitting around waiting to collect a pension." Katharine replied: "We don't have a lot of people like that." For many people, she said, the pension was "incredibly meaningful." I recently asked Dauber for his own recollection of the dispute. "I don't recall, Marty, as that was many years ago," he emailed me. Katharine's account "doesn't sound right to me, but I truly don't recall."

Staff resentment simmered for months—so much so that as late as February 2016, Bezos was pressed on the issue by employees at a staff town hall. "It's important for businesses not to have uncapped liabilities," Bezos replied. "You know, it's a strongly held opinion, it's a philosophical point for me. It has never made sense . . . It's really that simple."

I was no fan of newsroom unions. I appreciated their often-necessary role in our business as a negotiator for well-deserved better wages, benefits, and working conditions. Over years, however, I had seen the newspaper guild stubbornly resist needed workplace transformation when journalism's success—survival, really—urgently depended on it. Newsrooms routinely suffer from a strong gravitational pull back toward what used to be at the expense of what needs to be. Unions had reinforced that intransigence. Plus, I had diminishing tolerance for their belligerent portrayal of managers as malefactors, willful ignorance of what's required to run a sustainable business, self-righteous moralizing, and reflexive opposition to enforcing customary standards for employee behavior, including standards that staffers agreed to upon being hired. But the pension confrontation seemed unnecessary, with low monetary stakes and high costs in terms of morale. It struck me as a warning shot: A new sheriff was in town.

There were other tensions, too. Before Bezos's acquisition, *The Post* had been making plans to sell its historic but obsolete headquarters building at 15th and L Streets NW and move elsewhere. Bezos elected not to purchase the building along with *The Post* itself. Senior *Post* management had concluded that building a new structure in a location near Union Station in the "NoMa" district, where CNN had its D.C. studios, would deliver substantial savings. New construction, though, carried the risk of costly delay, and the location away from downtown's core didn't offer high visibility for *The Post* in a city that was filled with visitors from around the world.

At one point, as the Newseum—a private exhibition space on Washington's famous Pennsylvania Avenue dedicated to free expression and media history—was suffering financially, a portion of its building was put up for lease. The Bezos team considered having the newsroom work there while situating *Post* business operations at another location. The idea was fiercely resisted by Katharine. Severing the newsroom from business operations would undercut a long-standing goal of having the entire organization work as one. The idea ultimately was abandoned.

Oddly, Katharine could not just pick up the phone and call Bezos to hash things out. She had no direct number for him. Nor did she have a private email address. Her emails went to the same address any Amazon customer could use to write him. And though there was obviously a system for Bezos to detect emails from *The Post*, hers would often go unanswered for days, occasionally not at all.

Throughout his first year at *The Post*, Bezos had held no one-on-one meetings with Katharine. He was invariably accompanied, on the phone or in person, by Dauber, who was so averse to public attention that, when his boss first visited our newsroom, he requested (unsuccessfully) that we not publish a photo that included him. Katharine, by her account, had asked Bezos for private meetings without Dauber's presence, but to no avail. The request, she told me at the time, worsened her relationship with Dauber—tension that mystified me because my own dealings with the Bezos aide were uniformly pleasant. Dauber told me for this book that he was "surprised" by Katharine's account. "I never felt any friction working with Katharine," he wrote me. "I certainly wasn't driving any major decisions at *The Post*, personnel or otherwise, and Katharine was always welcome to speak directly and privately with Jeff."

Katharine's own relationship with Bezos could not have been helped when she once missed a flight to Seattle. The rest of the "Pancakes" group held the scheduled meeting in an Amazon conference room without her.

In mid-August 2014, we were told that Bezos was headed to a family gathering in New England but that he'd be making a stopover in Washington, D.C. *Post* executives scrambled to put together a briefing for him. When the session with Bezos ended, I continued speaking with Katharine while Bezos took a bathroom break. Upon his return, Jeff asked to meet with Katharine privately. I knew instantly that something unusual was about to happen. This was the first time they would speak without anyone else present. I suspected the news would not be good.

The private meeting lasted no more than five minutes. Bezos reminded Katharine of what she had told him when he bought *The Post*: He might wish to choose his own publisher. Now, yes, in fact he did. Bezos asked Katharine whether she had considered a "second chapter" for her career. She said she had, accepting the decision to dismiss her while showing no immediate emotion. "You're very unflappable," Bezos told her.

A few hours later, Katharine stepped into my office to tell me what had transpired. I can attest that she was not as unflappable as Bezos imagined. Less than a year had passed since Bezos had taken ownership of the paper. Now, no member of the Graham family, which had controlled *The Washington Post* for eight decades, would be working there. Regime change was complete.

Katharine today exhibits no bitterness. "It makes sense. I came from the [Graham] family," she told me when I asked her to replay her dismissal for me. "Of course, he was going to pick his own publisher." Some days after her first and only private meeting with Bezos, she sent him an email. "I appreciate your grace in doing it in person," she recalls writing. In an interview with a *Post* reporter in early September once her ouster was publicly revealed, Katharine conceded an additional thought: "I just was expecting to at least finish this year. And we are having an awesome year." Bezos was entitled to have a publisher of his choosing, of course. More than anything, though, I was struck by the abrupt and icy dismissal. The same, I figured, could be in store for me when her successor was announced. So many of my contemporaries as editors had become casualties of the turmoil in our business and seemingly inevitable conflicts with publishers over budget cuts and editorial direction.

Upon announcement that Katharine would exit *The Post*, Bezos immediately named Fred Ryan, fifty-nine, our new publisher. Fred had been CEO of Allbritton Communications and founding CEO of its most widely recognized media property, *Politico*, a major rival of *The Post* in the intensely competitive arena of political coverage. He was to be my boss.

Although Fred had spent many years in media, his career was closely tied to the political fortunes of Ronald Reagan. He had been an advance man for Reagan after graduating from law school at the University of Southern California. In the White House he had overseen the president's scheduling operation. He was particularly close to Nancy Reagan, and he followed the Reagans to California to be the former president's chief of staff in the years after he left office. He became chairman of the Ronald Reagan Presidential Foundation and Institute, was an honorary pallbearer at Reagan's funeral, was editor of a book titled *Ronald Reagan: The Wisdom and Humor of the Great Communicator*, and took charge of a yearlong series of events celebrating the hundredth anniversary of Reagan's birth.

Fred made encouraging statements at the outset. "Since I've been in Washington at every incarnation," he declared, "*The Washington Post* has been the dominant news institution in Washington. There's no question about it." And he added that, under Bezos, "*The Post* is better positioned than any other media organization because it's got a mandate to innovate, to experiment, and to do it for the long term."

Fred called me promptly, inviting me to meet with him at the Four Seasons hotel in Georgetown. In the lounge of the Bourbon Steak restaurant, amid the opulent environs of a hotel that proudly boasts its "legacy of intuitive hospitality for high-profile guests, including global leaders and captains of industry," his manner was cordial and genial. Our meeting was nearly as brief as it was hasty. Over nuts and sparkling water, we made some small talk—how we were both natives of Tampa, Florida, for one—and Fred had some nice things to say about me. Fred tells me today they were genuine, though at the time they struck me as perfunctory. Then came the words that, for me, were most substantive and memorable. *The Post*, he said, suffered from "low metabolism."

I took in the remark without comment of my own, but I didn't take it well. That was not *The Post* I knew. I left sore and anxious. Is this what Bezos thought of us, too? I was uncertain I'd last the year.

4

BADASS

Fred Ryan and I couldn't be more different. Fred is perfectly groomed and impeccably attired, invariably with a tie, cuff links, and monogrammed shirts. My hair is unruly, and I opt for casual clothing unless left with no alternative. Sleeves are rolled up.

Fred worked infinitely harder at staying fit. He was a family man, I was single. Fred was a Washington insider, I was an outsider, never having worked in Washington until I joined *The Post*. Fred was a frequent presence at Washington parties where power brokers mingled. I was allergic to that social scene, attending only what I had to.

He was an avid viewer of political shows on television, particularly MSNBC's *Morning Joe*, frequently sending attaboys to *Post* staffers on their broadcast appearances (once sending congratulations for their landing two spots on Sunday's *Meet the Press*). I had little taste for television of any sort, regularly sending notes to staffers about their stories in *The Post* itself. Fred had a sparkling smile. I was known for not smiling nearly enough.

Even as he took charge of *The Post*—which on its editorial page proudly proclaimed itself "An Independent Newspaper"—Fred continued as chairman of the foundation honoring Ronald Reagan that is, as its website declares, "charged with continuing his legacy." It was a role that, surprisingly, didn't draw particular attention until the summer of 2020, when conservative commentator Mark Levin screamed "conflict of interest" after the foundation demanded that Donald Trump and the Republican National Committee stop using Reagan's likeness to raise money. "So the *Washington Post* is running the Reagan Foundation," the president tweeted in outraged reaction, yet without dislodging Fred from the post. The only legacy I was promoting was *The Post*'s. My sole fleeting dalliance with politics was in my senior year of high school, when I volunteered briefly for centrist Democratic senator Henry M. "Scoop" Jackson in his failed 1972 Florida presidential primary campaign. I never again felt an affinity for any candidate, party, or political movement and was deeply mistrustful of politicians generally. I regarded myself as entirely independent. I saw value in being an outsider. As it turned out, there was.

I quickly came to wonder how well Fred and I would work together. Fred was disciplined at keeping emotions in check. And although I had become practiced at doing the same over many decades, I easily lost my cool in early encounters with him. Our first full meeting, in mid-October, was a discomfiting one for me. Fred spoke for a half hour in my office, working off a list on his notepad, about his agenda and perspective on *The Post* and his expectations for our relationship: He'd likely be more involved in the newsroom than his predecessor. What did that mean? I was wary.

Our coverage should never be ideological, he said, adding that he'd stood up before to critics of coverage. I said I was nonideological and didn't care whose ox was being gored. We had stung politicians of both parties, no matter what our critics said about our purportedly liberal leanings. If stories had merit, that's all I cared about. I wondered: Why is he bringing up this subject?

I told him the staff was pissed over the pension suspension. He said the decision was irreversible. Fred said news staffs always suspect a hidden agenda targeted at them. I could scarcely argue. At that very moment, I, too, feared a hidden agenda.

Then Fred asked: What did I want? I spoke immediately of his remarks when we first met: *The Post* did not have an overall metabolism problem, I said, even if there were some pockets of *The Post* that were laggards in adapting to the digital world. I pointed out that per capita *The Post*'s newsroom exceeded *The New York Times* and *Politico* in the online traffic we produced. We couldn't just keep asking reporters and editors to do more and more, I argued. I called for better technology, such as big-data tools that could aid our efforts to boost traffic.

I should have stopped but I went on: I preferred bosses who were straightforward and told me what they thought, ones who didn't conceal the real issues bothering them. It would help if he told people what they were doing right, not just what they were doing wrong. And he needed to show empathy for reporters when many were working under stressful and even risky conditions, especially in overseas conflict zones. It felt to me like we were testing each other, poking wherever we thought the other might be vulnerable. Though we were mutually civil and respectful, neither of us seemed much inclined to defer to the other.

The publisher has responsibility for every aspect of the news organization, including and perhaps especially for its profitability and growth. The top editor's primary responsibility is the strength and integrity of the news report. There is also an editorial page editor—at *The Post*, it was Fred Hiatt—who worked independently of me, overseeing the opinion pages and reporting straight to the publisher himself.

The relationship between a publisher and the top editor for news coverage is almost built for conflict. Journalism is both a profession and a business, but commerce and journalism can make uncomfortable, even incompatible, bedfellows. Publishers typically rise or fall on whether their media outlets succeed commercially. Big advertisers get upset when they come in for negative press coverage. At times they threaten to withhold their business; sometimes they follow through. Politicians can make misery for owners whose fortunes may hinge on their good graces. Some (like Donald Trump) try to make financial mischief for owners (like Jeff Bezos) if coverage isn't to their liking. Advocacy groups often call upon readers to cancel subscriptions if they take offense at even a single story (or phrase). Charges of bias—from all political corners—are common, as are threats of litigation for defamation.

Over my fourteen years as the top editor before Fred became my boss, I had been at loggerheads at one time or another with just about every publisher I'd worked for. Arguments were a constant. Over the size of the staff, their productivity, layoffs, so-called efficiencies, how the newsroom was organized, the pace and nature of digital transformation, and whether we were covering the right subjects in the right way and with the right people. Pressure to do more at lower cost never ceased. I typically felt that publishers and their business teams didn't understand the effort and resources required to practice quality journalism—and that their metrics were, with occasional exception, bullshit.

I was loath to have a publisher intrude too much into news operations. What constituted "too much" made for some nasty disputes. Managing up to one publisher had always been harder for me than managing hundreds of reporters and editors. Remarkably, I hadn't been fired. When Fred now made a nod to the fact that I had worked with many publishers, I interjected, "Yeah, you're my sixth." He chuckled. It came off as impertinent. I kicked myself. I had adapted, more or less, to other publishers. I would have to figure out how to work collaboratively with, yes, my sixth.

When Fred was announced as *The Post*'s publisher, the news department reported the story as it would any other. Then-reporter Karen Tumulty sought to uncover how his selection came to be. In short order, she secured a highly reliable account. Fred has never confirmed it. Neither has he denied it. But my own sourcing backs up what Karen wrote.

Fred had announced in September 2013 that he was stepping down as president of the media company Allbritton Communications and as CEO of the news site *Politico*, which Allbritton owned. Fred retained his membership in the Alfalfa Club, an exclusive Washington social club that holds one massive black-tie banquet annually that is attended by the capital's elite. (Shortly after his own induction in January 2016, Bezos cracked at a newsroom gathering that it was exactly his kind of club—"where you only meet once a year—for dinner.") Membership entitled Fred to invite guests. In January 2014, his guest was a longtime friend, Jean Case, a philanthropist, former technology executive, and the wife of AOL founder Steve Case.

As Karen told the story in a multi-bylined *Post* profile of Fred, Jean Case asked him what he wanted to do next in his career. "I want to be publisher of *The Washington Post*," Fred replied. Case recommended him effusively to Bezos, and by September Fred was handed the job of his dreams. In Fred, Bezos saw an executive with relevant digital-first experience who wouldn't be trapped in the old way of doing things, contrary to the impression he acquired of Katharine as still a creature of *The Post*'s system. Fred was someone he expected to push relentlessly for change and experimentation, and against inertia.

Though Fred and I were not a natural fit for each other, over time we would settle into a constructive, friendly, mutually supportive groove. In the years ahead, he backed me when our newsroom was under political attack. He supported robust hiring of additional news staff. I admired his resolute advocacy for journalists held captive overseas—in particular, our Iran correspondent Jason Rezaian, who was finally released after 544 days in prison there, and Austin Tice, a freelancer who wrote for *The Post* from Syria and has not been liberated since his kidnapping near Damascus in 2012. But first we argued, incessantly and furiously. About almost everything. Whenever Fred entered my office, my executive assistant, sitting just outside my door, knew she would soon hear me shouting. I was stunned that staff and media didn't pick up on the friction between us.

We fought over finding "efficiencies," the need to reorganize (he said yes; I said we did that before he showed up), the number of "midlevel editors" (he said we could use fewer; I said we needed more), whether the newsroom suffered from "silos" (he said yes; I said some but not as much as he imagined), whether we needed to work as assiduously as he insisted at trying to sponsor a presidential debate (he said yes; I doubted it was worth the enormous effort), whether my ethics standards for compensating personnel with dual business and newsroom responsibilities were, as he put it, "antiquated and knee-jerk" (I said they were everlasting), and even who would get invited and where they'd all be seated at the annual White House Correspondents Dinner, an event of unseemly extravagance that was of exactly no interest to me. It went on and on.

Relations were especially frosty when we both showed up as guests at a small dinner party at the home of Chris Matthews—the political commentator, TV host, and author—and his wife, Kathleen, an executive at Marriott and former local TV news anchor. I was seated next to Fred's delightful wife, Genny. She happened to mention, curiously enough, that her husband and I were bound together, our success dependent on each other. Indeed, we were. And her remark gave me something to think about. The Post's success, and our own, depended on the two of us getting along.

At a December 2014 employee town hall, where questions were submitted on note cards, Fred had been asked, "Are you going to keep Marty?" First, he cracked a joke: "This looks like Marty's handwriting." And then he answered the question: Yes, he said. "Why ditch a leader when you have a winning team?"

I clung to that prospect in the months that followed, though it was shy of an ironclad commitment. Somehow, Fred tolerated my combativeness, imposing no penalty. And today he shrugs off our clashes as normal for "people who are passionate." In time we navigated the contentious issues. Tensions dissipated (with episodic flare-ups). He treated me honorably and generously. And after that first very rocky year together, to my astonishment he gave me a handsome bonus, declaring that the newsroom had exceeded every metric set for us, morale was high, and I had made *The Post* better. It wasn't going to be easy, but maybe this pairing of two very different personalities would work out after all.

The area where Fred and I found the most early common ground was in how *The Post* should cover politics. In an echo of Bezos's previous question about how *The Post* might "dominate 2016," Fred now urged us to "win 2016." Fred was a politics junkie—no other subject came anywhere close to interesting him as much—and he wanted us to crush the competition. When I told him we would need even more staff, busting the budget, he was nonplussed. Find "impact players," he said, and submit a plan. Senior editors were only too happy to do so.

Nothing is more central than politics to the identity of *The Post*, which remained, for all its lost luster, the leading news organization in the nation's capital. For the sake of its reputation, political reporting would have to shine; for the sake of its business, too. Politics drew more readers across the country to *The Post* than any other subject.

The Post's coverage of national politics remained strong but faced severe challenges. Only a couple of years before I landed at *The Post*, editors were anguished over the potential departure of revered political writer Dan Balz to the Reuters news service, which had kicked off a hiring spree. Although Balz was persuaded to stay, even journalists within *The Post* feared that the newsroom had ceded its preeminence in precisely the territory where it could least afford to. From his perch at the *Politico* news site of Allbritton Communications, Fred had witnessed an erosion of *The Post*'s competitive position. In one early conversation with me, he took a swipe at prior *Post* management for having allowed *Politico* to be birthed in the first place.

Politico won fans at *The Post*'s expense almost immediately after two *Post* political reporters decamped to create it in 2007. Jim VandeHei and John Harris had pressed *The Post* to set up a separate site with a single-minded focus on politics. When they concluded that support would be more robust, promising, and lucrative outside *The Post* than from within, they took their idea elsewhere. Backing arrived in the person of Robert Allbritton, whose prosperous family had interests in media and banking.

With its web-savvy journalism, granular coverage of politics and policy, multiplying morning newsletters, and a goal to "drive conversation" in official Washington, *Politico* in short order was generating buzz. As early as 2008, the *American Journalism Review* declared that *Politico* "lives up to its hype," quoting *The Post*'s own media writer at the time, Howard Kurtz (later to become media commentator at Fox News), as calling it a "must-read for anyone who follows politics." In 2010, *The New York Times Magazine* placed the author of *Politico*'s influential Playbook newsletter, Mike Allen, prominently on its cover, crowning him "the man the White House wakes up to." *The New Republic* magazine in 2011 called *Politico* "the obsessive-compulsive news organization that has changed journalism in D.C." The plaudits for *Politico* kept coming while *The Post*'s image sagged under a series of dispiriting buyouts.

Bezos's call to "dominate 2016" was a lifeline, and we eagerly grabbed on to it. In preparation for the senior executives' first meeting with Bezos at his Seattle-area home, then–politics editor Steven Ginsberg assembled a memo for beefing up staff and coverage titled "A Path to Dominance." To dominate, he wrote, "requires an aggressive expansion and a commensurate readjustment in structure. It is both an extraordinarily ambitious and eminently achievable goal. Our political team has been built to own the story of the day and most days it delivers on that promise. But while we are very much in the conversation each day, we have a limited ability to lead it. We are also constrained in our ability to wow with graphics and other visual elements. We have almost no capacity to answer the biggest questions before the country. And in every respect, we absolutely must break more news. *The Post* also suffers from an unforced error: our persistent inability to create momentum or buzz behind our stories. That too needs to change if we are to dominate."

Ginsberg's 2013 memo came with a request for fourteen additional journalists of various specialties in his own department and others. He did not immediately get everything he requested, but in the lead-up to the 2016 election he got that and more—just-in-time delivery of heightened politics coverage for one of the most tumultuous chapters in American history. Time and again, Bezos and Fred would authorize us to hire more high-impact politics reporters. Before Fred but especially after his arrival, we were adding impressively to *The Post*'s solid but generally less seasoned roster of political reporters. Among the new high-impact hires: Robert Costa from *National Review*; Matea Gold from the *Los Angeles Times*; Ashley Parker from *The New York Times*; Josh Dawsey, James Hohmann, and Seung Min Kim from *Politico*; Dave Weigel and Toluse Olorunnipa from *Bloomberg*; Philip Bump from *The Atlantic*; Michael Scherer from *Time* magazine; and Matt Viser, Michael Kranish, and Annie Linskey from *The Boston Globe*, among others. By the summer of 2015, media reporter Michael Calderone of *Huffington Post* wrote that *The Washington Post* was "once again laying claim to housing some of the nation's top political reporting talent after years of concern about its future." The politics staff, which numbered roughly two dozen for the 2012 presidential election, doubled during my time at *The Post*, reaching the highest level ever. The muscular journalism that followed put us on a collision course with the next president of the United States. It would also bring us readers in astounding numbers. Before long *The Post* was gaining as many as five thousand additional subscribers every day.

Fred's experience with *Politico* appeared to serve as his template for *The Post*. He imported the site's ideas, its language, and its culture of ceaseless preening. We were to "win the morning" with a series of political and public policy newsletters—seeking to solidify our influence with Washington's power players, gain a greater share of the "leadership" and "advocacy" ads directed at them, siphon off revenue from his previous employer, and get people buzzing about our scoops immediately after they woke up. His early comments about *The Post*'s "low metabolism," he recently acknowledged, arose from contrasting "legacy media companies that can have slower metabolisms" with "lean digital-centric companies" like *Politico*.

Fred shared Bezos's fondness for metrics. One that attracted his resolute attention during my entire tenure was the speed of alerts to readers via apps and email of breaking news and exclusives. A PhD on the technology team had cooked up a system to compare our speed in sending out alerts to that of competitors. These were punishing measurements for every weekday daytime, every weekday night, weekdays overall, and weekends overall. If our alert registered a mere second behind a competitor, we were ranked below it. For the most part, we held the No. 1 position. But when we went several weeks as No. 2 or 3, Fred insisted on knowing why we had "slipped," usually with some taunting reference to how our overall news staff was bigger than that of our competitors'. The explanation often had to do with anomalies and outright flaws in the metric, but that didn't earn us absolution.

Self-promotion—the "bragging" that Bezos wanted—became a top priority. Fred had a special knack for that, and he rarely missed an opportunity for good PR. Reporters needed to be "all over" news programs on television and radio, just as *Politico*'s reporters had been. When I worried that a sharp increase in TV and radio appearances would mean less time for reporters to actually report, Fred said they should consider broadcast appearances part of their jobs. Eventually, *Post* journalists were collectively making a thousand television and radio appearances every month. Once, after Fred copied me on a thank-you note to a politics reporter for being on cable news throughout an entire day—it would allow our work to reach "a larger national and global audience"—she promptly wrote me, "For the record, I actually spent most of the day reporting . . . Honestly!" I was glad she had a sense of my priorities. But true enough, promotion mattered: Getting reporters on TV and radio was how we advertised ourselves to potential readers across the United States. Unlike our most direct competitor, *The New York Times*, we had no national advertising campaign.

Perhaps nothing on television was more important to Fred than MSNBC's *Morning Joe.* In mid-November 2014, hosts Joe Scarborough and Mika Brzezinski, then not yet married to each other, were scheduled to visit Fred, with whom they were friendly. He made plans to roll out the red carpet. The idea was to show off the new energy and direction at *The Post.* Fred would walk them through the newsroom, have them meet with the technology team, and drop in on a team developing the new, supremely visual tablet app that would appear exclusively at first on Amazon's Kindle Fire. A schedule for where they would be escorted and when was distributed to relevant staff. It was to be, as Fred put it, a "full State Visit."

"The eagle has landed," his executive assistant emailed us when they arrived for coffee in Fred's ninth-floor office, which he had selected for having the best view of the Washington Monument from our new headquarters building. But we were reminded that Fred did not want this to look "dog and pony show–ish" and that it should flow "as organically as possible" and "look like a regular working day." Scarborough would be presented with a Kindle Fire loaded with a new app so that he could test it. Instructions were for that bit of gifting to look "spontaneous," too.

It all worked as choreographed. The next day, on *Morning Joe*, Scarborough lavished praise on the "pretty amazing app out there this morning" from *The Washington Post*. Brzezinski called it "gorgeous, beautiful." It was great PR for an initiative in which Bezos was deeply involved, that constituted our first big play for a national paying audience, and that endeavored to incorporate many of a newspaper's best qualities (visual cues, hierarchy, simplicity, sense of completion) into digital form while reducing "cognitive overhead" (a favorite Bezos term often used to describe the numerous decisions that customers had to make for even the most minor tasks).

In plans to publicize the app, Bezos urged us to "talk slightly less about how cool the app is and more about how cool the *Post* is." We needed to "lean on the heritage of *The Post*." As Bezos put it, "Any app can have new features . . . Only *The Post* can have *The Post*." It was reassuring that Bezos saw *The Post*'s journalism, not strictly superior technology features or dazzling self-promotion, as central to our success.

As involved as I was in marketing, new products, strategies, and tactics, it was the journalism that consumed the vast bulk of my attention and interest. *The Post*'s newsroom needed to regain its mojo. As it turned out, we were on a streak.

Only days after Fred assumed his position as publisher, *New York Times* columnist David Carr declared in his media column that *The Post* was "in the middle of a great run, turning out the kind of reporting that journalists—and readers—live for." Carr's assessment was a full reversal from the column he'd written only two years earlier, weeks before I became editor, excoriating *The Post* for bungling and decline. In a column headlined "*The Washington Post* Regains Its Place at the Table," Carr wrote, "Nothing in God's creation is ever as good as it once was, but *The Washington Post* is coming pretty close."

He added, "The killer app . . . is real, actual news. And *The Post* has generated a ton of it."

The Post was setting the nation's news agenda with gratifying regularity. Investigative work put a spotlight on mismanagement and malfeasance. As Carr noted, the streak started with *The Post*'s Pulitzer-winning reporting on the Edward Snowden leaks and the National Security Agency's surveillance.

The Post was now, in late 2014, in the midst of coverage that would win us another Pulitzer. National investigative reporter Carol Leonnig had been reporting episodically on failures and blunders by the Secret Service. There were enough embarrassing stumbles to suggest to me that the agency, its reputation polished to a high shine over decades, suffered from systemic problems. Penetrating the Secret Service, one of the nation's most under-covered and least transparent government agencies, would pose enormous hurdles. But if the Secret Service was a mess, the safety of all those it protected—the president, vice president, other leading political figures and their families—was at risk. I asked Carol and her editors to meet, inquiring if the Secret Service failures constituted a pattern that deserved deeper investigation. Carol said she had become aware of other serious potential lapses, and she happily agreed to spend full time investigating more deeply.

Carol delivered a stunning series of revelations about the performance and mismanagement of the Secret Service: failure to identify and properly investigate shots fired at the White House; how a man with a knife was able to get inside the White House and run through much of the main floor; how a security contractor with a gun and an arrest record was allowed on the same elevator as President Obama, violating Secret Service protocols; how agents purportedly assigned to work on a White House surveillance unit were sent instead to rural Maryland to monitor a dispute involving the Secret Service director's administrative assistant. The director quit amid the revelations. Other supervisors were soon forced out as well.

Additional *Post* investigations landed with similar impact. Aggressive reporting in 2013 led to former Virginia governor Robert F. McDonnell's conviction the following year on charges that he had corruptly used the prestige of his office to help a company executive in exchange for gifts and sweetheart loans. (The conviction was overturned nearly two years later by the Supreme Court, with Chief Justice John G. Roberts Jr. describing McDonnell's behavior as "tawdry" but contesting the government's "boundless interpretation" of the federal bribery statute.)

Another investigation showed how police around the country had seized cash totaling hundreds of millions of dollars from motorists and others who were never charged with any crimes, forcing them to embark on long legal battles to get their money back. Yet another documented the Obama administration's catastrophic mismanagement of the rollout of the Affordable Care Act and the federal health insurance marketplace it established.

Post reporters also had taken huge risks in covering the brutal civil war in Syria, the deadly Israel-Gaza conflict, ongoing wars in Iraq and Afghanistan, and that year's Ebola epidemic in West Africa, where beloved *Post* photojournalist and three-time Pulitzer Prize winner Michel du Cille tragically died in December 2014 at age fifty-eight from an apparent heart attack as he was reporting on the outbreak in remote Liberia. "Sometimes, the harshness of a gruesome scene simply cannot be sanitized," Michel had written in *The Post* that October, "but I believe that the world must see the horrible and dehumanizing effects of Ebola." And then he added: "The story must be told," a simple and stirring declaration that has stayed with me ever since.

With an eye on *The Post*'s storied history, *The New York Times*' Carr took in the totality of *The Post*'s journalism in the first full year of the Bezos era. "*The Post* has been guilty of boring its readers in the past," Carr wrote, "but the current version is a surprising, bumptious news organization—maybe not the pirate ship that Ben

Bradlee helmed as executive editor, but it is a sharp digital and daily read. It's creating challenges for, ahem, its competitors, and bringing significant accountability to the beats it covers."

Ben Bradlee will forever be the reference point for any executive editor of *The Washington Post*. Everyone who has held his position since has been compared, or contrasted, to him. Every editor in the decades ahead almost certainly will be, too. The Watergate investigation he oversaw and his determination to publish the Pentagon Papers in defiance of the Nixon administration will always be considered *Washington Post* swagger at its apogee.

I could not be Bradlee. I did not try. We were starkly different in personality, and journalism had changed radically since he retired as executive editor in 1991. I was periodically asked whether I was intimidated by his legacy. Intimidated, no; inspired, yes. As far back as the early 1970s, when I was an aspiring journalist in college, I had observed his fierce independence and courage. The principles stayed with me.

I did not get acquainted with Bradlee in any meaningful way. I met him on a few occasions at a party at his Georgetown home and at one of the lunches organized by his former colleagues as a way of staying in touch with the man who had defined the modern-day *Post*. His faculties were failing. And on October 21, 2014, the man who had elevated *The Post* to one of the world's leading newspapers died at home of natural causes at age ninety-three. Though his death did not come as a surprise, it sent a shock through a newsroom that had always been lifted by his spirit. There was no longer a Bradlee at *The Post*. No member of the Graham family remained either. An era was over, a new one was now firmly in place.

Bradlee was eulogized eight days later at Washington National Cathedral, where funeral or memorial services have been held for nearly all presidents since its charter was approved by Congress in

1893. "He pulled off being Bradlee because he wasn't afraid," Watergate reporter Carl Bernstein said at his funeral service. "Of presidents, of polio, of political correctness, of publishing the Pentagon Papers . . . of making mistakes." Watergate's Bob Woodward called him a "journalistic warrior" who "made you want to be better." *Post* columnist David Ignatius advised, "Future journalists should ask, 'What would Ben do?'"

Bezos did not know Bradlee, and had not planned to attend the service. When Woodward learned that, he fired off an email: "Understand you're not coming to the Bradlee funeral. He was the soul of the institution that's now yours." Bezos immediately got the picture. "Understood. Thanks. On my way," he responded. And soon he was on his private jet to Washington.

Several times afterward Bezos spoke movingly about the Bradlee funeral service as an awakening. He acknowledged not having fully appreciated the culture of *The Post* until he listened to what its journalists had to say about their longtime leader that morning in the cathedral. He began to better understand *The Post* as a special place with a special role. When he shared those thoughts with me one evening at dinner, I offered up the word "calling" to describe how *Post* journalists feel about their work. He embraced the word as apt, wondering whether *The Post* was different in that way from other newspapers. I said it had been largely the same in every newsroom where I had ever worked.

On another occasion, he confessed to a *Post* executive, "I didn't get it before. Now I get it." And when he spoke to employees upon the February 2016 grand opening of our sleek new headquarters on K Street facing Washington's Franklin Square, he brought the subject up again, elaborating in remarks to employees about the memorial service as a "formative" experience.

"I came, and I didn't really know what to expect," he said. That's where I really started to understand a piece of the culture of this institution . . . What I started to figure out is this is a badass newspaper . . . I think it's very distinctive . . . I'm not sure exactly where it comes from. Probably some of the characters in the past who led this institution. Maybe we were always a little hungrier because we weren't the paper of record. Maybe there's a little more ambition of a different kind. That swagger, that swashbuckling character—but combined with what is really a very professional team of reporters and editors."

Bezos had discovered the quality that made *The Post* exceptional, the intangible but essential ingredient that had been key to its success over decades. Over time he would call *The Post* "badass" many times. He meant it in the sense of fearless, driven, daring, tough, uncompromising on principles, confident, even intimidating. He admired what he saw. And they were qualities that would be key to our continued success, most notably when a president sought to bully us.

"The most important things about institutions, once they've been around for a while," he said, "cannot be imposed from the outside. They are already built in. If you try to change them, you're just squandering a resource. Instead, what you do is you try to figure out what they are, and kind of uncover them, and eventually learn to articulate them."

As the year 2015 got underway, the still-new *Post* owner kept investing. We were delivering results. We had acquired business momentum for the digital age. Our journalistic capacity and power were growing. Ambitious, agenda-setting journalism at *The Post* was holding the powerful to account. The NSA. The Secret Service. Who had really penetrated these organizations before? We were trumpeting our achievements. Our sense of purpose was strong. Spirits were up. We had come a long way fast. And just in time.

5

SHOWTIME

Donald Trump was not on our list of expectations for 2015. Our opinionated politics blog, The Fix, led by Chris Cillizza, who later left for CNN, had begun ranking leading presidential candidates as early as 2013. A look back shows the pitfalls—folly, really—of political forecasting.

That February, Senator Marco Rubio of Florida led the first ranking of Republican presidential prospects, "christened—by us and others—as the new de facto leader of the Republican Party." By September, Senator Rand Paul of Kentucky had ascended to the top of Chris's ranking: "Underestimate him at your peril." In October, attention turned to the rising prospects of New Jersey governor Chris Christie: "No one weighing a run for the Republican presidential nomination has had a better year than Chris Christie—and it's about to get better." Soon, a scandal made his year, and his presidential prospects, much worse.

It might have made sense at that point for The Post's politics blog to cease ranking candidates. But political punditry resists restraint: Jeb Bush surged, only to quickly collapse. Then: Mitt Romney might run for the presidency a third time. No, he wouldn't.

Notwithstanding the errant rankings, The Post was early to the prospect that Trump might be the one to rise. Trump told The Post's Robert Costa in late February 2015 that he was "more serious" than ever about running for the presidency. He had hired an election attorney and some impressive staff in key states, and he had pushed off signing for another season of NBC's *The Celebrity Apprentice*. While acknowledging the political challenge for Trump—until then he had been largely "a provocateur on the sidelines of Republican politics"—Bob envisioned how the race might shape up: Trump "would bring into the race a colorful contender with deep pockets and a national following—attracting media attention and forcing others to respond to his views."

Bob's interview with Trump drew skepticism and chuckles from political operatives as well as media. The *Christian Science Monitor*'s Peter Grier wrote that "Trump will move to Maine and raise beets before he runs for president. It's not happening, no way, no chance, let's be real." Other outlets chose to ignore what Trump told Bob, giving his interview no attention whatsoever. Trump, after all, had hinted at running several times before and then didn't—except for a flirtation with the Reform Party nomination in 2000, when he abandoned the Republican Party as "just too crazy right."

But Bob understood the Republican base as well as anyone. It had been his beat previously at the conservative *National Review*. As far back as 2011, he witnessed Trump whip a gathering of the Conservative Political Action Committee (CPAC) into a frenzy as he called the United States a "laughingstock" and "whipping post" in its trade deals. Trump gave him his personal cell phone number afterward, and they regularly stayed in touch. Bob suspected the Republican Party might move "in this populist, nationalist, nativist direction."

When *The Post* and ABC News in May 2015 conducted their first joint poll that included Trump among prospective candidates, only 4 percent of registered Republican voters listed him as their preference. There were clues even then, though, that the electoral landscape was due for a shock. Trump's standing was weak, but no one else looked strong. Scott Walker, the governor of Wisconsin, and Rand Paul, senator from Kentucky, barely led the field with 11 percent support each.

Still, few imagined that, when the pieces of the election puzzle fell together, they would display the image of Donald Trump. *The Post* was no exception. The depth of antiestablishment anger throughout the country eluded us. Washington media have long been faulted for living in a bubble, and there remains plenty of truth to that. Years before the 2016 presidential election, our reporters should have been traveling far from home base to take the country's mood. We had failed to do that. That was a mistake we would seek to avoid repeating. More reporters would have to go to more places and do more listening.

The Post has a long history of aggressively investigating major-party nominees for president. For good reason. They aim to occupy the most powerful position in the world. The time would come for us to dig deeply into Trump's personal and business histories, messy as both were. But in early 2015, no one was counting on Trump to be the nominee.

Hillary Clinton, though, was a solid bet to get the Democratic Party's nod, even if Vermont senator Bernie Sanders was working tenaciously to prove otherwise. Her record deserved a good scrubbing. So, before Trump started racking up primary victories, *The Post* devoted more of its investigative resources to her than to any other candidate. When you're a dominant front-runner, that's what you should expect.

The Post's reporting focused heavily on the Clinton Foundation, which by then had dominion over $440 million in assets and was raking in contributions of $200 million annually. In February 2015, *Post* staffers Rosalind Helderman, Tom Hamburger, and Steven Rich reported on the $2 billion that had been dispatched into the foundation. "The organization has given contributors entrée, outside the traditional political arena, to a possible president," *The Post* reported. Contributing lavishly were financial firms and "foreign donors and countries that are likely to have interests before a potential Clinton administration—and yet are ineligible to give to U.S. political campaigns." Millions came from foreign governments even as Clinton was secretary of state. In Canada, more than a thousand donors to a charity affiliated with the Clinton Foundation were undisclosed, contradicting pledges of transparency.

The Post's coverage also was directed at the origins of the Clintons' wealth, particularly since the presidential contender declared in 2014 that she and Bill Clinton were "dead broke" when his presidency ended in 2001. How they recovered from enormous debts and ascended to the ranks of the superrich was a story *The Post* was obligated to tell. And it did: the power couple's $25 million in speaking fees in little more than one year; how Bill Clinton himself earned nearly $18 million as the "honorary chancellor" of a for-profit college; how, all told, the former president collected more than $65 million in consulting, speaking, and writing fees during Hillary's four-year tenure as secretary of state.

A sweeping look at the Clintons' fund-raising machine in November 2015, titled "Two Clintons. 41 Years. $3 Billion," reported that the Clintons had built an "unrivaled global network of donors while pioneering fundraising techniques that have transformed modern politics." At issue was whether big-money donors were currying favor with a secretary of state and prospective president.

As early as March 2015, *The New York Times* disclosed that Clinton had used a private email server in her Chappaqua, New York, home to conduct government business during her time as secretary of state, raising questions about whether she had violated department rules on retaining agency records and had failed to safeguard classified information. *The Times*' scoop reinforced a common view of Clinton: obsessively secretive and disinclined to play by the same rules required of everyone else. Clinton allies would repeatedly argue that the issue was overblown, but it was a self-inflicted wound that never healed.

Clinton didn't help her standing with the press or the public by letting days go by with an initially stingy three-sentence statement: "I want the public to see my email. I asked State to release them. They said they will review them for release as soon as possible." Nor was her image helped when she attributed her email practices to mere "convenience" or by the revelation that half of sixty thousand emails from her time in office were deleted as personal on the sole say-so of her team and herself.

Coverage of Clinton's private server began to dissipate after a few weeks. But it would be given fresh life in late July, when the inspector general for the intelligence community declared that his office had reviewed a small sample of forty Clinton emails and identified four that contained information that should have been designated as classified, even if it wasn't marked as such. The FBI began its investigation based on a referral from the IG's office.

The drip-drip-drip release of information about Clinton's State Department emails, the monthslong delay in her delivery of an apology (not until September), the discovery that additional emails on her server contained classified information, and an extraordinary ongoing FBI investigation of a major presidential candidate commanded our attention.

As always, we made coverage decisions in real time, not knowing what ultimately would be revealed. In that context, in my view, our own reporting was not overdone. With the benefit of hindsight, however, it's easy to argue that coverage by the press overall was disproportionate to the transgression, given the overriding stakes in the election. Clinton's practices were not materially worse than those of former secretary of state Colin Powell, with whom she once exchanged emails on communications practices.

The Post's own editorial page, over which I had no responsibility, finally expressed exasperation after NBC's Matt Lauer insistently pressed her on the issue at a national security forum in the election's closing months. "The Hillary Clinton Email Story Is Out of Control," read the headline. The editorial writers lamented that "one would think that her homebrew server was one of the most important issues facing the country this election. It is not."

This was the same editorial page, however, that had declared in March that Clinton's email decisions "were based on what was best for her—what was 'convenient'—and not so much for the public trust." Fourteen months later, *The Post*'s editorial page said that Clinton "had plenty of warnings to use official government communications methods, so as to make sure that her records were properly preserved and to minimize cybersecurity risks. She ignored them." That later editorial was headlined "Clinton's Inexcusable, Willful Disregard for the Rules." There was one sure way Clinton could have ensured no coverage, and no FBI investigation, at all. She could have followed those rules in the first place.

Roughly two months into the furor over Clinton's private email server, her allies would be labeling the investigation by a House Republican-led committee into the matter a "witch hunt." It wouldn't be long before her Republican opponent-to-be would use identical language when a harsh spotlight fell on him.

Trump had spent his decades in Manhattan real estate cultivating the press, feeding stories to New York's tabloids to mold an image as a rakish, glamorous, and cunning entrepreneurial success—notwithstanding a series of defaults and bankruptcies that would have been humbling, if not humiliating, for anyone else. His business record had not escaped tough scrutiny over the years, however. Journalist Wayne Barrett was the pioneer in truth-telling about Trump. Barrett reported doggedly on Trump for the *Village Voice* since 1977 and for his own landmark book, *Trump: The Deals and the Downfall*, in 1991, tracking chicanery and bombast in virtually every facet of his life. "Donald Trump is a user of other users," he wrote as early as 1979. Barrett would later write, "He had prided himself on never having met a public official, a banker, a lawyer, a reporter, or a prosecutor he couldn't seduce. Some he owned, and others he merely manipulated."

Trump entered the presidential campaign having shaken off journalists who dug into his muddy business record and with his public image burnished by his starring role as host of *The Apprentice*. As *The Post*'s Marc Fisher wrote, the show "turned Trump from an easily caricatured Richie Rich who had just weathered some difficult years into a pop-culture truth-teller, an evangelist for the American gospel of success, a decider who insisted on standards in a country that had somehow slipped into handing out trophies just for showing up."

Trump was a showman, and while *The Post*'s political staff concluded early on that Trump shouldn't be ruled out as a serious candidate, his announcement on June 16, 2015, was expected to be the ultimate expression of his showmanship. Which is how *The Post* covered it. Even the crowd in the glistening gold atrium of Manhattan's Trump Tower was spectacle and fakery. "In reality," *The Post*'s Ben Terris wrote, "members of team Trump spent the hour before the event out in the streets of midtown Manhattan trying to lure tourists in to fill out the crowd. A man in a pressed suit who would say only that he 'worked for Trump' offered passersby free T-shirts and already-made signs, many handwritten, to hold if they would come on in and see the show."

Ben's story cited Trump's call for a border wall, his attack on the nuclear deal with Iran, and his signature blend of the pugilistic (America is run by "losers") and the apocalyptic ("The American dream is dead"). And yet it overlooked some notable substance, making no mention of Trump's most incendiary words: "When Mexico sends its people, they're not sending their best . . . They're sending people that have lots of problems, and they're bringing those problems with us. They're bringing drugs. They're bringing crime. They're rapists. And some, I assume, are good people." Ben recalls seeing Trump's rant about Mexicans go viral and feeling that he didn't need to be the "zillionth" reporter to quote it. Now he feels remorse at the omission. "I think about this all the time, actually," he told me. "For history's sake, I wish it were in there, and I regret not seeing how important it would become."

Trump's crude, racist, and regularly revolting language sent shudders through the media, political, and cultural establishment. But it worked. A *Washington Post*–ABC News Poll in mid-July showed Trump surging ahead of all Republican Party opponents. Trump suddenly had the support of a quarter of registered Republicans and Republican-leaning independents. Almost six in ten Republicans viewed Trump favorably. Only two months earlier, just about the same percentage regarded him unfavorably.

Almost nothing Trump said or did—no matter how boorish, malicious, or misleading—would make a long-lasting difference in his popularity. Not his disparaging comments about John McCain. ("He's not a war hero. He was a war hero because he was captured. I like people who weren't captured.") Not his call months later to ban all Muslims from entering the United States. The press, including *The Post*, would be awash in stories about the "storm" and "outrage" he had provoked. But as Marco Rubio's campaign manager, Terry Sullivan, would say, "Whatever we call them—snafus, faux pas, misstatements—I certainly don't think the Republican primary electorate was nearly as offended by any of these statements as the media." The question before GOP voters was this, he said: "Should I side with Donald Trump, who said something I may not fully agree with, or the media, who's just kicking the crap out of him for saying it?"

We in the establishment press focused on his bigoted smear of people who had come from Mexico. Republican voters saw a candidate who would do something about immigration. We honed in on the questionable constitutional grounds for banning all Muslims and the discriminatory animus behind his proposal. The GOP primary electorate saw a candidate who would do something about terrorism. Our concerns, no matter how justified in law and fact and fairness, were not those of most Republican voters. Among GOP voters and those who leaned Republican, his support continued to surge: 33 percent by September and 38 percent by December, according to *The Post*–ABC News poll, leaving sixteen opponents to fight over the remaining pieces of the pie. Trump's piece was "made out of titanium," Todd Harris, a strategist for Rubio's presidential campaign, remarked after the election.

The more worked up we in the press became, the more delighted Republican voters were. They wanted someone to punch us in the face, and Trump was eager to take a bare-knuckled swing. "One of the things we saw consistently in our research," Trump pollster Tony Fabrizio would say, "is voters overwhelmingly preferred to have somebody who spoke their mind, even though it wasn't politically correct. Every time Donald Trump said something, and he went downstairs and doubled down, that only proved to those voters that he would speak his mind and not lie to them." Trump did lie, routinely. To much of the public, though, he sounded like a straight shooter.

The Post's Dave Weigel reported in December 2015 on a focus group in Alexandria, Virginia, of twenty-nine voters who supported Trump or used to. Frank Luntz, a Republican media consultant, tried everything possible—every ad, attack, or wild statement by the candidate himself—to make Trump look bad. Nothing worked. "To Luntz's amazement, hearing negative information about the candidate made the voters . . . hug the candidate tighter," Dave wrote. "Participants derided the mainstream media, accusing reporters of covering snippets of Trump quotes when the full context would have validated him . . . None in the group wanted to find themselves on the side of the mainstream media—or of President Obama." It was one of the most telling stories of the presidential campaign. To my regret, it wasn't pitched for publication on the front page.

Trump and his campaign's relationship with *The Post* went through wild swings, from courtship to condemnation and back again. A month before Trump announced for the presidency, he spoke in Des Moines at the Lincoln Dinner of the Iowa Republican Party. White House reporter Phil Rucker recalls observing Trump and his entourage meeting in a side room of the Iowa Events Center when he was approached by an elegant young woman. It was Hope Hicks, who became the Trump campaign's communications director. "If you ever need to reach Mr. Trump," she said, offering her Trump Organization business card, "here's my number. Call me." Trump was seeking the credibility that comes with major media attention.

Courtship turned to confrontation in July. Phil and Bob Costa were in Phoenix for a rally at the convention center where Trump gave a defiant seventy-minute speech, slamming immigrants, NBC, Macy's, NASCAR, U.S. ambassador to Japan Caroline Kennedy, and Hillary Clinton, among others. Bob accompanied Trump back to New York's LaGuardia Airport on his Boeing 757, having filed material to Phil while in transit to the plane. In midair, after Hicks handed Trump a printout of the co-bylined story, he stomped to the back of the plane to unleash a tirade against Bob. Trump was livid that the story had set the crowd size at a number he considered far too low—4,200—and that his speech had been described as "rambling." Bob hadn't seen the final story as written by Phil and hadn't chosen the adjective, even if it was anything but inapt. But he and Phil had diligently checked how many people the convention center could accommodate.

"He exploded at me . . . kind of waving the article around, berating me and *The Washington Post* for not understanding how big the crowd was outside the arena," Bob remembers. "I think to myself, 'I'm alone as a reporter. There's no one else on this plane going across the country. Stay cool.' I said, 'Mr. Trump, we checked, that's the capacity of the arena. It was full.' And he said, 'Well, there was tens of thousands of people outside. That's the real crowd size.' And he kind of tossed the paper toward me."

Bob was still able to get an in-flight interview with Trump, though the candidate cut off questions with a profane flourish after a mere eight minutes: "What the fuck else do you have? Are you finished yet?" After landing at LaGuardia, Trump barred Bob from joining him and his staff on the bus that carried private-plane passengers to the terminal. "You wait for the next bus!" he commanded.

"So petty and childish" is how Bob remembers the episode. "His anger was out of control." Bob returned to the newsroom, telling his direct editors and me that Trump was "kind of unhinged" on the flight. Phil remembers the moment as the "very first flash point" in Trump's conflict with *The Post*, reflecting "his temper, his pique, his thin skin when it came to how the media viewed him."

Only a few months later Trump was Mr. Congeniality. Bob, Phil, and Dan Balz were in Trump Tower to meet with the candidate for an hour. That October day, he was, as Phil remembers it, "solicitous and trying to charm us," giving them a tour of sports memorabilia and framed magazine covers—"real and fake"—on his office wall. As party leaders theorized that his candidacy might fade, Trump was outlining the next chapter of his campaign, with more TV advertising and a beefed-up infrastructure. Trump, Phil says, "was trying to prove to us he would be a durable candidate."

The Post's independent editorial page, incensed over Trump's resentful, race-baiting populism and unending falsehoods, made him a regular object of rebuke. On December 5, 2015, a searing editorial declared Trump "corrosive to the U.S. political debate in at least two ways." One was "his basic contempt for facts." The other was that he "sees people as caricatures and stereotypes to be poked at and exploited rather than as individuals with dignity." The editorial argued that "these are among the reasons that no mainstream party should associate with Mr. Trump."

In the newsroom, we were documenting those Trump traits every day. His disdain for truth was constant fodder for *The Post*'s Fact Checker team, led by Glenn Kessler, which would enter its busiest years ever as Trump embarked on a course of historic mendacity that got a running start with his June 16 announcement of a presidential run. "Businessman Donald Trump is a fact checker's dream . . . and nightmare," Glenn and Michelle Ye Hee Lee had declared in June while debunking one statement after the next in his announcement speech. On December 7, Glenn took on another Trump doozy. Trump had repeatedly claimed that he predicted in his 2000 book that Osama bin Laden would attack the United States and that "you need to take him out." Glenn awarded him "Four Pinocchios," meaning it was off-the-charts false, or a "whopper."

Nobody's quite sure what set Trump off that same December 7, but he apparently had enough of *The Post* and, for the first time, targeted our multibillionaire owner, Jeff Bezos, in a ten a.m. Twitter threesome. "The @washingtonpost, which loses a fortune, is owned by @JeffBezos for purposes of keeping taxes down at his no profit company, @amazon," he tweeted. "The @washingtonpost loses money (a deduction) and gives owner @JeffBezos power to screw public on low taxation of @Amazon! Big tax shelter," he followed up. And then: "If @amazon ever had to pay fair taxes, its stock would crash and it would crumble like a paper bag. The @washingtonpost scam is saving it!"

The tweets could not have been more detached from reality. Amazon, a company with public shareholders, doesn't own *The Post* and never did. *The Post* is Bezos's personal property. But verifiable facts weren't the point. Payback was. "I love getting even when I get screwed by someone," Trump said in one of his books years before ever running for president. "When you are in business you need to get even with people who screw you. You need to screw them back

15 times harder. You do it not only to get the person who messed with you but also to show the others who are watching what will happen to them if they mess with you."

Bezos at the time was a Twitter novice, having posted his maiden tweet on November 24, 2015, celebrating the successful flight of the New Shepard rocket ship built by Blue Origin, his commercial space company. Twitter newcomers often have itchy fingers, and Bezos certainly did on December 7. "Finally trashed by @realDonaldTrump. Will still reserve him a seat on the Blue Origin rocket. #sendDonald-tospace," he wrote on Twitter. Witty, yes, but a rookie mistake. Trump doesn't take well to humor at his expense, as Bezos would learn the hard way.

In February 2016, he made explicit that he would punish Amazon because of *The Washington Post* if he became president. "I have respect for Jeff Bezos, but he bought *The Washington Post* to have political influence," Trump said at a rally in Fort Worth, Texas. "He wants political influence so that Amazon will benefit from it. That's not right. And believe me, if I become president, oh, do they have problems." Bezos by then knew better than to offer a retort. Trump was a genius at getting under people's skin, and Bezos was resolved not to let it happen to him again.

Despite vilifying *The Post* and its owner, the very next month Trump was in our new offices on K Street, having accepted an invitation of the editorial board to meet. The editorial board oversees the opinion pages, including the very editorials that had eviscerated Trump. The news department that I ran plays no role in the opinions department. Nor does the opinions department have any influence over how reporters and their editors cover the news. In that way, *The Post* maintains the independence of news coverage. So I wasn't invited to attend. No one from the news department was. Hours later, the editorial board provided us a transcript.

Trump began with a conciliatory remark that contradicted what he'd been saying on the campaign trail: "I think we're all in the same business of trying to make our country better, a better place. So, we have something in common." But then he quickly shifted into grievance mode: "I've been treated very, very badly by *The Washington Post*." While voicing his sour view of NATO, China, American military investments in Asia, "nation-building" in places like Iraq, and the U.S. economy—with a lengthy monologue on the size of his hands (so bizarre that it was reenacted verbatim on *The Daily Show with Trevor Noah*)—Trump reiterated a recent threat of his: He'd toughen up libel laws. "All I want is fairness," he said. "The laws are really impotent."

Trump's rhetoric on the stump may have struck us as outrageous and dangerous, but a large segment of the American public felt what he was saying was long overdue. Reporters were assigned to take the measure of his supporters. We needed to understand and communicate what made him so popular.

One former employee of a liberal arts college in Ohio who showed up at a Trump rally told *The Post* in early 2016 that Trump was "saying what a lot of Americans are thinking but are afraid to say because they don't think that it's politically correct" and that people were "tired of just standing back and letting everyone else dictate what we're supposed to think and do." The story, by Karen Tumulty and Jenna Johnson, was headlined "Why Trump May Be Winning the War on Political Correctness." Critics saw the campaign against "political correctness" as a cover for racism, sexism, and intolerance, while Trump supporters claimed legitimate policy and cultural differences.

Jenna recounted that January how Trump was taking his rallies to places, even in blue states, that rarely saw a presidential candidate so early in a campaign. "In each crowd," she wrote, "there's an overwhelming feeling that the economy is still not doing well enough—and a resignation that it might never get better than this without some sort of dramatic change." Although the recipient of vast family wealth—an estimated $413 million, much of it from dodgy tax schemes, as *The New York Times* documented—Trump cast himself, Jenna wrote, as "an underdog of sorts who beat the system with some basic common sense, and his biggest cheers often come when he bashes Democrats, the Republican establishment, the media, money-grubbing corporations or any other institution that has let people down."

Left-leaning critics of press coverage argued that *The Post* and other news outlets spent too much time talking to supporters like those. We were accused of amplifying and normalizing racism and intolerance. Stories like these didn't do that at all. These were stories that deserved our attention. We didn't anticipate a Trump-like candidacy because we hadn't spent enough time listening to the people who now saw him as speaking for them. We couldn't keep making that mistake.

Though casting himself as a no-holds-barred truth-teller, Trump had made the truth itself his enemy. His political career was built on that. Trump was already infamous for his leading role in promoting the "birther" lie that Barack Obama was not born in the United States, claiming in 2011 that he had sent investigators to Hawaii ("and they cannot believe what they're finding") and asserting the following year that an "extremely credible source" had told him Obama's birth certificate was a "fraud."

Ever fond of fabrications, dark innuendo, and baseless character assassination, Trump would intimate that Senator Ted Cruz's father had some sinister connection to the 1963 assassination of President John F. Kennedy, based solely on a *National Enquirer* story asserting that a man in a photo that year with Lee Harvey Oswald looked like Rafael Cruz, a claim that independent experts could not corroborate. "What was he doing—what was he doing with Lee Harvey Oswald shortly before the death? Before the shooting? It's horrible," Trump said. Cruz would call it "false tabloid garbage," and it was.

Trump's disregard for truth—disdain, really—had been his life-long pattern. He was a master of the mirage. In *The Art of the Deal,* Trump extolled what he called "truthful hyperbole," which he de-fined as "an innocent form of exaggeration." He seemingly could not appreciate that distortions of the truth, by definition, are not true. He misrepresented the number of floors in his buildings, by a lot. He portrayed himself as having a Midas touch when he had suffered a half dozen corporate bankruptcies. He disclaimed any commercial ties to Russia when evidence showed otherwise, including his lawyer Michael Cohen's pursuit of a Trump Tower project in Moscow right through the presidential election.

There was no chapter in Trump's life that didn't deserve to be thoroughly investigated. Odds were high that his story wasn't the true story.

With Trump's campaign gaining momentum, *The Post* directed its attention to his business empire. In October 2015, reporters exam-ined how, in his real estate projects in Manhattan and his casinos in Atlantic City, Trump regularly did business with known Mafia figures. Trump was never accused of being a participant in a mob-connected criminal enterprise, and organized crime so infiltrated the construction industry at the time that it was nearly impossible to avoid business relationships with it. Yet, as *Post* reporter Robert O'Harrow noted, "No serious presidential candidate has ever had Trump's depth of documented business relationships with mob-controlled entities."

Post journalists poked into the failed Trump Mortgage, the de-mise of Trump University (a nonuniversity that many attendees ended up suing as a rip-off), and the use of cheap foreign labor for his clothing line. Reporters Tom Hamburger and Roz Helderman also took note of a strikingly large number of connections to Russian individuals. His interest in doing business in Russia was long-standing. One associate was Felix Sater, a Russia-born businessman whom Trump anointed to pursue projects in Moscow, Florida, and New York. While the proposed Moscow venture never got off the ground, Trump was left with the stink and stain of partnering with someone who, in addition to his conviction for participating in a Mafia-connected stock scheme, did time in prison for stabbing a man in the face with the stem of a margarita glass. Sater described a familiar and friendly relationship with Trump. He was given Trump Organization office space and business cards, which identified him as a "senior adviser" to Trump. Trump said he barely knew the guy.

In mid-June 2016, *The Post* followed up with a thorough examination of Trump's thirty-year pursuit of business in, and from, Russia: how he brought his Miss Universe pageant to Moscow with the support of one of the country's billionaires; his continuing pursuit of a Trump Tower in Moscow; his effort to develop luxury hotels there; his son Donald Jr.'s repeated business trips to Russia and revelatory boast in 2008 that "Russians make up a pretty disproportionate cross-section of a lot of our assets . . . We see a lot of money pouring in from Russia"; the pursuit of Russian buyers for a Trump condo project in Panama; and how Trump flipped a Palm Beach mansion in less than four years to a Russian oligarch for $95 million after paying $41.4 million for it.

There was good reason for *The Post* and other media to be exploring all these Russian ties. Trump aspired to immense power. His default measure of the world was through opportunities for profit. He was angling for business deals even as he ran for president. Any gains for the Trump Organization would benefit him. Voters deserve to know about potential conflicts of interest for an occupant of the White House.

Editors at *The Washington Post* had assigned a series of stories to thoroughly examine key chapters in the life of Donald Trump, from his purchase of a team in the United States Football League, an organization that collapsed several years later, to his failed Atlantic City gambling operations and his marriages that dissolved. It was almost enough to write a book. And then *Post* reporter Michael Kranish proposed we do just that.

Before joining *The Post*, Michael had been a longtime reporter in Washington for *The Boston Globe*. While I was *The Globe*'s editor, he had co-authored biographies on Massachusetts senator John Kerry and the state's governor, Mitt Romney, when each sought the presidency eight years apart. When staffers launched the Kerry biography, I urged them to "leave no crumbs on the table." Nothing should be left unexamined. That is how journalists should cover someone who might well occupy the Oval Office. And there is a long history of that sort of deep reporting. Kranish's outline for a book on Trump proposed the same. We made a commitment to the publisher to deliver a manuscript in time for publication shortly after the Republican convention in July 2016. To do a thorough job so quickly we would have to assign twenty additional reporters to help.

When a book deal was signed, co-author Marc Fisher contacted Hope Hicks, Trump's campaign spokesperson, seeking a series of interviews. Before he could finish explaining the project, Hicks cut him off, protesting that *The Post* was being "incredibly disingenuous" and was "profiteering off Mr. Trump." She made it instantly clear that Trump absolutely would not participate, certainly not with *The Washington Post*. That was on a Friday in April. The following Monday an upbeat Hicks called Marc back. "I told Mr. Trump about your project, and he loves it," Hicks said, as Marc and Michael recounted in a story published in August, after Trump officially became the Republican nominee. "He's happy to meet with you."

Trump would go on to participate in twenty hours of interviews with *Post* reporters for *Trump Revealed: An American Journey of*

Ambition, Ego, Money, and Power. He shaded, evaded, and misstated the truth, but he made himself available. Of all the presidential candidates we had ever encountered, he was the most accessible, often extending interviews from a scheduled hour to two or three. "He's insatiable in his desire to get press. Also, he loves trying to mold the story," Marc said.

Trump didn't set aside his brutish impulses. If the book wasn't to his liking, he told them, he would cut *The Post* off from access. He would "destroy" their lives. Soon, what Trump was hearing about the book wasn't to his liking at all. In May, he and his allies erupted after the *Washington Examiner*, a right-leaning news outlet, reported that celebrated *Post* investigative journalist Bob Woodward had told the National Association of Realtors in Washington that the project to "dig into every facet" of Trump's life had been "urged on by new owner Jeff Bezos," who wanted *The Post* "to reveal everything about the potential nominees." Those were the *Examiner*'s words. The paper quoted Bob saying of Bezos, "He said, 'Look, the job at the *Washington Post* has to be tell us everything about who the eventual nominee will be in both parties, 15-part, 16-part series, 20-part series, we want to look at every part of their lives and we're never going to get the whole story of course but we can get the best attainable."

Bob described the story as "a classic example of a manufactured controversy." He had merely indicated that *The Post* and Bezos supported in-depth, exhaustive reporting on both the Republican and Democratic nominees. Bob is the nation's best-known investigative reporter and a prolific, bestselling book author; he gets scoops and brings Watergate-era fame. But Bob, by then seventy-three years old, hadn't been an actual *Post* employee for years, though he retained the honorific title of "associate editor." He hadn't participated in our decision to deploy a big team of reporters on a biography of Trump. Nor had I or anyone in our newsroom spoken to Bezos about it. If Bezos said anything like what Bob quoted him as saying, I sure never heard it.

Ever since Bezos had acquired *The Post*, we had to bat away suspicions that he was meddling in our news decisions. Here we were once again, and I had to speak up, responding to reporters' queries with a statement: "I can say categorically that I have received no instructions from Jeff Bezos regarding our coverage of the presidential campaign—or, for that matter, any other subject."

Trump was never one to miss an opportunity for attack. He seized on the *Washington Examiner* story about Bob to denounce Bezos. Trump knew *The Post*'s newsroom would never cave to his pressure. So why not lean heavily on the owner who might worry more about his commercial interests? Maybe that would work.

Trump took to Fox News' Sean Hannity to unload with a blast of wild, but by now familiar, accusations: Bezos was using *The Post*, he said, "as a tool for political power against me and against other people and I'll tell you what, we can't let him get away with it." Trump's supporters followed up by sending ugly, profane emails to Bezos. Though taken aback by the vitriol, Bezos gave no hint of being intimidated. "I'm glad I bought *The Post*," he reassured us in an email, and he expressed appreciation for the "incredibly important" job of "looking closely at the candidates for President of this treasure of a country."

Six days after Trump's broadside on Fox I was scheduled to interview Bezos at one of *The Post*'s live events. I gave Bezos's staff a heads-up that I would be asking about Trump's attacks. His remarks would be the first made publicly about Trump's denunciations.

"Most of the world's population," Bezos said, "live in countries where, if you criticize the leader, you can go to jail. We live in the oldest and greatest democracy in the world, with the strongest free-speech protections in the world, and it's something that we are, I think, rightly proud of . . . We want a society where any of us, any individual in this country, any institution in this country, if they choose to, can scrutinize, examine, and criticize an elected official, especially a candidate for the highest office in the most powerful country on Earth."

Then he added: "We have fundamental laws, and we have constitutional rights in this country to free speech, but that's not the whole reason that it works here. We also have cultural norms that support that, where you don't have to be afraid of retaliation. And those cultural norms are at least as important as the Constitution." As for Trump's threats against Amazon itself: "My view is that's not an appropriate way for a presidential candidate to behave."

I could not have been more gratified by Bezos's remarks. In all my time as a working journalist I had never witnessed a presidential candidate so determined to demolish an independent press and exact vengeance on a media owner. Trump's threats recalled the administration of Richard Nixon in 1973, when I was studying journalism in college. Nixon's allies, with his blessing, sought to challenge the licenses of *The Post*'s Florida television properties to avenge the newspaper's Watergate coverage.

Trump's attacks on Bezos were also a cynical turnabout. In August 2013, five days after the announcement that Bezos would buy *The Post*, Trump heaped praise on both Bezos and the paper. "I think it's a great move for him, I think it's great for *The Washington Post*," Trump said. He called himself a "fan" of *The Post* and Bezos an "amazing guy," predicting he would take the news organization to "that next plateau." Having now experienced our political coverage, Trump's affection for *The Post* and Bezos was instantly extinguished. Bezos's purchase of *The Post* was now portrayed as subverting the national interest.

Trump's campaign activities gave us fresh material to investigate. The candidate had ducked out of a January 28, 2016, Republican debate on Fox News ahead of the Iowa caucuses, still griping of supposed mistreatment by Megyn Kelly at the GOP debate the previous August. Instead, his campaign said he'd be raising money for veterans "who have been treated so horribly by our all-talk, no-action politicians." Two and a half miles from the debate venue in Des Moines, Trump held a benefit rally, declaring that he had raised more than $6 million for veterans. One million dollars, he said, came straight out of his own pocket.

The Post's David Fahrenthold decided to take a look months later at what became of the money Trump said he was giving away. Since that rally, small donations had been made by the Trump Foundation. As far as Dave could figure, though, they only added up to $1.1 million. What happened to the rest of the $6 million? What became of Trump's own $1 million?

When he posed the questions to Trump's campaign, at first there was silence. And then campaign manager Corey Lewandowski gave him a call. "The money is fully spent," Lewandowski said in May 2016. "Mr. Trump's money is fully spent." But, as Dave later recounted, "He wouldn't say which groups Trump had donated to. Or when. Or in what amounts." Lewandowski was asserting that Trump had lived up to a campaign pledge, but he wouldn't offer proof.

Dave's next move was an inspired use of social media for journalistic ends. It was also a lesson in why the press shouldn't take what candidates say at face value and in how they can be held to account. In this instance, Dave's work would win a Pulitzer Prize, both for his ingenuity and for showing that Trump had misused charitable funds for personal and political purposes. It would ultimately cost Trump $2 million in fines and lead to the shutdown of the Trump Foundation for misusing funds in a tax-exempt charity.

On Twitter, Dave spent a day asking veterans groups to let him know if they'd received the money, using Trump's handle of @realdonaldtrump to alert the candidate to what he was doing. Trump called him the next day, declaring that he'd just given away his

$1 million in one lump sum. That meant, as Dave reported in *The Post* in late May, that Lewandowski hadn't told the truth when he said that the money already had been donated. Dave asked Trump whether he would have given away the money if Dave hadn't been looking into it. "You know, you're a nasty guy," Trump responded.

When Trump was asked a few days later at a press briefing what had become of the other money that was supposed to go to veterans charities, he said disbursements had just been made. That meant the funds had been sitting in the Trump Foundation for months.

What happened next was classic Trump. Held accountable for what he promised, he castigated his media inquisitors. "You're a sleaze," he told one reporter, and followed up with "You're a real beauty" for another. As *The New York Times* described it, for forty minutes Trump had "assailed those reporting on his candidacy with a level of venom rarely seen at all, let alone in public, from the standard-bearer of a major political party . . . Historians reached back to the Nixon administration, with its reporter-stocked enemies list, for a fair comparison." Trump was asked whether the encounter is what White House press briefings would be like. "Yes, it is," he said. "It's going to be like this." Finally, Trump was telling the truth.

Shortly afterward Dave and I encountered each other at the elevator bank in *The Post*'s headquarters. I posed a question: If Trump was dishonest about charitable giving that he announced at a highly publicized rally, what might he have done with other purported charitable donations when no media were paying close attention? With that, David was off and running, digging along with researcher Alice Crites into the as-yet unexamined world of Trump's supposedly good deeds. Over the years, Trump had announced charitable pledges totaling about $8.5 million—from the profits of his books, *The Apprentice* show, Trump University, and other ventures. But the Trump Foundation reported receiving only $5.5 million, far short of what was required to fund the pledges. The Trump Organization's chief financial officer said Trump wanted to keep the foundation's donations secret. So Dave once again turned to Twitter to see where the foundation money went, if anywhere at all. "What has set Trump apart from other wealthy philanthropists," Dave would write, "is not how much he gives—it is how often he promises that he is going to give." He didn't always follow through. Notoriously, one donation was for a portrait of himself, which ended up hanging in his Doral golf resort in Florida. Funds were also used to pay off his businesses' legal expenses and help his presidential campaign.

On June 13, Trump announced that he was revoking *The Post*'s press credentials for covering his campaign. Trump's peeves with *The Post* were adding up, but the reason he cited was a headline. We had, in fact, published a lousy one. The day before, twenty-nine-year-old Omar Mateen, who had pledged fealty to the leader of ISIS, walked into an Orlando gay nightclub called Pulse just after two a.m. and began shooting with a semiautomatic assault rifle and pistol. Forty-nine people were slaughtered, fifty-three wounded. Never before in the United States had there been a mass shooting so deadly.

Trump promptly sought to tie Obama to the massacre with cryptic and eerie insinuation. "Look, we're led by a man that either is not tough, not smart, or he's got something else in mind," Trump said the day after the shooting. "And the something else in mind—you know, people can't believe it. People cannot, they cannot believe that President Obama is acting the way he acts and can't even mention the words 'radical Islamic terrorism.' There's something going on. It's inconceivable. There's something going on."

The Post's initial online headline read, "Donald Trump Suggests President Obama Was Involved with Orlando Shooting." Without ever hearing from the Trump campaign, *The Post*'s staff recognized that it had blundered in its phrasing, changing the headline to something less categorical and more nuanced: "Donald Trump Seems to Connect President Obama to Orlando Shooting." But the ninety minutes that passed before the revision played into Trump's hands. We had given him another chance to bludgeon *The Post*. Of course, he took it.

Trump posted on Facebook that he was immediately revoking press credentials of the "phony and dishonest *Washington Post*" for its "incredibly inaccurate coverage" of his campaign. *The Post* joined the ranks of other media outlets—among them *Politico*, *BuzzFeed*, *Huffington Post*, and the *Daily Beast*—that were being denied press access to news conferences, campaign events, and the media charter flights that followed Trump as he campaigned across the country. Trump's retaliatory action imposed arduous logistical burdens on *Post* reporters covering the campaign, but its impact on the substance of our coverage was nil. Rallies were televised, and we could attend them just like any member of the public—as long as we got in line early enough. Staff and freelancers around the country were deployed to do that.

I had no intention of approaching Trump or his campaign staff to request a reversal of the decision. It was too easy to imagine what would happen if I did: At a rally Trump would parody me as begging him to give us back our credentials. Senior politics editor Steven Ginsberg saw things a bit differently. He agreed that we shouldn't ask for reinstatement, but he saw value in at least talking with the Trump team. He had reached out to the campaign to determine the specific reasons for its ban but got no response. Yet he was able to set up a meeting with the candidate himself in Trump Tower for July 5, immediately upon his return from a long-planned trip to Zimbabwe and Botswana. "It was too extreme of a move, with too many implications for a free and fair press, to let it go," Steven told me later. "What would happen if he became president?"

Steven received loads of advice from colleagues prior to the meeting, mostly not to proceed with it. "There was a sense that there was little to gain and legitimate fears that he would make a public spectacle of it and use it as another way to attack *The Post* and the media," he recalled. "My then 6-year-old son cried and asked me not to go, fearing that Trump would shoot me." But Steven said he wanted a "straight answer" about why *Post* reporters had been banned.

Soon enough, fresh from observing elephants, rhinos, and predatory beasts in the wild, Steven was facing Trump in his office, with its panoramic view of Central Park. Seated beside Steven was Hope Hicks, Trump's spokesperson. Trump put on the charm, remarking on Steven's preternaturally youthful appearance. Before long, Trump brought up *The Post*'s owner. Why didn't Bezos like him? Steven made clear that he had scarcely spoken with Bezos. He had never talked to him about Trump. And he had no idea whether Bezos liked him or not. He also assured Trump that Bezos stayed out of the newsroom's decision-making. Trump didn't buy it, moving on to the stories that most aggrieved him. Steven, annoyed, finally told Trump he had assigned each of those stories himself. Trump, he said, should blame him, not Bezos. And then Trump asked Steven to convey a message to Bezos, as if he were some sort of courier: "Tell him that I like him."

Trump complained about the bad headline and yet acknowledged that *The Post* had altered it on its own, without hearing at all from the campaign. Steven wondered why the campaign hadn't called to complain. "It's been so bad with *The Washington Post* that I didn't even ask you to change it . . . Because we've given up." (For all his grousing, two months later Trump would explicitly call Obama the "founder" of ISIS and Clinton a "co-founder.")

Trump had a range of other gripes, but nothing seemed to provoke Trump more than David Fahrenthold's stories about his charitable giving. "If I would have given $100 million on day one, he would have made me look bad. It was terrible." Steven reminded him that *The Post*'s first story reported straight that he had raised $5.6 million for vets. The issue was whether he followed through.

Hicks called *The Post*'s coverage "vicious" and finally asked Steven, "Are we looking to resolve sort of the status of our relationship, or proceed as is?" Steven responded, "I think our relationship is fine. It's up to you guys what you want to do about it." She was clearly exasperated. "What do you mean by 'resolve'?" Steven asked. "What are we trying to resolve?" There was nothing to resolve. Our coverage would continue as it was.

Something more momentous than the Trump-*Post* spat was about to unfold. The candidate, Hicks, and Steven walked outside Trump's office to watch. FBI Director James Comey was on television to announce the conclusion of his investigation into Hillary Clinton's use of a private email server. The three of them—joined by Ivanka Trump, Jared Kushner, the Trump security detail, and others—watched on an old small television that sat in a nook. Comey announced that he was recommending no criminal charges against Clinton, though he upbraided her for "extreme carelessness," poor judgment, and incurring national security risks. Comey said, however, that she had not intentionally or knowingly mishandled classified information. So she wouldn't be charged. Trump immediately pronounced the system "rigged."

Turning back to Steven, Trump said he would be watching *The Post*'s reporting about him. *The Post*'s coverage, Steven told him, would not change in any way. And for another two months, the Trump campaign kept us—and a dozen other outlets—on the blacklist. Finally, eight weeks before the November election, Trump lifted his vengeful ban. "I figure," he told CNN, "they can't treat me any worse."

6

"DON'T WORRY ABOUT ME"

News judgments are made in the moment, often amid competitive frenzy. Time allows us a chance to reflect on how well we did our jobs. I've done a lot of thinking about coverage of the dramatic news that began to break in the summer of 2016 with the hack of the Democratic National Committee servers.

There was genuine news in the Democrats' emails that spilled out in the months before the election. Coverage was unavoidable; necessary, too. But the stories during those first several months after the hack fell short of all that the public needed to understand.

There was a far more significant story taking shape, and it took the press too long to fully communicate it: Russia was aggressively interfering in a presidential election. A superpower adversary was doing what it could to propel Donald Trump into the White House. At *The Post* we learned a lesson: If there was a hack like this in the future, we would be putting greater emphasis on who was behind it and why, not letting the content of stolen information distract us from the motives of the hackers.

The story of the hack began in June 2016 when *Post* national security reporter Ellen Nakashima took a call from a lawyer, Michael Sussmann, who was representing the Democratic National Committee. Soon he, Democratic National Committee CEO Amy Dacey, and Shawn Henry, the head of the cybersecurity firm CrowdStrike

Services, would fill her in on a grave security breach: Intruders had acquired access to all email and chat traffic along with the Democrats' opposition research on Trump. Two Russian intelligence agencies were the leading suspects.

At first it looked like the aim was "classic political espionage," Ellen recalled to me—a desire to get opposition research on Trump. This sort of spying had become routine, as she wrote when publishing her scoop about the hack, "much as American spies gather similar information on foreign candidates and leaders." But in July, just days before the Democratic National Convention where Hillary Clinton was about to receive her party's nomination for president, London-based WikiLeaks released nearly twenty thousand hacked emails. There was little doubt about who had supplied them.

The emails suggested that the purportedly neutral DNC was in league with the Clinton campaign and sabotaging rival Bernie Sanders. They also revealed how the Democrats wrangled big-money contributions—including, as *The Post* wrote, "how the party has tried to leverage its greatest weapon—the president." The Sanders camp, incensed at evident favoritism toward Clinton, focused on the emails' content far more than on their provenance. So did we in the press, while also keeping busy with the warring within the Democratic Party that followed. I wish we could get a mulligan: Russia deserved at least equal weight. No political dogfight was bigger than its malicious election interference.

The Post's stories typically cited Russia's suspected involvement in the hack. Clinton's campaign chairman, Robby Mook, however, wanted the press, the public, and politicians to focus not just on who but also on why: Russia, he alleged, was intervening to help Trump. Mook might have gotten his wish if intelligence and law enforcement officials had spoken up. But no one within those agencies that summer would say anything conclusive about why the emails were leaked—or, remarkably, even about who extracted them. Months would pass before they had something notable to say. The impact of the WikiLeaks email dump, however, was immediate. Debbie Wasserman Schultz announced her resignation as chair of the Democratic National Committee. Three top DNC officials, including CEO Daccy, quickly followed her out the door.

One month after voters cast their ballots for president, emotions still inflamed, the Institute of Politics at Harvard Kennedy School brought together campaign managers and the press for a quadrennial "behind the curtain" look back at what transpired during the election. I joined other newsroom leaders in a discussion about the role of the press. Journalist Sasha Issenberg, as moderator, asked about the hacked emails. "Did you ever think about not covering the contents of those because of their origins and how they came to light?"

My answer was direct and honest but, in retrospect, too narrow. "No, I can't say we ever said we were not going to cover them. The Clinton campaign never said that they had been falsified." And I added later: "If we had chosen not to cover them, then somebody else would have covered them and, certainly, the ideologically motivated websites would have covered them. At the very least, we made a sincere effort to put them in proper context, find out what they were really all about, not exaggerate what the material was, talk to the campaign as best we could about them and put them in perspective." Not enough perspective, I came to believe.

Issenberg identified the central issue: "In a sense you are creating a marketplace for people who want to steal content and get it out without great reservations on the part of editors." CNN president Jeff Zucker responded: "We did debate whether or not we should be reporting on them because there but for the grace of God go we . . . In the end, we quickly, we decided that the newsworthiness outweighed not doing it. But it is a very slippery slope, and it's not completely clear-cut."

Four years later, in 2020, *The Post*'s then–politics investigations editor, Matea Gold, expressed concern that we might again be confronted with bad actors seeking to exploit our natural news instincts. She offered ideas for better balancing newsworthiness against the prospect of being manipulated. Reflecting her thoughts, I sent a memo to the staff with five "principles for covering hacked or leaked material ahead of the election." A key principle among them: "If a decision is made to publish a story about hacked or leaked information, our coverage should emphasize what we know—or don't know—about the source of the information and how that may fit into a foreign or domestic influence operation." We weren't forswearing coverage of hacked material. But why it was being hacked would have to command equal, if not greater, attention.

On the first day of the Democratic convention in Philadelphia, hours before First Lady Michelle Obama's admonition that "in this election, we cannot sit back and hope that everything works out for the best," the media were ordered to evacuate tents set aside for the press corps that threatened to collapse under a torrential storm. Lightning might strike.

The following afternoon, a political storm began to take shape. *The Post*'s Tom Hamburger received a call from Glenn Simpson, cofounder of a private investigations firm known as Fusion GPS. The two knew each other well, having worked together years earlier as reporters at *The Wall Street Journal*. Simpson had left *The Journal* in 2009 to go into business. The idea behind Fusion GPS was to pursue the sort of investigations that journalists take on, though now in the interests of private clients. "I call it journalism for rent," Simpson would say later, breezing past the principle that journalism for rent is not journalism at all.

Tom had high regard for Simpson's work at *The Journal*, and as a private investigator Simpson had been a source of solid information.

There is an entire tribe of people like him in Washington. Private investigators are common figures among the warrior class on both the political left and right; in the world of Wall Street finance, too. Digging up dirt on opponents has a ready market. So despite their long-standing relationship, Tom knew that Simpson's story pitches came with an agenda. "Hired guns," as Tom says. But everyone who seeks out a journalist does so for a reason. Some are public-spirited, more are self-interested. If we're doing our jobs right, we keep that in mind and follow up with independent reporting.

Simpson asked Tom if they could meet at the Franklin Bar in Center City Philadelphia. "This is urgent. You're going to want to hear this," Simpson told him. When they met, Simpson flipped open his laptop and read from what he described as a report from "one of the most credible people in the world" when it came to deciphering Russia. Simpson would only describe him as "a senior former Western intelligence official" known to U.S. counterparts. No name provided.

"I'm just going to read you part of this," Simpson said, and he began with lines from the top, which read in full: "Russia has been cultivating, supporting and assisting TRUMP for at least five years. Aim, endorsed by PUTIN, has been to encourage splits and divisions in the western alliance. So far, TRUMP has declined various sweetener real estate business deals offered him in Russia in order to further the Kremlin's cultivating of him. However he and his inner circle have accepted a regular flow of intelligence from the Kremlin, including on his Democratic and other political rivals. Former top Russian intelligence officer claims FSB [a Russian intelligence and security service] has compromised TRUMP through his activities in Moscow sufficiently to be able to blackmail him. According to several knowledgeable sources, his conduct in Moscow has included perverted sexual acts which have been arranged/monitored by FSB."

He allowed Tom to take a glance. The information, Simpson said, would be provided to top Democratic officials and law enforcement and intelligence authorities. Tom was bound by the conditions of his conversation to keep Simpson's name—and his company's—secret. Nor would Simpson give him a copy of the report. To begin verifying the document, Tom sought a face-to-face interview with its author. "Can you arrange a meeting?" Tom asked. "Probably not, not now anyway," Simpson responded.

Tom knew by then that Simpson was doing work for Democrats, and he correctly suspected Simpson had been retained by Perkins Coie, the Washington law firm whose partner had disclosed the hack of Democrats' computers to his colleague Ellen Nakashima. On deadline to complete another story, Tom rushed back to work with his editors. Later that evening, he passed along what he had heard in the Franklin Bar. Tom confided in his editor, Peter Wallsten, who then oversaw political investigations, that Simpson was his contact and that the information originated with a "former intelligence official."

The following morning brought a shocker. *The Post's* political reporters and editors were crowded into the lounge of the Alexander Inn, a boutique hotel in the historic heart of Philadelphia where our journalists were housed while they covered the convention. After wrapping up the morning's daily planning meeting, heads turned to the TV screens for a press conference by the Republican nominee.

Trump bellowed what no one in that room ever expected a presidential candidate to so much as whisper. He invited Russia to find and release tens of thousands of emails that passed through Hillary Clinton's private server when she was secretary of state. "Russia, if you're listening, I hope you're able to find the 30,000 emails that are missing." Trump was calling upon America's superpower rival to target his opponent—even if it meant illegally fishing through computer systems—and to help him win.

A meeting of *Post* journalists that afternoon had already been organized by senior politics editor Steven Ginsberg. The purpose was to discuss how to investigate the seeming symbiosis between Trump and Russia—along with what Tom had been told the night before by Simpson and was hearing from senior Democrats at the convention. Trump was all flattery when it came to Russia and Putin. And Russia, in turn, was suspected of hacking emails that injured his opponent. Trump's mind-blowing remarks that morning added to the alarm. An "aha moment" is how Steven later described it. "We felt like, 'Holy shit, this is different.'"

Post journalists covering the convention gathered in the hotel room of national editor Scott Wilson. Members of our national security staff joined via teleconference. Tom recited what he was hearing at the convention about concerns over possible Russian support for Trump and suspicions that the Russians were even attacking the computers of delegates and donors gathered in Philadelphia. He also passed along the unconfirmed allegations he had picked up the previous evening: Russia might possess compromising information on Trump and might have cultivated the GOP candidate as an intelligence asset. He didn't go so far as to mention the report's reference to "perverted sexual acts" by Trump that supposedly occurred at Moscow's Ritz-Carlton hotel, a bizarre tale of Trump allegedly paying prostitutes to pee on a bed in the presidential suite where President and Michelle Obama had once stayed. "Golden showers," as the report called the purported episode.

Politics editors asked the national security staff to help chase down the leads. Nothing would be published unless verified. The message, Steven recalls, was, "We have got to mobilize."

The response they got was not what he and the politics team hoped for. At first they were met with silence; then with incredulity and exasperation: Mobilize based on what exactly? Who was saying all this? Why can't we know? How do we know this is at all credible? When you say it's an intel source, do you mean a current official who has access to signals intelligence or a former one who no longer does? We're supposed to buttonhole national security officials to ask whether Trump is a Russian asset? Really?

The Russia investigation would bring months of sharp clashes among *Post* journalists over what deserved investigating, the reliability of sourcing, whether reporters were being sufficiently energetic in pursuing possible stories, and the significance of what they were learning.

I hadn't been at the meeting in Philadelphia. I was back in Washington. Stunningly, no one bothered to tell me about it—or even about the tip from Simpson, or about the staff rancor it touched off. Months of reporters chasing down leads—and quarreling with each other—would pass before I was finally clued in. As I reported for this book a half decade later, I finally learned what I didn't know then, including the full depth of division among the staff that this line of reporting had opened up. There had been, to say the least, a failure to communicate. Sometimes the top editor is the last to know—last by a long shot, in this case.

Critics would come to suspect a craftily coordinated effort by *The Post* to take down Trump. It was anything but. Newsrooms are often a wellspring of conflict, dissent, and grievance. Such was the case when it came to investigating Trump and Russia.

"Deep skepticism" is how national security reporter Greg Miller described his own reaction to what he heard from Tom, along with frustration that his colleague was so guarded about where the reports were coming from. "Run down what?" Greg asked, unclear what precisely he was supposed to confirm. The response, as he sums it up: "See what they're saying about Trump and Russia." Greg remembers "just biting my tongue during the call." Researcher Julie Tate recalls Greg asking, "Are we chasing ghosts? Or am I chasing something real?"

The response from national security reporter Adam Goldman was testier still. Fifteen minutes into the meeting, he bolted out of a conference room in D.C., boiling and disinclined to pursue tips he regarded as "far-fetched." Julie told me, "I've never seen him act that way."

"They wouldn't tell us where it was from," Adam later recalled. "And if you can't explain where you got this from I'm not sure I can take it seriously ... I hated the secrecy bullshit."

Memories of that Philadelphia meeting differ on key points. Tom insists he made clear that information was coming from a former Western intelligence official, even as he honored a pledge to keep other details confidential. Others say he wasn't clear at all.

The politics staff was floored by the pushback. How could others not see things their way? The reports about *kompromat*—compromising information—on Trump might be farcical. They could well be false. But the country might also be facing an unprecedented national security threat. And, not incidentally, our competitors might break this explosive story, leaving *The Post* humiliatingly in the dust.

As the Philadelphia meeting drew to a close, Greg declared, "I'll see what I can get." Greg was attending the Aspen Security Forum, a three-day nonpartisan venue for discussing intelligence, defense, and foreign affairs. That gave him an opportunity to do some checking. National security officials told him they, too, had been picking up scuttlebutt about Trump's connections to Russia but had yet to see anything that substantiated the worst suspicions. Nobody at the national security conference, he told me, "was giving me even a wink or body language" of something treasonous.

Not that intelligence officials weren't worried about Trump. Some were hesitant to give Trump classified briefings that, as a nominee for president, he would be eligible to receive. So Greg wrote that story. But intelligence officials were not yet prepared even to confirm that Russia was behind the hack of Democrats' emails, even though it easily qualified as Suspect No. 1. Nor would they confirm then that the hack was intended to assist Trump, or even that Americans should be particularly alarmed.

At the Aspen conference, Director of National Intelligence James Clapper advised the public—and particularly the media—to just calm down, declaring himself "taken aback a bit by ... the hy-perventilation" over the hack of the DNC. Americans, he said, "just need to accept" cyber intrusions as a long-term challenge and "not be quite so excitable when we have another instance of it." When asked whether Russia intended to undermine American elections, he said matter-of-factly that Putin's government fears "we're trying to influence political developments in Russia, we're trying to effect change, and so their natural response is to retaliate and do unto us as they think we've done to them."

Ever since the Democratic convention, Tom Hamburger had been asking his source Glenn Simpson for direct contact with the au-thor of the riveting report about Trump. Opportunity came in mid-September. Simpson and his Fusion GPS colleagues were arranging for journalists to meet with the source on September 22 at the Tab-ard Inn, a small century-old hotel that was a popular dining and drinking destination for Washington journalists. The source was revealed there as Christopher Steele, a former British intelligence agent.

Steele was recruited out of the University of Cambridge to Brit-ain's overseas spy service, known as MI6. Early in his career, he had served undercover in the British embassy in Moscow for several years. Serving in London and Paris, he continued to focus on Russia until he departed the spy agency in 2009 after a few years heading up the intelligence service's Russia desk. He went on to set up a consulting and investigations business, shopping his experience and contacts to private clients. After assisting the FBI in its investigation of FIFA, international soccer's governing organization, he became one of the agency's paid confidential sources.

At the Tabard Inn, each news outlet was given a one-hour slot in separate rooms. Simpson required the meetings to be "on back-ground," meaning reporters were bound by certain ground rules set by Fusion. Steele's name and nationality could not be published. If they wished to quote him, he could only be identified as a "former senior Western intelligence official."

Instead of meeting at the hotel, Tom invited Simpson to bring the former intelligence officer to *The Post*'s headquarters. Later that day, the report's author—accompanied by Simpson—entered *The Post*'s newsroom. Feeling spurned by the national security staff, Tom invited none of them to join him. Instead, he asked only Dana Priest, a two-time Pulitzer Prize winner who had long specialized in national security investigations, to participate. Dana had left *Post* employment almost two years earlier to be a professor at the University of Maryland but continued to maintain a professional relationship with us.

After taking the elevator to the newsroom on the seventh floor, Steele was walked past one glass office after the next and into a space that, for no good reason, had been drearily named the "Patent Room," also all glass. The lack of privacy unnerved Steele. "Don't you have any meeting space without glass walls?" he asked.

Until he introduced himself that September day, no one at *The Post* had known his name. Nor had any of our journalists yet been able to read the full text of the seventeen memos that became known as the "Steele dossier." Looking suave with his swept-back graying hair, his tailored suit, and cuff links, the newsroom guest introduced himself. "If you google me, you'll see there is a British porn star by that name. I'm not that Christopher Steele," he quipped.

Steele said Putin was personally interfering in the election, that Trump was financially compromised and Russian investors were propping him up, that the Russians had cultivated Trump. He described his own relationship with the FBI as solid, and said the agency was investigating his findings. What he was giving *The Post*, he said, required further corroboration. But he also claimed multiple sources.

After two hours, Steele and Simpson left, yet again declining to turn over a copy of the full report. Fifteen minutes later, Tom took a call. The former spy obsessed with secrecy had left behind his laptop. Keys to the kingdom had been sitting unattended in *The Post*'s glass-walled conference room. Steele and Simpson were scurrying back.

Steele and Simpson returned again on October 6. This time, Tom arranged for greater privacy. The secrecy about Steele was so complete that not until months later did full-time national security reporters become aware that he had even been in our office. Steele and Simpson were testier on the second visit. "Their basic message," recalls Dana, "was, 'Maybe we didn't make ourselves clear. Donald Trump is an agent of Russia, and he could be president.'" The message was perfectly clear, but the proof was missing. *The Post* had its standards and principles: Before anything could be published, corroboration was required. Reporters were still coming up empty.

On October 7, 2016, news came in colossal waves. First, the Department of Homeland Security and the director of national intelligence finally released their assessment of the hacks of Democratic National Committee computers and other political organizations. The intelligence community declared itself "confident" that the Russian government directed the computer intrusions, and it cited a motive: "These thefts and disclosures are intended to interfere with the U.S. election process." The agencies added: "We believe, based on the scope and sensitivity of these efforts, that only Russia's senior-most officials could have authorized these activities."

That afternoon at about four p.m., *The Post*'s David Fahrenthold broke a story that delivered a brutal blow to the Trump campaign. Dave obtained a 2005 hot-mic recording of Trump bantering on a bus with Billy Bush, then of the *Access Hollywood* program, as they arrived on the set of the soap opera *Days of Our Lives*. The presidential candidate's remarks on the video were so grotesque that we wrestled with the proper words to describe them, settling on "lewd" and "vulgar." With beautiful women, Trump said, "I just start kissing them. It's like a magnet. Just kiss. I don't even wait. And when you're a star, they let you do it. You can do anything." Billy Bush responded, "Whatever you want." Trump went on, "Grab 'em by the pussy. You can do anything."

As if to counteract the explosive impact of such a story on the Trump campaign, WikiLeaks almost immediately released two thousand emails from the account of Clinton's campaign chairman, John Podesta. The email dump actualized Trump ally Roger Stone's open prediction of an "October surprise" from WikiLeaks and its leader, Julian Assange, with whom Stone claimed to have been in contact. (Assange denied they were in touch.) The emails revealed excerpts from Clinton's closed-door speeches before Wall Street bankers that with her support for a "hemispheric common market, with open trade and open borders"—would prove severely damaging. The campaign wouldn't confirm their authenticity. Nor did it contest them.

Yet another angle to the Russia investigation had emerged that fall. *The Post*, along with other media outlets, was receiving word that computer scientists had detected internet traffic showing regular "pinging" between a server purportedly belonging to the Trump Organization and two servers registered to Alfa Bank of Moscow, founded and controlled by Russian billionaire Mikhail Fridman, whose ties to Putin were said to be close.

We knew that other media outlets were working feverishly on this story. If there were surreptitious communication, it would be a hell of a scoop. The politics staff had crafted a very rough draft of a story to get a sense of what a published version might say. Such an exercise can clarify what is missing. And, in this instance, it was a lot: Did this "pinging" mean there was something nefarious going on, or was it meaningless? We had no idea.

Reporters had contacted the bank for information and comment. Fridman wanted to speak directly with me, and colleagues asked if I was available. I was, but my whereabouts—on the last stop of a tram in Medellín, Colombia, where I was giving a speech—weren't ideal for such a complex and sensitive conversation. With spotty cell service, I listened as Fridman insisted the bank had nothing to do with the Trump campaign. What was being observed on the internet was inconsequential, he said. I asked about his willingness to speak directly with our reporters. He was willing, and later spoke with Tom Hamburger.

When Tom finished up with Fridman, a group of us gathered on a phone call to confer. I asked what computer experts thought. Some considered the network connections suspect, and others considered them innocuous. Would we be able, I asked, to do anything more than raise suspicion? The answer was no. *The Post*'s news department wasn't in the speculation business. So we agreed to put the story on ice unless and until we could say something definitive. If someone beat us to the story, so be it. No journalist likes to be beat, but it's better than being wrong.

The online magazine *Slate* in October and, two years later, *The New Yorker* would go on to publish extensive stories about the mysterious pinging, raising abundant questions but coming up short on answers. A *Time* magazine piece in 2019 would do the same. *Slate*'s writer, Franklin Foer, took immediate heat for his piece and revisited the subject a mere two days later. His second story carried a different flavor: Many computer scientists and technology journalists had "simpler, more benign explanations" for the server activity.

The FBI concluded by February 2017 that, in fact, there were no cyber links between the Trump Organization and Alfa Bank. The agency, according to a 2021 indictment, found that the email server wasn't even owned or operated by the Trump Organization but rather by a marketing company that handled advertisements for hundreds of companies, including Trump's. It was yet another investigative dead end for journalists.

Because of the strict separation between the news department that I led and the opinions department headed by Fred Hiatt, it was rare for me to gain any insight into the deliberations of the editorial board. But in late October 2016, Fred confided in me.

The *Post*'s editorial board had published one scorching editorial after the next about Trump throughout his campaign. "The growing ugliness of Donald Trump's campaign poses a challenge to us all," the editorial board wrote in November 2015. "We have seen the likes of him before, in the United States and elsewhere: narcissistic bullies who rise to prominence by spreading lies, appealing to fears and stoking hatred." A day before the first presidential debate between Trump and Hillary Clinton in late September 2016, they wrote, "Mr. Trump has amply demonstrated his unworthiness to occupy the Oval Office."

On September 30, *The Post* launched into a series of editorials "on the damage he could wreak unilaterally as president." With the headline "The Clear and Present Danger of Donald Trump," they practically pleaded with those considering voting for him not to do so: "If you know that Donald Trump is ignorant, unprepared and bigoted, but are thinking of voting for him anyway because you doubt he could do much harm—this editorial is for you."

As Fred Hiatt's department was set to embark on that series, he raised with publisher Fred Ryan the scheduling of an endorsement for president. The editorial page editor told me he was astonished, and infuriated, with the response. "Do we really have to make an endorsement?" Hiatt told me he was asked. Fred Ryan, by Hiatt's telling, still regarded Hillary Clinton as profoundly flawed. While Hiatt had serious differences with Clinton on her policies and her record, he saw her as amply qualified. He could not imagine withholding an endorsement for her in this race. He told me he had contemplated quitting if *The Post* failed to make one.

In a scheduled teleconference with Bezos, Fred Hiatt laid out the planned series of editorials making the case against Trump. And then he slipped in the line, "If or when we make an endorsement . . ." That elicited no immediate response, and *The Post*'s editorial page editor kept describing the series. When the conversation concluded, Bezos, always an attentive listener, backtracked. "You said, 'If or when you make an endorsement.' Why wouldn't we make an endorsement?" The matter was settled.

I asked Fred Ryan for his account. He adamantly disputed what Hiatt told me, firmly asserting that he "didn't have any hesitation in *The Post* making that endorsement." Perhaps, he told me, there was some misunderstanding, and he expressed frustration that, with Hiatt's death from cardiac arrest in December 2021, it was not possible to clear things up.

On October 13, *The Post*'s endorsement was published. Though detailing at length Clinton's "genuine flaws, missteps and weaknesses," *The Post* declared: "In the gloom and ugliness of this political season, one encouraging truth is often overlooked: There is a well-qualified, well-prepared candidate on the ballot. Hillary Clinton has the potential to be an excellent president of the United States, and we endorse her without hesitation."

Even with the election only a couple of months away, Trump hadn't backed off his five-year history of raising baseless doubts that President Obama was born in the United States. Asked on Labor Day where Obama was born, he declined to say. *The Post*'s Bob Costa was scheduled to get a one-on-one interview with Trump aboard his private plane late on September 14. It had been a long while since Trump agreed to speak with our reporters. Not until a week earlier had he lifted a ban on access to his events by *The Post* and some other outlets. As the plane idled on the tarmac in Canton, Ohio, Bob took his editors' advice and pressed Trump on the birther issue once again. Trump still wouldn't acknowledge Obama's birth in the United States. "I'll answer that question at the right time," Trump said. "I just don't want to answer it yet."

Bob's interview brought heightened attention to Trump's stubborn refusal to either reaffirm his lie or renounce it, adding pressure for an answer at long last. It came in a five-sentence press statement during a September 16 appearance Trump organized at his new hotel on Washington, D.C.'s Pennsylvania Avenue. Trump kept the press waiting an hour. Then he pulled a stunt. With cable networks airing the event live in anticipation that he would address his Obama fabrication, Trump instead turned the stage over to military veterans so they could endorse him on national television. When finally discussing Obama's birth, he lied again, falsely blaming Hillary Clinton for starting the "birther" conspiracy. Then, at long last, Trump declared: "President Barack Obama was born in the United States. Period." Taking no questions, he walked off the stage. For Trump, there was only one way to put an end to the lie he had promoted for years—by choreographing a cynical, mendacious, and manipulative press spectacle and shifting blame away from his own contemptible behavior.

Bob's questioning of Trump on the birther conspiracy had gotten under his very thin skin, and Trump lashed out in a way that went unmentioned in *The Post*'s story. Bob vividly remembers the encounter: "Trump said to me at one point, 'Jeff Bezos decides everything you do, doesn't he?' I said, 'What are you talking about? No, he does not. I don't even know Jeff Bezos.' And he goes, 'Oh no, Bezos tells you to do everything.' I said, 'Mr. Trump, if that was true, I would resign.' He said, 'Ah, no. Bezos runs everything.'"

In October, *The New York Times* got a look at what many Americans had long been waiting for: Trump's tax returns, at least a slice of them. Despite once declaring in January that they were "all approved and very beautiful" and would be released ("absolutely"), Trump was still refusing to disclose them. *The Times* obtained records showing that a $916 million loss on his 1995 return yielded him a tax deduction so gargantuan that it could have allowed him to avoid federal taxes—legally—for up to eighteen years. It was a major revelatory story. The repercussions for Trump's campaign, however, were slight to nonexistent.

Less than a week later, with only a month to go before the general election, it appeared that Trump might finally have suffered the debilitating damage he had eluded from one controversy to the next over a long campaign. *The Post*'s Dave Fahrenthold broke his story about the *Access Hollywood* tape ("Grab 'em by the pussy"). Trump was boasting, after all, of nothing less than sexual assault.

Dave had been called at about eleven a.m. on Friday, October 7, by a source offering unaired video of Trump. Minutes later, he was watching the tape. We just needed to authenticate it. One concern was that the most offensive words were recorded when Trump and Billy Bush were on a bus and not visible on camera. Dave promptly sent the campaign a transcript of the two key minutes at the beginning of the video. When aide Hope Hicks interrupted Trump while he was preparing for his next debate, Trump dismissed the idea that the words could possibly be his. A campaign official got back to Dave: "That doesn't sound like Mr. Trump. Can you send us a video?" With the video in hand, Hicks played it for Trump and his team. "It's me," Trump admitted. At four p.m., with its authenticity confirmed, the video was posted to our website, racking up what was then the highest digital traffic for any single story in *Post* history.

In his initial statement, Trump said, "This was locker-room banter, a private conversation that took place many years ago. Bill Clinton has said far worse to me on the golf course—not even close. I apologize if anyone was offended." It was typical Trump; no contrition, only deflection. But for once, Trump couldn't blow it off so easily. He was forced into a second statement, apologizing for the first time that anyone could recall: "I said it, I was wrong and I apologize."

Bob Costa had been sitting next to Dave Fahrenthold in the newsroom as his colleague broke his explosive story. The next day, on Saturday, Bob came into the office and called Trump directly, having held on to his personal cell phone number from his reporting days at the *National Review*. Trump picked up. "What do you want?" he asked. "On. The. Record," Bob responded. Trump: "Yes." Bob: "Will you withdraw?" Trump: "I'd never withdraw. I've never withdrawn in my life." And Trump added, "I've been here before, I'll tell ya, in life. I understand life and how you make it through. You go through things." Less than two hours before Trump was to participate in a debate with the Democratic nominee on October 9, he was on the offensive again, assembling for the cameras women who had accused Bill Clinton of sexual misconduct.

The Post's Access Hollywood story had unquestionably hurt Trump. The Real Clear Politics average of presidential polls showed Clinton increasing her lead over Trump from 4.6 percentage points to 6.7 points. And then came FBI Director James Comey, again. Eleven days before the presidential election, on October 28, the FBI director informed Congress that the agency was once again reviewing Hillary Clinton's email traffic, having become newly aware of emails on the computer of former congressman Anthony Weiner, the estranged husband of top Clinton aide Huma Abedin. A mere two days before the election, Comey declared that those emails revealed nothing new, reaffirming his conclusion that Clinton should not face charges. The Clinton email investigation was finally closed.

Clinton's loss can be attributed to a wide variety of factors, from widespread antiestablishment anger and Russian hacking to many mistakes of her own making. But Nate Silver, the founder of

FiveThirtyEight, the data-analysis site, assessed Comey's eleventh-hour letter to be the decisive blow. "Hillary Clinton would probably be president if FBI Director James Comey had not sent a letter to Congress on Oct. 28," he wrote the following May. *The Post's Access Hollywood* story had threatened to knock Trump out. Along came Comey to clobber Clinton's campaign instead, allowing Trump to recover and raise his fist in victory.

I was not among those in the press, including most of my colleagues, who felt certain that Clinton would win. She had never proved herself a skillful candidate. Her message was muddled, disproportionately centered on how horrible Trump was. Unlike a Teflon-coated Trump, she suffered for her blunders. And the nation was split in half politically anyway, with most people immovable in their views. Trump, I predicted to friends, had a 40–50 percent chance of winning.

Traditionally on election night, because results come in so late and deadlines loom, news staffs often write stories in advance of the vote counts, based on expectations. If things turn out differently, newsrooms scramble to adjust. At *The Post* the politics staff fully anticipated that Clinton would prevail. An entire suite of stories had been crafted with the expectation that she would. Not so for Donald Trump.

By eight p.m., however, results from Florida and North Carolina were beginning to signal that Clinton was in trouble. No matter the preference of most voters, a president is selected via the Electoral College, and Trump was showing strength in states that Clinton needed to lock up. Steven Ginsberg began directing politics reporters to start drafting stories premised on a Trump win. By 9:00 and 9:30, everyone could see for themselves that the race would be far closer than predicted. An hour later, Trump's victory was secure.

The gravity of the evening set in. This election would be historic, but not in the way that so many expected. Some women in the newsroom who had envisioned, and hoped for, the first woman president teared up as it became apparent 2016 would not be the year for that. A news staff that had endured Trump's threats and insults faced the prospect that we were in for four, or eight, more years of the same or worse. Few expected Trump to be any different as president than he had been as a candidate. With *The Post*'s video department aiming its cameras at our news hub for a live webcast, I made one request of the people within view: Show no emotion.

After a few days had passed, Steven asked if I would speak with the politics staff. Many were in shock that so much of what we reported about Trump apparently had been disregarded by voters. There was a "disconnect between the reality of what we saw and the reality of what they saw," Steven recalled. "I think the really strong feeling was, 'What difference did our work make?'"

The next Monday the politics team poured into the main conference room, named after legendary editor Ben Bradlee. My message was brief. I said what I genuinely believed: All we could do now was to keep doing our jobs. We give the public the information they need and deserve to know. They decide what to do with it. That's how democracy works. We should remember that this is the same democracy that allows us to publish with the freedom we do. All that we had reported about Trump was now in the public domain. Citizens would have to process it over time. "Just do our job. It's that simple," I said.

There was only so much assurance I could provide. Trump, we knew, would stop at nothing to question our credibility and integrity, even our humanity. "With any election, you just see election day as the end," Steven recalled. Now, "The finish line was the starting point. That was overwhelming to think about . . . It was hard to imagine that we were going to have to muscle up for the four years we knew were coming."

On November 10, Jeff Bezos posted a tweet that was dramatically different from his first regarding Trump: "Congratulations to @realDonaldTrump. I for one give him my most open mind and wish him great success in his service to the country." Bezos was scheduled to visit *The Post* a month later, on December 9, on business matters. I suggested he carve out some time to thank journalists who had worked so hard through an arduous campaign.

Before editors and reporters joined us for a forty-five-minute lunch of deli sandwiches in the ninth-floor "publisher's suite," Bezos asked me what he should know in advance. I told him the staff was suffering a bit of PTSD from the incessant attacks by Trump. They wondered whether their work resonated at all with the public. They were anxious about enduring four to eight more years of vilification, harassment, and obstruction in a Trump presidency. That middle finger he had given the press was about to become a fist.

My own mood was one of stoic acceptance. *The Post* had experienced plenty of friction with the Obama administration, and I had expected relations with the White House to be fractious even if the presidency was assumed by Clinton. I had told my publisher that there would be a ton to investigate regardless of whether victory went to Trump or Clinton. We had just doubled the size of our investigative team on that premise, adding a "rapid response" unit to turn out work more quickly.

At lunch Bezos expressed gratitude for the coverage and empathy for what the staff had endured. He urged them to just keep at their work. As to Trump, Bezos manifested no animosity, judging him an "innovator" who follows no traditions: When people say that's the way it's always been done, Trump says, "So what?" That was a quality that Bezos, famous as a disrupter, seemed to value.

All of us, of course, wanted to know how he himself was handling Trump's attacks. *Post* journalists naturally feared that Bezos might cave to pressure with Trump about to wield enormous power. Bezos showed no particular concern. He surmised that Trump, in blaming him for *The Post*'s coverage, was projecting: If Trump owned *The Post*, he would use it to advance his own commercial, personal, and political objectives. So he imagined that Bezos had to be doing the same. "Don't worry about me," Bezos said. "I can take care of myself." A wary and weary political staff took heart, practically levitating out of the room.

7

THE RUSSIA RIDDLE

On the first day of his presidency, Donald Trump pledged to end "American carnage." The next morning, Trump traveled to CIA headquarters, where there was some major patching up to do. He had accused the intelligence community of Nazi practices, suspecting them of having leaked reports of his allegedly compromising behavior in Russia. Somehow, while standing before a wall that honored agents who died in service, Trump found it proper to invoke his favorite villain: the press. "The most dishonest human beings on earth," he called us, and then belligerently declared, "I have a running war with the media."

Later that day, press secretary Sean Spicer, egged on by the forty-fifth president, falsely accused the press of deliberately inaccurate reporting when it observed that the inaugural crowd at the National Mall fell short of the attendance at Barack Obama's first inauguration in 2009. Spicer lied in asserting that Trump enjoyed "the largest audience to ever witness an inauguration—period—both in person and around the globe." The next day, challenged on *Meet the Press* about Spicer's fact-free assertions, Trump senior adviser Kellyanne Conway notoriously argued that Spicer had given "alternative facts." To which NBC News' Chuck Todd fittingly responded, "Alternative facts aren't facts, they are falsehoods."

The Post would soon report that on his first morning in the White

House, facing the staggering responsibilities of his new position, Trump was so fixated on the inaugural crowd comparisons that he personally called the acting National Park Service director, pressuring him to find photographic proof that the media had lied. The agency found more aerial photos, but they showed the press had told the truth. No matter. Trump told ABC's David Muir days later that his was the "biggest crowd in the history of inaugural speeches." Truth be damned.

Trump and his team were behaving as expected. The campaign for the presidency was over, but the campaign against the press—and verifiable fact—would never end. And his goal was obvious. He admitted to it before he took office. When Lesley Stahl of CBS met with him in Trump Tower in preparation for a post-election *60 Minutes* interview, she asked why he persisted in denigrating the press. "You know why I do it?" he told her, as she disclosed in 2018. "I do it to discredit you all and demean you all so that when you write negative stories about me no one will believe you."

When I was asked several weeks into Trump's presidency about his declaration of war on the press, I gave a response that caught fire with journalists: "We're not at war with the administration. We're at work." We were doing our jobs. Every president should be held accountable. When this one trampled on the truth, as he did so shamelessly and often, we had a duty to make that known. Journalism isn't stenography. Lying about something as minor as an inauguration crowd was a sign, as if we needed another, that this new president would regularly demolish truth on matters far more consequential. Covering this White House would require even more than the usual hard work.

Trump began his presidency with the Russia story casting a dark cloud. We and other media were aggressively investigating Russia's election intrusion, what Trump campaign operatives knew about it, whether there was coordination, and whether Trump's links to Russia went deeper than we already knew.

The reports from Christopher Steele set journalists on a path to see what they could confirm about his allegations. That led to many dead ends. But many investigative avenues didn't begin with Steele and had nothing to do with him. Those investigations bore fruit.

At *The Post*, the intelligence community's formal assessment in October 2016 that Russia actively interfered in the presidential election had served to galvanize our national security staff. We had also just welcomed into our newsroom another national security reporter, Adam Entous from *The Wall Street Journal*, who brought fresh energy and additional sources to the investigative effort. The political investigations staff was reassured by his eagerness to hear what they were picking up.

Because the October assessment by intelligence agencies was still vague on some points, Adam started pumping sources to check on any follow-up. In weekly meetings with one source, he repeatedly asked, "Has that assessment changed?" One day, Adam recounts, the source "was not willing to say it was the same," instead merely raising an eyebrow. The small gesture said a lot.

The Post soon reported that the intelligence assessment had become far more definitive and far more damning. In early December, six weeks before Trump was inaugurated, Adam, Ellen Nakashima, and Greg Miller disclosed the conclusions: Russia's goal in intervening in the United States went beyond eroding Americans' faith in the electoral process. The objective was to get Trump elected.

Trump would never allow for the possibility that Russia helped him get elected. By his reckoning, victory could only be due to his own superior abilities. The hacking, Trump told *Time* magazine earlier that week, "could be Russia. And it could be China. And it could be some guy in his home in New Jersey." And he waved away *The Post*'s scoop, once again taking a swipe at the intelligence agencies.

Time, he said in late December, to "move on to bigger and better things."

The Post's reporting was confirmed in early January when the intelligence community released its unclassified report: "We assess Russian President Vladimir Putin ordered an influence campaign in 2016 aimed at the US presidential election. Russia's goals were to undermine public faith in the US democratic process, denigrate Secretary Clinton, and harm her electability and potential presidency. We further assess Putin and the Russian Government developed a clear preference for President-elect Trump. We have high confidence in these judgments." The report—a product of the CIA, FBI, and office of the director of national intelligence—also expressed "high confidence" that Russia's military intelligence service had hacked Democratic officials' computers and relayed the material it stole to WikiLeaks, which then released it.

No way were we just going to "move on." There was much more to know. Our standard, though, would remain the same: Publish only what we could corroborate.

By the second week of December 2016, Tom Hamburger and Roz Helderman finally got their hands on a full copy of the reports written by Steele. Their source, as later revealed in court documents, was David Kramer, a Russia specialist, former State Department official, and adviser to Senator John McCain. He had received the documents from Glenn Simpson of Fusion GPS, who wanted McCain to press the FBI for an investigation.

Kramer was providing the reports to Tom and Roz for investigation purposes only, not for publication. *The Post* had set out to see if it could confirm what Steele had alleged. Other media outlets were on the hunt for supporting evidence, too. Kramer, unnerved by what was alleged in the Steele memos, was secretly sharing the documents with a number of reporters and government officials. And Fusion gave a copy, on an off-the-record basis, to the Washington bureau of *The New York Times*.

The Post's staff in Moscow was asked to chase down leads. But the request out of our D.C. headquarters was met there with profound skepticism. No one was more dubious than David Filipov, who had only started as *The Post*'s Moscow bureau chief in September 2016. David was hired from *The Boston Globe*, where he had covered Russia for years. He had specialized in Russian studies in college and learned to speak the language fluently, well enough to be selected as the American journalist on Russia's one-hour political talk show *60 Minut*. Just as he landed at *The Post*, the Russia investigation was thrust upon him.

David accepted that there had been an effort by Russia to sow chaos and portray American politics as dirty and divisive. That would be straight out of Russia's traditional playbook to discredit and disrupt democracies. The Russians probably kept a file on Trump, too, he says, just as they do on many prominent foreigners. And David also allowed that many condos in Trump-branded buildings were paid for with the cash of crooked Russians. But when presented with the names of the Trump campaign's Russian contacts, he had serious reservations about their significance. In David's mind, these were not the sort of people who would serve as conduits for Putin and Russian intelligence. Journalists were looking at hills, he says today, and "making them into Mount Everest."

David recalls the reaction from Russians when he inquired into allegations against Trump: "When did you lose your journalistic objectivity and standards?" On the other hand, he says, the politics staff was dissatisfied with the energy he was devoting to a story he judged to be highly improbable. While his reporting helpfully debunked some unfounded rumors, his self-assessment is straightforward: "No one would ever say 'you let us down' [but] . . . I didn't add value to the investigation." David left *The Post* in 2018. Now retired, he remains as skeptical of collusion as ever.

Andrew Roth was also then a Moscow correspondent for *The Post*, later reporting for Britain's *Guardian*. Unlike David, he didn't see a meaningful distinction between an effort by Russia to create chaos in the U.S. election and helping Trump. "The way you'd create chaos is by upping his chances to win," he told me. But Andrew all along was doubtful of actual collusion between the Trump campaign and Russia. Though individuals in Russia had been communicating with Trump campaign aides, "We saw these people as bit players, people with their own narrow interests." Andrew described a "real gulf" between the Moscow bureau's perception and Washington's.

Dealing with *Post* headquarters, he said, left the Moscow staff feeling "almost like apologists for the Russia side, doubting Thomases." Meanwhile, reporting out of Russia that was unrelated to Trump became nearly impossible, as officials and high-profile media figures stiff-armed American journalists. "Their posture," says Andrew, "was that the Trump election had basically driven us crazy. And in order to explain it, we were trying to pin the blame on Russia."

The Post's Moscow correspondents made efforts to speak with employees of the Ritz-Carlton where Trump purportedly had engaged in "perverted sexual acts." But they came up empty in locating employees who could confirm anything. Washington colleagues felt they could have tried harder.

Just prior to Christmas, editors asked Andrew to get himself to Prague to check out the assertion by Steele, attributed to a Kremlin insider, that Trump attorney Michael Cohen had traveled there in the late summer of 2016 to meet with Russian officials. When Andrew was enlisted to pursue the claim, he was in Tomsk, a university city in Siberia, where the temperature was twenty-two degrees below zero Fahrenheit. Despite the temperature, Andrew was there on vacation, amazingly enough, and would have preferred to stay put. Instead, he flew to Moscow, then to the Latvian capital, Riga, and then to Prague, where he hooked up with a local journalist for assistance. Severely ill and working with a high fever, Andrew spent several days in the city. Every inquiry he and his reporting colleague made led nowhere. Cohen firmly denied making such a trip. No media outlet ever documented that he had. And the report of special counsel Robert Mueller ended up accepting that Cohen, as he attested, "had never traveled to Prague."

It would have been good for me to know by December, shortly after the election and months after the Democratic convention in July, what the staff was doing on the Russia story. And yet, astonishingly, no one had yet clued me in. Nobody had told me about the leads they were chasing. Nobody had even told me about the reports from Christopher Steele. I hadn't picked up on how the politics and national security teams were butting heads or the skepticism from our correspondents in Moscow.

In writing this book, I asked some editors why they had failed to keep me informed and get me involved in an investigation so sensitive, internally fractious, and potentially consequential: All told me they thought someone else had, or should have. My sense now is that they were waiting to see what they could confirm. They weren't confirming anything. But telling me nothing was a lousy call. The more I think about it, the more pissed I get.

That December, investigative reporters on the politics staff were working hard to see what they could learn about Christopher Steele's assertions. What they were picking up fell short of confirmation, but it was unnerving nonetheless.

For Tom and Roz, one mid-December day was especially disquieting. DNC chairwoman Donna Brazile tearfully described to them being under relentless computer attack, presumably by Russian operatives. Confidential information in her files and private communications could be released publicly at any time, she feared. When Tom and Roz met with a senior government official that evening, they were further rattled. That individual acknowledged rumors among Trump transition officials that his appointee as national security advisor, Michael Flynn, had held multiple secret conversations with the Russian ambassador. They were also told that certain elements of what Tom had heard from Steele were considered to be, at least, credible. Although still uncorroborated, the source said, the allegations were being looked into.

When they met with *The Post*'s national security team the next day, Roz read down the list of what she and Tom were hearing. Again, they were met with skepticism, deepening friction on the staff. Some days later Tom stopped by my office. "I want to make sure you know what's going on," he said, beginning to fill me in on all that I had been missing those many months. "Nobody tells me anything," I said.

On January 10, the long-simmering Russia story erupted into a bonfire. CNN reported at 5:09 p.m. ET that intelligence officials had briefed Trump on the allegations in the Christopher Steele memos, including that Russian operatives claimed to possess "compromising personal and financial information." CNN's eleven-minute report said not only that the information in those documents had come from a former British intelligence official who was considered a "credible source" by U.S. agencies but also that "his Russian sources" had been "vetted" and were regarded as credible. CNN allowed that the allegations had not been verified and that the material arose out of work for Trump's political opponents. (Some of the allegations in Steele's memos had been reported a week before the election by *Mother Jones* magazine but had received scant attention in other media.)

Seventy-one minutes after CNN's report, *BuzzFeed News* raced to publish the full, uncorroborated text of what it labeled a "dossier" on Trump, including its most inflammatory claims about "perverted sexual behavior" and *kompromat*. *BuzzFeed* noted that it contained "specific, unverified, and potentially unverifiable" allegations. Instantly, the Russia story threatened to dominate the inception of Trump's presidency.

The media is not a monolith. Each outlet makes its own judgments about what to publish or broadcast. *BuzzFeed News* had taken a step that we at *The Post* and many other major media outlets were determined not to. The rest of us were sticking to a traditional standard: No verification, no publication.

To this day, I consider *BuzzFeed*'s decision to publish the so-called dossier in full that January a serious mistake. It circulated incendiary and salacious allegations without any evidence that they were true. And it gave Trump a rewarding opportunity to smear the entire press. He would forever be able to falsely equate the entire Russia investigation with Steele's claims, leaving much of the public with the idea that they were one and the same. It was a gift to Trump, one that looked ever more reckless over the years when the press proved unable to corroborate Steele's most provocative assertions.

The Post confirmed CNN's report without detailing specific allegations in the dossier's full text, pointing out that reports "compiled by the former British intelligence official have been circulating in Washington for months" and that "several news organizations, including *The Washington Post*, have been attempting to confirm many of the specific allegations without success." The president-elect reacted to *BuzzFeed*'s disclosure by calling it a "failing pile of garbage." CNN was labeled, as usual, "fake news." As for the intelligence community, which he falsely suspected of leaking the allegations, they were compared to "Nazi Germany."

BuzzFeed's explanation for publicizing highly specific accusations against Trump that it couldn't vouch for unspooled over time. In its initial story, *BuzzFeed* said it published "so that Americans can make up their own minds about allegations about the president-elect that have circulated at the highest levels of the US government." The public, of course, was in no position to assess the veracity of shocking allegations made by unidentified sources. *BuzzFeed*'s then–editor in chief, Ben Smith, followed up with a tweet an hour after publication, sharing a note to his staff: "Our presumption is to be transparent and to share what we have with our readers." Publishing the document "reflects how we see the job of reporters in 2017," he said.

Smith, a hotshot of "new media" in the digital era, promptly took to *The New York Times* opinion pages to dismiss criticism of his decision from within the press and elsewhere, attack others for holding to an old-school "instinct to suppress news" of significance, suggest that the press is incapable of confronting power when it engages in "a theater of traditional journalism," and lay claim to being "transparent with readers about our process of reporting." In a column one year later in *The Times*, where Smith in 2020 was awarded the prestigious role of media critic, he dismissed journalistic "traditionalists" and argued that publishing the full dossier "has helped journalists explain to their audience the investigation into Russian influence on the 2016 election."

Yet *BuzzFeed* knew for months that the document had been making the rounds within government. Just like other news organizations, it had withheld the dossier as it sought to corroborate key allegations. *BuzzFeed* declared in a 2018 court filing that, prior to CNN's report, it "had no plans to publish the Dossier, in whole or in part." After CNN's report, the calculus abruptly changed. "The story we wanted to report in light of these new developments," Smith testified, "was not the story we had been investigating up to that point, which was trying to ascertain the truth or falsity of underlying allegations within the Dossier. Rather, the story we now wanted to report was a different one, a story explaining to readers what the Dossier was and how it was affecting government actions."

The rush to publish, along with subsequent court testimony, has long suggested that other, less high-minded factors were central to

BuzzFeed's decision: the very traditional journalistic urge to beat the competition and the contemporary media craving for a surge in digital traffic. Smith admits as much in his 2023 book, *Traffic: Genius, Rivalry, and Delusion in the Billion-Dollar Race to Go Viral.* Ken Bensinger, the *BuzzFeed* reporter who obtained the dossier, testified he was just getting off a theme park ride at Disney World in Florida when he received a phone call from editors telling him the dossier would be published. At the time, he "understood that we were still working on reporting" on the dossier. Though he said in his court declaration that he "was and remains convinced that publishing the dossier was the right thing to do," he had never imagined that such a document would be published without first verifying its allegations. The decision to publish, I've learned, was essentially foisted on him, the only choice being whether he would allow his name to be included among the story's authors. Although Bensinger asked for time to give sources a heads-up about *BuzzFeed*'s decision, according to his testimony, Smith said he "could not" because he "felt time was of the essence given the information CNN had reported."

For this book, I went back and asked *Post* journalists involved in the Russia investigation how they viewed *BuzzFeed*'s decision to publish the full dossier. A couple who had never been given a copy were pleased to finally have the opportunity to read it. The vast majority were harshly critical: "Terribly damaging." "I think it was bad for journalism. It just gave all sorts of ammunition to paint the media with a broad brush as out to get Trump." "I don't think you put unvetted information out in the world just because everybody is talking about it." It was reassuring to hear *Post* staff embrace customary strict standards. Count me an unabashed traditionalist.

While *The Post* had wisely refrained from publishing claims in the Steele dossier when it couldn't verify them, I've concluded that we did fail in one significant respect. It was a failure of omission. Given that *Post* reporters had repeatedly come up empty in their monthslong efforts to find corroboration for Steele's most sensational claims, we owed the public a very different story: a tough examination of Steele and his work. If key elements of the dossier couldn't be verified, maybe they just weren't true. By 2021, Barry Meier, a former *New York Times* investigative reporter, delivered a scorching assessment of the reliability of Steele's reports in his book *Spooked: The Trump Dossier, Black Cube, and the Rise of Private Spies.* As *The Post*'s top editor, I should have pressed years earlier for coverage of that sort.

Steele, we would learn, relied overwhelmingly on a Russian American analyst, Igor Danchenko, who appeared to have no special pipeline into the Kremlin. Nor did a network of friends and acquaintances who supplied Danchenko with stories about Trump. During interviews with the FBI in early 2017, Danchenko said Steele had misstated or exaggerated what he had passed along, which itself was predominantly hearsay. As for the infamous "golden showers," Danchenko said he told Steele that was "rumor and speculation"— not, as the Steele memos had it, "confirmed" by a senior Western staff member at Moscow's Ritz-Carlton.

There was always reason to wonder how one former intelligence officer could know so much so quickly—more than all U.S. intelligence agencies and their worldwide partners combined. Steele's tenure in Russia was limited to a few years. He had retired seven years earlier from active spy work and had no access to Western governments' formidable surveillance network.

Our most severe critics on the right will say we didn't do enough to publicly raise doubts about Steele because of a deep-seated hostility toward Trump. Meier posits in *Spooked* that reporters hesitated to debunk it "because they didn't want to look like they were carrying water for Trump or his cronies." The primary reason, in my view, was something else: Just because the Steele accusations hadn't been proved didn't mean they wouldn't be someday. We would end up looking foolish if we discredited them and they were later verified.

Yet the media environment, and the passage of time without solid supporting evidence, justified cranking up the skepticism. Influential outlets were suggesting that the dossier was acquiring corroboration over time when, in fact, it wasn't. In a masterful series of columns in late 2019 and early 2020, *Post* media critic Erik Wemple took a penetrating look at how media outlets had been loudly beating the dossier drum or claiming to have found supportive "evidence." Among them were MSNBC, where Rachel Maddow, as late as October 2017, said that "a lot" of the Steele dossier was "dead to rights," and CNN, where host Don Lemon declared in November 2017 that "much of the dossier has been corroborated." In December 2017, even after a Justice Department inspector general's report threw cold water on Steele's incendiary allegations, a CNN anchor asserted that "many parts of that dossier were later corroborated."

Much of the media, including *The Post*, gave weight to Steele's memos because senior intelligence officials in the United States and Great Britain, as well as the FBI, did so. They vouched for his professionalism and expertise. The FBI had gone so far as to rely on Steele and his reports as central support for getting approval from the FISA court to wiretap Carter Page, who early on had been identified as a Trump campaign foreign policy adviser. Yet, according to the DOJ inspector general's report in December 2019, the FBI knew of questions about Steele's reliability and failed to share them with other Justice Department officials or the secret U.S. court. The IG's report said much of the material in the Steele reports "could not be corroborated" and that "certain allegations were inaccurate or inconsistent with information gathered" by FBI investigators. As for the "limited information that was corroborated," the report said it "related to time, location and title information, much of which was publicly available."

———

Steele's most startling allegations couldn't be verified. But separate journalistic investigations that had nothing to do with Steele documented how members of Team Trump consistently lied when the subject involved communications with Russian officials.

Reporters for *The Post* had been hearing for weeks that incoming national security advisor Michael Flynn spoke periodically during the transition period with Russia's ambassador to the United States, Sergey Kislyak. The conversations were reported to have occurred as President Obama was imposing severe sanctions on Russia. Obama, belatedly, was responding to interference in the 2016 presidential election.

As a tempestuous 2016 neared its final days, Obama announced that he would expel from the United States thirty-five Russians suspected of being intelligence operatives and penalize four top officers of Russia's military intelligence unit and three entities that purportedly assisted in the hacking. Russia's lavish waterfront compounds on the Eastern Shore of Maryland and New York's Long Island, which it had designated as relaxation retreats, were targeted for shutdown, too. The U.S. government considered them intelligence hubs. "These data theft and disclosure activities could only have been directed by the highest levels of the Russian government," Obama said.

Russia at first pledged that it would retaliate with equivalent measures. But in a sudden reversal Putin announced that there would be no retaliation whatsoever. The question within the administration, and among the press, was a natural one: What the hell happened? Why didn't the Russians follow through on their threat?

Word of Flynn-Kislyak conversations attracted understandable suspicion. Did they discuss the sanctions? Did Flynn say something that explained Russia's puzzling failure to retaliate? Was the Trump team interfering with Obama's foreign policy before actually taking office?

Flynn had been ousted by Obama in the spring of 2014 as director of national intelligence, leaving him furious over his treatment.

Sources at the time attributed his removal to a chaotic management style, while he blamed a political purge based on his views of
militant Islam. More recently, his seemingly chummy interactions
with Russians had provoked dismay within national security circles. Breaking with former military colleagues, Flynn fully aligned
himself with Trump in calling for a closer relationship with Russia. And his attendance in December 2015 at a tenth-anniversary
party in Moscow for the state-controlled RT television network, a
propaganda arm of the Kremlin, met with particular alarm. Flynn
had been paid more than $45,000 by RT to give a speech at its
celebration. And at dinner he sat shoulder to shoulder with Putin, a
juxtaposition memorably captured in a photograph that circulated
widely on the internet. Putin later claimed that he and Flynn barely
talked and hardly knew each other. An image of impropriety stuck.

Between the national security and politics staffs at *The Post*, there
was a divide on whether simple confirmation that Flynn and Kislyak
had been talking would warrant a story. Tom Hamburger, who says
he shared word of the Flynn-Kislyak conversations along with everything else he was hearing in mid-December, pressed to have the tip
investigated for a possible story. But if reporters could only confirm
calls between Flynn and Kislyak, what did that really amount to?
How could *The Post* know that it signified anything more than ordinary diplomatic courtesies? "We need more than 'there were a bunch
of phone calls,'" Adam Entous recalled to me.

That was a reasonable position. If we didn't know what Flynn and
Kislyak talked about, it would be hard to explain why we thought
it was so newsworthy. Opinion columnists, however, have far more
leeway than news reporters. They get to openly express their views.
They can raise provocative questions when there are no readily available answers. That is what *The Post*'s David Ignatius did in a column
published in the final days of the Obama administration.

Citing a "senior U.S. government official," Ignatius reported
that Flynn had "phoned Russian Ambassador Sergey Kislyak sev-

eral times on December 29, the day the Obama administration announced the expulsion of 35 Russian officials as well as other measures in retaliation for the hacking." And then David asked: "What did Flynn say, and did it undercut the U.S. sanctions? The Logan Act (though never enforced) bars U.S. citizens from correspondence intending to influence a foreign government about 'disputes' with the United States. Was its spirit violated?"

The next day, Sean Spicer, then the transition spokesman, acknowledged contact between Flynn and Kislyak but portrayed the calls as entirely innocent: extending holiday greetings and setting up a phone call with Trump for the days after he took office. "That was it," he said, "plain and simple." Two days later on Sunday's *Face the Nation* program, CBS News' John Dickerson questioned Vice President–elect Mike Pence about the Flynn calls. Pence was categorical: "They did not discuss anything having to do with the United States' decision to expel diplomats or impose censure against Russia."

But people in the national security establishment knew otherwise. Pence was either lying or had been lied to. Ignatius's column and the administration's duplicitous response "opened the floodgates, emboldened people to go a little bit farther," remembers Greg Miller of the national security staff. *The Post* became the vehicle for getting the truth out. "When the administration lied about it, it motivated people to contest the lies."

Greg had sought to interview Kislyak about Flynn through normal channels. On every try he was blocked. Greg discovered that on January 31 Kislyak would be speaking at the Marriott Wardman Park hotel in northwest Washington. Odds that Greg would get to the ambassador were slim. But the ambassador was sitting in the front row when Greg arrived. When Kislyak got up to speak, Greg headed for an empty chair next to his. To Greg's surprise, when Kislyak wrapped up his remarks, he didn't make an immediate exit but returned to his seat. As the next speaker launched into his remarks, Greg introduced himself and questioned the ambassador about

Flynn. Kislyak acknowledged communicating often with Flynn before and after the election, though he portrayed their conversations as routine. He wouldn't say whether the two had discussed sanctions. But Greg now had confirmation that Flynn and Kislyak were talking more frequently than the White House had acknowledged.

Adam Entous pursued the Flynn-Kislyak story with an old reporting technique of his. Meeting with intelligence officials, Adam pulled from his pocket a piece of paper. It contained a few typed statements, bullet points that ran counter to what Pence and other administration officials had been saying: (1) The FBI was listening to Kislyak, picks up Flynn. (2) On the call they discussed sanctions. (3) Not sure but probably, Pence and others lied or were misinformed by Flynn. "I don't have a problem with that," one source declared. "You're not going to look stupid," another said. When the conversation turned to Pence's assertions in his Sunday interview with Dickerson, sources would say, "That's not true." That was a sign: Flynn's conversations with Kislyak had been intercepted during the U.S. government's regular surveillance of Russian officials.

Fortuitously, *The Post* had a golden opportunity to get to Flynn directly. Karen DeYoung, a veteran foreign affairs and national security correspondent, was scheduled to meet with him about his priorities and approach to the job. With only minutes left in Karen's hour with Flynn, she advised him that, based on intelligence agencies' intercepts of his conversations, *Post* colleagues were planning to publish a story declaring that he had discussed sanctions with Russia's ambassador. "How can they listen to the intercepts? How can they do that?" Flynn said. A summary of the intercepts was in circulation, and *The Post*'s sources were familiar with it.

Still, Flynn stood his ground. No, he hadn't discussed sanctions. No, he hadn't signaled to the ambassador that Russia should hold off on any retaliation. Karen got permission to put all of that on the record.

A small clutch of us were waiting anxiously when Karen returned to the office—Adam, Greg, national security editor Peter Finn, and myself. We were taken aback by Flynn's flat-out denial. Normally, officials at that level will equivocate rather than lie outright. In my office, we discussed how to proceed. "Our reputation is on the line. There's no being 90 percent sure," as Peter later put it to me. I felt as he did, temporarily putting the brakes on publication. Reporters would have to check back with sources to ensure there was no misunderstanding.

When Greg returned the next day to meet with Cameron Barr, managing editor for news, and me, he spoke for all the national security reporters. They had checked again. Flynn was lying. "We are positive," he said. "Okay," I replied, "we need to go ahead." Greg would inform National Security Council spokesman Michael Anton. "Make it explicit," I said, "that we are proceeding with the story despite the denial."

Anton asked for time to respond. He came back with a revised statement. Flynn, he said, "indicated that while he had no recollection of discussing sanctions, he couldn't be certain that the topic never came up." Anton also wanted to retract Flynn's previous unqualified denial, requesting that it not be published. When reporters rightly balked, Anton asked to speak with a senior editor. Cameron took the call, giving him the blunt answer he deserved: Trump was always accusing us of "fake news" but now the administration was proposing that we pretend that Flynn hadn't lied. "I'm not now going to misrepresent what your boss told us," Cameron told Anton. "He tried to obscure the truth. He tried to hide what was done."

Within an hour, after some final polishing, the story was published. Citing as sources "nine current and former officials, who were in senior positions at multiple agencies at the time of the calls," *The Post* reported that Flynn's clandestine conversations with Kislyak were regarded by some government officials as "an inappropriate and potentially illegal signal to the Kremlin that it could expect a reprieve from sanctions that were being imposed by the Obama administration." The story also noted that the "emerging details contradict public statements by incoming senior administration officials," including Pence.

Four days later, as Trump officials reacted by issuing inconsistent pronouncements about Flynn's standing in the administration, *The Post* reported that Acting Attorney General Sally Yates had previously advised the White House that Flynn "misled senior administration officials about the nature of his communications with the Russian ambassador to the United States, and warned that the national security advisor was potentially vulnerable to Russian blackmail" because Russia knew that Flynn had lied. Within hours of that follow-up story, Flynn was no longer in the Trump administration, having been forced to resign after only twenty-four days in office.

Trump's statements in the days ahead were a study in incoherence, contradiction, and deceit. At first, he instinctively lashed out at the press—the "fake media," naturally—first declaring that Flynn had been treated "very, very unfairly." The following day, Trump said he "asked for his resignation" because Flynn had not been truthful with Pence. Another eleven days later, obviously alluding to *The Post*'s investigation into Flynn, he alleged that reporters had fabricated sources. "Because they have no sources," he declared in a speech to the Conservative Political Action Conference (CPAC). "They just make them up when there are none. I saw one story recently where they said nine people have confirmed. There are no nine people. I don't believe there was one or two people."

It was a bizarre thing to say. Only nine days earlier, Trump had called for a criminal investigation, railing against the "documents and papers that were illegally—I stress that—illegally leaked." And notwithstanding his call for an investigation and his claim that we had no sources, he also told CPAC that he already knew who our sources were: "I know who they talked to." If the president really believed the story was fabricated, then how could he allege an illegal leak of classified information? And if he already knew to whom our reporters spoke—after just saying we had "no sources"—any investigation would be over in no time at all. Trump could not have been more nonsensical.

Over the course of months *The Post* would produce scoops that shook the Trump administration. In March, our reporters disclosed that Attorney General Jeff Sessions, even when asked directly, had failed to disclose in his confirmation testimony that he had spoken twice with the Russian ambassador. That forced his immediate recusal from any investigation of Russia's intervention in the U.S. election, infuriating Trump, who expected the nation's top law enforcement officer to act as his personal protector. Also that month, *The Post* reported that Trump had revealed highly classified intelligence to the Russian foreign minister and ambassador when they met at the White House, alarming national security officials. Later, in May, *The Post* revealed that Russian ambassador Kislyak relayed to Moscow that Trump's son-in-law and close adviser Jared Kushner had sought to set up a secret communications channel between the incoming administration and the Kremlin—using, astoundingly, Russia's own diplomatic facilities to escape notice.

By then, Trump was feverishly trying to discredit and impede the investigation of his campaign aides' contacts with Russians. *The Post* reported how the president had tried to get two top intelligence officials to publicly discredit the idea of collusion between his campaign and Russia. In June, *The Post* was the first to report that the special counsel's office was beginning to investigate the president himself for possible obstruction of justice.

A July 31 story of ours carried immediate relevance for an obstruction inquiry: Trump, while aboard Air Force One flying back from Germany, had personally dictated his son's highly misleading statement about a meeting with a Russian lawyer that was set up with the promise of damaging information about Hillary Clinton. In a bombshell story, *The New York Times* had previously revealed that meeting in Trump Tower. In mid-July, it reported that Donald Trump Jr. gladly accepted an invitation to get together with the Russians after receiving an email from an intermediary pledging information that "would incriminate Hillary and her dealings with Russia and would be very useful to your father." The email continued, "This is obviously very high level and sensitive information but is part of Russia and its government's support for Mr. Trump." While the meeting never lived up to its promise, Trump's eldest son clearly saw nothing wrong, and a lot to celebrate, about getting campaign help from Russia. "If it's what you say I love it especially later in the summer" was Donald Jr.'s enthusiastic response to the idea.

The Times' coverage was especially strong on Trump's persistent efforts to quash investigations of his campaign and administration. It disclosed that FBI Director James Comey had written a memo on how Trump asked him to shut down the investigation of National Security Advisor Flynn—and how Trump had effectively admitted in an Oval Office meeting with the Russian foreign minister and ambassador that Comey ("a nut job") was fired because of the FBI's investigation into possible Russian collusion with his campaign. *The Times* documented how Russia, using fake accounts on Facebook and Twitter, had exploited social media to launch a cyber campaign against Clinton in the months before the presidential election.

So fierce was the day-to-day competition between *The Times* and *The Post* that *Vanity Fair* magazine asked in a headline, "Is *The New York Times* vs. *The Washington Post* vs. Trump the last great newspaper war?" Writer James Warren observed, "Two revived bastions of Old Media are engaged in a duel that resembles the World War II rivalry of American general George S. Patton and British general Sir Bernard Montgomery as they scrambled to be first to capture Messina." It certainly felt that way.

8

DEMOCRACY DIES IN DARKNESS

Dear *Washington Post* Newsroom staff," read the letter sent to me one week after Donald Trump took residence in the White House. "In the short (and very long) few days since the inauguration, it has become painfully clear that our democracy is on the line, and your work—your words, your integrity, your pursuit of truth and good storytelling—is essential to holding it up. We admire and deeply appreciate your effort and your ongoing commitment to keeping us informed. We hope in the doubtlessly long hours you are putting in, that you remember good journalism is an act of patriotism. Ignore the insecurities of the Critic in Chief, and remain brave. We need you."

The letter began with one reader in Berkeley, California. She shared it with others, who signed. They passed it along to still others. After collecting eighty signatories—from Idaho, Oregon, California, and Nevada—they sent it to me. With Trump's inauguration, letters like that came in a flood, cresting again a month later after he declared the nation's news media "the enemy of the American people" notwithstanding his pledge to "preserve, protect and defend the Constitution of the United States."

Never before had I witnessed such an outpouring of support for journalists' work. By then I had gloomily concluded that American citizens took a free and independent press for granted. They had no reason to believe it would be endangered and had scarcely thought about the consequences if it faced extinction. People were now awakening to the risks.

Many readers encouraged me to communicate their appreciation to the entire staff. So, I papered the glass wall of my office with thank-you notes, with readers' gratifying words facing outward toward the newsroom corridor. For staff anxious after the election that their work had not resonated with the public, here was evidence that it had. The wall became a popular waystation on newsroom tours given to family, friends, and other visitors.

"The Free Press is our only hope in times like these," read one letter. "You are our only defense against alternative facts!" a retired middle school teacher wrote. "Please tell all the stalwart souls who work for this grand paper how much they are appreciated and how much we the people depend on them," urged another reader.

Many Americans now understood that this new president was taking aim not only at the press but also at the very concept of verifiable fact. "These past several months (& especially last week) have been concerning for many reasons, not least of which because facts don't matter to this administration. I'm glad they matter to you," as one put it. "I subscribed to the *Washington Post* today because facts matter," said another.

Some readers suggested *The Post* find a way to accept even more money from them, despite the mind-boggling wealth of our owner. "I can't believe we're at a point where it's necessary to say this," one wrote, "but thank you for your paper's service to this country . . . I would like to suggest *The Post* have a donate button on its website . . . I for one would enjoy the opportunity to support your mission over and above a subscription." Americans wrote to stiffen our spine and boost our morale: "Just continue. We are with you!" "We in the streets have your backs. Don't stop."

A journalism professor at a community college in the South wrote in late February: "My students come from all walks—and economic conditions—of life. Some are poor, some are middle class. Few are rich. Many come from different countries . . . My students are young and smart and are working incredibly hard to get their Associate of Arts degree. But they are also afraid. Like the *Post*, they've, too, been criticized and they've been told they are enemies of the state. Some have been told they are less than human. Others worry for their safety. Each day, they brace themselves for another tweet vilifying their chosen profession . . . The reason I'm telling you all this is that when the fear gets too much for them, which it often does, I pull up the *Washington Post*'s website. I show them the *Post*'s stories. I show them the work you reporters do. I show them the best journalists in the nation. I show them how brave and resourceful the men and women of the *Post* are. We talk about your coverage. We analyze your newspaper's writing and we discuss the *Post*'s incredible legacy. And their fear goes away."

Critically for our business fortunes, readers were showing their support in a tangible way. They bought subscriptions. Almost overnight, we vaulted past one million digital-only subscriptions by the fall of 2017, more than double what we had secured at the start of the year. We were closing in on the 1.27 million digital subscribers at *The Wall Street Journal*, a longtime success story in digital circulation marketing. *The New York Times* was still far ahead at 2.3 million paid digital subscribers; so, something to strive for.

The Post would steadily reduce the number of free articles available to the public, putting the squeeze on casual readers to subscribe. As Bezos saw it, we now had an opportunity to recover from years of giving away our journalism for free on the internet, in contrast to how we had always charged for print newspapers. Setting up a "paywall," as we called it, was finally yielding impressive results. "Put the genie back in the bottle that we let out 20 years ago," Bezos said. Remarking on the paradox of Trump's attacks boosting our commercial fortunes, he invoked the elephant-headed, potbellied Hindu god Ganesha. Ganesha is revered as a remover of obstacles, but Ganesha also places obstacles in people's path so they develop the determination, resilience, and ingenuity to overcome them.

Many of our new readers clearly were looking for *The Post* to help secure democracy. A new motto for *The Post* seemed to promise just that. One month into Trump's presidency, *The Post* affixed the words "Democracy Dies in Darkness" under its nameplate on the printed newspaper, at the top of its website, and on everything it produced.

As Bezos envisioned it, this was not a slogan but a "mission statement." With its timing and grimly aggressive tone, Trump's allies saw it as a shot at the president, which it was not. The timing was only proof of the tortuous, and torturous, process of coming up with something sufficiently memorable and meaningful that Bezos would bless.

Beginning in early 2015, Bezos's instructions were to imagine a phrase that would convey an idea, not a product; fit nicely on a T-shirt; communicate a club that people would want to belong to; make a claim uniquely ours, given our heritage and base in the nation's capital; and be both aspirational and disruptive. "Not a paper I want to subscribe to," as Bezos put it, rather "an idea I want to belong to. I'd easily pay $100 to be associated with that idea." The idea: We love this country; so we hold this country accountable. "We have such high standards that we're outraged when those standards are not met."

No small order. And Bezos was no distant observer as we struggled. "On this topic," he told us, "I'd like to see all the sausage-making. Don't worry about whether it's a good use of my time."

Bezos, so fixated on metrics in other contexts, now advised ditching them. "I just think we're going to have to use gut and intuition." And he insisted that the chosen words recognize our "historic mission," not a new one. "We don't have to be afraid of the 'democracy' word," he said; it's "the thing that makes *The Post* unique." And he alluded to a year-old quote of mine: "We have to communicate to the public that we are essential, not just through writing columns saying, 'Boy, you know, you're going to miss us if we're not around.'"

Staff teams were assembled. Months of meetings were held. Frustrations deepened. Outside branding consultants were retained, to no avail. ("Typical," said Bezos, who rarely missed an opportunity to diss consultants.) Failure begat embarrassment. Expectations were that someone in the marketing department might get fired.

Desperation led to a long list of options, venturing into the inane. The ideas totaled at least a thousand: "A Bias for Truth," "Know," "A Right to Know," "Unstoppable Journalism," "The Power Is Yours," "Power Read," "Relentless Pursuit of the Truth," "The Facts Matter," "It's About America," "Spotlight on Democracy," "Democracy Matters," "A Light on the Nation," "Democracy Lives in Light," "Democracy Takes Work. We'll Do Our Part," "You Have a Right to Know," "The News Democracy Needs," "Toward a More Perfect Union" (rejected lest it summon thoughts of our own workforce union).

By September 2016, an impatient Bezos was forcing the issue. We had to settle on something. Nine *Post* executives and Bezos met in a private room at the Four Seasons in Georgetown to finally get over the finish line. Due to Bezos's tight schedule, we had a half hour, starting at 7:45 a.m. A handful of options remained on the table: "A Bright Light for a Free People" or, simply, "A Bright Light for Free People"; "The Story Must Be Told" (recalling the inspiring words of the late photographer Michel du Cille); "To Challenge and Inform"; "For a World That Demands to Know"; "For People Who Demand to Know." None of those passed muster. Instead, we settled on "A Free People Demand to Know" (subject to checking the grammar with our copy desk, which subsequently gave its assent).

Success was short-lived—mercifully, no doubt. Late that evening Bezos dispatched an email in, as he put it, the "not what you're hoping for category." He had run our consensus pick by wife MacKenzie (a novelist and "my in-house wordsmith"), who had pronounced the phrase clunky. "Frankenslogan," she sneered.

By then, we needed Bezos to take unilateral action. Finally, he did. Let's go with "Democracy Dies in Darkness," he decreed. It had been on our list from the start, and a phrase Bezos had used previously in speaking of *The Post*'s mission. Without announcement, it would appear in mid-February 2017 on the front page of *The Post* and at the top of our digital homepage. I'd never seen a slogan—er, mission statement—get so much reaction. It even drew attention from *People's Daily* in China, which tweeted, "'Democracy dies in darkness' @washingtonpost puts on new slogan, on the same day @realDonaldTrump calls media as the enemy of Americans." The *Merriam-Webster* dictionary reported a sudden surge in searches for the word "democracy." Comedian Stephen Colbert cracked that some of the rejected phrases included "No, You Shut Up" and "We Took Down Nixon—Who Wants Next?" The digital magazine *Slate* weighed in with "15 Metal Albums Whose Titles Are Less Dark Than *The Washington Post*'s New Motto." Twitter commentators remarked on *The Post*'s "new goth vibe." Media critic Jack Shafer tweeted a handful of "rejected *Washington Post* mottos," among them "We're Really Full of Ourselves" and "Democracy Gets Sunburned If It Doesn't Use Sunscreen."

Bezos couldn't have been more thrilled. The "mission statement" was getting notice. "It's a good sign when you're the subject of satire," Bezos said a couple of weeks later when we took stock of how the phrase was being received. The point was that "we are actually doing something important." The four words atop our journalism had drawn attention to our mission. Much worse would have been a collective public shrug.

Bezos had heard *Washington Post* legend Bob Woodward use the phrase. It was a twist on a ruling in 2002 by federal appellate court judge Damon J. Keith, who wrote that "democracies die behind closed doors." Like others at *The Post*, I questioned the wisdom of branding all our work with death and darkness. All I could think of at that point, though, was the Serenity Prayer: "God grant me the serenity to accept the things I cannot change." Truth was, it was magnificent marketing. The phrase stuck with readers. Many could recite it from memory—and many also saw it as perfect for the era of Donald Trump, even if that was not its intent.

Millions of Americans were prepared to participate in supporting democracy at that moment in U.S. history. They saw a subscription to *The Post* as a way to join the democracy club. "We are deeply grateful for your remarkable investigative reporting as you seek the truth about abuses to our cherished democracy," several dozen self-described "members and friends" of the First Congregational United Church of Christ wrote me. "We know that 'democracy will not die in darkness' as long as *The Washington Post* is at work. In the face of hate and threats of violence to our Nation's free press, we pray for your continuing strength and resolve to find the truth."

Now our job was to deliver the accountability promised in the mission statement. Hundreds of thousands of new subscribers were counting on us.

Editorial page editor Fred Hiatt was once again confiding his concern to me. If "Democracy Dies in Darkness" seemed like a slap at Trump, Fred was suddenly getting a different vibe from Bezos himself. *The Post*'s owner had never ordered up an editorial, quashed one, or even reviewed one before publication (and, from what I've been told, hasn't done so since). In Bezos's twice-monthly meetings with top opinions department editors, the conversations routinely dealt in generalities about issues likely to be addressed, gently testing whether they were in overall agreement. So it came as a surprise to Fred that, in the days before Trump took office, Bezos urged showing support for Trump on whatever issues he could. Publisher Fred Ryan firmly agreed. It was not an unreasonable request. Whenever

The Post editorial board's view coincided with Trump's, why not say so? *The Post's* editorial page editor, however, feared that Bezos was anxious to smooth things over with the new occupant of the White House.

Nine days before taking office, Trump held his first post-election press conference. In one line, he declared, "I have great respect for the news and great respect for freedom of the press and all of that." Bezos, by Fred Hiatt's account, had seized hopefully on that as a promising sign. It was a slim reed to lean on. *The Post's* own story noted that Trump had "returned to a theme that was a hallmark of his campaign: He flayed and belittled the news media." Irate over reporting on the Christopher Steele dossier, Trump refused to take a question from a CNN reporter ("fake news") and attacked *BuzzFeed* ("a failing pile of garbage").

"Freedom of the press and all of that" was perfunctory and doubtlessly insincere, but it appeared *The Post's* editorial page would at least take a stab at finding something to commend in the new president. On January 18, *The Post* published an editorial headlined "Five Policies Trump Might Get Right," which kicked off with a milquetoast understatement about why *The Post* endorsed Trump's opponent—"because we thought she offered better policy solutions and was better-suited by experience and temperament for the job." But the editorial then added, "Nevertheless, his election was legitimate, and his inauguration is inevitable. All of us have a duty to oppose Mr. Trump when he is wrong, but also to remain open to supporting him when he and the Republican-majority Congress make worthy proposals. How often might that be? Well, not never: We can identify a number of areas in which Mr. Trump and his fellow Republicans have ideas worth taking seriously."

The Post editorial offered encouragement, with significant caveats, on tax reform, school choice, a stronger military, infrastructure, and deregulation. "As full of risk for our democracy as the Trump presidency is," the editorial declared, "it would be folly to ignore any opportunities for progress it presents, if and when it does." *The Post* editorial page would rarely find reason to be so hopeful again.

Nine days into his presidency, fresh from signing an executive order that suspended refugee admissions to the United States for 120 days while barring any citizen of seven Muslim-majority countries from entering for 90 days, Trump was scheduled for what was expected to be an hourlong call with the prime minister of Australia, Malcolm Turnbull. Australia ranks among the strongest allies of the United States, one of only four other countries included in an espionage alliance known as "Five Eyes."

With any normal newly elected president, such a call would be cordial. And, as the administration recounted it, that's exactly what happened. The official word was that the conversation "emphasized the enduring strength and closeness of the U.S.-Australia relation-ship that is critical for peace, stability, and prosperity in the Asia-Pacific region and globally." Within five days, *The Post*'s Greg Miller and Philip Rucker reported what really transpired. Trump was seek-ing to renege on an Obama-era pact that created an exception to his executive order that temporarily forbade the admission of refugees. The United States had agreed to accept 1,250 refugees who had been detained by Australia in horrific conditions on two remote islands. Trump declared it "the worst deal ever," protested that he was "going to get killed" for accepting the refugees, alleged that Australia was sending the "next Boston bombers," and said categorically that he didn't want to accept them. The anticipated one-hour call ended in twenty-five minutes. In contrast to the official White House ac-count, Trump told Turnbull that, of his five conversations with world leaders that day, "this was the worst call by far."

By summer, *The Post* published the full transcript of Trump's call with Turnbull and another call of his on January 27 with Mexican president Enrique Peña Nieto. Trump insisted that Peña Nieto stop declaring "we will not pay" for a wall, substituting instead "we will work it out." Otherwise, Trump said, "I do not want to meet with you guys anymore because I cannot live with that." His overriding considerations were politics and PR. Peña Nieto's outright refusal to pay would run counter to Trump's claim to being a master deal-maker who could pressure Mexico into footing the full cost of a border wall. "You cannot say that to the press," Trump told him.

Trump reacted with rage to *The Post*'s reporting. His conversations—the entire transcripts, imagine that—had found their way into the hands of our journalists.

Trump's government was shaping up as the leakiest in memory. Trump would blame the "deep state," but the reasons were more varied. Trump had assembled his administration haphazardly, en-listing many individuals who had no government experience and no history of previously collaborating with each other—"kind of a crowd of misfit toys," as Josh Dawsey, a White House reporter for *The Post*, put it to me. Many were mere opportunists. "Part of it," said Ashley Parker, another White House reporter for *The Post*, "was that some of them weren't loyal to Trump at all." Plus, she noted, "He had no loyalty to them." And, for all Trump's grousing about "anonymous sources," he and his aides were regular leakers, too, insisting on an-onymity for themselves.

Many administration officials, Ashley observed, came to believe that working in the administration resembled being a character in the HBO program *Game of Thrones*. Better to knife others before you got knifed yourself. Odds were high that Trump would do the stabbing someday on his own. "Most of them knew that at some point he was going to turn on them," Dawsey said, and officials had their own reputations to protect.

Ideologies and personalities were in conflict, too. Administra-tion officials with genuine policy beliefs were competing for Trump's attention and favor. The best way to persuade the president, Ashley said, was to fight their battles in the media. "That was far more likely to sway him than staying up all night to prepare a briefing book." Deep reading wasn't his forte.

Finally, some people leaked out of principle. They were astonished at the norms of governance and democracy being violated—and at the pervasive lying. "People saw a lot of astonishing things," Josh recalls. Officials would call and say, "You're not going to believe what happened today . . . They just thought it was a bizarro place to work." Reporters often served, Josh sensed, as "people's therapist."

The torchlit rally of white nationalists in Charlottesville, Virginia, in August 2017—with hundreds chanting racist and anti-Semitic slogans and a neo-Nazi plowing his car into counter-protesters, killing thirty-two-year-old Heather Heyer—weakened allegiance to Trump and led to even more leaks. The president's response to the violence—"you also had people that were very fine people, on both sides"—infuriated many even within his administration. Josh remembers it as a "seminal moment," with some officials thinking "this guy may be way further out there than I'm willing to go."

Reporters were not merely passive recipients of inside information, however. *Post* journalists had cultivated strong sources over years covering politics and government agencies, including the most secretive ones. Tips couldn't be taken at face value, especially when officials were pressing their own agendas and pursuing their own grudges. Each tip often required calling a dozen or more people to nail down the facts. "People think incorrectly we just sat at our desks and just took dictation," Ashley says. And yet Trump surrounded himself, she adds, with people who "were certainly less disciplined than the Obama White House, the Biden White House, or the Bush White House."

Trump had come into office obsessing over loyalty and secrecy, demanding key administration figures sign nondisclosure agreements (NDAs) that might subject them to being sued if they revealed what he wanted kept confidential. Now, with the president furious over *The Post*'s publication of the transcripts of his conversations with Australia's prime minister and the president of Mexico, the administration acted on his obsession by declaring war on leakers.

On August 4, Attorney General Jeff Sessions, eager to please a president he had infuriated by recusing himself from the Russia investigation, made a show of announcing that he was zealously pursuing leakers. Sessions stood at a Justice Department podium with Daniel Coats, director of national intelligence, to declare that leak investigations had tripled since the end of the Obama administration, which itself had been aggressive in hunting down leakers. Referring to *The Post*'s publication of the transcripts, Sessions said, "No government can be effective when its leaders cannot discuss sensitive matters in confidence or talk freely in confidence with foreign leaders."

With that, Sessions suggested that the Justice Department would roll back Obama-era reforms that had limited the government's efforts to secretly subpoena journalists' emails and phone records. The secrecy denied media outlets an opportunity to raise legal objections. "We respect the important role that the press plays and will give them respect, but it is not unlimited," Sessions said. "They cannot place lives at risk with impunity."

It was a preposterous statement. Nothing in *The Post* had put anyone's life in jeopardy. Sessions didn't cite a single story of ours, or anyone else's, that did so. It was a phony justification for prying into journalists' communications. Soon, the Reporters Committee for Freedom of the Press, which advocates for First Amendment freedoms and news-gathering rights, mobilized media executives, including myself, to meet with Deputy Attorney General Rod Rosenstein. Sessions's announcement was designed to terrify potential sources, intimidate the press, and keep the truth about the Trump administration from becoming public.

In 2021, *The Post* learned just how far the administration had gone to investigate our revelations about Trump and his team. On May 3, 2021, the Justice Department wrote reporters Ellen Nakashima, Greg Miller, and Adam Entous (by then a writer for *The New Yorker*) to inform them that their phone records for the period April 15 to July 31, 2017, had been secretly obtained. The letter from the Justice Department indicated that it had received access to the phone records from Ellen's work, cell phone, and home numbers; Greg's work phone and cell phone; and Adam's cell phone. The records did not include the content of the phone calls but did reveal who was called, when, and for how long—potentially invaluable data for identifying sources. The DOJ had also sought access to the logs of the reporters' emails but was unsuccessful. *The Post* had prepared years earlier for leak investigations just like this one. National security reporters' emails were stored on *The Post*'s own private servers. The DOJ couldn't grab them secretly from a third party, as it had done with the phone records.

Court records that were later unsealed showed that the Justice Department sought the reporters' communications records on December 22, 2020, one day before then–attorney general William Barr resigned his position. Those records also revealed exactly what the DOJ was investigating as a leak of classified information: *The Post*'s May 2017 article about Trump son-in-law Jared Kushner wanting to set up a secret communications channel with Russia; a June 2017 article about how the Obama administration struggled to respond to Russia's election interference the previous year; and the July 2017 article about Sessions's communications with Sergey Kislyak, Russia's ambassador. No lives had been threatened with those stories, only falsehoods.

The Post was not the only target of the Justice Department's aggressive tactics. In short order, *The New York Times* and CNN learned that the department had also seized records of their reporters. In the case of CNN, emails were also obtained. The DOJ had also sought *The Times'* emails, but Google, which runs its email system, resisted the subpoenas, and the Justice Department backed down. The DOJ had allowed *Times* lawyers and some executives to know about their legal maneuvers. However, in a highly unusual step, the government successfully obtained a court order that prohibited them from sharing that information with colleagues in their own newsroom.

The Justice Department hadn't formally rescinded reforms of the previous administration on seeking reporters' communications, but at the very least it was encroaching on them. The Trump administration had been more belligerent toward the press than we even knew at the time. Only after Trump left office did we discover that it was at its most warlike, in secret, in his final weeks.

There were many tools in Trump's toolbox for trying to get the press coverage he wanted or to keep adverse coverage at bay. At the dinner that owner Jeff Bezos, publisher Fred Ryan, editorial page editor Fred Hiatt, and I had with him at the White House on June 15, 2017, we observed one technique. He put on the charm. There was never a doubt in my mind, however, that Trump saw that dinner as more than an occasion to get acquainted. If Trump gives—in that case, a dinner with himself—he expects something in return.

For all his gripes about *The Post*, Trump had never before contacted me. Now that we had sat elbow to elbow, he did. I would be subjected to another tool of his: jawboning the top editor while denigrating the reporters who regularly covered him. The first post-dinner call came to my cell phone on June 26 at nine p.m., shortly after I had gotten home from work.

Trump was steaming over a story that had recently appeared on our front page. White House correspondents Ashley Parker and Philip Rucker had reported on how Trump was adapting to the

Russia investigation "that he complains hangs over his presidency like a darkening cloud." Based on interviews with twenty-two administration officials, advisers, and allies, Ashley and Phil wrote of "a White House still trying, after five months of halting progress, to establish a steady rhythm of governance while also indulging and managing Trump's combative and sometimes self-destructive impulses."

Trump had just wrapped up his dinner with Indian prime minister Narendra Modi when he called me. "I think we'll do better with India," he said, and then turned to the purpose of his call, slamming *The Post*'s story and its authors. "It was so wrong." As he'd done on many previous occasions, he recounted his against-the-odds electoral victory. "I beat seventeen senators, governors, top of the line . . . I beat the Hillary Clinton machine, I beat the Bush machine." He boasted of the size of his rallies, including his latest in Iowa, where the crowd was so big "they sent people away." He recited his Electoral College numbers more than once. He pointed to the strong economy and a rising stock market. And he brought up Russia: "There was no collusion, no obstruction."

Of Ashley and Phil, he said, "They don't know me." And he was keeping score. Of Ashley in particular, he said she "has never written a good story, even when she was at *The New York Times*," her employer before she joined *The Post* in reporting on the White House. He said that Phil had written only one good story—a piece in April 2016 about commuters on the Staten Island Ferry as a portrait of Trump's base of support: "After that, he went bad," adding, "I used to like Phil." He complained that Ashley hadn't called him ("not that I would have taken her call") and that I should call anytime, checking in first with aide Hope Hicks. (I never took him up on the offer.)

Mostly he grumbled about how his demeanor and physical appearance were represented. "That's not the person who has won all his life." The story reported that he appeared to have gained weight. (Trump said he was "five pounds lighter.") He said he wasn't in a gloomy mood. ("Just the opposite. I don't have time to be depressed.")

The story depicted him as "some kind of fool, like I'm some sort of slob," Trump said, taking issue with the idea that he watched television. "I am the president . . . They have me moping around like an idiot." And, in a line that has stuck with me like no other because I could never have imagined it being uttered by the president of the United States, Trump said, "I read that article, and it's like I'm a little boy. I'm not a little boy." The call lasted fifteen minutes, with my thanking the president for sharing his perspective. And then I typed up the notes I took during the call.

The next call from Trump came two days later, at 9:57 a.m., as our morning news meeting was breaking up. The complaint this time was another story by Rucker and Parker, along with co-author Robert Costa. In a story headlined "Who's Afraid of Trump? Not Enough Republicans—At Least for Now," the three *Post* reporters had written that Trump was yet to be revered or feared on policy matters such as health care. "I know when people respect or don't respect," he protested.

Trump said a health-care meeting he held with Republican senators the previous day had been a "love fest." Speaking of himself in the third person, he said, "Did Trump display leadership? He ran the meeting." He disputed the idea that he didn't know policy details. "I know as much about health care as anybody in that room . . . I think we're going to get health care passed." (He never delivered a health care plan to replace Obamacare.) Over the course of nearly half an hour, he railed against the story, the reporters, *The Post,* and—not to be left out—Bezos.

Trump declared that *The Post's* journalists must be "controlled" by me, and that I could tell Phil, Bob, and Ashley "on behalf of me that they're very dishonest reporters." Once again, he complained that the reporters hadn't called him for their story. I suggested that perhaps our reporters should call him on every story they wrote about him. "I don't think it would do any good," he snapped. Of *The Post*, Trump said, "I know you're controlled by Amazon." Irritated at having to listen to that nonsense directly from Trump himself, I pushed back. "It's not, and you know it's not." Profanity from the president ensued. *The Post* was a "hate machine" and a "fucking joke." And he concluded that *The Washington Post* is "a big fat lie." Saying that, he said, "makes me feel good."

Trump wasn't getting anywhere with these calls. He must have known that. That was the last I ever heard from him.

Although Bezos was outwardly unflappable in the face of Trump's bilious rhetoric, there had been signs since the election that it had set his nerves on edge at least a bit. He began to sense that we might need allies in the face of intensifying pressure.

Bezos's thinking emerged from a small, late-November 2016 dinner on my behalf after I won the Hitchens Prize, which celebrates a commitment to First Amendment rights and truth. I was stunned, and honored, to discover that evening that Bezos had flown to New York to attend. It was one of several instances when he showed appreciation, in a personal way, for my editorship. The following year, he donated $1 million to the Reporters Committee for Freedom of the Press, which provides pro bono legal representation for journalists, when I won its award for career achievements. A couple of years later, he flew to Washington to present me with a bike on my sixty-fifth birthday.

In the back room of Greenwich Village's Waverly Inn that November, I said in my prepared remarks that we were now "compelled to fight for free expression and a free press," even though those were rights guaranteed in the Constitution. "Many journalists wonder with considerable weariness what it is going to be like for us during the next four—perhaps eight—years. Will we be incessantly harassed and vilified? Will the new administration seize on opportunities to try intimidating us? Will we face obstruction at every turn? If so, what do we do? The answer, I believe, is pretty simple. Just do our job. Do it as it's supposed to be done."

A few days later, before his post-election lunch with the politics staff in December, Bezos sent an email suggesting that the speech had him focused on how we might prepare for the worst. Our most natural ally in defense of the press was also our most ferocious competitor, *The New York Times*. Despite our battles on journalistic and business fronts, Bezos proposed building a relationship that could be called upon if there were ever the need.

My own relationship with the hierarchy of *The New York Times* was strong. Arthur Sulzberger Jr., as CEO of the New York Times Company, had been my ultimate boss when I was the top editor of *The Boston Globe*, which it owned. Dean Baquet, the top editor of *The New York Times*, had been a personal friend since my three-plus years in the late 1990s as a senior editor at that paper and his tenure as national editor. When we both reached the top ranks of our newsrooms, we regularly confided in each other and compared notes about the pressures we faced, even on occasion when we led outlets that were archrivals.

Bezos had no connection with the senior leaders of *The Times*, and he came to feel one was warranted. Sulzberger had sent Bezos an email after his purchase of *The Post* proposing a get-together (even inviting him to speak at an offsite meeting of *Times* executives). To Sulzberger's frustration, there was no response. Now, though, the relationship-building would begin. Our first meeting was in February 2017 at a dinner in the downstairs private room of the Dovetail restaurant on Manhattan's Upper West Side. Another dinner followed in May at publisher Fred Ryan's Georgetown town house. A third was held in March 2018, amid Trump's escalating war against Bezos, in a curtained-off room at the Ribbon, also on the Upper West Side.

The third encounter gave us away. The Ribbon was boisterous

The sale of *The Washington Post* to Jeff Bezos was announced to employees on August 5, 2013, by Katharine Weymouth, its publisher, and Donald Graham, her uncle and CEO of the parent company. (Photo by Marvin Joseph / *The Washington Post*)

Publisher Katharine Weymouth had established a strategy for being "for and about Washington." Bezos immediately changed course, declaring that *The Post* should be a national, and even global, news organization. (Photo by T. J. Kirkpatrick / Bloomberg via Getty Images)

A banner headline announced *The Post*'s sale to Bezos on its front page, displayed at the Newseum in Washington, D.C. (Photo by Brooks Kraft LLC / Corbis via Getty Images)

Bezos took questions from newsroom staff for the first time on September 4, 2013. Among his comments regarding news coverage were "Don't be boring." (Photo by Matt McClain / *The Washington Post*)

Top leadership, past and present, attended Bezos's September Q&A with *Post* journalists. From left to right: Fred Hiatt, editorial page editor; former executive editor Len Downie; former managing editor Robert Kaiser; managing editor Kevin Merida; publisher Katharine Weymouth; me; and former executive editor Ben Bradlee. (Photo by Matt McClain / *The Washington Post*)

Bezos sat next to me when he observed a daily news meeting on September 3, 2013, his first day in the newsroom. (Photo by Matt McClain / *The Washington Post*)

Bezos rang a triangle, participating in *The Post*'s traditional ritual for calling a daily news meeting. From left to right: Scott Vance, deputy managing editor; Eric Rich, then the universal news desk editor; designer Christian Font, seated; and MaryAnne Golon, director of photography. (Photo by Matt McClain / *The Washington Post*)

Journalist Barton Gellman shook hands with me in April 2014 after *The Post* was awarded the Pulitzer Prize for Public Service for its coverage of National Security Agency surveillance. Former intelligence contractor Edward Snowden leaked highly classified documents to Gellman. Deputy national editor Anne Kornblut and national editor Cameron Barr applauded. Investigations editor Jeff Leen stood in the background, at right. (Photo by Katherine Frey / *The Washington Post*)

Bezos attended the funeral service for legendary *Washington Post* executive editor Ben Bradlee at the Washington National Cathedral on October 29, 2014, and later described it as a "formative" experience. (Photo by Chip Somodevilla / Getty Images)

Senior executives met with Bezos at his home in Medina, Washington, in late October 2013 to begin planning a new direction for *The Post*. Joining Bezos, from left to right, were me, publisher Katharine Weymouth, president and general manager Steve Hills, and chief information officer Shailesh Prakash. (Photo courtesy of Shailesh Prakash)

The Post's Tehran bureau chief Jason Rezaian, right, was held in an Iranian prison for 544 days. After Rezaian recovered at a U.S. Army medical facility in Germany, Bezos brought him and his wife, Yeganeh Salehi, left, who also had been imprisoned, back to the United States on his private plane on January 22, 2016. (Photo by Douglas Jehl / *The Washington Post*)

New *Washington Post* offices were dedicated on January 28, 2016. Bezos, center, and his then-wife MacKenzie talked with *Post* publisher Fred Ryan, right. (Photo by Bill O'Leary / *The Washington Post*)

Presidential candidate Donald Trump met with *The Post*'s editorial board on March 21, 2016. He was accompanied through the office by Fred Hiatt, editorial page editor, in foreground. (Photo by Bonnie Jo Mount / *The Washington Post*)

Bezos spoke for the first time about Donald Trump's attacks on him, Amazon, and the press during an interview with me at a *Post*-sponsored conference on May 18, 2016. Every individual or institution, he said, should be able to "scrutinize, examine, and criticize an elected official, especially a candidate for the highest office in the most powerful country on Earth." (Photo by Linda Davidson / *The Washington Post*)

Wesley Lowery addressed the newsroom in April 2016 after *The Post* won the Pulitzer Prize for a major project he inspired that closely examined police shootings. After receiving a disciplinary letter for his social media activities, he announced in January 2020 that he would leave *The Post*. (Photo by Manuel Balce Ceneta / AP)

Glenn Simpson, right, and Peter Fritsch of the Fusion GPS investigations firm hired former British intelligence agent Christopher Steele to investigate Trump's connections to Russia. When Steele's allegations were disclosed, they touched off a furor. (Photo by Stephen Voss / Redux)

and packed. There was no way to avoid being detected, and media reporter Oliver Darcy disclosed that Bezos, Ryan, and I had met with Baquet, Arthur Sulzberger Jr., his son and new *Times* publisher A. G. Sulzberger, and Times Company CEO Mark Thompson. *Times* and *Post* executives conferred on a response to deflect attention from the summit-like appearance of our gathering. "Leaders of the *Post* and *The Times*," Baquet said in an artful statement, "have gotten together periodically for decades and still do. Arthur and Don Graham were friends, as were Katharine Graham and Arthur's father. When Jeff Bezos bought *The Post*, Arthur thought it was a tradition worth maintaining. So we have."

That was all true, but it was not the full story. The occasion for these meetings, from Bezos's perspective, was a concern that the Trump team might escalate its assault on the press in a far more damaging way. Corey Lewandowski, a close confidant of Trump's and his first campaign manager, had declared in December 2016 that Dean "should be in jail" because *The New York Times* had gotten its hands on several pages of Trump's 1995 tax returns and published them, also calling for *The Times* to be sued "into oblivion." (Dean had declared in September that he'd publish Trump's tax returns at the risk of incarceration.)

So *Times* and *Post* executives spoke about our common concerns: the prospect of litigation, including libel suits; how reporters had come under threat online, with their personal information disclosed in a practice known as doxing (or doxxing); and the overall posture of the administration toward the press. In our final meeting at the Ribbon, Bezos was asked by our *New York Times* competitors whether owning *The Post* had helped him or hurt him. "Net-net," he allowed, using business jargon for "in the final analysis," it had probably hurt. He didn't elaborate, and he professed not to care, saying he was proud of *The Post* and enjoying his ownership. Most of the conversation was social. We never reached any mutual-aid pact, nor was it ever clear what that might have looked like even if we had wanted to. But the executives of both organizations knew each other better—and knew we had each other's backs.

Before acquiring *The Post,* Bezos had closely read the autobiography of Katharine Graham, taking special note of how she and *The Post* had come under threat from the Nixon administration. In one instance, as *The Post*'s Carl Bernstein and Bob Woodward prepared to publish another Watergate-era scoop, Attorney General John Mitchell barked, "Katie Graham's gonna get her tit caught in a big fat wringer if that's published."

In a note to staff when his *Post* purchase was announced, Bezos wrote of "two kinds of courage" the Grahams had demonstrated over the years that he now hoped to channel. One, he said, was "the courage to say wait, be sure, slow down, get another source. Real people and their reputations, livelihoods and families are at stake." The second, he said, was "the courage to say follow the story, no matter the cost. While I hope no one ever threatens to put one of my body parts through a wringer, if they do, thanks to Mrs. Graham's example, I'll be ready."

Bezos had that incident with Katharine Graham very much in mind one Sunday in late October 2017, when he made a personal delivery to *The Post.* He was in D.C. for non-*Post* business and told me he would be bringing a gift for our newsroom. He wanted zero fuss over his presence, which would be very brief. Someone on duty just needed to meet him for the few minutes required to drop it off. But Bezos left strict instructions not to unveil the gift until our Monday-morning news meeting. On October 30, I pulled off the cover in the news conference room named for Ben Bradlee. Bezos had acquired an antique clothes wringer for us and ordered up a right-sized oval wood table made especially for its display. The wringer carried a plaque engraved with words that Bezos later told me were inspired in part by remarks of mine about how journalists should respond to attacks: "If it comes, so be it. Just do the work, as best you can, wherever it may lead." The wringer remains in that conference room as a reminder of *The Post*'s task in the face of any menace—and ideally, in Bezos's words, as "more of a ward than an omen."

9

EXPLOSIONS

Deep into his tenure as president, Donald Trump paid homage, surely unintended, to the contribution that investigative reporting makes to good government. Seemingly out of nowhere, Trump had something favorable to say about the media's "vetting" of his appointees.

"I give a name. I give it out to the press. And you vet for me. A lot of times you do a very good job, not always," Trump said in August 2019. "The vetting process for the White House is very good. But you're part of the vetting process, you know. I give out a name to the press, and you vet for me. We save a lot of money that way."

Though not especially coherent—the White House vets well, but your vetting allows us to save money?—Trump had just attested to journalism as a public service, even as he happened at the time to be fulminating over what the press had most recently dug up regarding a national security appointee. In his disordered way, Trump helped highlight a central task of ours: scrutinizing people who aspired to positions of enormous power.

I had long been a champion of investigative reporting. But so much investigative journalism takes months to complete, at times lasting half a year or longer. Enlightening and effective as the work might be, that is too infrequent a signal to the public that the press holds the powerful to account. And news routinely doesn't allow for long waits. That's certainly the case when the president makes appointments and during the feverish pace of elections.

Well before the 2016 election, I had spoken with *The Post*'s publisher, Fred Ryan, about setting up a SWAT team of investigative reporters to respond quickly to the news, working closely with reporters on other teams whose missions were very different. More "accountability journalism," as we called it, would both serve our "Democracy Dies in Darkness" mission and win us more subscribers. Fred agreed—as did the ultimate decision-maker on budget matters, Jeff Bezos—and we received the green light to create an eight-person "rapid-response investigative team." That almost doubled the size of our investigative unit.

After the staff was fully assembled in August 2017, results were instantaneous.

Stephanie McCrummen was a member of a team of *Post* reporters who worked full-time on long-form narratives that typically explored the fissures in American society through the lives of ordinary people. The tools have been deep reporting and nuanced, literary-level craftsmanship. Journalists nationwide long coveted the opportunity to work on that team and with Stephanie's revered editor, David Finkel, a Pulitzer winner and the rare recipient in our profession of the so-called genius award from the MacArthur Foundation, which paid tribute to his "finely honed methods of immersion reporting and empathy for often-overlooked lives."

Under David's direction in the fall of 2017, Stephanie traveled to Alabama, aiming to understand and communicate the passion for Republican Senate candidate Roy Moore among his most fervent supporters. Moore's candidacy had been championed by Steve Bannon, the far-right nationalist and former chief strategist in Trump's White House, as a step toward jettisoning the Republican Party's ruling establishment. In 2003 Moore had been removed from his position as chief justice of the Alabama Supreme Court after refusing a federal court order to dismantle a granite monument of the Ten Commandments that he had installed in the judicial building. After being reelected, he ordered probate judges not to issue marriage licenses to same-sex couples, defying the landmark U.S. Supreme Court ruling that gave them the right to marry. For that, he was suspended in 2016 for the rest of his term.

Moore was now running in a special election to fill the Senate seat left vacant when Jeff Sessions was tapped to become attorney general of the United States. He had defeated the candidate favored by Trump in the Republican primary and now faced Democrat Doug Jones, a former U.S. attorney.

Stephanie was a natural for the assignment. She was a Birmingham native, raised there in the Southern Baptist faith, and the granddaughter of a Southern Baptist preacher. The story she ended up with, however, was far from what she initially imagined.

Stephanie traveled to the Gadsden area in Etowah County, where Moore was born. She had in mind immersing herself in the life of a family who supported him, illuminating their view of America and Christianity's role in it. She began by stopping in on places that were flying Christian flags. At an old burger joint called the Big Chief, she was talking to one man when another passed by and said, "Oh, you're writing about Roy Moore. You should come to lunch with me. I'm meeting with a bunch of guys. They all love him. So you should come meet them." She went along. And as those men talked, one happened to remark, "Oh, Roy Moore, he likes the young girls." It was a casual comment, but Stephanie noted how "the other guys there kind of laughed. It was as if everybody knew this."

Stephanie didn't rush to investigate. For a day or two, she contemplated what she'd heard. "I guess my initial reaction was, 'It's probably just a rumor.' I don't know, is there any truth to it?" she recalled to me. "I'm here to do this other story. I wasn't, like, chomping at the bit exactly." But she had received the name of one woman who might have information. It was worth hearing what she had to say. Introduced to fifty-three-year-old Leigh Corfman, a customer service representative at a payday loan business, she met Corfman at a bar, initially off the record.

At first, Stephanie said, "I didn't take any notes. I didn't record anything . . . She told me her story. My initial impression was that she seemed real. She seemed nervous. The story she told me even that day was fairly detailed. I didn't ask her to go into every single, solitary detail. But it was specific enough that I thought this might be real." Corfman told Stephanie in that interview and subsequent ones how then-thirty-two-year-old Moore first met her when she was only fourteen and how he lured her into what became a sexual encounter.

Stephanie is not an investigative journalist in the narrow, conventional sense. But good reporters investigate if they learn of wrongful behavior. So Stephanie embarked on a journalistic path that was outside the norm for her assignments.

After Stephanie conferred with Finkel, *The Post* dispatched a second reporter to assist. If *The Post* was going to dig into Roy Moore's past, time was running short. It was already late September. The election was to be held in early November. Another reporter would help move the reporting along more quickly. Beth Reinhard, a veteran journalist recently named to the rapid-response investigative team that I had established early that year, was soon on a plane to Alabama.

The pair, I was told, were finding more women who knew of Moore's attraction to teenagers. Those women pointed to still others. In time they identified several women he had sought to engage in a relationship when they were between the ages of sixteen and eighteen and he was an assistant district attorney in his thirties. They learned that he would walk the Gadsden Mall, allegedly hitting on teens to go out with him.

With a subject so sensitive, exceptional rigor was required. Nothing could be taken as true without corroboration. Corfman was up front about messy aspects of her own life: several divorces, multiple bankruptcies with an ex-husband, a fine for driving a boat without lights, a misdemeanor count (ultimately dismissed) for selling beer to a minor. *Post* reporters dug into the court records to unearth everything about her they could. Same for the other women who recounted Moore's behavior.

"My feeling throughout was terror, sheer terror that we would get something wrong, that we would make some kind of misstep," Stephanie told me when I asked her to relive those days. Beth recalled in one interview the reporters' care in "making sure that the people we were talking to didn't have any axes to grind."

Excavating Roy Moore's personal history represented an affront to the power structure of Alabama. It threatened to undercut a Republican candidate who could solidify allegiance to Trump in the Senate and who had strong ties to Trump ally Bannon and his media outlet, *Breitbart News*. But we had no inkling that Trump-aligned interests would wage war against us as fiercely as they did. There were few limits to what they would do.

Moore's campaign argued that it needed time to respond to *The Post*'s reporting. "They kept asking for another hour, another hour, another hour. And we kept giving it," Stephanie recalled. We were erring on the side of generosity, doing everything possible to be fair. But the Moore team was playing games, scheming to have *Breitbart News* publish a preemptive story designed to cast suspicion on what *The Post* was about to report. Minutes before *The Post* was to publish on November 9, *Breitbart* released its own story: "After Endorsing Democrat in Alabama, *Washington Post* Plans to Hit Roy Moore with Allegations of Inappropriate Relations with Teenagers; Judge Claims Smear Campaign." Never mind that the news department I led had no involvement in editorials, *Breitbart* would suggest a connection nonetheless.

A *Post* story by Stephanie, Beth, and researcher Alice Crites was promptly published online under the headline "Woman Says Roy Moore Initiated Sexual Encounter When She Was 14, He Was 32": Corfman recounted how Moore one day "picked her up around the corner from her house in Gadsden, drove her about 30 minutes to his home in the woods, told her how pretty she was and kissed her." On a second visit, "he took off her shirt and pants and removed his clothes. He touched her over her bra and underpants, she says, and guided her hand to touch him over his underwear." And the story added that three other women interviewed by *The Post* said Moore "pursued them when they were between the ages of 16 and 18 and he was in his early 30s, episodes they say they found flattering at the time but troubling as they got older. None of the three women say that Moore forced them into any sort of relationship or sexual contact." Moore denied the allegations, and continues to, and neither he nor Corfman prevailed in subsequent defamation suits against the other.

The story set off a political explosion. As leading Republicans called for Moore to quit the race, the candidate and his allies mobilized to disparage *Post* journalists and the women who had bravely come forward. It was as shameless a campaign against creditable journalism as any I had ever witnessed. *The Post* had delivered bulletproof reporting. The retaliatory weapon of Moore allies was deceit.

Citizens in Alabama began receiving calls that falsely purported to be from our news staff. "I'm a reporter for *The Washington Post* calling to find out if anyone at this address is a female between the ages of 54 to 57 years old, willing to make damaging remarks about candidate Roy Moore for a reward of between $5,000 and $7,000," the caller said in a voice mail recording. A reporter's name was given, but no one by that name worked at *The Post*. An email provided was fake. About the same time, *Gateway Pundit*, a conservative site that frequently trafficked in conspiracy theories, amplified an allegation from a Twitter account that was known for spreading misinformation. The story relied entirely on one tweet that said, "A family friend in Alabama just told my wife that a WAPO reporter named Beth offer [*sic*] her 1000$to accuse Roy Moore." *Gateway Pundit* wrote, "Of course this is HUGE news if true." A big if: It wasn't true. *The Post* never pays people for information, and no one was encouraged to say anything untrue.

Moore partisans also aimed to smear Stephanie personally. A right-wing website dredged up minor incidents from her distant past, including some civil traffic violations and what one website called a history of "faking." What was the faking? As a college student at the University of North Carolina, Chapel Hill, Stephanie had once written a check for $6.93 that bounced. She ended up pleading guilty to a misdemeanor charge, paid off the check, and ponied up a $50 fee. "I was a starving college student. I bounced a check for groceries. I used to sell my CDs for money," Stephanie told me.

We would also learn months later of an astonishing scheme to discredit Corfman. Only days after her accusations against Moore were made public by *The Post*, her attorney told our reporters in March 2018, he was approached by two of the candidate's supporters offering $10,000 in exchange for dropping Corfman as a client and declaring publicly that he did not believe her account.

And then came the effort to sabotage *The Post* itself.

After our first story about Moore was published, calls came in to *Post* reporters from women alleging unsavory experiences with Moore. One email received by Beth was particularly cryptic. "Roy Moore in Alabama . . . I might know something but I need to keep myself safe. How do we do this?" The account carried the name "Lindsay James," but its author later fessed up that her real name was Jaime Phillips. Phillips, who claimed to live in New York, said she would be visiting family and friends in Annapolis, Maryland, over Thanksgiving and proposed meeting at a shopping mall in Tyson's Corner, Virginia.

When they met, Phillips, then forty-one, said she first came across Moore in 1992 when she moved in one summer with an aunt in the Talladega area of Alabama and was attending a church youth group. She described a secret sexual relationship that led to her being impregnated by Moore. Moore, according to her account, drove her to Mississippi to get an abortion. Phillips pressed Beth to guarantee that Moore would lose the election if she came forward with her allegations, a pledge that Beth didn't make and never would.

Post journalists quickly grew doubtful of Phillips's account: Why had she used a fake name? ("This is not normal behavior," as Eric Rich, editor of the rapid-response investigative team, put it. "People don't really lie to us. They might not give us their name initially. But most people don't come out with a fake name.") Why was she pressing so hard for a promise that Moore would be defeated? Why was she being so vague on details? Why was she proposing to meet in Virginia if she was visiting Annapolis, some fifty miles away? (*Post* journalists suspected that Phillips planned to record the conversation. Maryland requires that all parties to a recorded conversation give prior consent while Virginia requires only one party's approval.) With *The Post* under attack for its Moore story, Eric recalled, "Our radar was up."

Pressed for specific verifiable information, Phillips wrote Beth complaining of "anxiety & negative energy" from the meeting and asked to meet with Stephanie instead. Meantime, research into Phillips's background was anything but reassuring. Most alarming was a GoFundMe pitch dated May 29, 2017, that Alice had discovered on the internet. "I'm moving to New York!" Phillips wrote. "I've accepted a job to work in the conservative media movement to combat the lies and deceit [*sic*] of the liberal MSM." All signs pointed to a sting operation by a far-right media outlet. Who was fucking with us and why?

Stephanie McCrummen, just back from Alabama, agreed to meet on November 21 with Phillips, who had chosen Souvlaki Bar, a Greek restaurant in Alexandria, Virginia, as a place to talk. Steven Ginsberg, recently promoted to national editor, proposed a video recording of the meet-up, thinking Stephanie would use her own iPhone, but Eric approached me about something more elaborate and ambitious: a full-scale sting of our own, with the video staff sent to clandestinely film the whole encounter. Videographers were to sit undetected at an adjacent table to document what unfolded. Stephanie would be wired up with an audio device. I quickly gave my consent.

Phillips was even less willing at that meeting to share details. She pressed Stephanie to commit that, if she came forward, Moore would be "completely taken out of the race." No commitment was forthcoming. When Stephanie confronted Phillips with the GoFundMe account, she claimed to have sought work at the conservative *Daily Caller* (an assertion that didn't check out) and now no longer aspired to be part of the "conservative media movement."

"At some point in the conversation," Stephanie said, "I remember thinking I want her to tell me how she came to be doing whatever she was doing . . . I was trying to get her to tell me more about her life. How does one get involved in this thing? How are you trained?"

The Post would learn more about Phillips in the days ahead. First came a bizarre pursuit by our journalists that evening. In addition to the video team, investigative reporter Aaron Davis had been sent to tail Phillips when she left the restaurant. Aaron had parked his car in the darkened lot of an auto body shop next door, watching Stephanie and Phillips through his rearview mirror. He identified three possible departure routes for a driver seeking to travel either north or south. But Phillips, obviously schooled for the possibility she might be tracked, walked down the shoulder of a divided highway, crossed it, and disappeared into a line of trees. Aaron hurried from his car, scrambled across the highway, and caught sight of her entering a Target store a quarter mile away. He made like a shopper, tucking some toilet paper under his arm. But Phillips made a quick U-turn in the aisle and walked out the front door. When he could safely exit and begin following again, Aaron saw Phillips at the far corner of the parking lot, rushing to a black car parked alone.

Aaron remembers my words when he reported back to the office, and they stung. "So you lost her," I said. And, worst of all, "we can't write anything." Without knowing who had put Phillips up to this, what story did we really have at that point? But the story still had life in it. Research showed that Phillips lived in Stamford, Connecticut, not New York as she had claimed. That was only sixteen miles from what Alice Crites had identified as the unmarked headquarters in Mamaroneck, New York, of our leading suspect to engage in such shenanigans, Project Veritas. Led by James O'Keefe with millions of dollars in right-wing funding, Project Veritas is infamous for setting up stings to expose what it considers the liberal bias of mainstream media. I gave my approval to keep watch on Phillips's home, track where she drove, and stake out Project Veritas's office. The expectation was she'd be reporting back to headquarters the Monday after Thanksgiving.

That Sunday, four *Post* reporters—two from video, two from the rapid-response investigative team—took the train to Connecticut and rented cars, requesting ones with plates from Connecticut and New York to deflect suspicion. Aaron drove by Phillips's home, spotting the same black Prius he had observed in the Target parking lot. "My heart leapt," is how he remembers the moment.

By early Monday morning, videographers Dalton Bennett and Tom LeGro had taken separate positions at Project Veritas's headquarters that would allow them to keep an eye on all entrances. Investigative reporter Shawn Boburg parked two hundred yards from Phillips's car on a tree-lined street that had only one outlet. Aaron positioned himself near the on-ramp to the Merritt Parkway, which they suspected she would take to the Project Veritas office. At 8:57 a.m., Boburg, spotting a woman getting into the Prius, texted his colleagues: "Movement."

Trailing her on a local street, Boburg was pulled over by a cop for talking on his cell phone, illegal under Connecticut's distracted driving law. Aaron picked up the tail at the on-ramp. Sure enough, Phillips made her way to Project Veritas's office, where our two videographers were waiting. "When she entered a locked side entrance, we were nearly certain. When O'Keefe exited the building minutes later, it was a lock," Aaron remembers. We had our story. We knew whom Phillips worked for. And we could describe the scheme they had engineered—and bungled—in an effort to discredit our investigation into Roy Moore.

The normally loquacious O'Keefe went largely mute when confronted by *The Post* outside his office. In a second attempt at an interview, O'Keefe wouldn't say whether Phillips worked for Project Veritas or if Project Veritas was collaborating with Moore, Bannon, or Republican allies. But our story about Phillips, O'Keefe, and his failed operation that was published on November 27 spoke volumes about the devious tactics being used to attack *The Post* and its work.

Many of us at *The Post* had long harbored suspicions that professional investigators were being used to spy on our staff on behalf of Trump and other far-right interests. Reports in other media ultimately yielded support for our concern: Project Veritas employees were, in fact, being trained by former spies. *The New York Times* reported in March 2020, based on court documents, that Project Veritas staffers had been taught a variety of espionage techniques by former U.S. and British intelligence agents recruited by Erik Prince, the former head of security contractor Blackwater Worldwide, brother of Trump-era education secretary Betsy DeVos, and an ally of Trump and his family. *The Times'* story followed a May 2019 report in *The Intercept*, a nonprofit investigative news outlet, that O'Keefe had boasted on social media about learning "spying and self-defense" in Wyoming, with the goal of making Project Veritas "the next great intelligence agency." The training took place,

The Intercept said, at Prince's family ranch and was conducted by a former MI6 agent.

I couldn't have been more satisfied that Project Veritas's effort to discredit our Roy Moore investigation ended up backfiring. O'Keefe's sanctimonious pronouncements about exposing the liberal media had brought his outfit bundles of money from rich right-wing donors—and our story didn't shut the spigot—but at least the public could see for itself the duplicitous tactics being underwritten. They had been recorded by *The Post* for all time on video.

The Post's work was cheered by journalists nationwide, and hundreds of readers wrote in to celebrate. "This is why I subscribed to *The Post*," one wrote. "Absolutely popping with glee and admiration at your paper's busting of Project Veritas and the (not nice adjective) people in their employ. Y'all are my heroes." Another: "Chilling and heroic . . . Keep taking your vitamins!"

I took the greatest pride in how well *The Post* had executed its investigation of Moore himself. Those sorts of allegations are among the trickiest to report. They tested our ability to be dogged, fair, and forthright all at the same time. Allegations needed to be checked to the nth degree. We published only when confident of being on solid ground. Then we didn't hesitate to say what we had uncovered.

The investigation into Roy Moore had an outsized impact. On December 12, Democrat Doug Jones defeated Moore by a close but decisive margin. He became the first Democratic senator from Alabama in twenty-five years, reduced the Republicans' narrow majority in the Senate to only one seat, and delivered a humiliating defeat for Trump and the Bannon-run *Breitbart* media outlet. Curiously, eight days later, *Breitbart*'s editor in chief said in an interview that he actually believed Corfman's accusations against Moore. Her account, he said, had "a lot of credibility."

Years after the Moore coverage, I asked Stephanie what lessons she had taken from this episode. We could not have been more in sync. Stephanie cautioned that, even though we feel empathy with proclaimed victims, we need "to be skeptical, to not be on a crusade . . . to just never get caught up in anything other than making sure that you're right." Stephanie has used this episode to remind her fellow journalists of the obligation to be fair to the accused. "We were writing about people's lives," Stephanie said on one occasion, including "the candidate himself whose reputation also was on the line and who deserved also to be treated fairly, who deserved our skepticism about the allegations initially, who deserved to know who his accusers were and exactly what they were accusing him of, and a chance to respond."

When *The Post* went on to win a Pulitzer Prize in 2018 for its reporting on Moore and Project Veritas, I was tempted to write O'Keefe a thank-you note for all his help. In February 2023, he was ousted from Project Veritas in a dispute with its board about his management behavior and whether his spending practices jeopardized its nonprofit status. But O'Keefe will surely have ample support for his next act. Leading figures of the far right immediately rallied behind him.

That same year we also won a Pulitzer for our Russia-related investigation of Trump. Bezos tweeted his congratulations. "Great reporting requires patience, grit and a willingness to follow a story wherever it leads, whether Alabama or Moscow." The tweet, especially its reference to Moscow, could not have made Trump happy. CNBC's interpretation was that Bezos had "taken a shot" at Trump. Though it came across that way, my guess is Bezos had in mind nothing more than congratulating both teams of reporters on winning journalism's most prestigious prize.

Behind that Pulitzer for the Moore investigation were women who had displayed impressive courage. One was a payday loan employee, another a retired elementary school teacher, a third an entrepreneur just then aiming to expand her business in Alabama. In early 2018, Stephanie spoke eloquently about their bravery in going on the record:

"These women were not part of any sort of movement, were not on any bandwagon, weren't gunning for any kind of political outcome. They didn't know each other. They didn't talk to each other. Each of these women had to decide whether to come forward on their own . . . And they did so without knowing whether they would be believed. They did so without knowing whether anyone would care about what they had to say. Not knowing what the consequences might be to them personally . . . They did so knowing that the allegations they had were likely to upset some very powerful people . . .

"They had every reason not to come forward, including that we're at this very strange moment . . . where people are telling them that journalists are not to be trusted, that they're going to take what you say and they're going to spin it this way or that way, or God knows what. But they did come forward. And I just think it's worth remembering how stunning that is . . . Perhaps the reason they did was . . . to satisfy their own conscience. They just wanted the truth out there."

In the fall of 2018, the rapid-response investigative unit would break another explosive story. Once again, the subject would be sexual behavior. The spotlight would fall on a Supreme Court nominee.

The first message came in to *The Post*'s tip line on July 6, 2018, at 10:26 a.m. via WhatsApp. "Potential Supreme Court nominee with assistance from his friend assaulted me in mid 1980s in Maryland. Have therapy records talking about it. Feel like I shouldn't be quiet but not willing to put family in DC and CA through a lot of stress." At 11:47 a.m. there was a follow-up on the tip line with clarifying detail: "Brett Kavanaugh with Mark Judge and a bystander named PJ." Coming after the Fourth of July holiday, reporters in the newsroom were scarce. The tip didn't get passed along immediately. That lapse in a newsroom that has to be on full alert twenty-four/seven nearly cost us one of the biggest, most provocative stories of the year.

Three days later, Trump nominated Kavanaugh, fifty-three, for the Supreme Court to replace retiring justice Anthony M. Kennedy, with seismic consequences. "No president," Kavanaugh declared as he stood beside Trump, "has ever consulted more widely or talked with more people from more backgrounds to seek input about a Supreme Court nomination." It was an oddly ingratiating remark to hear from a nominee who would be expected to exercise judicial independence. And there was a story about Kavanaugh that Trump hadn't picked up in all those supposed phone calls. It was sharply at odds with the image of a respected judge on the powerful U.S. Court of Appeals for the District of Columbia Circuit. There was no way Trump could have known. Our tipster had never told her story publicly.

On July 10 the tipster left another message. "Haven't heard back from *WaPo*," she wrote, suggesting she might take her information elsewhere, maybe to the Senate or *The New York Times*. This time, reflexes at *The Post* were better. The tip was handed immediately to Emma Brown of *The Post*'s rapid-response investigative team. Emma quickly followed up with a phone call. The tipster wouldn't identify herself at first, but by fall the name of Christine Blasey Ford would be known nationwide. With a story by Emma published on September 16, Ford would touch off arguably the most fiery hearing ever for a nominee to the Supreme Court.

Emma's own role in the saga would be memorialized when Ford finally testified before the Senate Judiciary Committee that was to vote on Kavanaugh's nomination. *The Post* reporter, she declared on September 27, "had gained my trust. It was important for me to describe the details of the assault in my own words."

In May 2016, when candidate Trump made the clever (or crass) campaign gambit of listing his prospective Supreme Court nominees to shore up his conservative bona fides, Kavanaugh's name didn't appear among them. Nor was it on an expanded list released in September that year. But Kavanaugh's sizable fan club tenaciously lobbied on his behalf, and his name showed up on a list of five additional prospects released in November 2017.

Kavanaugh had to overcome nagging doubts. Although unquestionably a conservative jurist, Kennedy had left a sour taste with the right by providing the swing vote in cases that preserved abortion rights, legalized same-sex marriage, and upheld a university affirmative action plan. Trump, insistent that his choice never deliver such unpardonable disappointments to his base, was assured that Kavanaugh would be a safe pick, despite his deep establishment roots and many friendships in what Trump called Washington's political "swamp."

Two months later, the safe pick came to look like less than a sure thing. Ford, a professor in clinical psychology at Palo Alto University, had sought to make contact with her congresswoman, Anna Eshoo, prior to the Kavanaugh announcement. On July 5, a day before texting *The Post*'s tip line, she left a message with a receptionist in Eshoo's office about having been assaulted by him. She wasn't called back until after Trump's announcement, didn't meet with an Eshoo staff member until July 18, and didn't speak with Eshoo herself until July 20. Ford asked Eshoo, as she had with *The Post*, to keep her identity confidential. She wished to fulfill her civic duty, she said, but publicity could be devastating for herself and her family.

A day after speaking with Ford, Eshoo shared her story but not her name with Dianne Feinstein, the California senator who was the ranking Democrat on the Senate Judiciary Committee. "You know this is very serious," Feinstein told Eshoo, according to a narrative in *Supreme Ambition*, a book by *The Post*'s Ruth Marcus about the Kavanaugh nomination and Ford's experience. "Have her write a letter to me." Not until July 30 did Eshoo's aide get back to Ford, advising her to write to Feinstein and the Republican chairman of the Senate Judiciary Committee, Chuck Grassley. Her name, she was told, would be required if there was to be follow-up about her accusations. Ford immediately composed a letter but addressed it only to Feinstein, fearing Grassley would not honor her desire for confidentiality.

"Brett Kavanaugh physically and sexually assaulted me during High School in the early 1980s," she wrote. "He conducted these acts with the assistance of his close friend, Mark G. Judge. Both were 1–2 years older than me and students at a local private school. The assault occurred in a suburban Maryland area home at a gathering that included me and 4 others. Kavanaugh physically pushed me into a bedroom as I was headed for a bathroom up a short stairwell from the living room. They locked the door and played loud music, precluding any successful attempts to yell for help. Kavanaugh was on top of me while laughing with Judge, who periodically jumped onto Kavanaugh. They both laughed as Kavanaugh tried to disrobe me in their highly inebriated state. With Kavanaugh's hand over my mouth, I feared he may inadvertently kill me." When Judge jumped on the bed, she said, she was able to get away from the boys, lock herself in a bathroom, and ultimately run outside the house and get home.

In early August, Washington attorney Debra Katz, who had been referred to Ford, contacted *New York Times* reporter Jodi Kantor. Kantor and colleague Megan Twohey had exposed the sexual harassment scandal that brought down Hollywood mogul Harvey Weinstein in late 2017. Katz "raised the prospect of her client telling her story" to the two of them, "getting ahead of any possible leak," as the reporters revealed in their 2019 book *She Said: Breaking the Sexual Harassment Story That Helped Ignite a Movement.* "Her client had sent a tip to the *Washington Post* and spoken with a reporter there," they wrote, "but it wasn't clear if the *Post* was moving on the story."

The Post was moving on the story, as fast as Ford would allow us. Emma had been speaking with Ford all along but was constrained by our pledge not to publish without Ford's consent. If Feinstein was in a bind because she had promised confidentiality, so were Emma and *The Post*.

"I stayed in touch with her as she wrestled with how to proceed," Emma wrote in the prologue to her 2021 book *To Raise a Boy*, "talking and texting whenever possible—in the windowless room at work where I pumped milk for my son, or in the driving rain on the shoulder of a mountain in Vermont while backpacking with my family. She decided not to speak out, figuring her story probably wouldn't make a difference."

In late August, Ford told Emma, "Why suffer through the annihilation if it's not going to matter?" After Labor Day, though, any notion that Ford's name would remain secret was fantasy. In early September, a *BuzzFeed* reporter had called and texted her, dropped by her house to leave a package of sexual harassment stories she'd written, and then showed up at her statistics class trying to interview her. *The Intercept* was calling around. And *The New Yorker*'s Ronan Farrow was outside Ford's home, too.

With the dam about to break, Ford invited Emma to interview her face-to-face in California. The two met for an early dinner at the Ritz-Carlton in Half Moon Bay on September 11, and the interview continued at breakfast the next morning.

Ford told Emma she had first spoken of the incident when she was in couples therapy in 2012, and she permitted Emma to review portions of her therapist's notes. They described an attack by students "from an elitist boys' school" who became "highly respected and high-ranking members of society in Washington." An individual therapy session a year later described a "rape attempt" in her late teens. Ford's husband, Russell Ford, told Emma he had a detailed memory of what she related in couples therapy: Two boys had trapped her in a room. One leaped on top of her, molesting her and preventing her from yelling for help. He recalled her identifying Kavanaugh by name and worrying that the federal judge might someday end up on the Supreme Court. After the assault, Ford had not told her parents or anyone else, and there were many specifics Ford said she didn't remember: the year (although she believed it was 1982, when she was fifteen and Kavanaugh was seventeen), the precise house and who owned it, who organized the party, how she got there, and how she got home.

As Emma headed to the airport on September 12 to return to Washington, *The Intercept* reported that Feinstein possessed a Kavanaugh-related document and that Democrats on the Senate Judiciary Committee were livid that she refused to let them see it. Details were scarce in that story, but "the one consistent theme was that it describes an incident involving Kavanaugh and a woman while they were in high school." Two days later, *The New York Times* reported that "the incident involved possible sexual misconduct between Judge Kavanaugh and a woman when they were both in high school." And then Ronan Farrow and Jane Mayer disclosed the disturbing allegations in detail: Kavanaugh at a party "attempted to force himself" on the young woman. He and his classmate had "turned up music that was playing in the room to conceal the sound of her protests." Kavanaugh "covered her mouth with his hand." Kavanaugh issued a statement "categorically and unequivocally" denying the accusation. "I did not do this back in high school or at any time."

It was an unnerving and frustrating period for Emma and her editors. Others were breaking news on Ford's allegations, though without her identity. *The Post* was sitting on a complete story, save for comment from the White House and Kavanaugh. Emma had spoken with Ford directly, and had pressed her for corroborative evidence. *The Post* had committed, however, to maintaining her confidentiality.

We had no strict rulebook governing which allegations of sexual abuse were considered credible enough to publish. But I had outlined general guidelines on previous stories as the #MeToo movement took off, felling prominent politicians and business executives, notably in the media industry: At least one individual who had been victimized would agree to be identified, letting the accused and the public know who was making allegations and allowing for a defense. There had to be corroborative evidence well before we were informed of the allegations. Ideally, corroboration would take the form of emails, texts, conversations with family or friends, a diary, or documents related to a legal settlement or a formal complaint. We would seek to determine if there was a pattern of behavior, meaning more than one person experienced or witnessed similar abuse. And details of an abuse survivor's account had to be investigated and verified. Not all guidelines had to be met. But we needed enough for us to stand behind the allegations as credible. And if we were presented exculpatory information, we would take that into account in deciding whether and what to publish.

In Ford's case, many of those elements were missing. She had made no formal complaint. She had not informed her parents or friends of an assault at the time it allegedly occurred. Moreover, the alleged attack occurred as far back as high school. Even as the #MeToo movement gained momentum, cases had centered on the behavior of adults in the workplace. Reaching back to teenage years was unusual. Also, Ford didn't recall many details. And yet the gaps in memory could be viewed as making her account more believable. Too-perfect stories of long-ago events can be cause for suspicion.

Her husband's recollection and the therapist's notes offered significant support. And Kavanaugh's selection for a lifetime position of immense power meant he warranted extra scrutiny. Serious allegations of assault deserved a thorough airing and investigation. Finally, Ford's letter was already becoming major news, with reverberations for Senate Democrats and Republicans, the White House, and Kavanaugh himself. There was no question we would publish the accusations—if only she would give us permission.

Emma had made no effort to encourage Ford to go public. She

made no promises about what impact a story might have. She told Ford that concerns about the impact on her life were valid. Emma felt, rightly, that it wasn't her role to persuade or pressure. She would listen and report. She would wait for Ford to make her own decision. That decision came on the night of September 15.

With the flurry of stories in *The Intercept*, *The New York Times*, and *The New Yorker*, disclosure of her name seemed only a matter of time. "Your agony will end if you just go ahead and say it," her husband, Russell Ford, told her, according to Ruth Marcus's book. "Let's call Emma; we'll end it." The call to Emma came that night. At nine the following morning, *The Post* sought comment from the White House, which sent along Kavanaugh's previous denial. Through the White House, Kavanaugh declined to answer then whether he even knew Ford in high school. *The Post*'s story was published online at 1:30 p.m.

Now there was an identified individual standing behind the allegations against Kavanaugh. She could not be ignored, certainly not in the era of #MeToo and not with the unforgettable history of how poorly Anita Hill had been treated when she accused Clarence Thomas of sexual harassment at his Supreme Court confirmation hearing in 1991. A confirmation process for Kavanaugh that had been moving apace would now have to slow down. A hearing for Ford to detail her accusations before senators and the American people—and for Kavanaugh to defend himself—would be scheduled for September 27. Her life would come under a microscope, as would Kavanaugh's, with accounts of his excessive drinking in high school and college. The calm, earnest testimony of Ford and the enraged, indignant defense by Kavanaugh are now seared into the public's consciousness. So, too, is the despicable mockery of Ford by Trump at a rally in Mississippi on October 3 before Kavanaugh was confirmed, despite having previously called her a "very credible witness" and a "very fine woman" after her "compelling" testimony.

Ford had talked about fulfilling her "civic duty" in coming for-

ward. At *The Post*, we felt we had performed ours in allowing her
to tell her story. Hers was a credible accusation. It deserved thorough investigation, even though it received a severely limited and
shamefully incomplete one from the Senate and the FBI, which
took direction from the White House on whom to interview and
thus pursued none of the thousands of tips it received over a tip line.
There is no better time to investigate the possibility of grave wrongdoing by Supreme Court nominees than before they are awarded
lifetime positions that affect every American.

The Post's reporter, Emma Brown, had focused single-mindedly
on getting the facts right and checking out Ford's account as best
she could under the circumstances at the time. She had no idea
how accusations by one woman with uneven memories from long
ago would be received. "Perhaps naively," Emma wrote in her book,
"I did not expect what came next: a polarized political brawl that
played out on cable news talk shows, on President Trump's Twitter
account, and in the Senate Judiciary Committee hearing room."

Emma also became acutely aware of how her story had given rise
to sensitive, and at times emotional, conversations among teenagers
and parents. Some teen boys called for greater responsibility and
sensitivity toward girls while others expressed fear that they might
one day be falsely accused of improper behavior. And Emma's email
in-box filled with the stories of women who related the decades-
long traumatizing effect of sexual assault in their teen years. "I know
what I experienced was rape and blamed myself for it for years,"
one wrote. "I said no, no, no . . . He did what he wanted and left me
laying on that floor," said another.

Ford's accusations, along with those by women earlier in the year
against Republican Senate candidate Roy Moore, also threw into
sharp relief the issues we at *The Post* would have to confront on other
stories involving sexual abuse and harassment: What was the threshold of corroboration necessary in order to publish? How might we
give voice to women who alleged lifelong harm by abusive men,

seeking to finally hold them accountable? How, at the same time, might we be fair to men who adamantly asserted their innocence while expressing fear for the devastating lifelong harm of wrongful public accusations? Debate and discord about how to respond to these accusations would not unfold only in the arena of national politics and business. Those tensions would surface as well in our newsroom.

In June 2020, *New York Times* media critic Ben Smith began his weekly column with an anecdote that I had taken initiative to block "an explosive story" by Bob Woodward that might have derailed the Kavanaugh nomination. According to Smith, Woodward was "planning to expose" Kavanaugh as a liar but that I had "stepped in" as the story was "nearly ready," prevailing on him to withhold publication. Smith wrote that Kavanaugh had denied—"in a huffy letter in 1999 to *The Post*"—an account in a Woodward book about independent counsel Kenneth Starr's investigation of President Bill Clinton. However, Smith wrote, Woodward was getting set to disclose that Kavanaugh, who had been a lawyer in Starr's office, was himself the confidential source for that account. Just as Kavanaugh was "fighting to prove his integrity," Woodward's story would have revealed him as duplicitous.

Smith's description of the possible story and my advice was accurate. Everything else in his telling was false or misleading. The facts are these: Woodward came to my office to inform me that he had a story he was considering publishing. He had not made up his mind on whether it should run. He sought my opinion, and he was doing the same with other key editors. I had no inkling such a story might be in the works, but I read what he provided me. Contrary to what Smith described as a story "nearly ready" for publication, it was a rough early draft outlining what Bob wrote in his book, what

Kavanaugh's letter disputed, and what Bob's notes reflected about his interviews with Kavanaugh.

Neither I nor several other *Post* editors found the story "explosive," certainly nothing that had any prospect of torpedoing Kavanaugh's nomination because it would weigh heavily in senators' assessment of his integrity. Would the Senate judiciary Committee have voted against Kavanaugh because he was a confidential source for Bob's book? Would it have done so because the nominee took issue with how Bob narrated events for which Kavanaugh provided information? Would it have caused Republicans to see Kavanaugh as a liar and Ford as a truth-teller about an alleged assault in high school?

I gave Bob my advice: He had spent his entire career arguing for the sanctity of protecting confidential sources. I didn't see why he would break that rule for this particular story. His rule would now appear to be nothing more than situational: Under certain political circumstances, he would be willing to breach confidentiality. Bob would be the one to come in for criticism, not Kavanaugh.

Finally, I told Bob, the decision was his to make, not mine. After all, Kavanaugh had been a source for a book he published on his own years earlier, not for work he did on *The Post*'s behalf. Other *Post* editors' counsel was the same. Bob thought it over for a couple of days and came to his own conclusion. He would not publish.

The advice I gave then is the same I'd offer today. And, in fact, I gave Bob the same advice on another matter when Trump's lies were contradicted by "deep background" interviews he had conducted with close aides for another book. "I understand and sympathize with your frustration—similar to what we're dealing with every day with this administration," I told Bob in an email. But "your sources expected that, no matter what the president later said, the conditions negotiated with them would be honored. You and they knew that Trump could very well lie later on, denying what was true. That's his pattern and practice." Bob responded that I had been "very wise and thoughtful," and he was coming to the same conclusion.

The day after Ben Smith's column was published online, I received a call from Bob. He allowed that the decision not to publish was his and that he was in complete accord with my advice. His own wife, he said, had argued against proceeding with the story. Nodding to the age-old anger-management technique of pausing before doing something you might later regret, Bob said the decision-making process was "in the great tradition of counting to 10."

The falsehoods in Smith's column subjected me to the wrath of readers who felt that I deserved blame for Kavanaugh's ultimate confirmation. "This sucks," wrote one reader who went on to suggest I consider resigning. "My faith in the paper as a whole, and in you, are badly shaken." Bob Woodward's long-ago agreement with Kavanaugh became public via Smith's column. But Bob's policy of honoring confidentiality pacts with sources was a sound one. I never heard him express regrets over his Kavanaugh decision. I had none either for my own advice.

10

THE OWNER

In March 2018, at the final of our three dinners with senior leaders of *The New York Times*, executive editor Dean Baquet appeared to be doing some reporting amid the socializing. He asked Jeff Bezos whether Donald Trump called him regularly to apply pressure. The president, Bezos said, had pretty much given up on him.

Trump's direct call to Bezos after our dinner at the White House in the summer of 2017 was, in fact, the last he made to our owner. In Trump's binary thinking, you were either friend or foe. When Bezos refused Trump's demand to rein in our coverage, the Amazon founder was immediately tagged as foe. Trump's attacks on Bezos were now routinely public, more frequent, and more barbed. Within weeks, the threats became more real.

Trump framed his criticism as a matter of public policy: Amazon needed to pay more in taxes and pony up more to the U.S. Postal Service for package delivery. But everything about his tirades made plain that his real aim was to bully Bezos over *The Washington Post*.

"The #AmazonWashingtonPost, sometimes referred to as the guardian of Amazon not paying internet taxes (which they should) is FAKE NEWS!" he screamed into the Twitterverse on June 28, 2017. In July, he charged on Twitter that there had been an illegal "intelligence leak" by the "Amazon Washington Post." Our national security reporters had just disclosed that Russia's ambassador told his superiors that Jeff Sessions had discussed "campaign-related matters, including policy issues important to Moscow" with him during the 2016 presidential race. That contradicted the attorney general's sworn testimony. The Russian ambassador's communications, *The Post* reported, "were intercepted by U.S. spy agencies."

By mid-July, Trump was salivating to have an antitrust case filed against Amazon. Hedge fund titan Leon Cooperman revealed in a CNBC interview that Trump had asked him twice at a White House dinner that summer whether Amazon was a monopoly. On July 25, Trump tweeted, "Is Fake News Washington Post being used as a lobbyist weapon against Congress to keep Politicians from looking into Amazon no-tax monopoly?"

Trump this time apparently was spun up over a *Post* report that he had decided to end the CIA's covert program to arm and train rebels in Syria fighting its president, Bashar al-Assad, with the goal of forcing him from power. Just exactly what Trump found objectionable was hard to figure, although perhaps it was because *The Post* noted that the decision was "long sought by Russia." Still, our story explained that the Syria program's "efficacy" had been questioned, even by its supporters. Nuance be damned, Trump was quick with the Twitter trigger: "The Amazon Washington Post fabricated the facts on my ending massive, dangerous, and wasteful payments to Syrian rebels fighting Assad," Trump wrote on July 25, thus confirming *The Post*'s report as factual even as he assailed it as false. "So many stories about me in the @washingtonpost are Fake News. They are as bad as ratings challenged @CNN. Lobbyist for Amazon and taxes?" he tweeted on the same day.

At a Phoenix rally in August, where he sought to deflect criticism of his vile response to the violence by right-wing hate groups in Charlottesville, Virginia, Trump faulted the media for schisms in American society and incited the crowd against the "failing *New York Times*," CNN (with the crowd chanting "CNN sucks"), and

The Washington Post, which he once again called a "lobbying tool for Amazon."

The president's real agenda was hard to miss. As Arizona State University law professor Adam Chodorow wrote in *Slate*, Trump was "clearly trying to discredit one of his most dogged chroniclers in the press by claiming that its owner is somehow disreputable because he takes advantage of the tax laws to avoid taxes others are required to pay. Not only is that desperate, but it is also hypocritical, coming from someone who bragged during the campaign that he's fought like hell to pay as little in taxes as he could and whose advisers claimed that his ability to avoid taxes was a sign of his genius."

As 2017 drew to a close, Trump became increasingly venomous. "Why," @realDonaldTrump complained on Twitter, "is the United States Post office, which is losing many billions of dollars a year, while charging Amazon and others so little to deliver their packages, making Amazon richer and the Post Office dumber and poorer. Should be charging MUCH MORE!" Secretly, three individuals told *The Post*, Trump agitated over the course of 2017 and into 2018 to get U.S. Postmaster General Megan Brennan to unilaterally double the rate that was charged to Amazon and other shippers.

By March 2018, the online publication *Axios* reported what was becoming obvious by then: "He is obsessed with Amazon," a source told the news site's Jonathan Swan. "Obsessed." *Axios* revealed that Trump had discussed somehow changing Amazon's tax treatment "because he's worried about mom-and-pop retailers being put out of business," bringing an antitrust action against Amazon, and ending "cushy" pricing by the U.S. Postal Service for the delivery of Amazon's packages. "The president would love to clip CEO Jeff Bezos' wings. But he doesn't have a plan to make that happen." Trump's rich buddies, including retail executives and shopping mall owners, were griping that Amazon was "destroying their businesses."

Axios's story was generous to Trump in suggesting that some serious policy thinking was in motion. But the story also nodded to the real reason for Trump's bellyaching: "Trump also pays close attention to the Amazon founder's ownership of *The Washington Post*, which the president views as Bezos' political weapon." "Close attention" was an understatement, "political weapon" was nothing but a Trump contrivance.

Two days after the *Axios* report, *The Post*'s White House bureau chief, Philip Rucker, told me that he had spoken with an individual who had been in the Oval Office "no short of 20 times when the president has raged about Bezos and Amazon." Chief economic adviser Gary Cohn estimated after leaving the White House that Trump had brought up Amazon's postal rates and sales taxes thirty times, according to an account in *The Divider: Trump in the White House, 2017–2021* by journalists Peter Baker and Susan Glasser. "It's total bullshit," Cohn told an associate, they reported. "He's just mad at Bezos for owning *The Washington Post*."

A negative story in *The Post* effectively guaranteed that Trump would get worked up about Bezos and Amazon. "In case there were any doubt," Phil emailed me, "this has nothing to do with mom & pop retailers and everything to do with the *Washington Post*." Trump's stated rationale for the policy attacks was a charade. "Over time, his rationale has shifted from antitrust to internet taxes to postal shipping rates," wrote Jonathan Chait in *New York* magazine. "The constant in all these complaints is the *Post* and its 'fake'—i.e., real—news . . . Whatever the merits of his case about Amazon, it has nothing to do with helping mom-and-pop shops and everything to do with his authoritarian desire to control the news media."

Amazon stock sank immediately after *Axios*'s report, losing $31 billion in value, a remarkable reaction given that Trump had been publicly attacking Bezos and Amazon since 2015. Wall Street's interpretation—correct, as it turned out—appeared to be that the past was mere rhetoric but that concrete action was now imminent. Trump followed up the *Axios* report with a days-long string of anti-Amazon/anti-*Post* tweets—on March 29, March 31, April 3, and April 5—further battering the company's stock. We at *The Post* were, in his words, the "chief lobbyist" for Amazon and "should so REGISTER." The tweets came as *The Post* reported that the Trump Organization was facing pressure to open its books from three different sources: special counsel Robert Mueller, investigating Russian influence in the 2016 election; Stormy Daniels, the adult-film actress whose real name is Stephanie Clifford, seeking internal correspondence to free herself from a nondisclosure agreement linked to an alleged affair with Trump; and the District of Columbia and the state of Maryland, which were suing on grounds that Trump was improperly accepting gifts, or "emoluments," through his businesses.

Trump's claims about Amazon ripping off the Postal Service were inaccurate; Amazon shipments were a moneymaker, not a money-loser, for the post office. His claims about *The Post* were ludicrous. It wasn't owned by Amazon. Bezos didn't tell us what to write. And *The Post* didn't lobby. (Amazon was doing plenty of lobbying on its own, deploying 105 lobbyists and spending $14.2 million in 2018 alone, a sum that would continue to rise sharply.)

Our general policy at *The Post* was to refrain from comment when a manic Trump went on the warpath against us. What would be the point of responding to his eruptions? Exceptions were made only when he named individual reporters, with the obviously malicious intent of setting them up for harassment and physical threats.

Trump's Twitter storm in March and April 2018, however, drew a flurry of media attention. *The Guardian*, based in Great Britain but with a major U.S. presence, published a story that described Trump and Bezos as "locked in a personal feud," even though only one man was doing any feuding. Bezos had remained silent, no doubt practicing what I'd heard him describe in another context as "strategic silence."

Vox's Matt Yglesias had it right when he attributed Trump's venom to "a form of systemic corruption where the success or fail-ure of a business enterprise hinges fundamentally on whether its owners and managers are aligned with the ruling regime. The fact that Trump is explicitly injecting the *Post* into the debate certainly suggests that aspiration on his part."

When *The New York Times* solicited a reaction to Trump's inces-sant framing of Bezos, Amazon, and *The Post* as an axis of evil, our public relations staff conceded it might be time to say our piece. Still, I had to resist expressing what I genuinely thought: Trump pursued power with the very purpose of abusing it. He was an as-piring authoritarian. My job, however, required me to be diplomatic. "I don't even know how to describe what goes through my mind," I told *The Times* in April 2018 when discussing my reaction to his lies about us. "It's completely made up." As for Bezos: "I can't say more emphatically he's never suggested a story to anybody here, he's never critiqued a story, he's never suppressed a story." When *The Post* itself wrote about Trump's attacks, publisher Fred Ryan said with unusual directness, "Most everybody recognizes it's Trump fiction."

Sally Quinn, widow of Watergate-era editor Ben Bradlee and a former writer for *The Post*, thought maybe Bezos needed some bucking up. She went about it in her own idiosyncratic way. "As Ben would say," she emailed Bezos, "keep your pecker up!" An amused Bezos allowed that he had.

In late July, investigative journalist Bob Woodward contacted Bezos to warn him that Trump would have another reason to go bal-listic. Woodward, as he recounted to me, had his own way of commu-nicating directly with Bezos: send an email to then-wife MacKenzie, who told Bezos, who would then call. Within six weeks, Woodward told Bezos, he would be releasing his book *Fear*, advertised as reveal-ing the "harrowing life inside Donald Trump's White House." Bezos, in Woodward's account, was matter-of-fact. "So," he told Bob, "Trump hates me. He hates *The Post*. And now he'll hate you."

At the start of Bezos's ownership, I had reason to fear that he might interfere in our news coverage, if only because there was a long history of wealthy media owners doing so. By the time Trump took office, however, years had passed without Bezos's intervention. I could judge him by his record. As Trump sought to tighten the screws, Bezos made plain that we had no need to fear that he might capitulate due to pressure.

In March 2018, as we concluded one of our business meetings, Bezos offered some parting words over the speakerphone: "You may have noticed that Trump keeps tweeting about us." The remark met with silence. "Or maybe you haven't noticed!" Bezos cracked. He wanted to reinforce what I had publicly said before. "We are not at war with them," Bezos said. "They may be at war with us. We just need to do the work." By July of that year he once again spoke up unprompted at a business meeting. "Do not worry about me," he said confidently. "Just do the work. And I've got your back."

In all my interactions with him, Bezos showed himself to have integrity and spine. Early in his ownership he displayed an intuitive appreciation that an ethical compass for *The Post* was inseparable from its business success. There was a ton about Bezos and Amazon that *The Post* needed to vigorously cover and investigate—from his company's escalating market power to its heavy-handed labor practices and the ramifications for individual privacy of its voracious data collection. We were determined to fulfill our journalistic obligations with complete independence. And yet I was coming to like *The Post*'s owner as a human being. I had opted not to read Brad Stone's *The Everything Store: Jeff Bezos and the Age of Amazon*, published only two weeks after Bezos acquired *The Post*, so that my own impressions would be free of outside influence. As driven, disciplined, and demanding as Bezos was on business matters, I found him to be a far more complex, thoughtful, and agreeable character than routinely portrayed.

Our business meetings took place typically every two weeks by teleconference, only rarely in person. During the pandemic that took hold in 2020, we were subjected to Amazon's exasperatingly inferior videoconferencing system, called Chime. The one-hour sessions were a lesson in his unconventional thinking, wry humor ("This is me enthusiastic. Sometimes it's hard to tell."), and some fantastic aphorisms: "Most people start building before they know what they're building." "The things that everybody knows are going to work, everybody is already doing." "Show me a company where people don't disagree, and I'll show you a place where people don't care." At one session, we were discussing group subscriptions for college students. Bezos wanted to know the size of the market. As we all started to google, Bezos interjected, "Hey, why don't we try this? Alexa, how many college students are there in the United States?" A-plus for Alexa: She pulled up the data from the National Center for Education Statistics (which was among the leading results when I googled it).

His instincts about news organizations could defy expectations. Media pundits speculated that he would push to personalize the news experience as he had done with purchasing on Amazon's site, but instead he argued that readers were looking for editors' curation. "You can way over-index on personalization," he once said. "It's not what people actually want."

In informal settings, he was always self-assured but also delightful company. With the food and wine, unsurprisingly, he spared no expense. In 2018, at the restaurant A Rake's Progress in D.C.'s trendy Line Hotel, he instructed waiters to bring whatever they wished, saying he was taking a breather of sorts: "I don't want to make any decisions." You need to have the right bank account for a mental respite of that sort.

That dinner was the equivalent of a single canapé at the star-

studded weekend Campfire gatherings Bezos hosted in the fall at
the Four Seasons Resort (The Biltmore) in Santa Barbara. I first
attended in 2017 when I was to be interviewed there on media issues
by Bob Woodward and then was invited back with no responsibilities the following year. The wonky morning programming (biome-
chatronics from MIT technologist Hugh Herr, disaster-driven food
distribution from celebrity chef and philanthropist José Andrés, etc.)
was followed by afternoon excursions (hiking, whale-watching, art
tour) and some serious nighttime food, drinks, music, and partying.
I was thoroughly out of my element with boldface names such as
Jon Bon Jovi, Jamie Lee Curtis, Tom Ford, Neil Gaiman, Amanda
Palmer, Jon Hamm, Cyndi Lauper, Norman Lear, Oprah Winfrey,
Ron Howard, and Reese Witherspoon. No guest excited my assistant as much as jazz singer Gregory Porter. I emerged with a lovely
friendship with fashion designer Diane von Furstenberg. Our family
heritage in what was once Bessarabia (now Moldova) is similar, and
she would later check in with me regularly on the 2020 presidential
election. ("What now?" she'd email worriedly every few days.) If it
had been hosted by anyone other than Bezos personally, my attendance at Campfire would have violated *Post* conflict-of-interest rules
that prohibited my accepting gifts or compensation from anyone
we covered (or even potentially might cover). But Bezos, whom we
covered a lot, was my boss. He already paid my salary and bonus.
Conflict of interest, in relation to him, came preinstalled in my professional life until I left *The Post* some years later.

In conversation, Bezos was witty and self-deprecating ("Nothing
makes me feel dumber than a *New Yorker* cartoon"), laughed easily,
and posed penetrating questions. When he was asked once by a *Post*
staffer whether he'd join the crew of his space company, Blue Origin,
on one of its early launches, he said he wasn't sure. "Why don't you
wait a while and see how things go?" I advised. "That," he shot back,
"is the nicest thing you've ever said about me." Bezos can be star-
tlingly easy to talk to. Just block out any thought of his net worth.

Science fiction—Isaac Asimov, Robert Heinlein, Larry Niven—was a huge influence on Bezos in his teenage years. He has spoken of how his interest in space traces to his childhood absorption in the *Star Trek* TV series. *Star Trek* inspired everything from the voice-activated Alexa to the name of his holding company, Zefram LLC, drawn from the fictional character Zefram Cochrane, who developed "warp drive," a technology that allowed space travel at faster-than-light speeds. "The reason he's earning so much money," his high school girlfriend Ursula Werner said early in Amazon's history, "is to get to outer space."

From the moment Bezos acquired *The Post*, he had made clear that its historic journalistic mission was at the heart of its business. It was refreshing. I had been in our field long enough to witness some executives—unmoored by crushing pressures on circulation, advertising, and profits—cutting the cord with our journalistic culture, even shunning the vocabulary we used to describe our work. Many publishers took to calling journalism "content," a term so hollow that I sarcastically advised substituting "stuff." Journalists were recategorized as "content producers," top editors retitled "chief content officers." Bezos was a different breed.

With *The Post*'s new tablet app, Bezos appeared to more thoroughly be reading our work, serious and not-so. Nothing was a higher compliment than to be told a story was "riveting," a favorite Bezos word. It was an adjective he bestowed, for example, on a character study by national arts reporter Geoff Edgers of comedian and actor Bill Murray. He obviously valued some relief, sparkle, and fun in our report, having already pronounced it a sin for us to be "boring." At one dinner in late 2015, he specifically cited lighter first-person fare about family and relationships. ("I'm a Diehard Liberal. It Ruined My Parenting," read one headline. "How to Find a Feminist Boyfriend" was another.) On the same occasion, he lavished praise on *The Post*'s coverage of his lifelong obsession: space. He had previously taken note in September 2015 when reporter Joel Achenbach posted an online story headlined "Elon Musk Just Got a New Cape Canaveral Neighbor: Jeff Bezos. Hare, Meet Tortoise." If Bezos took umbrage at being portrayed as a laggard to an archrival, he didn't say so. His only comment concerned how a potential conflict of interest for *The Post* was addressed. Typically, *The Post* formulaically noted Bezos's ownership in one dry sentence. Achenbach, though, broke the mold: "Disclaimer: This blog item discusses Jeff Bezos, whose position within our news organization is 'Owner.' Potential conflicts of interest permeate this blog item the way the Higgs Field permeates the fabric of the universe." Bezos dashed off a note: "This is *by far* the best disclaimer I have ever seen."

Donald Trump had to be a less pleasurable subject for Bezos, though he was obviously giving stories about him a close read. When David Fahrenthold published a magazine piece in December 2016 recounting his year covering Trump—including the *Access Hollywood* blockbuster—Bezos couldn't have been more flattering in his assessment. But his comments focused not at all on the man at the center of the story but rather on Dave's writing style. Bezos loved "everything about this story," he wrote in an email, citing its humility, humor, and how it "shows (but never brags about)" Dave's innovative use of Twitter for reporting. And he loved the story's ending, which clearly reflected how Bezos conceived our role as journalists (and, thankfully, mirrored my own). Dave had co-authored *The Post*'s lead story on Trump's election victory in 2016. A few days later, Dave recounted at the end of his magazine story, he was interviewed by a German reporter: "He asked if these past nine months, the greatest adventure in my life as a journalist, had been for naught. 'Do you feel like your work perhaps did not matter at all?' he said. I didn't feel like that. It *did* matter. But, in an election as long and wild as this, a lot of other stories and other people mattered, too. I did my job. The voters did theirs. Now my job goes on. I'll seek to cover Trump the president with the same vigor as I scrutinized Trump the candidate. And now I know how to do it."

As for scrutiny of ourselves, Bezos was no fan of an internal newsroom ombudsman, or "public editor," to regularly critique our work. "The internet is our ombudsman," he said. It was a sentiment I shared. Why anoint one person as investigator, prosecutor, judge, and jury? There were plenty of press critics—including our own in op-ed columnist Erik Wemple, who didn't hesitate to take a shot at the news staff—and the public could judge for itself. *The Post*'s publisher ended the role of ombudsman in February 2013, shortly after I arrived and with no protest from me. I never saw any evidence that public editors enhanced trust in the press as they routinely claimed.

Bezos wasn't inclined to impose his politics on anyone. Though typically guarded about the views he held—at least until he started tweeting in May 2022 against President Joe Biden's rhetoric and policies on inflation—he once acknowledged to me some libertarian leanings but presented himself as pragmatic and nonideological. I've heard him characterized as a classic tech founder, liberal on social issues but conservative and even libertarian on economic issues. But what I've learned over time suggests more complexity than that: He believes in abortion rights and legalizing marijuana, convinced that any law routinely violated by millions of people—such as the Prohibition-era antialcohol laws—should not be a law in the first place. On economics, he believes business is overregulated, counterintuitively protecting incumbent businesses over upstarts. But he favors progressive taxation, raising the minimum wage to $15 an hour, and raising corporate tax rates. He'd get rid of corporate welfare (including tax breaks for Hollywood projects that bring benefits to film studios like Amazon's own). If he had his way, the tax code would be no more than twenty pages long. On personal taxes, he believes that setting the capital gains rate lower than the income tax rate is fundamentally unfair. He sees government as having an essential role in addressing certain mammoth societal problems. Climate change, a major focus of his philanthropy, stands out as an example of a threat that business won't tackle on its own.

Bezos seemed amused that his association with *The Post* could spin his image 180 degrees with some in the public. After a 2018 question-and-answer session in Washington, D.C., elicited vitriolic emails to Bezos because he said it was "dangerous" for Trump to demonize the media, the ultimate capitalist was in a sharing mood: "This one is special. It's not that often I get called a communist."

Bezos seemed averse to politicians who behaved rashly. One bad and unthinking move, as he saw it, could get the country into deep, long-lasting trouble. As best as I could tell, he values stability and moderation. He seemed confident of the nation's future regardless of whether it leaned a bit to the right or left but not if it went to extremes. Presidents, he once declared, "don't have to be smart but they do have to be sane." When *The Wall Street Journal* in 2022 published a story headlined "How Children Use Conflict to Win Popularity," Bezos tweeted, "Too many of our elected officials are still using these techniques." That seemed to best capture what I divined to be his view of many politicians: performative. On that, our opinions were aligned.

Bezos was frustrated by a culture of personal vilification in the public sphere. And although he tends to shrug off attacks on himself, suggesting an extra glass of fine wine dissolves any hurt feelings, I was told he considered ad hominem attacks directed at him from politicians like Senators Elizabeth Warren and Bernie Sanders akin to Trump's own demonizing rhetoric. If the political class felt he should pay more in taxes, his view was they should change the law while declaring it the right thing to do for the country, rather than berating him or anyone else personally. Meantime, he didn't deploy exotic tax schemes and paid what he legally owed. (In 2007 and 2011, that was zero, according to tax returns obtained by the ProPublica investigative journalism nonprofit that attributed the result in those years to investment losses, no stock sales, and an Amazon salary that was set at a low level.)

As the primaries for the 2016 presidential election neared, he theorized like many others that the public would grow weary of Trump as unacceptable. And as revealed in Brad Stone's 2021 book *Amazon Unbound: Jeff Bezos and the Invention of a Global Empire*, Bezos saw a prospective Trump presidency as a reason for dread: In December 2015, he rejected his aides' advice to stay silent even as Trump directly attacked him on Twitter. He emailed Jay Carney, senior vice president for global affairs and former White House press secretary under Obama: "Feel like I should have a witty retort. Don't want to let it go past. Useful opportunity (patriotic duty) to do my part to deflate this guy who would be a scary prez. I'm an inexperienced trash talker but I'm willing to learn. :) Ideas?" The result was the #sendDonaldtospace tweet—written by Craig Berman, Amazon's vice president of global communications—that a petulant Trump probably never forgot and that Amazon executives came to regard as a mistake with long-term damaging implications for the company. Less than a year later, within weeks of the election, Bezos expressed regret for taking Trump's remarks so "lightly" when they fit into a pattern of behavior that "erodes our democracy around the edges."

Bezos was struck at times by Trump's wily political instincts, even though it was evident he didn't see him as remotely qualified to be president. And yet for a couple of years into the Trump administration, Amazon executives would hear Bezos give credit to Trump for having some sensible ideas about business. Bezos saw Trump as rightly arguing against overregulation, making some solid points about China, and correctly warning Germany against building a gas pipeline that would make it more dependent on Russia, even if Trump's pugnacious manner often did more to repel his audience than persuade them.

Bezos's own political contributions to federal candidates have been paltry, and the Amazon political action committee's donations split fairly evenly between Republican and Democratic congressional candidates in the 2019–2020 election cycle. The $2.5 million contribution he and his then-wife MacKenzie made in 2012 to a Washington state referendum in support of gay marriage was widely reported. Six years later, he contributed $33 million to a scholarship fund for "dreamers," undocumented immigrants who were brought to the United States as children and remain vulnerable to deportation despite identifying as Americans. The fund had been set up by Don Graham, the former *Post* publisher whose family had controlled the newspaper for eight decades before selling it to Bezos.

Bezos found U.S. immigration policy particularly nutty in key respects: Why would we give talented foreign students coveted seats at America's top universities, educate them, and then force them to leave the country upon graduation when many longed to remain? In his view, the country could only benefit from their intellect and energy. "We should require them to stay for ten years!" he once said.

Bezos brought up immigration the first time he met Trump. Trump was scheduled to gather with tech CEOs in Trump Tower just over a month after his election. Jared Kushner had called Bezos, telling him the president-elect wanted to get together privately a half hour earlier. When Bezos entered Trump's office, Trump reached over his jumbo-sized desk, stretched out his hand warmly in greeting, and declared, "Love Amazon! Love Amazon! *Washington Post*, not so much." Both laughed. The discussion turned to Bezos's ideas for an immigration policy akin to Canada's, which includes provisions that are welcoming to skilled workers. After a few questions, Trump said, "This is a great idea!" Then he turned to Vice President–elect Mike Pence: "Can we do this with an executive order, or do we need an act of Congress? How does this work, Mike? Mike knows how all this stuff works." Pence, silent until then, explained that Congress needed to act. "Okay," the president-elect responded, "let's figure out how to get this done." Nothing got done.

Bezos's views on immigration are unsurprising. Tech companies benefit immensely from foreign-born talent. And Bezos knows in the most personal way that immigration can bring extraordinary individuals to American shores. His adoptive father, Miguel (Mike) Bezos, was sent alone in 1962 to the United States from Fidel Castro's Cuba at age sixteen as part of the mass children's exodus known as Operation Pedro Pan. For three decades he worked as an engineer and manager domestically and overseas for what is now Exxon-Mobil, cherishing the education and opportunities he received in a country that welcomed him.

Bezos, in his donations, seems to yearn for a bipartisan or nonpartisan world: $10 million in September 2018 to a political action group that supports veterans running for office as either Republicans or Democrats; and several years later $100 million each to chef and World Central Kitchen founder José Andrés, TV analyst and Dream Corps founder Van Jones, and singer-songwriter and philanthropist Dolly Parton as a "Courage and Civility Award" so they could donate it to their own causes. "We need unifiers and not vilifiers," Bezos said in July 2021 when announcing the first two of those gifts after his trip to space aboard a Blue Origin rocket. "We live in a world where sometimes instead of disagreeing with someone's ideas, we question their character or their motives. Guess what? After you do that, it's pretty damn hard to work with that person. And really what we should always be doing is questioning ideas, not the person." He had to be imagining a time when someone like himself didn't become the target of someone like Trump—or Warren or Sanders. Bezos, I've been told reliably, was the rare voter showing enthusiasm for business titan and former New York mayor Mike Bloomberg as a presidential candidate.

I felt Bezos spent too little time becoming acquainted with *Post* journalists, learning more about their ideas and concerns along with the particular challenges of their work. Visits to our headquarters were rare and brief, and his personal security detail was always nearby whenever he was anywhere in the office. His knowledge of *The Post* was sharply limited, defined by one-hour teleconferences with key managers and private discussions with publisher Fred Ryan. I never had a conversation with him without others present until he called to thank me and wish me well within days of my retirement in February 2021. Though I fully appreciated the heavy demands on his time, I was left disappointed that he didn't make an effort to know *The Post* and its people in greater depth.

And yet Bezos seemed to value and enjoy his highly infrequent encounters with the news staff in small groups. He spoke fondly of a four-hour dinner in May 2015 at D.C.'s fancy Fiola Mare restaurant with winners of *The Post*'s Pulitzer Prizes. National investigative reporter Carol Leonnig told Bezos she felt sorry for him—everyone perked up—because he must always be the focus of every meeting. She invited him to ask anything rather than be required to do all the talking. Bezos, entertained, took her up on the offer.

Bezos had read their stories in depth and inquired thoughtfully into their reporting. He asked Bart Gellman why he brought the story about the National Security Agency's surveillance practices to *The Post*. (Because, Bart said, *The Post* would "stand up to power.") He expressed admiration for how Eli Saslow wrote about the prevalence of food stamps without passing judgment. He quizzed Carol, who won for exposing security lapses by the Secret Service, on how she was able to get people to talk to her when the risks for them were so high. It had to be a subject of understandable curiosity for the head of Amazon, which routinely rebuffed reporters' inquiries with "No comment." Carol told him she was straightforward about what she was seeking and directly addressed individuals' fears and motivations: *The Post* would protect their identities. If they wanted injustice or malfeasance revealed, we needed their help. *The Post*'s reputation for serious, careful investigative reporting, she told Bezos, carried a lot of weight with potential sources. *Post* journalists concurred that Bezos was charming, fun, and, as one put it to me, "a Class A listener."

In a 2018 meeting with Pulitzer winners, he asked reporters who had covered the Trump-Russia investigation what stories they had chosen not to publish. It was a damn good question, one I'd never been asked. We cited our decision not to publish anything regarding suspicions that computer servers of Russia's Alfa Bank were communicating with the Trump Organization's servers. We couldn't verify anything, and the suspicions ended up proving baseless. Also mentioned: the Steele dossier. We had refrained from publishing its accusations because we couldn't verify them—although, when *Buzz-Feed* released the full document and Trump responded with a tirade, we were obligated to outline for readers what was being alleged.

Bezos's ambitions for *The Post* were limitless. He declared on *CBS This Morning* in November 2015 that "we're working on becoming the new paper of record," proudly boasting of *The Post*'s "gigantic accomplishment" in passing *The New York Times* in online monthly readers—66.9 million, more than one million beyond our leading competitor, in October 2015. In a much-discussed Innovation Report in March 2014, *The Times* mentioned *The Post* only in passing, brooding instead on the threat from celebrated digital-only media upstarts. Now, as media analyst Ken Doctor noted, word was that *The Times* was "paying significantly more attention to the competition rising from the southern end of the northeast corridor." When *Fortune* magazine wrote in 2015 about a plan for Amazon Prime members to get a free *Post* subscription for six months and then get a discounted rate after that, Bezos celebrated the magazine's assessment that the initiative put *The Post* and *The New York Times* on a "collision course." That "meme," he declared, "is really good for us."

Having surpassed *The Times* in digital traffic, *The Post* was quick to run ads declaring itself "America's new publication of record." Too quick. For Bezos—always hyperattentive to the nuances of branding (or what he preferred to call "reputation")—the ads went too far. In lieu of saying "we *are* the publication of record," he advised us to show "more humility" and say instead that "we are *working hard* to become the American paper of record." The idea was more "aspiration and goal—not a self-appointment," drawing on the "huge well of good will" from people who want us to win rather than demonstrating "hubris." Bezos called it a "strategic way to pick a fight with someone." In short, find a way to "let others say it."

Despite our success under Bezos, his stewardship of *The Post* drew varied reactions from its journalists. There was appreciation for our commercial achievements and expansion as well as for his embrace of our journalistic mission. One thank-you note from a reporter emailed in 2017 read, "Your decision to buy this place and to invest in its growth—which led the editors here to offer me a job—changed my life . . . A great many of my colleagues appreciate your faith and support just as much as I do."

Still, the union representing nonmanagement employees—whose membership numbers had reversed direction under Bezos, swelling because of our growth—portrayed him as a corporate villain during years of contentious bargaining over contracts. A "21st-century poster boy for income inequality and predatory capitalism" was what union leader Fredrick (Freddy) Kunkle tweeted in September 2018. The union, of course, was entitled to press hard for more pay and whatever job protections its members felt were necessary. Management was also within its rights to negotiate equally hard for conditions that would allow the company to earn a profit, continue investing, and gain more flexibility in staffing in a rapidly changing media environment.

Unions, of course, were anathema to Bezos, and *The Post*'s publisher, Fred Ryan, was loath to give the one in our shop victories it could crow about. Both men wanted to keep across-the-board contractual raises as modest as possible and favored compensating employees based almost entirely on performance. I also had a strong bias toward "merit raises." There was only so much money to go around, and our best journalists deserved and needed to be rewarded. Many were being aggressively recruited elsewhere. But merits weren't only going to "stars," as the union alleged. The high quality of our staff meant almost two-thirds were getting merits each year by the time I retired in 2021, compared to one-third when I arrived in 2013. Money for raises of that sort fortunately had grown fast, even faster than the staff itself had grown.

Still, Bezos, contrary to what many in the public and media punditocracy imagined, wasn't inclined to spend freely on *The Post*. He firmly believed in fiscal discipline. Amazon's "leadership principles" (fourteen at the time) applied equally to us, as far as I could tell. Along with "Customer Obsession" and "Think Big" was "Frugality": "Accomplish more with less. Constraints breed resourcefulness, self-sufficiency, and invention. There are no extra points for growing headcount, budget size, or fixed expense."

My beef with the union was not its existence. While I had never been a union member—no newsroom unions existed at the papers where I worked as a reporter—I believed they served an important role in arguing for greater pay, equitable treatment, and more generous benefits, including longer parental leave. But I was irritated by our newsroom union's impulse for stinging, highly personal attacks. In the midst of contract negotiations he led in 2017, Freddy wrote in *HuffPost* (previously called *Huffington Post*) that Bezos was guilty of "petty theft from the people who work for him." When interviewed for a 2019 *New Yorker* profile of Bezos, Freddy told writer Charles Duhigg that *The Post* owner "doesn't think companies have obligations to employees beyond paying wages while they work."

Comments like that rankled. It was a caricature, absurd and unjust. *The Post* wasn't a Bezos charity, even if some of its journalists felt his ownership gave them a rightful claim on his bulging bank account. Bezos saw us as an independent business that needed to pay its own way. So did I. If he treated us like a charity and later tired of us, we'd be in deep trouble, left with operations as unsustainable as the day he bought *The Post*. And I knew for a fact that our salaries and benefits were competitive, the work environment congenial. Hundreds applied every year for jobs in our newsroom, and we had a good record of retaining talented journalists who had received handsome offers to go elsewhere.

Duhigg, author of the *New Yorker* piece on Bezos, was an acquaintance of mine from Boston when he was getting a Harvard MBA. After his story was published, he asked for my reaction. "I haven't seen the hard-hearted man that's so often portrayed," I told him. "I have seen the man who is very hard-headed, unsentimental, disciplined, highly analytical, consistently strategic, and tactical. He sees limited resources and wants them allocated most effectively and efficiently so that we can grow. Does that mean people will feel they didn't get their proper piece of the pie or feel that the company didn't act with adequate empathy? I suppose. But does it foster an inhumane workplace? Not at *The Post* is all I can say."

Days into January 2016, news arrived that we had worried might never come: *The Post*'s correspondent in Tehran, Jason Rezaian, would be released from Iran's Evin Prison, notorious for horrific abuses of prisoners. He had been held there on bogus charges since the summer of 2014. *The Post*'s State Department reporter, Carol Morello, waved me out of a news meeting to share what she had learned from sources. We could say nothing publicly yet. There was still risk that a deal might fall apart. But suddenly there was cause for optimism that Jason would regain his freedom, finally permitted to fly out of the country with his wife, Yeganeh Salehi, an Iranian journalist, whose own imprisonment had lasted more than two months.

The coming days would be filled with unnerving uncertainty.

Real joy would have to wait until we knew for sure that he was out of Iranian airspace. After 544 days of incarceration, much of the time in solitary confinement, Jason would be on his way back to the United States, ferried on the final leg home in the company of Jeff Bezos on his private jet.

On July 22, 2014, Jason and Yegi were arrested by Iranian security forces who raided and ransacked their Tehran apartment and rummaged through computer and mobile phone records. A government official, as reported by the Islamic Republic News Agency, declared that "Iranian security forces are vigilant towards all kind of enemies' activities." Just exactly what activities made Jason or Yegi enemies of the Iranian state was a mystery.

If the outcome hadn't been so tragic, the Iranian authorities' accusations would have qualified as farce. "Do you know why you are here, Mr. Jason?" an interrogator asked, as Jason recounted in his book *Prisoner: My 544 Days in an Iranian Prison*. No, Jason responded. "You're the head of the American CIA station in Tehran. We know it. And you have a choice. Tell us everything and you'll go home."

"There's nothing to tell," Jason responded. "I'm just a journalist." And though the Iranians to this day have never acknowledged that truth, that's all he was. Jason had recently been reporting on nuclear negotiations between Iran and six world powers led by the United States. But much of his coverage had centered on the daily lives of ordinary people. In January that year, he authored a story headlined "Tehran Foodies Flock to American-Style Burger Joints." In March, he wrote about the rare few days of clean air in polluted Tehran, and in May his subject was how drug addiction among women was finally getting attention and treatment. But in May, he also focused on the arrest of young Iranians who produced a video that was set to the Pharrell Williams song "Happy."

As it happened, the "Happy" story highlighted an Iranian reality that was now relevant to his own predicament. "Many news reports and commenters on social media have simplified the arrests into some version of the headline that 'no one is allowed to be "happy" in Iran,'" he wrote. "But that does not illuminate a bigger issue, which is the complicated nature of Iran's power structure and what this case says about disagreements within it." Jason noted that Iranian president Hassan Rouhani had argued for loosening controls on social media and other forms of communication. "But it is not up to him," Jason wrote. "While many think of Iran's power structure as a monolith, it is anything but, with many checks and balances, some of them official and some blurrier."

Jason himself appeared to have fallen victim to those very divisions within Iran's hierarchy. Yegi was released on bail after seventy-two days, but Jason was sent to Evin Prison, held there by the intelligence wing of Iran's Revolutionary Guard Corps. The IRGC, which reports directly to Iran's supreme leader and exists to quash any internal or external threats, was at odds with Rouhani over his desire to strike a deal that would lift economic sanctions on Iran in exchange for restrictions on its nuclear program. Subsequent events in Jason's case signaled an effort to embarrass the Iranian president. Shortly after Rouhani accepted a preliminary nuclear agreement with six world powers, the Fars news agency, considered close to the IRGC, announced that Jason was facing charges of "espionage" and "acting against national security." A full seven months after his arrest, we finally knew what he was specifically accused of.

In addition to espionage, he faced grave charges of "collaborating with hostile governments" and "propaganda against the establishment." He also was accused of having collected information "about internal and foreign policy," providing it to "individuals with hostile intent." On top of all that, his case was assigned to a judge whose record of imposing long prison terms, lashings, and death sentences in high-profile cases had earned him sanctions by the European Union in 2011. Jason now faced a potential sentence of ten to twenty years in prison.

The stunning magnitude of the injustice needed to be made clear. "Jason was arrested without charges," I said in a statement in late May 2015. "He was imprisoned in Iran's worst prison. He was placed in isolation for many months and denied the medical care he needed. His case was assigned to a judge internationally notorious for human rights violations. He could not select the lawyer of his choosing. He was given only an hour and a half to meet with a lawyer approved by the court. No evidence has ever been produced by prosecutors or the court to support these absurd charges. The trial date was only disclosed to Jason's lawyer last week. And now, unsurprisingly but unforgivably, it turns out the trial will be closed."

In October, after a sham trial, Iranian media reported that he had been convicted. In November, a spokesman for the Iranian judiciary said Jason, already incarcerated for sixteen months, had been sentenced to prison, though he didn't specify for how long.

Throughout Jason's ordeal, *The Post* had been working hard publicly and behind the scenes to secure his release. The case was complicated by his dual U.S. and Iranian citizenship. His late father had emigrated from Iran two decades before he was born in the United States. His mother is American. San Rafael, California, was his hometown. But Iran does not recognize dual citizenship, treating anyone with an Iranian passport as Iranian only. The United States and Iran had severed diplomatic relations months after the Iranian takeover of the U.S. embassy in November 1979. Fifty-two American citizens were held hostage for 444 days. Iranian authorities now barred American diplomats or anyone representing the United States from visiting or communicating with Jason.

The Post's own efforts on Jason's behalf were captained skillfully by publisher Fred Ryan, a prelude to years of admirable advocacy on his part for press freedom worldwide. Fred had retained a team of lawyers at the law firm WilmerHale—led by Robert Kimmitt, a former U.S. ambassador to Germany with deep connections within the U.S. and foreign governments—to pull whatever levers they could. Fred himself set up periodic meetings with top-level White House officials—Denis McDonough, President Obama's chief of staff, Secretary of State John Kerry, and National Security Advisor Susan Rice—to ensure that Jason's release remained a top priority within the Obama administration. He requested help from every prime minister, president, or foreign minister who visited *The Post* for meetings with the editorial board. Foreign editor Douglas Jehl stayed in regular contact with Jason's family. Editorial page editor Fred Hiatt effectively marshaled the opinion page on Jason's behalf. My role was to be the public face and voice of *The Post*, ensuring that his case received worldwide media attention. President Rouhani and Foreign Minister Mohammad Javad Zarif deserved to be confronted with Jason's case wherever they traveled. I urged other news organizations to give Jason's imprisonment the coverage it needed. Gratifyingly, they did.

No one was a more persistent or effective public advocate for Jason than his brother Ali, who traveled the country and the world advocating for Jason with politicians and the press. President Obama could not have made a truer statement than when he told Jason upon later meeting with him at the White House, "Your brother made sure we never forgot you."

Even as Jason languished in prison, I was regularly extended warmly worded invitations by the Iranian government to attend its press briefings in the fall when Rouhani attended the United Nations General Assembly. About two dozen leading editors and reporters of major American news organizations were typically invited to pose questions to the Iranian president, a frustratingly stilted ritual at the UN Plaza hotel in Manhattan that was preceded by bountiful breakfast offerings. Incongruously, Iran's press representative would welcome me graciously as I stepped off the elevator to pass through security.

Iran's activities in those years yielded the media plenty of material for interrogating the Iranian president. My purpose, as I saw it, was to keep Jason prominently on the table, and I seized the chance to press Rouhani on his fate. On September 23, 2014, before his address to the United Nations, I had my first chance.

"First of all," I said to Rouhani, "I just want to take this opportunity to revisit the subject of our correspondent Jason Rezaian and his wife, Yeganeh. I would like to say to you personally that we believe that he deserves his freedom, and we ask the government of Iran to release him. But I want to ask you how the Iranian government can justify imprisoning a good journalist. I think you know he's a good journalist and a good person. And having him imprisoned for two months and interrogated for two months, how is that possible?" Without uttering Jason's name, Rouhani disclaimed any responsibility and dismissed the idea of his intervening. "I am not the judge of an individual who is being questioned by the judiciary at this point," he said.

I was heartened to learn upon Jason's release that he had witnessed my exchange with Rouhani from prison when it aired on Iran state television. His jailers, he recounted in his book, had told him that *The Washington Post* was "doing absolutely nothing on my behalf. Not even talking about me." Jason could see for himself in prison that he was being fed another Iranian lie.

On one occasion, an Iranian press officer at the UN displayed some empathy for Jason. "We at the mission," he told me after one of Rouhani's Q&As, "are very saddened by Mr. Jason's situation. We have met him many times before and consider him a good friend." I put my hand in my jacket pocket to pull out a #FreeJason pin, one of thousands that *The Post* had distributed to its staff and other journalists. "I'm sure you'll want to wear this," I told him. He refused the gift.

A year later, in September 2015, opportunity arose to speak with another powerful figure in the Iranian government. Ali Larijani, speaker of Iran's parliament and member of a highly influential family, was to be in New York for a United Nations meeting. Of keen interest to us, his brother headed Iran's judiciary. When Douglas Jehl was invited as *The Post*'s foreign editor to join a roundtable interview, he requested that the two of us also be granted a face-to-face meeting with Larijani. Surprisingly, the Iranians assented, a concession we found encouraging. When I was also allowed to attend the roundtable interview with Larijani, I raised Jason's imprisonment.

"Iranian law says no person may be detained without conviction for more than a year unless charged with murder," I said. "Jason has been in prison for well more than a year. Iranian law says a verdict must be issued within a week of a trial's conclusion. His trial concluded weeks ago. No verdict has been announced, and yet he continues to be imprisoned. Why is Iran violating both international law and its own laws in its treatment of a journalist who did nothing wrong?" The question did not go over well. When the roundtable session concluded, Iran's press officer informed me that the face-to-face meeting Larijani had promised us was being canceled. I had already asked about Jason, he said; there was no longer a need to meet.

Doug and I were exasperated, insisting Larijani not renege on his promise to see us. I had traveled hours from Washington solely for that reason, I pointed out. The press officer was unmoved but said he'd check again with Larijani. We were to wait in the UN Plaza's lobby. When he returned, the answer was no again. Larijani had no time for us. "That's unacceptable," I said. "We'll wait until he has time."

The press officer, remarkably, pledged to try once more. And when he returned, he announced that Larijani had consented to meet with us briefly. We took the elevator up to Larijani's room and were met by him and an aide at the door, permitted to step no more than a few feet inside. As we stood facing each other for several minutes, he made no promises, only expressing hope that Jason's case would be resolved "very soon." What that meant, we had no idea. But why would he meet with us, even briefly, unless he had a positive signal to send?

In an interview later with NPR, Larijani suggested a prisoner exchange might be one way to arrange for Jason and other Americans held on spying charges in Iran to go free. It was another hopeful sign, and we finally allowed ourselves to anticipate his freedom. Fred Ryan sent a note on September 19, 2015, to the team working for Jason's release: "Jeff Bezos, who has been kept informed throughout this process, wants to make sure that when the opportunity comes to get Jason out, we move quickly without letting complications of logistics or expenses get in the way. He has his plane ready to be dispatched to any pick-up location and will personally absorb any expenses to get Jason and his family home as expeditiously as possible."

When weeks passed in silence, our optimism began to dissipate. As Jason's period of imprisonment exceeded the 444 days that Americans were held hostage in 1979, Fred Ryan once again sought to have Obama meet with *Post* executives and Jason's brother Ali. Fred wrote White House chief of staff McDonough to follow up on our "multiple requests" for a meeting with the president. "We are increasingly asked if the President has met with Ali Rezaian and the *Washington Post* team that is assisting in his efforts to secure Jason's freedom. In response, we have attempted to be diplomatic and have evaded answering that question to date." When Fred received no immediate response, he raised the possibility of going public with how we'd been stymied. The consensus was that we should not, and we never did.

Despite the wait, the prisoner swap Larijani hinted at in September ultimately took shape. On January 16, 2016, just after international sanctions against Iran were lifted as part of a deal to limit its nuclear program, a Swiss plane carried Jason, Yegi, and his mother, Mary, along with two other Americans who had been imprisoned, out of Iran. A fourth American released as part of the prisoner exchange did not join them on the plane. For its part, the United States allowed seven Iranians being held for sanctions violations to receive clemency and go free while charges against fourteen Iranians outside the United States were dismissed.

In anticipation of Jason's release, Doug Jehl and I had flown to Switzerland, and then made our way to the U.S. Army–operated Landstuhl Regional Medical Center in Germany, where we learned he would receive care. Jason would need time to adjust to freedom and to recover from the longest period of imprisonment for any Western journalist held in Iran. But seeing him as a liberated man was a moment of overwhelming relief and pure joy.

Soon, Jason received word that Jeff Bezos wanted to visit him at Landstuhl and then fly him and his family home to the United States in his private jet. When Bezos arrived, they shared takeout schnitzel and beer at the medical center's Fisher House, a temporary residence for families of those receiving care. The next morning, Bezos arrived in a shuttle bus to take the Rezaian family back to the United States. A photo taken by Doug showed Jason and Bezos both smiling in the cabin of his jet, with *The Post* owner's right arm draped over Jason's shoulder and Jason's left wrapped behind Bezos's back. Streamers and #FreeJason posters could be seen in the background. The plane landed first in Bangor, Maine, where they were processed for entry into the United States. Yegi, whose passport had been seized by the Iranians and never returned, received an I-94 visa with her status designated as "humanitarian parole." It was the only official ID she now had.

There would be another leg to the trip. Bezos had already asked Jason, "Where do you want to go? I'll take you wherever you want." Jason responded, "How about Key West?" "I was like, 'Okay!' And that's what I did. I dropped him off in Key West," Bezos recalled to *Fortune* magazine in March 2016. "He and Yegi had only been married for just over a year before he got imprisoned. It was almost like a second honeymoon." A driver from Bezos's security firm picked them up, drove them to their hotel, where they checked in under fake names, and picked up the tab for all their restaurant meals and other needs throughout their stay. Good thing, too. They had no cash. Jason advised their protector that they also had no spare clothes. "He said he'd been instructed to buy us anything we wanted," Jason recalled. "I asked what the limits of that were and he said, 'We're probably not going car shopping, but anything else is fair game.'"

Bezos's gesture carried huge symbolic significance. Twenty months earlier, Bezos had to be advised to attend the memorial service of famed *Post* editor Ben Bradlee. Now he had an instinct for when to be present for the newsroom. Bezos had celebrated Jason, Yegi, and Mary's flight out of Iran with a tweet on January 17. But, as his jet carried them to the United States, he said nothing more publicly. The flight itself spoke volumes about his support for *The Post*'s mission and its journalists. Two months later, Bezos was asked by *Fortune* if he meant to make a statement with that trip. "I did it just for Jason. My motivation is super simple," he replied. "But I would be delighted if people take from it the idea that we'll never abandon anybody."

Until June 2017, I had yet to observe Bezos give a full interview exclusively devoted to his thoughts about *The Post*. A week after our visit to the White House for dinner with Trump, he did that in Turin, Italy, of all places. The occasion was a forum sponsored by the newspaper *La Stampa*, which was owned by his friend the billionaire John Elkann, who leads a family business empire with interests in Ferrari, Fiat, sports, and media. The forty-three minutes were, by my figuring, the most comprehensive public discussion ever of his vision for *The Post*.

Enthusiastic as he was about *The Post*'s technology team and our digital experimentation, he emphasized his own obligation to the organization. "I took it—and take it today—as a very serious responsibility. I'm very missionary about it. I care about it. I care about the independence of the newsroom."

Bezos made clear that he would not be running the newspaper as a "philanthropic endeavor," even though he was investing with an eye on the long run. We would be subjected to the discipline of budgets and profitability. "I really believe that a healthy newspaper that has an independent newsroom should be self-sustaining. And I think it's achievable. And it *is* achievable. We've achieved it. We made some money in 2016. We'll make money again here in 2017 . . . Remember, constraints drive creativity. The worst thing I could have done for *The Post*, I believe, is 'don't worry about revenue, whatever you need, just do the job' . . . I don't think that would lead to as much quality as you get when there are, in fact, constraints."

While we needed to attract lots of online readers so they could get a taste of our journalism, ultimately we had to deliver work they considered worth paying for. That, as Bezos pointed out, turned out to be journalism that involved a heavy investment of time and resources. "If you want to do investigative reporting and other kinds of very expensive reporting, you have to have a model where people will pay you for it. And I am super-optimistic about that . . . We see that our stories, the ones we put a lot of work into, those are more likely to drive subscriptions."

While he didn't envision print newspapers disappearing soon, he saw them diminishing to the status of mere curiosity. "One day, at some point," Bezos said, "it will be a luxury product. It will not be something that most people have. It'll be kind of exotic. It'll be like owning a horse. And you won't use your horse for transportation. You own it because it's a beautiful animal and you love to ride. And some people will still get physical newspapers. And it'll be a beautiful thing. You'll go over to your friend's house, and they'll have a physical newspaper. And you'll be like, 'Wow! Can I try that?'"

By the end of the interview, Bezos had boiled down his business philosophy about *The Post* to three simple, easy-to-remember elements.

"Be riveting, be right, and ask people to pay. They will pay. This industry spent twenty years teaching everyone in the world that news should be free. The truth is readers are smarter than that. They know that high-quality journalism is expensive to produce, and they are willing to pay for it. But you have to ask them."

Bezos was reviving an institution that Trump was determined to tear down. And yet the more Trump worked to crush *The Post*, the more he persuaded millions of Americans of *The Post*'s essential value. In his effort to dodge accountability, Trump proved how much it was needed. Readers would pay *The Post* to reveal what the president aimed to conceal.

After little more than a half year of the Trump administration, *The Post*'s digital-only subscriptions had climbed past one million. By the time he left office, *The Post* had reached three million, propelling the newsroom staff to more than a thousand, the most ever. An unwitting Donald Trump can legitimately claim to be the best salesman for *The Post* in its history.

11

WORK, NOT WAR

Everything about Donald Trump, starting with his campaign, told me that he had the makings of an autocrat. How he celebrated violence against protesters during campaign rallies. How he strove to dehumanize the press. His threats to use presidential power to punish, even imprison, opponents. His hateful language and racist dog whistles. His campaign's anti-Semitic imagery mixing cash, corruption, globalism, and power. His contempt for verifiable fact and democratic norms. His reckless, baseless claim that the 2016 election was being "rigged" against him—and his refusal, even then, to concede the outcome if he lost. How he conflated the public interest with his own. His praise for strongmen, first and foremost Russia's Vladimir Putin but also the Philippines' Rodrigo Duterte, Egypt's Abdel Fattah el-Sisi, North Korea's Kim Jong Un, Turkey's Recep Tayyip Erdoğan, and Hungary's Viktor Orbán.

"I can tell you, knowing the president for a good twenty-five or thirty years," the U.S. ambassador to Hungary at one point declared to Franklin Foer for *The Atlantic* magazine, "that he would love to have the situation that Viktor Orbán has." I myself listened as a Republican senator recounted how Trump, referring to the world's authoritarians, admitted that "he likes the strong ones."

As Trump took office, I felt the need to educate myself in a way I had never anticipated for an incoming president. The media had been unprepared for his brand of presidential campaign. I needed to get myself ready for his brand of presidency. All of my reading was concentrated on authoritarianism and the manipulation of public opinion.

On the list: *It Can't Happen Here*, the 1935 novel by Sinclair Lewis. (A populist president who ushers in the end of democracy and speaks of editors "in spider-dens" while "plotting how they can put over their lies.") *The Plot Against America*, the 2004 novel by Philip Roth. ("To have captured the mind of the world's greatest nation without uttering a single word of truth!") *The Origins of Totalitarianism*, Hannah Arendt's 1951 masterpiece on the subject. (Mass leaders who believe "fact depends entirely on the power of the man who can fabricate it.") *The True Believer*, the 1951 reflections of Eric Hoffer on mass movements. ("The effectiveness of a doctrine does not come from its meaning but from its certitude.") *The Image*, where in 1962 Daniel Boorstin highlighted mass media's addiction to "pseudo events." (How Senator Joseph McCarthy commanded "diabolical fascination and almost hypnotic power over news-hungry reporters" while "building him up in front-page headlines." They were "co-manufacturers of pseudo-events" and "were caught in their own web.") *Amusing Ourselves to Death*, the 1985 book by Neil Postman that observed politics entering an Age of Show Business. ("Political leaders need not trouble themselves very much with reality provided that their performances consistently generate a sense of verisimilitude.")

From more recent years: *On Tyranny*, the slim but powerful 2017 bestseller by historian Timothy Snyder. ("Post-truth is pre-fascism.") *How Democracies Die*, written in 2018 by Harvard professors Steven Levitsky and Daniel Ziblatt. ("We should worry when a politician [1] rejects, in words or actions, the democratic rules of the game, [2] denies the legitimacy of opponents, [3] tolerates or encourages violence or [4] indicates a willingness to curtail the civil liberties of opponents, including the media.") And over time, as I saw Trump's deceptions maintain their hold on many Americans, I read *Humbug: The Art of P. T. Barnum*, Neil Harris's 1973 biography. ("The bigger the humbug," Barnum reportedly said, "the better the people will like it.")

All these books drew a picture of someone like Trump. They anticipated a politician who could whip up fears and animosities with rhetoric that targets supposed elites. They documented how the press might prove impotent at holding such a man to account—advancing his prospects even when that was not their intent. They envisioned how truth could be easily trampled.

With Trump, American politics had shifted off its traditional foundations. Within the world of journalism, a debate had now gained urgency: Should our profession shift off its foundations, too? Could old standards be any match for Trump's demagoguery and deceit? Hadn't they failed already?

Trump's comment to CIA officials that he was in a "running war with the media" had elicited a quote from me that became widely celebrated by many journalists: "We are not at war with the administration. We are at work." A story in *Mother Jones*, an investigations-oriented news outlet with historically progressive values, called it "a shrewd bit of verbal judo." As time passed, however, many journalists and media critics became less confident of its wisdom.

In the critics' view, journalists had to acknowledge that we really were in a war with Trump—over facts, press freedom, and democracy itself. If he waged war and we didn't, victory would be his. Journalists, in their estimation, were behaving like wimps: Too polite. Too passive. Too deferential. Too circumspect in our language. Too constrained by old rules in the face of a determined rule-breaker. Traditional principles such as journalistic objectivity were, they assessed, ill-suited to the challenge, if not counterproductive. Cautious (or, as they would say, tepid) language—describing Trump's assertions as "falsehoods" instead of "lies," for example—meant the public wasn't being told the plain truth and that the president wasn't being held properly to account.

James Risen, a former colleague of mine, declared in August 2018 in *The Intercept* that "crusading journalism is what is needed now." And with that cri de coeur, he recalled a German publisher, Hermann Ullstein, who had fled Nazi Germany for New York. In a 1943 book, Ullstein had taken the German press to task for failing to confront Hitler more aggressively—"especially," Risen wrote, "in comparison to the aggressive right-wing media that was rising during the 1920s and boosting Hitler's political fortunes." The failure of the pre-Nazi mainstream press, Ullstein had written, was "to a large extent due to mildness of language, to the tired and cautious spirit in which they fought."

Jay Rosen, a New York University professor and a prolific writer, emerged as one of the most acidic critics of traditional journalistic standards. In an extraordinary series of eighteen tweets in August 2018, Rosen contested how I had framed our journalistic mission:

> *Here I share some thoughts about what has become a famous phrase. It originates with Marty Baron, editor of the Washington Post, whom I regard as the unofficial leader of the American press, the tribal chieftain. His famous phrase is this: "We're not at war; we're at work"... It's great word smithing, a little gem of English composition. It has compression, rhythm, insight, alliteration. And it is memorable. More impressive is how Baron's phrase, "We're not at war; we're at work," captures the consensus in American journalism, striking his colleagues as the very definition of wisdom about how to cover Trump—and respond to his provocations, his insults, his trolling, his attacks... You're supposed to stay cool. Letting your emotions show is unprofessional and unwise. The right pose is unrattled, laconic. Serene and detached when under attack... He's trying to throw you off your game. Don't take the*

bait. And do not get caught up in the politics of the moment. You're not a hero of the resistance. Just do your job . . . "We're not at war; we're at work" is genius. But its genius is incomplete . . . There is alive in the United States a campaign to discredit the American press and turn as many people as possible against it. It is led from the top. This campaign is succeeding. Before journalists log on in the morning, about 30% of their public is already gone. It is not easy to know what to do under these conditions. I certainly don't. But to say, "we're not at war; we're at work" does not speak to the enormity of the problem. Somehow the press has to figure out how to fight back.

Rosen's flurry of tweets was, most immediately, a response to a commentary in *The Atlantic* by Todd Purdum, who had been a longtime political writer of exceptional insight and elegance for *The New York Times*. Purdum had written of CNN reporter Jim Acosta's confrontation with White House press secretary Sarah Huckabee Sanders on August 2, 2018, when he called on her to declare "right now and right here" that the press was not the "enemy of the people." When Sanders repeatedly deflected Acosta's question-cum-demand, and after he interrupted her several times, Acosta walked out of the White House press briefing in protest, later tweeting that her non-response was "shameful." *The New York Times* reported that some White House correspondents "rolled their eyes" but that he was "cheered" by his CNN colleagues and liberals, particularly since he had just faced harassment at a Trump rally. Acosta's face-off was exactly the sort of adversarial approach many Trump foes—and a growing number of journalists—felt was overdue.

Purdum's article, however, called it a "dangerous brand of performance journalism." He concluded, "The last thing Trump—or the press, or the public—needs is another convenient villain in the performative arena of the long-running reality show that is his administration. Acosta's broadside blurs the line between reporting and performance, between work and war, at a time when journalists have a greater obligation than ever to demonstrate that what they do is real, and matters—and is not just part of the passing show."

Acosta, Purdum allowed, had "ample cause to ask Sanders whether she subscribed to her boss's Stalinist view of the press." Agreed. The public should celebrate when reporters ask serious, pointed questions and sharply follow up. Good journalism requires it. But tenacity is possible without spectacle. Lecturing, interrupting, and walking out aren't helpful additions to the journalist's handbook. They may earn lusty cheers from those craving a good fight, but they are a welcome gift to critics who want us to be seen by the public as partisan warriors.

"Whenever a reporter who has not been kidnapped by terrorists, shot by an assailant, or won a big prize becomes an actor in her own story," Purdum wrote, "she has lost the fight. Or in this case, reinforced the corrosive, cynical, and deeply dangerous feedback loop that has convinced Trump's most fervent supporters that his relentless brief against the press has merit."

Purdum was in my camp, and I in his. But as Trump laid siege to democratic norms, the opposing camp was gaining currency among mainstream journalists while ours was hemorrhaging support.

I never imagined words of mine gaining so much attention. Yet the phrase captured my feelings exactly. Trump was absolutely at war with us. I didn't feel at war with him. But I knew with certainty what our work was, and I was unhesitatingly committed to it: We had a duty to report vigorously on the president and tell the public without equivocation what he and his team were up to and what it meant for American citizens and the world. The American people would have to decide whether they wanted what he was selling.

We at *The Post* were not responsible for his election. There had been some lousy practices in the media, for sure: CNN and Fox News broadcasting his campaign rallies uninterrupted. Trump being allowed to prattle on during radio and TV interviews without being challenged on the facts. A nauseating revelry in Trump-driven television ratings. "It may not be good for America, but it's damn good for CBS," Les Moonves, then executive chairman and chief executive of the network, said in February 2016. "Man, who would have expected the ride we're having right now? . . . The money's rolling in and this is fun . . . I've never seen anything like this, and this is going to be a very good year for us. Sorry. It's a terrible thing to say. But bring it on, Donald. Keep going." Moonves would later say, "It was a joke! It was a joke!" Yeah, sure.

And, of course, there was the endlessly reverential coverage of Trump by right-wing outlets. Fox News and *Breitbart* effectively made lavish in-kind contributions to his campaign.

But at *The Post* we had vetted Trump closely during the campaign, devoting enormous resources to a lengthy series of stories about his life and business career. We had published a book, *Trump Revealed*, that investigated him even more deeply and drew the wrath of the candidate and his media allies. Trump's narcissism, vindictiveness, deceitfulness, and amorality were detailed for anyone who bothered to read it. Finally, our story about his vulgar comments on the now-infamous *Access Hollywood* tape had nearly torpedoed his campaign.

When Jonathan Chait in January 2019 published a *New York* magazine story headlined "Donald Trump Was Never Vetted," my reaction was, "Really?" New information about Trump was unearthed after his election, but that it wasn't uncovered before voters went to the polls wasn't for lack of trying by reputable media.

My sense was that Trump was elected not because of what the press did or didn't do but because so many Americans were in the mood for a bomb thrower. They wanted someone to upend the status quo. He talked like they did, thought like they did. And they counted on him to stick it to all the people (the "elite") they resented the most, with the news media high on the list. They cared less, if at all, about the subjects of our attention—his bankruptcies, Russian connections, philandering (even boasting of sexual assault), boorish behavior, incendiary language, or decades of suspect schemes at tax avoidance—a subject that *The New York Times* began to unpeel a month before the 2016 election and fully detailed with a masterful exposé in October 2018.

The reporting methods and standards of outfits like *The Post* and *The Times* didn't seem antiquated to me. You can't adequately measure the quality of our work by the magnitude of its impact, especially in the short run. And I wasn't about to react emotionally to Trump's election. Days after Trump's inauguration, strategist Steve Bannon had called the media the "opposition party." He hoped we would be seen as exactly that. The more we were viewed as partisans, the less our reporting would be believed. We could not fall into the trap that Trump and his close confederates had set for us.

Nor was it the time to discard journalism's fundamental principles. At a time of peril for democratic institutions, we needed to be good stewards of our own, reinforcing standards rather than abandoning them. The authors of *How Democracies Die* described how a demagogue who violates rules and norms can provoke others to do the same, further eroding democracy. Specifically, they cited a media that, feeling threatened, "may abandon restraint and professional standards." Much of the press was tempted to do just that.

Restraint and standards were, in part, the reason for our hesitancy to use the word "lie" in describing Trump's falsehoods, irritating press pundits and many readers. *The Post* had traditionally avoided using the word to describe the deceit of American presidents, although there had been plenty of it throughout history. "Lie," moreover, suggested we were certain that Trump knew what he was saying was false. And, for the most part, we couldn't be sure. Perhaps he was deluded, which hardly recommended him for the presidency. Or, being generous, he could have been grossly uninformed. Or maybe Trump was the ultimate bullshitter. A bullshitter "does not care whether the things he says describe reality correctly," as philosopher Harry G. Frankfurt wrote in his 2005 book, *On Bullshit*. "He just picks them out, or makes them up, to suit his purpose." By giving no attention whatsoever to truth, he argued, bullshit "is a greater enemy of truth than lies are."

Eventually, beginning for *The Post* in May 2018, there was no avoiding the word "lie." At the first major cracks in Trump's story that he knew nothing about hush money paid to women who alleged affairs with him, Dan Balz wrote, "Does it bother anyone that the president has been shown to be a liar?" *The Post*'s Fact Checker column in August pointed to the now-documented fact that Trump was fully aware of secret payments to silence porn star Stormy Daniels and *Playboy* model Karen McDougal over allegations that he had carried on affairs with them. "Not just misleading. Not merely false. A lie," declared the headline. Trump had denied making the payments, and he got aides to issue denials on his behalf. He also denied having affairs with the women. In a guilty plea that August, former Trump attorney Michael Cohen admitted to the payments, to being reimbursed by the Trump Organization, and to Trump's knowledge of it all. It was, as *The Post*'s Glenn Kessler wrote, "indisputable evidence that Trump and his allies have been deliberately dishonest at every turn." We were on rock-solid ground in using "lie." The word would make many more appearances in *The Post*'s coverage of Trump.

A change in vocabulary might mollify at least some of our critics. Aggressive and revelatory reporting, however, is the only genuinely effective way for the press to hold power to account. I had witnessed straightforward, fact-based journalism do just that, most notably after launching *The Boston Globe*'s investigation that exposed how the Catholic Church covered up sexual abuse by clergy for decades. It took time, process, and patience for the full scope of scandal to emerge and for the impact of the journalism to be felt. I had stripped stories of virtually all adjectives lest expressive language become ammunition for the Church and others to discredit our work. The facts alone could speak powerfully enough.

With Trump, my posture was the same: Report hard. Unflinchingly publish what we know. Avoid unnecessarily inflammatory language. Don't give Trump and his allies ammunition against us. The American people can then decide whether they want more of Trumpism. In a democracy, the call is theirs to make.

In the early months of his second year in office, Trump paid homage to a free press at a big gathering of Washington media, the annual white-tie Gridiron Club Dinner. It was an unusual statement, and an unusual setting, too. Trump had spurned other such events, every year declining invitations to attend the White House Correspondents' Dinner, the mammoth black-tie gala that traditionally draws thousands of journalists and a discordant heaping of celebrities. His staff would shun the event in "solidarity" with him in 2017, and two years later the president actually issued orders for Cabinet secretaries and senior staffers to stay away.

So it was a surprise when Trump agreed to appear in March 2018 at the Gridiron Dinner (an event I abhorred and avoided). And it was even more of a surprise when he had some praise for the press. "I have a lot of respect for a lot of the people in this room," he said, adding that there were "very few professions that I respect more." He granted that there were "some incredible, brilliant, powerful, smart, and fair people in the press." And, he said, "I want to thank the press for all you do to support and sustain our democracy. I mean that."

He didn't mean that. He would be back to his usual ways in no time at all. By July, he was accusing the "Fake News Media" of making up "stories without any backup, sources, or proof." Twenty-two minutes later, he claimed the media had distorted coverage of his relationship with Vladimir Putin because it "wants so badly to see a major confrontation with Russia, even a confrontation that could lead to war." Ten days later, the press he had praised in March for "all you do to support and sustain our democracy" was accused of being "very unpatriotic" and "driven insane by Trump Derangement Syndrome." The press, he said, had put people's lives "at risk" by revealing internal deliberations of government. "I will not allow our great country to be sold out by anti-Trump haters in the dying newspaper industry," Trump tweeted, specifically mentioning "the failing New York Times and the Amazon Washington Post."

In October, Trump all but encouraged violence against journalists when he applauded a Montana lawmaker for body-slamming a reporter, calling him a "tough cookie" and "my kind of guy." After sixteen pipe bombs were sent later that month to CNN, Trump critics, Democratic politicians, and former Obama administration officials, Trump went only as far as generically condemning "any acts or threats of political violence." And at a rally on the very night that news broke about the explosives, he blamed the media for "endless hostility and constant negative and oftentimes false attacks and stories."

The next day, Trump was, as usual, accepting no responsibility for inflammatory rhetoric that might have motivated such an attack, instead tweeting against the media for "a very big part of the Anger we see today in our society." That same day, authorities arrested Cesar Sayoc, a troubled resident of South Florida, who had plastered his van with stickers supporting Trump along with images of the president's critics that carried red targets over their faces. Five months later, Sayoc pleaded guilty to mailing the explosives. He told a federal judge that Trump's rallies "became like a new found drug." In August 2019, he was sentenced to twenty years in prison.

When news broke of the pipe bombs, Senator Ben Sasse of Nebraska, a Republican, argued for stopping "all this nonsense language about the press is the enemy of the people." Trump clearly didn't agree. To him, it was a good time to double down. When an ABC News reporter asked whether his rhetoric encouraged politically motivated violence, Trump suggested violence was the media's fault. "You're creating violence by your questions," he said, pointing to the reporter. A *Post* poll had just found that 49 percent of Americans felt "the way Trump speaks" encouraged violence. But Trump was speaking to his base. Two-thirds of Republicans felt "the way the media reports" encouraged violence.

By November, Trump was moving even more aggressively and vindictively against the press. The administration suspended the press credentials of CNN's Jim Acosta. It was, as journalists Peter Baker and Susan Glasser described in their 2022 book *The Divider*, "a brazen act of retribution unlike any taken by a modern White House."

The suspension came hours after a White House news conference, where Trump sought to cut off questioning from Acosta about the president's invective directed at a caravan of migrants. A White House intern attempted to grab the microphone from the correspondent, and press secretary Sarah Huckabee Sanders then accused Acosta of "placing his hands" on her. A video released by the White House to document her claim turned out to have come straight from *Infowars*, the site of right-wing conspiracy theorist Alex Jones, where a contributor manipulated it to portray Acosta as aggressive. Acosta had only raised his hand to shield the microphone, declaring "Pardon me, ma'am." Right-wing media personalities would spread the lie that Acosta had pushed and shoved the young woman. A federal judge rightly ordered the White House to restore Acosta's press pass on the grounds that it had been revoked without due process.

Trump's posture toward Black reporters was particularly ugly and disrespectful. When Abby Phillip, a CNN correspondent who had previously covered politics for *The Post*, asked Trump whether he wanted newly appointed acting attorney general Matthew Whitaker to "rein in" the special counsel's Russia investigation, Trump lashed out. "What a stupid question," he said, pointing his finger at her. "But I watch you a lot. You ask a lot of stupid questions." In Trump's mind, any question that put him on the spot was an offense.

By year-end 2018, Trump was ranking his war on the media as a signature achievement of his administration. "I think that one of the most important things I've done, especially for the public, is explain that a lot of the news is indeed fake," he told his advisers David Bossie and Corey Lewandowski in an interview for their book *Trump's Enemies: How the Deep State Is Undermining the Presidency.* (The following summer, he would envision his attacks on the press as "a big part of my legacy" in what he called the "Age of Trump.") The Committee to Protect Journalists, which typically monitored threats to press freedom in other countries, began to focus on Trump as a threat within U.S. borders. During the first two years of his administration, CPJ found, 11 percent of Trump's tweets denigrated the press. He insulted individual journalists via Twitter forty-eight times in the same period.

In September, *Axios*, citing a three-page fundraising pitch, reported that Trump's allies were raising $2 million to investigate reporters and editors. Damaging information would be furnished to "friendly media outlets" such as *Breitbart* and even traditional news organizations. Listed as "primary targets," *Axios* reported, were "CNN, MSNBC, all broadcast networks, *NY Times*, *Washington Post*, *BuzzFeed*, *Huffington Post*, and all others that routinely incorporate bias and misinformation into their coverage. We will also track the reporters and editors of these organizations." Days earlier, *The Times* had reported on a "loose network of conservative operatives allied with the White House" that was launching an "aggressive operation to discredit news organizations deemed hostile to President Trump by publicizing damaging information about journalists."

The operation, led by Arthur Schwartz Jr., a GOP consultant and adviser to Donald Trump Jr., had already dug up old social media posts by some journalists—anti-Semitic and racist tweets by a senior staff editor at *The New York Times* written while in college (he apologized); anti-Semitic tweets by a CNN photo editor (who resigned); antigay slurs by a CNN reporter when she was in college (she apologized); and an old, purportedly offensive tweet by a *Post* reporter that was actually written as irony (no action required). I had always expected Trump's allies to be digging through the backgrounds and old social media posts of our journalists. We scanned social media ourselves in researching job candidates. On occasion the results were startling and disqualifying. We did the same when vetting politicians and political appointees. The GOP effort, though, was designed with malicious intent. Some reporters' photos were posted by Trump allies merely to show they were being watched, as happened to *The Post*'s Josh Dawsey, when a photograph of him sitting at a bar was posted to Twitter. It was an act of intimidation. "They wanted all the reporters covering him to live in fear," Josh told me.

The president also persisted in lambasting reporters by name when their stories didn't match his own self-serving version of events. When *The Post*'s White House reporters Philip Rucker and Ashley Parker delivered a story describing Trump's "lost summer" of 2019, Trump went ballistic. Phil and Ashley wrote of "self-inflicted controversies and squandered opportunities" and went on to list them: "Trump leveled racist attacks against four congresswomen of color dubbed 'the Squad.' He derided the majority-black city of Baltimore as 'rat and rodent infested'... His visits to Dayton, Ohio, and El Paso after the gun massacres in those cities served to divide rather than heal ... His trade war with China grew more acrimonious. His whipsaw diplomacy at the Group of Seven summit left allies uncertain about American leadership."

A few days later, White House press secretary Stephanie Grisham and principal deputy press secretary Hogan Gidley condemned *The Post*'s journalism in an op-ed in the conservative *Washington Examiner* that was headlined, with childish mimickry, "*The Washington Post*'s Lost Summer." Covering the administration often seemed less like war than tit for tat in elementary school. The aides argued that *The Post* ignored a list of accomplishments provided by the White House when, in fact, their story had included the more consequential items on the list. Verbal sparring in the pages of a newspaper could never be enough for Trump, however. He promptly took to Twitter to rebuke Rucker and Parker as "two nasty reporters" who "shouldn't even be allowed" at the White House. When Trump called out our journalists by name, we spoke out forcefully. "*The Washington Post*," I said in a statement, "is immensely proud to have these two superb journalists on staff . . . The president's statement fits into a pattern of seeking to denigrate and intimidate the press. It's unwarranted and dangerous, and it represents a threat to a free press in this country."

Concerned about the president's "deeply troubling anti-press rhetoric," the young and still-new publisher of *The New York Times*, A. G. Sulzberger, accepted Trump's invitation to meet with him on July 20, 2018. "I told the president directly that I thought his language was not just divisive but increasingly dangerous," Sulzberger recounted. "I warned that his inflammatory language is contributing to a rise in threats against journalists and will lead to violence. I repeatedly stressed that this is particularly true abroad, where the president's rhetoric is being used by some regimes to justify sweeping crackdowns on journalists."

Sulzberger added, "I warned that it was putting lives at risk." Indeed, it was. When a brutal regime murdered one of our *Post* colleagues, we saw just how little Trump cared.

12

MURDER IN MIND

On October 2, 2018, word reached us that Jamal Khashoggi, a contributing columnist for *The Washington Post*, had gone missing after entering the Saudi Arabian consulate in Istanbul to obtain documents he needed for a marriage license. Although he set foot in the consulate at 1:14 p.m., he had yet to emerge by 5:00 p.m. when the consulate closed. His fiancée then called the police. As of midnight, there was still no sign of him.

Khashoggi had been added to *The Post*'s expanding Global Opinions online forum as a contributing columnist in January of that year, continuing his sharp criticism of the Saudi leadership, most notably Crown Prince Mohammed bin Salman. Khashoggi's column the next month highlighted how MBS, as the crown prince was commonly known, was exercising tighter control over the media despite cultivating an image as a reformer. "Over the past 18 months," Khashoggi wrote that February, "MBS's communications team within the Royal Court publicly has chastised, and worse, intimidated anyone who disagrees. Saud al-Qahtani, leader of that unit, has a blacklist and calls for Saudis to add names to it. Writers like me, whose criticism is offered respectfully, seem to be considered more dangerous than the more strident Saudi opposition based in London." The last *Post* column published before his disappearance called for the Saudi regime to end its "cruel war" in Yemen that had lasted more than three years: "The crown prince must bring an end to the violence and restore the dignity of the birthplace of Islam." For commentary like that, Khashoggi would be forever silenced.

Responding to reports of Khashoggi's disappearance, the Saudi government lied about his fate. "Mr. Khashoggi visited the consulate to request paperwork related to his marital status and exited shortly thereafter," it declared in a statement. The Turkish government insisted Khashoggi was still in the consulate, suspecting that he had been detained. "Where is Jamal Khashoggi?" *The Post* asked in an October 4 editorial, which also called upon the crown prince to "do everything in his power to ensure that Mr. Khashoggi is free and able to continue his work." That same day, *The Post* protested his disappearance by running blank space on its op-ed page under the headline "A Missing Voice."

As recently as April 2018, MBS had made a whirlwind three-week trip to the United States to fashion a more positive image of the kingdom and to stimulate business deals. In addition to meeting with Trump—where arms deals topped the agenda—he traveled to New York; Los Angeles; San Francisco; Seattle; East Palo Alto, California; and Cambridge, Massachusetts. He held meetings with actors, financiers, oil executives, educators, and technology bigwigs, including *The Post*'s owner, Jeff Bezos. A photo released by the Saudi embassy shows the two of them sharing laughs as they discussed "areas of cooperation in light of the Kingdom's Vision 2030."

Three days after Khashoggi visited the consulate, the crown prince gave an interview to *Bloomberg* in which he again insisted the writer had exited "after a few minutes or one hour"—and then invited Turkish authorities to conduct an inspection. "We have nothing to hide," he said. The communications director for the Saudi embassy in Washington turned to Twitter to "categorically reject any insinuations" of their holding Khashoggi. "Jamal Khashoggi's disappearance is a matter of grave concern to us all," he wrote.

On October 7 at about nine p.m., the Saudi ambassador to the

United States and brother of the crown prince, Khaled bin Salman, met with *Washington Post* publisher Fred Ryan at his Georgetown home, describing Khashoggi as always "honest" and dismissing the idea that the writer had been viewed by the regime as a threat. He also rejected as "baseless and ridiculous" suspicions that Saudi agents were involved in his disappearance. The embassy would later deny "any attempt to mislead" by the ambassador, even as they admitted his representations all "proved to be false." By then, Khashoggi had been savagely murdered in the consulate, his body dismembered and dumped somewhere that still has not been determined.

In the news department, we embarked on a fiercely aggressive investigation. Within the opinions department, veteran reporter and columnist David Ignatius wrote eloquently, and broke news, about the Saudi kingdom's brutal slaughter of someone he had known for roughly fifteen years. "Khashoggi understood that he could keep his mouth shut and stay safe, because he had so many friends in the royal family. But it simply wasn't in him," David wrote on October 7, when Khashoggi's fate was unknown but murder was feared.

With op-eds and advertisements, editorial page editor Fred Hiatt, global opinions editor Karen Attiah, and publisher Fred Ryan launched a relentless campaign for justice. A full-page ad in *The Post* on October 12 declared: "On Tuesday, Oct. 2 at 1:14 p.m. *Washington Post* columnist Jamal Khashoggi entered the Consulate of Saudi Arabia in Istanbul. He has not been seen since. DEMAND ANSWERS." On October 24, a revised ad was published. The phrase "has not been seen since" was replaced with "was brutally murdered." "DEMAND ANSWERS" became "DEMAND TRUTH."

Turkish law enforcement had obtained surveillance video of a body double used as part of the Saudis' attempt to fake Khashoggi's departure from the consulate. A Saudi agent wore Khashoggi's clothes, glasses, and a fake beard as a disguise.

Not until October 20 had the Saudi government finally acknowledged Khashoggi's killing inside the consulate. Still, the leadership made the preposterous claim that the death occurred during a fist-fight. But Turkish authorities said fifteen Saudis had flown to Istanbul on October 2, participated in the assassination, and then quickly left the country. A dozen of the Saudis identified by the Turks were connected to Saudi security services, with several having close connections to MBS.

Although the Saudi government said it was firing five officials and arresting eighteen others, it sought to shift responsibility away from the crown prince himself. That defied what experts knew about how the kingdom truly operated, and by mid-November the CIA concluded that the crown prince himself had ordered the assassination.

It took days for President Trump to comment at all on Khashoggi's disappearance. When he finally spoke up, his remarks were initially perfunctory, then shifted over time to noncommittal, dismissive, tough-sounding, credulous, and ultimately indifferent. A man who routinely rushed to judgment was suddenly hesitant to judge. The president who liked to describe himself as speaking "very strongly" and "very powerfully" was a portrait in weakness.

After days of mixed and mealymouthed responses, Trump went on Fox News on October 11 and characterized the United States' relationship with Saudi Arabia as "excellent." On the same day, Trump seemed to be looking for a way to avoid confrontation with the Saudis—on the grounds that Khashoggi, while a permanent resident of the United States living in exile, was not a U.S. citizen; plus, his disappearance took place in another country. "It's in Turkey, and it's not a citizen, as I understand it," he said. "But a thing like that shouldn't happen." By October 13, Trump was sounding somewhat more combative, promising in a CBS interview that there would be "severe punishment" if it was determined that Saudi agents killed Khashoggi. But then he added, "As of this moment, they deny it, and they deny it vehemently. Could it be them? Yes." Two days later, he was sounding all-too-eager to accept the word of Saudi royalty. "I just spoke with the King of Saudi Arabia, and he denies any knowledge of what took place with regards to, as he said, to Saudi Arabia's citizen," he said. And then he suggested "maybe it could have been rogue killers, who knows?"

After an October 16 trip to Riyadh by Secretary of State Mike Pompeo, where he appeared chummy with MBS, *Post* editorial writers called the administration's accommodating posture toward the Saudis "a diplomatic cleanup operation conducted by the Trump administration for a regime and a ruler it has grossly indulged, despite its mounting excesses both at home and abroad." When Trump acknowledged two days later that Khashoggi was most likely dead, he said the consequences would have to be "very severe. It's bad, bad stuff." And then he added, "We'll see what happens."

Not much happened. There would be no "very severe" consequences for Saudi Arabia. It was all empty talk. Pompeo ultimately revealed just how unserious his Saudi trip had been on the matter of accountability for the crown prince. "In some ways I think the president was envious that I was the one who gave the middle finger to *The Washington Post*, *The New York Times* and other bed-wetters who didn't have a grip on reality," he wrote in his January 2023 book, *Never Give an Inch*. "He said, 'Mike, go and have a good time. Tell him he owes us.'" Who knew Pompeo could so thoroughly enjoy himself at a time like that?

On November 15, the Saudis released a report saying eleven Saudi citizens would be indicted for Khashoggi's murder, with death penalties sought against five. The report provided an account of what befell Khashoggi on the afternoon of October 2, contradicting in every detail what the Saudi government had said to that point: Saudi agents had orders to bring Khashoggi back to Saudi Arabia, either by persuading him or by force. Instead, he was given a lethal injection. His body was cut to pieces, taken from the consulate, and disposed of by a Turkish individual. The report said nothing about where his body might be found. (One Turkish official later concluded that his body was dissolved in acid. An Al Jazeera investigation found instead that it was burned in a large outdoor oven at the Saudi consul general's residence.)

The U.S. Treasury imposed sanctions on seventeen Saudis for Khashoggi's death. But Trump followed up days later by expressing his strong support for the Saudi government, notwithstanding the CIA's assessment that the crown prince had ordered his killing. We "may never know all the facts surrounding the murder," Trump said in a statement bizarrely titled "America First!" and began "The world is a very dangerous place!" As-to the culpability of MBS, Trump's response was classic: "Maybe he did and maybe he didn't!" But Trump made clear that other U.S. interests had to prevail: Saudi oil, arms purchases, and support for Trump's Middle East policies. "They have been a great ally," Trump said.

And that was that. Trump, of course, wasn't directly responsible for Khashoggi's killing. But he was responsible for emboldening autocrats who intended to extinguish their press critics one way or another. In this instance, the chosen method was a bone saw. Crown Prince Mohammed bin Salman had ample reason to anticipate impunity from Trump, and he got exactly that. As for the Saudis charged, it's not clear that anyone has served time in prison despite convictions in a closed-door trial. The five death sentences were commuted.

Trump and his secretary of state saw *The Post* as irrationally obsessed with Khashoggi's brutal murder. Pompeo related in his book how, months later, he "lost it" at a dinner with journalists when he was asked about administration policy toward Saudi Arabia, telling them they had "lost your minds" over Khashoggi. Pompeo described a "recurring dinner party where the members of the establishment media sit for a chat." Other media figures and I recognized Pompeo's account as a reference to what had been, until then, an off-the-record dinner we attended. But Pompeo, despite my nineteen inquiries through intermediaries, would not respond to confirm or deny that.

Pompeo definitely "lost it" in my presence. But his book continued with quite the tale: how he was made to endure an "inquisition" over Khashoggi; how he dressed down the journalists as "you crazy Lefties"; and how he deserved gratitude for "defending our Jewish friends" from Iran and "protecting your Georgetown cocktail parties from radical Islamists." Then, in his account, he and his wife, Susan, "hastily made our exit from that dinner party—a mean, nasty world of its own." Nothing of that sort happened at the dinner I attended. *Post* opinion writer Ruth Marcus politely asked about U.S.-Saudi policy post-assassination. Pompeo exploded that we at *The Post* had lost our minds about Khashoggi. His temper tantrum quickly subsided, and the dinner, always civil and subdued, continued. It concluded with a normal good night.

I was proud when publisher Fred Ryan demonstrated that our fixation on the monstrous killing of a colleague came without an expiration date. He responded to Trump's inaction with an in-your-face statement in November 2018: "President Trump is correct in saying the world is a very dangerous place. His surrender to this state-ordered murder will only make it more so."

Trump would come to acknowledge doing Mohammed bin Salman a big favor. "I saved his ass," Trump told Bob Woodward for his 2020 book, *Rage*. "I was able to get Congress to leave him alone. I was able to get them to stop." So, it was not terribly surprising to see Trump's company and the Saudis in early 2022 discussing a moneymaking opportunity, where his golf courses would be named as sites for a tour of a new Saudi-financed golf league. Nor was it entirely a shock to learn in 2022 from *The New York Times* that an investment fund led by the crown prince had placed $2 billion with a private equity fund run by Trump son-in-law Jared Kushner only six months after he left the White House, even though the kingdom's financial advisers had cautioned against it. Kushner had been a leading MBS defender after the Khashoggi murder. Did Trump and Kushner consider prospective business deals when they went easy on the crown prince? Trump's own words come to mind: Maybe they did and maybe they didn't.

On the one-year anniversary of the murder, Jeff Bezos and Fred Ryan gathered with other mourners, including Khashoggi's fiancée, Hatice Cengiz, outside the Saudi consulate in Istanbul. "Leaders across the globe," Fred declared at the memorial, "must come to understand that journalists are not 'enemies of the people.' As Jamal's work so clearly showed, they are servants of the people—and of the democratic principles that empower the people. When people have access only to information supplied or approved by their governments, their worlds and their possibilities are limited to what the government allows them to know. The only way to escape this tyranny—the only way to have free and independent lives—is to guarantee a free and independent press."

Bezos's business interests by then had suffered as a result of *The Post's* unrelenting coverage of Khashoggi's murder. Saudi citizens were boycotting a Dubai-based e-commerce site, Souq.com, that Amazon had acquired in 2017 for $580 million in its largest foreign purchase. One Saudi media figure had condemned a "media campaign" that "defames" his country and its top officials. "Let's defend our nation . . . boycott Amazon to send a message to its owner so he is aware of the scale of the damage," he wrote. Meantime, an ambitious plan by Amazon to invest $1 billion to build data centers in Saudi Arabia came to a sudden halt.

At the memorial in Istanbul, none of that seemed to matter. Turning to Khashoggi's fiancée, Bezos said, "No one should ever have to endure what you have . . . It is unimaginable. You need to know, you are in our hearts. We are here. You are not alone." While Bezos's words were brief and personal, his widely covered appearance was powerful symbolism. His business interests might pay a high price, but his purchase of *The Washington Post* required an inviolable

commitment to free expression and the safety of those who practiced it.

Jamal Khashoggi's murder was arguably inevitable after Trump
showed indifference to the safety of journalists in the United States.
Worse than that, in fact. Trump's rhetoric had incited his followers
against journalists for several years.

In the final weeks of the 2016 campaign, amid concerns that
their man might lose the election and with Trump openly theorizing
that the results would be rigged, Trump supporters drew on the language of Nazi Germany to vilify the press. "Lügenpresse," meaning
"lying press," entered the vernacular of Trump supporters at his rallies and in their Twitter posts. The hashtag #TheList also started to
surface on social media, including on 8chan, an online forum popular
with the so-called alt-right, nationalists who feel "white identity" is
under attack. The faces of journalists were posted, crossed out with a
red X. "For your part in misleading the American public by spreading
lies and false information you have been added to #TheList," read
one post. Another: "Watch the lists below for a constant stream of
Lügenpresse shilling. Wait [for] one of them to speak out against
Donald Trump, for Hillary Clinton, or other forms of Kikery . . .
Sit back, enjoy tears." Such posts were often accompanied by language suggesting no violence was intended—most likely to shield
against criminal charges—but they acknowledged the purpose was
to harass. The inescapable interpretation of the X was that these
journalists might be assassinated. *Post* journalists were among those
who appeared on #TheList.

The image of a Jewish reporter for *Politico* was posted to Twitter
with a cartoonish blood-soaked bullet hole photoshopped onto her
forehead. "Don't mess with our boy trump or you will be first in line
for the camp," read one message with an anti-Semitic twist. Writer
David French, then at the *National Review*, said he was sent an im-

age of his daughter's face in a gas chamber, with "a smiling Trump in a Nazi uniform preparing to press a button and kill her."

After David Fahrenthold published his *Access Hollywood* story in early October 2016, one man left a voice mail at *The Post* declaring, "I wanna kill him." Dave met with the D.C. police, the FBI, and a security consultant who was retained by *The Post* to recommend safety measures at his home. Dave made light of the experience in a story he wrote for *The Post* about his year covering Trump, no doubt his way of dealing with the job's pressures. After the consultant dispensed her advice, Dave wrote, "I had to get back to work. My wife—who hadn't complained about any of this, the long hours or the missed bedtimes or the early-morning TV appearances—stopped me, shaken at what I'd gotten us into."

As President Trump doubled down on his antimedia venom, *The Post*'s senior executives leaned on the owners of our headquarters building to harden security. A former U.S. Marine who had protected embassies and high-level government personnel went on full-time duty as our director of security. In the summer of 2018, I was offered shatterproof glass for my office but declined, given that no one else in the newsroom would be receiving it. By September, *The Post* began paying for armed off-duty D.C. police officers to stand guard at turnstiles, retrofitted with higher glass gates, that led to the elevator bank. Security consultants already had counseled *Post* journalists to regularly alternate their commuting routes, advice I intermittently followed for my twenty-minute walk to the office.

One individual had tracked down my unlisted home phone number, leaving a voice mail that took objection to my acceptance of an award. "You, sir, are a whore. You have sold out the American people, truth, and journalism for cash . . . You are better suited for an award in the name of Dr. Goebbels." I had also seen my home address publicized on social media along with those of other top editors, with the poster slyly declaring that no one should do anything "illegal like . . . ," followed by a list of various forms of vandalism. The practice of revealing private information, known as doxing, would be used to harass innumerable journalists.

My personal experience at the time was far from the most unsettling, although things would get worse during the 2020 election and its violent aftermath. In August 2018, an anonymous caller into the Los Angeles bureau of the Associated Press declared, "At some point we're just going to start shooting you fucking assholes." Later that month, sixty-eight-year-old Robert Darrell Chain of Encino, California, was arrested for making fourteen threatening calls to *The Boston Globe*'s newsroom. The man was apparently worked up over *The Globe*'s effort to get other news organizations to sign on to an editorial condemning Trump for his attacks on journalists. "Hey," he said in one call, "how's your pussy smell today, nice and fresh? We are going to shoot you motherfuckers in the head, you *Boston Globe* cocksuckers. Shoot every fucking one of you." In another, Chain said: "You're the enemy of the people, and we're going to kill every fucking one of you . . . What are you going to do motherfucker? You ain't going to do shit. I'm going to shoot you in the fucking head later today, at 4 o'clock." Chain was certainly well stocked with weapons for such an attack. An FBI SWAT team found twenty firearms in his home. One, a semiautomatic rifle, had been purchased only a few months earlier.

A Boston University student working in *The Globe*'s newsroom took some of the calls. He told the FBI that the days until Chain's arrest were "undoubtedly some of the most frightening in my life." He was uncertain whether the threats were credible. "In a time when members of the media are constantly being attacked for doing their jobs . . . it seemed anything was possible." Facing a potential five years in prison, Chain pleaded guilty in May 2019 and expressed remorse. "Making those phone calls was the worst decision I've ever made. I really can't believe I said those things," he said prior to sentencing in October. "I just hope that those . . . people can forgive me. I truly wish them nothing but the best." It was quite the conversion from what he insolently told reporters as he left the federal court-house in Los Angeles back in August 2018, released on $50,000 bond. "Yeah, I'm making a statement," he said. "The United States got saved by having Donald J. Trump elected as president. Now take a hike, you bozos." Prosecutors had recommended ten months in prison; he received four. Prosecution for such threats against the media was infrequent. My impression in D.C. was that law enforcement, overwhelmed with the rise in threats of all types during the Trump era, made a record of the worst and only followed up if there was indisputable urgency.

Two months before the threats against *The Globe*, a mass shooting at the *Capital Gazette* in Annapolis, Maryland, had put all newsrooms on guard. Four journalists and a sales assistant were shot dead. While the attacker's vendetta had nothing to do with Trump's antimedia rhetoric, the attack had sensitized journalists everywhere to our ongoing exposure to fatal attacks. Trump's vilification of the media had dramatically increased the number of armed individuals who felt they had scores to settle with us. Having proclaimed journalists "horrible," "disgusting," and "scum," an American president had effectively given them permission to consider their cause a righteous one.

In the early evening of January 1, 2019, a pellet was fired into the lead-glass front door of the home of two *Post* journalists. One had just been on television, and her appearance was immediately followed by vile misogynistic Twitter postings revealing where she lived. Police arrived and filed a report. The following night, someone left a bright red Christmas tree ornament outside the journalists' front door, a signal that they were vulnerable and being surveilled. *The Post* promptly implemented security measures at the residence.

It was not uncommon for potential assailants to leave reminders that they knew where we lived. One *Post* reporter received mail at his home calling him a "tool," slang for asshole, along with a tool catalog. Another, in 2020, reported that his parents had received a call on their home landline threatening his brother. *The Post* had security cameras installed there and provided a security escort for the reporter.

There were periodic reminders of the proximity of the danger and its potential for devastating harm. In February of that year, a U.S. Coast Guard lieutenant living in Silver Spring, Maryland, was arrested for plotting to attack prominent Democratic politicians and hosts on MSNBC and CNN. Fifteen firearms and more than a thousand rounds of ammunition were seized from his basement. After pleading guilty to firearms and gun charges, Christopher Paul Hasson was sentenced to thirteen years in federal prison. "I'm embarrassed by these things and ashamed of the pain I caused," the defendant told the judge. Curious how these defendants always turned contrite at the moment of sentencing.

The ugly emails and phone calls, the doxing and the outright threats became more frequent as we got closer to another election year. Any one of them could have been dismissed as the ravings of a nutcase. But no more than one enraged zealot is required to inflict tragic harm.

The rhetorical attacks on *The Post* from more conventional corners were unending but largely an annoyance. Denunciation from Fox News commentators was, of course, regularly scheduled programming for that network. Others in the right-wing media universe hectored us in their own way. *FrontPageMag.com*, a website run by far-right theorizer David Horowitz, suggested in 2017 that I should be hauled to prison for an opinion essay whose meaning they distorted. "Arresting the editor of the *Washington Post*," they wrote, while identifying my neighborhood and publishing an inflated value for what was then my residence, "will send a message that there are limits to the abuses that the democratic institutions of this country will tolerate from the undemocratic institutions of the radical left."

Trump allies also regularly threatened to file defamation lawsuits against us and other major media outlets. Some of his acolytes headed promptly to the courthouse. Representative Devin Nunes, a prolific litigant against the media (MSNBC, McClatchy, CNN, Hearst, and reporter Ryan Lizza), filed two lawsuits against *The Post*. One was dismissed. The other was allowed to proceed, and continued to be litigated as this was being written. The Trump campaign itself sued us in 2020, but that was dismissed in February 2023. Trump-friendly media outlets and personalities also threatened to sue. And Project Veritas, the right-wing sting operation, regularly dispatched its lawyers to send us menacing letters alleging defamation with the implicit threat of litigation.

To me, it all smelled of a loosely coordinated effort to burden us with legal expenses, hefty settlements, or court judgments. We never came across proof of anything like that, but the appetite for litigation certainly matched up neatly with rhetoric dating back to Trump's campaign. "We're going to open up those libel laws. So when *The New York Times* writes a hit piece which is a total disgrace or when *The Washington Post*, which is there for other reasons, writes a hit piece, we can sue them and win money instead of having no chance of winning because they're totally protected," he said in February 2016 at a rally in Fort Worth. "We're going to have people sue you like you've never got sued before." That prediction of his was being borne out.

Trump had a hearty appetite for litigation, even well before he became president. A *USA Today* calculation in 2016 found that in the previous three decades he and his businesses had been involved in at least 3,500 legal actions, 1,900 of them as a plaintiff. "The sheer volume of lawsuits is unprecedented for a presidential nominee," the newspaper noted. "No candidate of a major party has had anything approaching the number of Trump's courtroom entanglements."

And libel cases, as James D. Zirin observed in his 2019 book, *Plaintiff in Chief: A Portrait of Trump in 3,500 Lawsuits*, were "apparently his favorite tort."

Most notoriously, in 2006 he brought a $5 billion lawsuit against former *New York Times* writer Timothy O'Brien over his book *Trump Nation: The Art of Being the Donald*. The book asserted that Trump's personal wealth was a fraction of the many billions of dollars he repeatedly claimed. Trump lost that suit, and it remains an enduring testament to his propensity for serial fabrications. A December 2007 deposition by Trump drew attention to thirty instances when Trump had invented or exaggerated facts related to his wealth and businesses. When interviewed by *Post* reporters during his 2016 presidential campaign, Trump said he "never read" O'Brien's book and expressed no regrets over the lawsuit because he only wanted to hurt O'Brien. "I liked it because I cost him a lot of time and a lot of energy and a lot of money . . . I said: 'Go sue him. It will cost him a lot of money.'" Trump never progressed beyond that bullying mentality and abuse of the court system.

That interview with Trump by *Post* reporters was for their own book, *Trump Revealed*, published in August 2016. As Trump responded to questions about O'Brien, he didn't miss an opportunity to suggest to the authors that they and *The Post* might face similar headaches. "I will be bringing more libel suits—maybe against you folks. I don't want to threaten," he said even as he threatened, "but I find that the press is unbelievably dishonest." He warned again that libel law would be on his agenda if he won the presidency.

In January 2018, Trump was at it once more, openly mulling the prospect of libel suits at his first official Cabinet meeting of the year. "We are going to take a strong look at our country's libel laws, so that when somebody says something that is false and defamatory about someone, that person will have meaningful recourse in our courts," Trump said, calling existing laws a "sham and a disgrace." The catalyst for Trump's remarks that day appeared to be publication of

Michael Wolff's book *Fire and Fury: Inside the Trump White House*, which described an administration awash in intrigue and infighting while stumbling badly on serious governance. Charles Harder, Trump's lawyer, had dashed off an eleven-page letter demanding that publisher Henry Holt (an imprint of Macmillan, which also released this book) stop publication of Wolff's manuscript and issue "a full and complete retraction and apology to my client as to all statements made about him in the book and article that lack competent evidentiary support." Harder said a *New York* magazine excerpt of the book contained falsehoods that "give rise to claims for libel" that could result in "substantial monetary damages and punitive damages." The sole result of his threat was to prompt the publishing house to accelerate the publication date. Condemnation from Trump was a surefire way to boost book sales, and naturally Wolff's book shot to No. 1 on the bestseller list.

Much of Trump's ire was directed at former chief strategist Steve Bannon, whose damning quotes about Trump and his family were attributed directly to him and never disavowed. But also high among Trump's grievances was one he had aired many times before—the use of anonymous sources or, as Trump put it in Wolff's case, "sources that don't exist." Trump's gripes about anonymity weren't based on the rigor of the reporting—or even, for that matter, its veracity. Leaks that reflected poorly on him were condemned as false, the sources nonexistent, even as he pressed for investigations to identify the supposedly nonexistent sources. With his followers' distrust of the media, he had little trouble persuading them that the stories were fabrications by media out to get him and them. Conflating his political self-interest with the public interest, he was prone to labeling the leaks as treasonous.

Anonymous leaking out of government didn't begin with the Trump administration, of course. It has a long tradition in Washington. It's often the only way for journalists to learn and report what is happening behind the scenes. If sources come forward with their

identities, they risk being fired, demoted, sidelined, or even prosecuted. The risks were heightened with a vengeful Trump targeting
the so-called deep state, what he imagined to be influential government officials conspiring against him. The Department of Justice
had announced early in his administration that it would become
even more aggressive in its search for leakers of classified national
security information. And Trump's allies and supporters could be
counted on to make life a nightmare for anyone who crossed him.
Meantime, senior Trump officials leaked regularly, typically as a result of internal rivalries. Trump himself leaked to get news out in
a way that he viewed as helpful, just as he had done as a private
citizen in New York. Washington journalists would much prefer to
have government sources on the record, but anonymity has become
an inextricable feature of Washington reporting. Sources rely on it;
reporters, too. Though Trump administration officials claimed to
be unjust victims of anonymous sourcing, they were skillful practi-
tioners and beneficiaries as well.

Trump's rhetoric and his pressure tactics had a profound impact
on what his supporters understood to be fact. They would take his
word—and his word only—for what was true and what was false.
He was aided in that by right-wing media outlets, Fox News above
all, that amplified his voice while assailing us. But he and his allies
were ineffective in dissuading us from doing our job. No one at
news organizations like *The Post* was deterred by incessant threats
of harm, the uninterrupted prospect of litigation, or the calculatedly
persistent attacks on our integrity and professionalism.

As Trump and the press knocked heads, Americans became ever
more divided in the media they watched or read. Polarization of
news media consumption in the United States had been scored already in 2017 by the Reuters Institute at Oxford University as the
world's worst. Our own readership numbers were striking in terms

of political leanings, although I was not really surprised. By the fall of 2018, the percentage of our digital subscribers who considered themselves somewhat or very conservative was in the single digits, with slightly more than 80 percent "very" or "somewhat" liberal. Even before the 2016 election, our readership among conservatives had not been large, but it was continuing to shrink. The Reuters Institute found that our readership was almost as left-leaning as Fox News's audience was right-leaning. Holding the middle ground were Yahoo! News, ABC News, and CBS News.

What we experienced at *The Post* was typical. Toward the end of 2019, Pew Research Center found that 93 percent of the people whose main source for political and election news was Fox identified as Republican. By contrast, 95 percent of those who listed MSNBC as their main political news source were Democratic. The numbers for *The New York Times* and NPR were similar, 91 percent Democratic for the former and 87 percent for the latter. CNN stood at 79 percent Democratic.

But those who liked *The Post* liked us a lot, and more people every day liked us enough to purchase a subscription. The number of digital subscribers at *The Post* was surging, as it was at *The New York Times*, where overall subscriber numbers were even larger. By the end of 2018, we exceeded 1.5 million digital-only subscribers. In March 2020, we topped two million. Just about all of them said they expected to renew, and satisfaction metrics among subscribers soared to record levels. "In this 'Age of Alternative Facts' I want to support mainstream media," one subscriber told us. "Facts are important right now," said another. "Keep fighting for the truth. Americans like me care!"

Our aim was to get at the facts, no matter the obstacles Trump and his allies put in our way. And a very determined *Post* staff did just that time and again. In January 2018, Josh Dawsey reported that Trump, during a discussion with lawmakers about protecting immigrants from Haiti, El Salvador, and African countries as part of an immigration deal, asked: "Why are we having all these people from shithole countries come here?" In March, reporters Dawsey, Carol Leonnig, and David Nakamura reported that Trump defied cautions from his national security advisors not to congratulate Russian president Putin on winning reelection to another six-year term. "DO NOT CONGRATULATE," warned briefing material that Trump may, or may not, have read. Such capitalized advice should have been unnecessary in the first place. After all, it was anything but a fair election. Prominent opponents were excluded from the ballot, and much of the Russian news media is controlled by the state. "If this story is accurate, that means someone leaked the president's briefing papers," said a senior White House official who, as was common in an administration that condemned anonymous sources, insisted on anonymity.

By early January 2019, national security reporter Greg Miller reported that Trump had gone to "extraordinary lengths" to conceal the content of his conversations with Putin, even to the point of confiscating his interpreter's notes and demanding that no one else be told what was said. As Greg noted, it was "part of a broader pattern by the president of shielding his communications with Putin from public scrutiny and preventing even high-ranking officials in his own administration from fully knowing what he has told one of the United States' main adversaries." Trump later told Fox News host Jeanine Pirro that Greg's story was "ridiculous," yet again calling *The Post* "basically a lobbyist" for Bezos and Amazon. For good measure, he added, "*The Washington Post* is almost as bad, or probably as bad, as *The New York Times*."

Trump would never let go of his smears and name-calling. But millions of ordinary Americans had a greater hold on our attention. They were counting on us to keep at our work. Every day, along with the threats and harassment, came expressions of gratitude in notes and calls and messages left by readers who had just purchased a subscription. Personal encounters were among the most heartening.

Reporter Joe Heim sent me an email about one in September 2018. "I'm on the road in Albuquerque," he wrote. "Was standing in line yesterday to pick up my rental car and started chatting with an older man in front of me. After a few minutes he asked what I did and I told him I was a reporter. He asked who I worked for and I told him *The Washington Post*. He looked at me and didn't say anything for a few seconds, but he had a strange look in his eye. I said, 'You're not gonna punch me, are you?' No, he said. 'I want to fall down on my knees and thank you for what you and your paper are doing.' I told him I'd make sure the boss got the message." Message received.

13

TRUTH AND LIES

In a late May 2018 ceremony at Columbia University, *Washington Post* journalists who often had been at loggerheads throughout our Russia investigation stood side by side to accept the Pulitzer Prize for national reporting, sharing the stage with our *New York Times* archcompetitors as co-winners of that prestigious award. The Pulitzer board credited "deeply sourced, relentlessly reported coverage in the public interest that dramatically furthered the nation's understanding of Russian interference in the 2016 presidential election and its connections to the Trump campaign, the president-elect's transition team, and his eventual administration."

That reporting was conducted over the course of the first year of the Trump presidency, a period in which Special Counsel Robert Mueller launched his investigation of Russia's election intrusion and whether Trump illegally obstructed the federal investigation it touched off. Nearly a year after the Pulitzer Prizes were announced and less than six weeks after he was sworn in, Attorney General William P. Barr released his summary of Mueller's key conclusions. The press, the public, and members of Congress were eager to see the full 448-page report for themselves, but the only word on its contents came via Barr's four-page letter, dated March 24, 2019, to Congress. The entire report, still with major redactions, would not be released for almost another month.

The press had to immediately report what Barr said that day even though we were unable to immediately verify whether his was an entirely faithful account. Barr could not have exploited our handicap more skillfully. In that moment he chose not to be a profile in candor and completeness but rather a master of political spin and selective disclosure.

Barr wrote that the special counsel "did not find that the Trump campaign, or anyone associated with it, conspired or coordinated with the Russian government" in its election interference "despite multiple offers from Russian-affiliated individuals to assist the Trump campaign." And the special counsel "did not draw a conclusion— one way or the other" on whether the president's actions constituted obstruction of justice. Though allowing that Mueller's report said it "does not exonerate" Trump, Barr asserted that it now fell to him to decide whether Trump criminally obstructed justice. And he determined that Trump had not, supplying Trump the vindication he hungered for.

Trump and his allies seized the opportunity gifted to them for attack. Sean Hannity tweeted: "MSNBC CONSPIRACY NETWORK LIARS FAKE NEWS LIARS FAKE NEWS CNN LIARS FAKE NEWS NY TIMES WAPO LIARS." And, hyperventilating as he does, Hannity added, "Starting Monday we will hold every deep state official who abused power accountable. We will hold every fake news media liar member accountable."

The attorney general misled the public about the totality of the Mueller Report. But perhaps worse, we were witnessing Trump and his enablers set a new, lower standard for the public and the press on how to judge a president, or any political leader: As long as behavior wasn't criminal, it was okay. Norms for a clean and fair election could be ignored. The practice and principle of conducting American elections without foreign interference could be abandoned. A presidential candidate who, along with aides, encouraged a rival superpower to help his campaign should escape censure. Illegal computer hacking and the sharing of campaign information with an individual tied to Russian intelligence services deserved nothing but a collective shrug. American politics was being further debased.

The Post was not about to be complicit. Traditionally, voters have set a higher bar than "not criminal" for those we entrust with government power; rightly so. The press, on the public's behalf, should keep its eye on abuse, dishonesty, connivance, and immorality regardless of whether it meets the standards for criminal prosecution. At *The Post*, we had been boosting our investigative firepower for the very purpose of tracking such transgressions.

The scandal isn't what's illegal, an old saying goes, it's what's legal. Trump and his team were a case study. The invitations, public and private, for Russia and WikiLeaks to interfere in the 2016 election and the president's efforts to kill a government investigation were scandalous even if the special counsel didn't pronounce them criminal. By any traditional measure of journalism's mission, that deserved our vigorous investigation. If anything, politicians should be judged on standards that are set high and not, as they might prefer, low.

One standard has always been whether political leaders are being straight with the public they serve. The president and his attorney general weren't. How a special counsel report that said it "does not exonerate" the president on obstruction became twisted into what Trump called "complete and total exoneration" was a stunning bit of legerdemain, so much so that Mueller felt compelled to correct the record. Three days after Barr sent his letter to Congress, Mueller sent Barr a letter of his own complaining that his statement "did not fully capture the context, nature, and substance" of his team's "work and conclusions."

The Post reported in early April that members of Mueller's team were "frustrated with the limited information" that Barr released and complained that "the evidence they gathered on obstruction was alarming and significant." Mueller's team had found ten instances of potential obstruction of justice by Trump. "If we had confidence after a thorough investigation of the facts that the President clearly did not commit obstruction of justice, we would so state," the report said. But Mueller, we learned when his report was later released, wouldn't even consider bringing criminal charges against the president because of Justice Department legal opinions that proscribed them on constitutional grounds. He argued that the Constitution "requires a process other than the criminal justice system"—that is, impeachment by Congress—to "formally accuse a sitting president of wrongdoing." And finally, there was the issue of fairness. In Mueller's estimation, it would have been "unfair" to allege a crime of obstruction when it could not be adjudicated in court. The ball was in Congress's hands if it cared to bring its own charges through impeachment. Congress took a pass.

Many television and newspaper commentators had speculated endlessly—and expectantly—that Mueller's prosecutors would find criminal "collusion." They had gotten out way over their skis. The law doesn't address "collusion," and criminal "conspiracy" is tightly defined in federal law. The sharp criticism pundits received when Mueller's conclusions became public was predictable and often warranted. But in their news reporting on the Russia investigation, *The Washington Post* and *The New York Times*—both of which led in breaking major stories—had unearthed the central facts: unprecedented Russian intervention to benefit Trump through computer hacking and manipulation of social media; numerous contacts between Russians offering help and Trump campaign officials expressing interest and encouragement; repeated efforts by Trump to quash any federal investigation; and chronic lying by Trump aides and Trump himself. The Mueller Report—and an especially damning 2020 report by the Senate Intelligence Committee led by members of Trump's own Republican Party—confirmed all of that.

Trump and his allies accused the FBI, the special counsel, and the press of pursuing investigations out of political animosity. The Mueller Report itself, however, put the lie to insinuations about the special counsel's own motives. With its exceptional caution, strict interpretation of the law, and scrupulous attention to fairness, it was miles from a hit job. And any fair reading of the Mueller Report shows there was ample justification for the press and government agencies to investigate. It would have been negligent not to.

The Post's investigation of Trump and Russia was in the cause of clean elections and honest government. Mueller said the same about his own probe. "Russia's actions were a threat to America's democracy," Mueller wrote in an unusual July 2020 op-ed for *The Washington Post*. "Russian efforts to interfere in our political system, and the essential question of whether those efforts involved the Trump campaign, required investigation."

The Mueller team delivered thirty-seven indictments, seven guilty pleas, and fourteen criminal referrals to the Justice Department for a variety of offenses. On the question of obstruction of justice, more than a thousand former federal prosecutors who served under both Republican and Democratic presidents signed a letter declaring that, if there weren't a Justice Department policy against indicting a sitting president, Trump would have faced multiple felony charges. This was a direct rebuke to Barr's own pronouncement.

The Russia investigation also brought into sharp relief the Trump team's endemic mendacity. When embarrassing evidence was discovered, aides defaulted to deceit. One after another, they lied under oath, rightfully earning themselves convictions and prison time: Michael Cohen, Trump's longtime lawyer, for making false statements to Congress, among other offenses; Michael Flynn, the onetime Trump national security advisor who admitted to lying to the FBI about his discussions with the Russian ambassador and in his federal filings about lobbying on behalf of the Turkish government throughout the 2016 presidential campaign; Trump confidant Roger Stone, seen as a campaign conduit to WikiLeaks, who was found guilty on seven counts, five for lying to Congress; George Papadopoulos, the nominal Trump foreign policy adviser who pleaded guilty to lying to the FBI about his interactions with Russian nationals; Trump campaign official Rick Gates, who pleaded guilty to lying to federal prosecutors.

And then there was Paul Manafort, the former Trump campaign chairman who fell into a category all his own. He lied every which way—and even encouraged witnesses to lie. In their sentencing memorandum for a federal judge in Washington, D.C., prosecutors noted that he lied for "garden-variety crimes such as tax fraud, money laundering, obstruction of justice, and bank fraud," and on laws that covered foreign lobbying. He lied "to tax preparers, bookkeepers, banks, the Treasury Department, the Department of Justice National Security Division, the FBI, the Special Counsel's Office, the grand jury, his own legal counsel, Members of Congress, and members of the executive branch of the United States government." He lied about sharing Trump campaign polling data with a Russian associate whom the FBI linked to Russian intelligence. He lied while leading Trump's campaign and then later while awaiting trial and even after pleading guilty. In sentencing him to seven and a half years in prison for conspiracy and fraud, U.S. District Judge Amy Berman Jackson excoriated his endless "lying to the American people and the American Congress . . . It is hard to overstate the number of lies and amount of money involved."

This was the sort of man who won effusive praise as "brave" from Trump because, as the president put it, he "refused to 'break'—make up stories to get a 'deal.'" Manafort was pardoned by Trump, as was a lawyer who worked with him. So were Stone, Flynn, and Papadopoulos.

The liar in chief was Trump himself. Many of his own lies—and the lies made on his behalf and with his assent—had previously been documented in the press or elsewhere, but the special counsel confirmed them, adding detail. Throughout his campaign, Trump denied that he had any business interests in Russia. "I have nothing to do with Russia," he said in July 2016. "I don't deal there," he reiterated as late as October 2016. But the evidence showed he was actively pursuing a deal for a Trump Tower in Moscow until June 2016—five months before the presidential election and as he was about to secure the GOP nomination. A letter of intent for a Trump Tower Moscow was signed on October 28, 2015, the day that Republican primary candidates gathered for their third debate. Trump knew full well that his attorney Michael Cohen was lying when he testified in 2017 before Congress that negotiations for the project had ended in January 2016.

Trump's lawyer had flatly denied reports that he was involved in drafting a statement by son Donald Jr. about a meeting at the Trump Tower in New York with Russians who claimed to have dirt on Hillary Clinton. The White House later admitted that Trump was involved in composing the statement. The special counsel documented how Trump had deleted a line in the statement that acknowledged the true reason that Donald Jr. agreed to meet with the Russians.

Trump denied ordering White House counsel Donald McGahn to demand that the Justice Department fire special counsel Mueller, calling it "fake news." He even insisted that McGahn publicly repudiate the report. McGahn rebuffed Trump. The reports, after all, were true: Trump had "called McGahn at home and directed him to call the acting attorney general and say that the special counsel had conflicts of interest and must be removed," according to the Mueller Report. McGahn refused to press for the firing of Mueller.

The special counsel also found that the White House's explanation for firing James Comey as FBI director was untrue. The initial explanation, absurd on its face, was that he had mishandled the investigation of Hillary Clinton's use of a private email server. But Mueller's team found "substantial evidence" that the true reason was "Comey's unwillingness to publicly state that the president was not personally under investigation, despite the president's repeated requests that Comey make such an announcement."

Once the full Mueller Report was made public on April 18, 2019, it became clear that the document didn't qualify as "complete and total exoneration," as Trump had been crowing for weeks. So Trump offered an assessment of the report that differed radically from what he had proclaimed after Barr gave his initial summary. Now, big portions were "total bullshit." The bullshit, of course, was how Trump had falsely portrayed the report from the start.

One of the enduring questions is why, if there really was no conspiracy as the law defines it, Trump and his people lied so often. "They just lied about everything all the time," The Post's Roz Helderman told me. "Lying was easier than acknowledging hard truths." All of that lying signaled they had something to hide—and it was more than ample reason for news organizations like The Post to press harder for the truth.

The Mueller Report did dispute some press reports. Among the most notable was BuzzFeed's explosive report on January 17, 2019, that Trump had "directed" Michael Cohen to lie in his congressional testimony. The story was so sensational that it prompted some members of Congress to call for Trump's impeachment on the grounds that he was suborning perjury. Other news outlets, including The Post, scrambled to match BuzzFeed's account but were unable to verify it. A Mueller spokesman then took the unusual step of making a public statement, declaring unequivocally that the report was "not accurate."

BuzzFeed editor Ben Smith responded that "we stand by our reporting and the sources who informed it." But release of the Mueller Report didn't do BuzzFeed any favors. "The evidence available to us does not establish that the President directed or aided Cohen's false testimony," Mueller's prosecutors wrote. Smith called me to complain in mid-January when *The Post*'s media reporter, Paul Farhi, focused on the questionable accuracy of his outlet's report under a headline that read, "*BuzzFeed*'s Stumble Is Highest-Profile Misstep at a Time When Press Is Under Greatest Scrutiny." Smith argued that Trump talks like a mob boss, using coded language that left Cohen with no doubt about what the president wanted him to do. No doubt Trump speaks that way. But "directing" someone to lie in testimony means something different—and I told Smith so. (Cohen subsequently testified in a closed-door congressional hearing that Trump's personal counsel, Jay Sekulow, urged him to "stay on message" and not contradict the president, an assertion that Sekulow's own attorneys rejected.)

The Post itself had a regrettable blunder, misidentifying a central source for Christopher Steele's Russia reports as a Belarussian American businessman. In mid-November 2021, *The Post* corrected its stories, changed a headline, removed a related video, and posted an editor's note acknowledging the error.

Despite some missteps, the vast bulk of the reporting by news outlets about the issues dealt with in the Mueller Report was verified. The Poynter Institute, an independent organization focused on media training, performance, and standards, noted the remarkable amount of news reporting—heavily based on anonymous sources—that was confirmed by Mueller's team. "Mueller Proves 'Fake News' to Be True," it observed in a headline. One story after the next was validated in the Mueller Report, often cited in its footnotes. Among them were *The Post*'s story on June 14, 2017, that revealed for the first time that Trump himself was under investigation by the special counsel for obstruction of justice and *The Times*' story on January 25, 2018, about Trump's demand that Mueller be fired and his White House counsel's refusal to follow up.

The supposed "fake" anonymous sources in press reports were real and, with the rarest exception, reliable. While Trump claimed overall victory in the Mueller Report, the media, despite all the attacks against us by Trump and his allies, could point to numerous successes of its own. A huge volume of difficult reporting had proved entirely accurate. The journalism wasn't universally perfect, but it had been damn good. Our critics clamored for an apology. As the person who oversaw *The Post*'s news department, I saw no reason to offer one.

There were no lessons from the Russia investigation for Donald Trump, except for those he felt others should learn from the supposed offense of investigating him in the first place. The notion of impropriety, as opposed to illegality, didn't seem to enter into his thinking. He had busted norms as a presidential candidate. He would keep doing so as president.

On June 12, 2019, less than two months after release of the Mueller Report, Trump sat for an interview with ABC News' George Stephanopoulos, declaring that he would happily invite a foreign government to give him dirt on an opponent. Dismissing the idea that such assistance might constitute election interference and should be reported to the FBI, he unashamedly said, "I think I'd take it." Trump saw nothing wrong with that. "I think you might want to listen, there isn't anything wrong with listening," he went on. "If somebody called from a country, Norway, [and said] 'we have information on your opponent'—oh, I think I'd want to hear it."

It's a short step from inviting foreign countries' help against your opponent to insisting on it. That summer, we learned, Trump took the extra step. Not with his ludicrously implausible hypothetical, Norway; rather, with Ukraine. Again, he saw nothing amiss. Trump was sticking with his low standard for presidential conduct: If it wasn't criminal, it was acceptable. The power of the office was to be used and abused at will as long as he could escape prosecution.

With good reason, the press and Congress would soon launch

fresh investigations of the president, having picked up the early odor of a tawdry scandal that involved Trump pressuring a foreign leader for his own political gain. Trump would come to call his dealings with Ukraine "perfect." The more we discovered, the more it became evident that they were anything but.

In early May 2019, the president's personal lawyer, Rudy Giuliani, was openly acknowledging to *The New York Times* that he would be traveling to Ukraine to get its newly elected president, Volodymyr Zelensky, to launch investigations that could be "very, very helpful" to Trump. One investigation he was seeking involved what Trump partisans alleged was Ukrainian officials' purported interference in the 2016 election to help Hillary Clinton. The other was into whether Joe Biden, as vice president, interfered to block a Ukrainian prosecutor's probe into an energy company called Burisma, where his son Hunter sat on the board. Joe Biden was the prospective Democratic opponent Trump feared most.

As *The Times* noted, Giuliani's plans created "the remarkable scene of a lawyer for the president of the United States pressing a foreign government to pursue investigations that Mr. Trump's allies hope could help him in his reelection campaign. And it comes after Mr. Trump spent more than half of his term facing questions about whether his 2016 campaign conspired with a foreign power." In defending the trip, Giuliani said, "There's nothing illegal about it." Nodding to the issue of ethics only to dismiss it, he added, "Somebody could say it's improper." Indeed, somebody could have, should have, and did. Giuliani was working as Trump's lawyer, not as a representative of the U.S. government.

Facing furious criticism for seeking foreign assistance with Trump's reelection, Giuliani canceled plans for a trip to Ukraine, but his pressure campaign for investigations continued. On August 21, *The Times* reported that Giuliani had pushed for the investigations with a top aide to Zelensky, both in a phone call and during an in-person meeting in Madrid.

Then *Politico* reported that Trump was holding up $250 million in military aid to Ukraine that Congress had approved as essential for confronting aggression by Russia, which had invaded and annexed Ukraine's southern peninsula of Crimea in 2014 and was supporting separatist rebels in the east. A *Washington Post* editorial in early September declared that Trump was "attempting to force Mr. Zelensky to intervene in the 2020 U.S. presidential election by launching an investigation of the leading Democratic candidate" and "using U.S. military aid the country desperately needs in an attempt to extort it."

As congressional committees began to investigate what Trump and Giuliani were up to, they received a letter from Michael Atkinson, inspector general for the intelligence community. A whistleblower had filed a complaint with him, he wrote, and in Atkinson's assessment it qualified as credible and a matter of "urgent concern"—defined as a "serious or flagrant problem, abuse or violation of the law or Executive Order" that involves classified information, but "does not include differences of opinion concerning public policy matters."

As required by law, Atkinson informed the congressional intelligence committees of the complaint. The inspector general also wrote that he had forwarded the complaint to the acting director of national intelligence, Joseph Maguire. But, he added, Maguire was declining to provide congressional intelligence committees with a copy of the complaint on the grounds that it was not, in fact, a matter of "urgent concern." The inspector general said that view did not "appear to be consistent with past practice." On September 13, Representative Adam Schiff, chair of the House Intelligence Committee, then accused Maguire of "unlawfully" withholding the complaint and demanded with a subpoena that he turn it over.

On September 18, 2019, a trio of *Post* national security reporters published a story that began to flesh out the contents of the whistle-blower complaint. The story assembled by Ellen Nakashima, Greg Miller, and Shane Harris cited anonymous sources in reporting that the complaint involved "President Trump's communications with a foreign leader." The story said that "Trump's interaction with the foreign leader included a 'promise' that was regarded as so troubling that it prompted an official in the U.S. intelligence community to file a formal whistleblower complaint." The identity of the foreign leader wasn't then known, nor was the nature of the promise, though the incident was said to revolve around a phone call. Trump's "direct involvement in the matter," *The Post* reporters wrote, raised "new questions about the president's handling of sensitive information and may further strain his relationship with U.S. spy agencies."

That, as it turned out, undersold the implications. Step by careful step, news organizations were excavating key components of another scandal that would consume Trump's presidency and this time lead to impeachment, making him only the third president in American history to be formally accused by the House of Representatives of high crimes and misdemeanors. *The Post* reported on September 19 that the whistleblower complaint involved Ukraine. *The Wall Street Journal* reported on September 20 that Trump had pressured Zelensky to investigate Biden's son and to work with Giuliani on the probe. *The Washington Post* and *New York Times* then reported that the July 25 call between the two leaders was an essential element of the whistleblower complaint.

As *The Post* story aptly noted, the call was "the clearest indication to date that Trump sought to use the influence of his office to prod the leader of a country seeking American financial and diplomatic support to provide material that could aid the president's reelection. After spending much of his presidency fending off allegations that he welcomed 2016 campaign help from Russia, Trump now stands accused of soliciting political ammunition from a country next door to Russia."

The Times noted that there were "echoes of the dominant scandal of the first years of Mr. Trump's administration: whether his campaign sought help from Russia to benefit him in 2016. Ultimately, the special counsel found that although 'insufficient evidence' existed to determine that Mr. Trump or his advisers engaged in a criminal conspiracy with the Russians, his campaign welcomed Moscow's election sabotage and expected to benefit from it." Now Trump was demanding another country's help to sabotage a possible opponent's campaign and benefit his own. It was a variation on an old and sinister theme.

When questioned by the media about the whistleblower complaint and what precisely he had told Zelensky, Trump wouldn't say whether he had brought up investigating Biden's son. "It doesn't matter what I discussed," he said. Of course it mattered. But for Trump, the issue, as always, was coverage by the press: "It's another media disaster," he said, adding: "I think this is one of the worst weeks in the history of the fake news media . . . You're a joke." He labeled the whistleblower a "partisan person" engaged in a "political hack job" despite not then knowing the individual's identity, described his conversations with world leaders as "always appropriate," and overall characterized the phone call with Zelensky a "beautiful conversation."

After first resisting disclosure, the administration ultimately turned over to Congress a rough transcript of a key phone call and the whistleblower's memo. "I would like you to do us a favor because our country has been through a lot and Ukraine knows a lot about it," Trump told Zelensky, according to the transcript. Trump asked Zelensky to find a Democratic National Committee computer server that purportedly was hidden in Ukraine. (No such server exists.) And then he urged Zelensky to investigate the Bidens. And he suggested that Ukrainian authorities work on the investigations in tandem with Attorney General Barr and Giuliani, his private lawyer.

After the whistleblower complaint was finally turned over to

Congress, it was made public. It contributed mightily to the suspicion that government officials were covering up what they knew to be wrongdoing by the president. The whistleblower reported that officials had veered from normal procedure to limit access to the written record of Trump's phone call with Zelensky. "In the days following the phone call, I learned from multiple U.S. officials that senior White House officials had intervened to 'lock down' all records of the phone call, especially the word-for-word transcript of the call that was produced—as is customary—by the White House Situation Room. This set of actions underscored to me that White House officials understood the gravity of what had transpired in the call," the whistleblower wrote.

"White House officials told me they were directed by White House lawyers to remove the electronic transcript from the computer system in which such transcripts are typically stored for coordination, finalization, and distribution to Cabinet-level officials. Instead, the transcript was loaded into a separate electronic system that is otherwise used to store and handle classified information of an especially sensitive nature. One White House official described this act as an abuse of this electronic system because the call did not contain anything remotely sensitive from a national security perspective."

By mid-October, White House chief of staff Mick Mulvaney effectively admitted a quid pro quo that the administration had been denying—that unless there was an investigation of the Bidens by Ukraine, there would be no military funds. "Get over it. There's going to be political influence in foreign policy," he said, although five hours later he argued that the media "decided to misconstrue" his remarks.

In November, *The Post* disclosed that Trump was leaning on Attorney General Barr to hold a news conference declaring that he had broken no laws in his call with Ukraine's President Zelensky—and that Barr had declined. Trump, as usual, denied the truth. And once again, he condemned our staffers by name—in this instance, Matt Zapotosky, Josh Dawsey, and Carol Leonnig—slamming them as "three lowlife reporters." His clear purpose was to subject them to abuse by his followers. When Trump incited attacks on individual journalists, a sharp response was called for. Despite Trump's "repugnant attempt to intimidate and harass *The Post* and its staff," I said, "we will continue to do the work that democracy demands of a free and independent press." Our reporters' story was confirmed by *The New York Times* and ABC News.

After contentious hearings, the House voted to impeach Trump on charges that he abused his office and obstructed Congress. The December 18 vote split almost precisely along party lines: 230 to 197 on the abuse charge, 229 to 198 on obstruction. When the Senate took up the trial, the ultimate outcome was foreordained. Sixty-seven votes of senators present were required to convict Trump, but Democrats held only 47 seats. The vote on February 5, 2020, was 52 to 48 for acquittal on abuse of power, with only one Republican, Senator Mitt Romney of Utah, voting to convict the president. Romney voted against the obstruction charge, making that vote 53 to 47 for acquittal. In his remarks, the 2012 GOP nominee for president stated the facts and central issue as clearly and succinctly as anyone: "The President asked a foreign government to investigate his political rival. The President withheld vital military funds from that government to press it to do so. The President delayed funds for an American ally at war with Russian invaders. The President's purpose was personal and political . . . Corrupting an election to keep oneself in office is perhaps the most abusive and destructive violation of one's oath of office that I can imagine."

But this was no longer the Republican Party once led by Romney as its presidential nominee. Senator Lamar Alexander of Tennessee wanly deemed Trump's behavior "inappropriate" but undeserving of impeachment. Senator Susan Collins of Maine summoned similarly anemic vocabulary: Trump's behavior was "improper" and "wrong" but not grave enough for a conviction. Romney's niece, Ronna Romney McDaniel, the Republican National Committee chairwoman, outlined the position of all but a few Republicans: Trump did "nothing wrong."

What qualifies as conduct deserving of impeachment and removal from office? What constitutes a high crime or misdemeanor? During Trump's trial in the Senate, members were told by one of Trump's lawyers, Harvard Law School's Alan Dershowitz, that impeachment required commission of a crime. Many constitutional scholars vehemently disputed that. That academic debate ultimately yields to realpolitik: Members of Congress can set the standard for impeachment—and conviction—wherever they wish. Political self-interest carries greater weight than principle.

We in the press, however, are still obliged to try to distinguish right from wrong. In my own view, and in every newsroom where I've worked for more than four decades, abuse of power is a clear and grievous wrong—whether by a president or anyone else, whether prosecutable or not, whether impeachable or not. Our obligation was to investigate whether Trump had abused his power for personal gain. He had. The evidence was overwhelming.

The day after his acquittal, Trump appeared in the East Room in his most exultant and vengeful incarnation. "This is what the end result is," he said, defiantly holding up a front page of *The Washington Post* with the banner headline "Trump Acquitted." The audience stood to cheer as he waved the paper from side to side for twenty-five seconds. Leaning forward to hand his copy to the first lady, he said, "We can take that home, honey. Maybe we'll frame it. It's the only good headline I've ever had in *The Washington Post*."

So much of what transpired during the Ukraine chapter of Trump's presidency foreshadowed what we would see from him in the fateful year that followed: a president who was consumed with baseless conspiracy theories (Biden had quashed a Ukraine investigation to protect his son, Ukraine had interfered in the 2016 election to hurt Trump, a DNC computer server was secretly stashed away somewhere in that country); who conflated the nation's interests with his own; who could command unwavering allegiance among supporters and allies despite compelling evidence against him; and who aggressively asserted executive privilege to deny Congress access to officials with firsthand knowledge of his suspect behavior.

Trump also spared nothing in his efforts to crush those who dared cross him, even if they testified under subpoena and under oath and followed all proper procedure. At one point, Trump theorized that if he had done anything wrong, the whistleblower would not have been the only one to file a formal complaint about his phone call with Zelensky: "Strange that with so many other people hearing or knowing of the perfectly fine and respectful conversation, that they would not have also come forward. Do you know the reason why they did not? Because there was nothing said wrong, it was pitch perfect!" In a matter of months, it would become obvious why others might not come forward, and it wasn't because they thought Trump's conduct was perfect.

The entire universe of Trump allies endeavored to have the whistleblower's identity revealed—widely circulating a name—with the spiteful aim of subjecting that individual to fierce harassment and intimidation or worse. So menacing was their conduct that the whistleblower's lawyer sent a cease-and-desist letter to the White House: "Let me be clear: Should any harm befall any suspected named whistleblower or their family, the blame will rest squarely with your client," he wrote. Months after the impeachment trial, Trump continued with his attacks on the whistleblower, suggesting that "somebody ought to sue his ass off."

Others who ultimately went public with their concerns, as they responded to congressional subpoenas and provided sworn testimony, became targets of relentless attack and mockery. Trump made certain they lost their jobs. The same fate befell those who raised red flags through regular channels about Trump's actions and behavior or whose congressional testimony contradicted Trump's version of events.

Lieutenant Colonel Alexander Vindman of the National Security Council, a central witness implicating Trump during the impeachment hearings, was fired after having endured condemnation from the White House and deceitful insinuations by Trump allies that he might be a double agent. Vindman's twin brother, Yevgeny, an NSC staffer who had raised protests internally about Trump's phone call with Zelensky, was fired, too. Gordon Sondland—the hotelier, Trump donor, ambassador to the European Union, and emissary of sorts to Ukraine—was fired. He admitted in congressional testimony that there had been an explicit quid pro quo conditioning a Zelensky visit to the White House on a Ukrainian investigation of Biden. The Vindmans and Sondland were all dismissed within two days of Trump's acquittal. Just before their ousters, White House press secretary Stephanie Grisham had suggested on Fox News that "people should pay" for what Trump went through.

The acting Pentagon comptroller, Elaine McCusker, had her promotion rescinded, evidently for having merely questioned whether Ukraine aid could be legally withheld. She later resigned. The intelligence community's inspector general, Michael Atkinson, was fired, leaving with a plea for whistleblowers to "use authorized channels to bravely speak up—there is no disgrace for doing so."

If there remains any doubt as to why so many government officials require anonymity when they speak with the press and why we allow it when necessary, this chapter in American history makes plain the reasons: If officials speak openly—or do nothing more than fulfill their civic duty in responding to congressional subpoenas— the most powerful man in the world and his allies can make their lives pure misery, impugning their character while jeopardizing their livelihoods and even their physical safety. "*The Washington Post* is constantly quoting 'anonymous sources' that do not exist," Trump had said in 2018 in one of his familiar lines of attack. "Rarely do they use the name of anyone because there is no one to give them the kind of negative quote that they are looking for." The Ukraine episode made evident that real people with incriminating information existed in substantial numbers. If they went public, they risked unemployment and threats to their safety. If they chose anonymity, as the whistleblower did in filing a complaint through an official channel, Trump and his allies would aim to expose them and have them publicly and savagely denounced.

Throughout the months leading to impeachment, Trump embarked on a fresh round of vilification of the press. It had to be a challenge for the president to take his vitriol beyond previous extremes, but Trump was up to it. In September, he condemned the "animals in the press" as "some of the worst human beings you'll ever meet." On October 2, in an East Room news conference with the president of Finland, we were "corrupt people," of course. "If the press were straight and honest and forthright and tough, we would be a far greater nation," he said. "Go write some phony stories," he hectored reporters.

He also threatened on that occasion to file lawsuits against opponents while accusing Democrats generally of "bullshit" and Representative Schiff specifically of "treason." Trump assailed Schiff for criticizing Secretary of State Mike Pompeo. "You know, there's an expression: He couldn't carry his 'blank' strap. I won't say it, because they'll say it was so terrible to say. But that guy couldn't carry his 'blank' strap." Trump freely said "bullshit" but couldn't bring himself to say "jockstrap." His performance was one for the ages.

As *The Guardian*'s David Smith observed, "Impeachment, it seems, has got under Trump's skin like nothing else. Over the past week his tone has become more frantic, frenzied and apocalyptic." For forty minutes, as *The Washington Post*'s White House reporter Toluse Olorunnipa wrote, Trump "played host to a roller coaster display of the grievances, victimhood, falsehoods and braggadocio."

#TrumpMeltdown trended on Twitter. George Conway, the prominent lawyer who was both fierce Trump critic and husband to Trump aide Kellyanne Conway, tweeted, "So *NOW* can we *FINALLY* have a national conversation about the psychological condition of the President of the United States?"

In July 2019, around the time that Trump made his "perfect" call to Ukrainian president Zelensky, I received an unusual email from a former high-level editor of *The Washington Post* almost pleading with me to order up a story on whether the president was mentally ill. "I understand there isn't much respectable journalistic precedent for exploring a president's mental health," he wrote. "We tiptoed toward the issue with Nixon, but nervously and gingerly. But there is also no precedent for a president like this one." After Trump's bizarre news conference in October with the president of Finland, he pressed me again, "because I think there is an excellent chance that Trump's fate and his place in history will be defined by his mental condition, and not the series of scandals that the *WP* covers so well."

The second request was inspired by a long, powerfully argued essay crafted by George Conway in *The Atlantic* that cast Trump as "unfit for office" both because he was probably mentally disturbed and because he had repeatedly violated the public trust. "You don't need to be a weatherman to know which way the wind blows," Conway wrote, "and you don't need to be a mental-health professional to see that something's very seriously off with Trump—particularly after nearly three years of watching his erratic and abnormal behavior in the White House. Questions about Trump's psychological stability have mounted throughout his presidency. But those questions have been coming even more frequently amid a recent escalation in Trump's bizarre behavior, as the pressures of his upcoming reelection campaign, a possibly deteriorating economy, and now a full-blown

impeachment inquiry have mounted. And the questioners have included those who have worked most closely with him."

With Conway's piece, the former senior editor of *The Post* was
reiterating that I should abandon what he called the "final taboo" in
covering presidents.

As early as January 6, 2018, Trump felt compelled to defend his
psychological fitness, pronouncing himself a "very stable genius." He
did it in a tweetstorm, reacting to the just-released book by Michael
Wolff, *Fire and Fury*, that cast doubt on the president's mental stability. It was not a new subject. Throughout his presidential campaign
and as he grew increasingly agitated over the Russia investigation,
questions percolated about whether Trump's strange conduct could
be explained as a psychological disorder. As Trump's behavior turned
more erratic—aberrant, really—during the impeachment process in
2019, worries gained fresh traction. Trump once again defended his
mental condition.

The more Trump insisted that he was a "very stable genius,"
the less stable he appeared. Some *Post* staffers argued for tackling
head-on whether Trump was mentally ill. For more than two years,
this had been a delicate and somewhat contentious subject within
our newsroom. I had been resistant. With aggressive reporting, we
could inform the public of Trump's abnormal behavior, but in my
view we were ill-equipped to penetrate the mind that was behind it
all. Although psychiatrists had come forward with their own damning assessments, they had not personally examined Trump. I felt they
were in no position to diagnose him either. Giving great weight to
their opinions struck me as imprudent. Moreover, their principal professional organization—the American Psychiatric Association, with
37,000 members—considered assessments from afar to be a violation
of a core ethics principle, a position they restated in October 2017.

When Trump lashed out in January 2018 at Wolff and others
who openly questioned his mental faculties, *The Post* stayed carefully

within conventional journalistic boundaries by explaining the origins of those concerns. Trump's rage, after all, only invited greater attention to the subject. *The Post*'s story on Trump's outburst noted that it had "served to elevate the question of Trump's fitness for office that some in Washington have privately—and some publicly—wondered about since before he took office." Concerns deepened, the story noted, when Trump engaged in a fiery verbal duel with North Korean leader Kim Jong Un, at one point boasting of a "much bigger & more powerful" nuclear button.

Politico reported that January that a Yale University psychiatry professor had met the previous month with more than a dozen members of Congress about her worries over Trump's mental fitness. "He's going to unravel, and we are seeing the signs," Dr. Bandy X. Lee was reported as saying. She cited "his going back to conspiracy theories, denying things he has admitted before, his being drawn to violent videos." Lee told *Politico* that "the rush of tweeting is an indication of his falling apart under stress. Trump is going to get worse and will become uncontainable with the pressures of the presidency."

Lee had edited a book, first published in the fall of 2017, titled *The Dangerous Case of Donald Trump: 27 Psychiatrists and Mental Health Experts Assess a President.* The specialists variously judged Trump as exhibiting signs of "sociopathy," "malignant narcissism," "extreme present hedonism," and other illnesses. *The Post*'s review of the book on the front page of its Outlook section included an illustration showing Trump in a straitjacket and an Oval Office of padded walls. This earned me an email of sharp, and reasonable, criticism from a former top-level *Post* executive for its disrespectful, over-the-top image of the president, and complaints from some readers for its stereotypical, insensitive portrayal of the mentally ill.

By then, some members of Congress were already poring over the Constitution's Twenty-Fifth Amendment, ratified in 1967, which established procedures for removing a president considered "unable to discharge the powers and duties of his office." The debate over whether removal was called for—and whether the amendment was even applicable—was picking up steam.

Some psychiatrists also had started to rebel against the American Psychiatric Association's "Goldwater Rule" that proclaimed it unethical for members of the profession to diagnose a public figure without a personal evaluation and permission to release the findings. The rule was established after a magazine surveyed psychiatrists on their views of Republican nominee Barry Goldwater during his 1964 presidential campaign. The separate and smaller American Psychoanalytic Association told its thirty-five hundred members in the summer of 2017 that they could ignore the rule.

In deciding whether we should launch a full-scale evaluation of Trump's mental state, however, I deferred to the dominant, long-standing ethical standards of the psychiatric profession. I was especially attentive to the view of Dr. Allen Frances, a psychiatrist who, in 1978, had helped determine the criteria for narcissistic personality disorder for the profession's bible, the *Diagnostic and Statistical Manual for Mental Disorders*. Frances wrote on the *Stat* medical news site that "the three most frequent armchair diagnoses made for Trump—narcissistic personality disorder, delusional disorder and dementia—are all badly misinformed." While he deemed Trump an "undisputed poster boy for narcissism," he added, "lots of people are extremely narcissistic without being mentally ill . . . To qualify for narcissistic personality disorder, an individual's selfish, unempathetic preening must be accompanied by significant distress or impairment. Trump certainly causes severe distress and impairment in others, but his narcissism doesn't seem to affect him that way." And he concluded: "I believe that Trump is a mirror of the American soul, a surface symptom of our deeper societal disease. He may not be crazy, but we certainly were for electing him."

I was sticking to my position that we should stay away from stories that allowed speculation on what was going on in Trump's head. "I'm comfortable with pushing as hard as we can to find out what he does and how he behaves and not beating around the bush about what we learn," I responded to the former *Post* editor who was urging us to aggressively weigh in on Trump's mental state. There was plenty about Trump's behavior we could document with traditional reporting. What we learned, and published, became ever more unnerving. Armed with that knowledge, ordinary voters could decide for themselves whether Trump was mentally fit to continue in the White House. After the impeachment trial, the election was less than ten months away.

14

SCANDALS

Democrats and Republicans gathered on January 25, 2020, at the Capital Hilton, just three blocks north of Trump's White House residence, for the annual black-tie party of the invite-only Alfalfa Club. The club, founded in 1913, is arguably Washington's most exclusive, though with no genuine purpose other than holding its yearly reception and dinner. Members include senators, military commanders, corporate heavyweights, diplomats, and Supreme Court justices; also, my superiors at the time, *Washington Post* publisher Fred Ryan and owner Jeff Bezos.

Not even an acrimonious impeachment trial, with the fate of the president and the country in play, could deter political and business elites from those festivities. At least a show of merriment continued deep into the night at an after-party. The setting for the latter was the 27,000-square-foot property in Washington's Kalorama neighborhood that Bezos had acquired three years earlier for $23 million. By 2020 Bezos had spent another fortune restoring the former Textile Museum, which incorporated two historic mansions. Renovation plans reviewed by *Washingtonian* magazine showed that it would have "191 doors (many either custom mahogany or bronze), 25 bathrooms, 11 bedrooms, five living rooms/lounges, five staircases, three kitchens, two libraries/studies, two workout rooms, two elevators—and a huge ballroom."

The guest list that evening, to judge from press accounts, leaned toward top-tier executives and White House officials whose boss had endlessly demonized their host. Among them were Ivanka Trump and Jared Kushner, Kellyanne Conway, Mitt Romney and guest Ben Stiller, former George W. Bush chief of staff Josh Bolten, Microsoft founder Bill Gates, JP Morgan Chase CEO Jamie Dimon, Goldman Sachs CEO David Solomon, former defense secretary Jim Mattis, Transportation Secretary Elaine Chao, Carlyle Group founder David Rubenstein, Norah O'Donnell of CBS, and Jonathan Karl of ABC. "I can't imagine why most voters are deeply cynical about politics and think all the fighting is just a game," tweeted Jon Favreau, former Obama speechwriter and liberal podcaster, upon seeing a guest list published by *Politico*.

The extravagant after-party came in the middle of a hellish stretch for Bezos himself. His private life, normally guarded from public curiosity, had spilled into view in the most sensational, embarrassing manner imaginable. President Trump, meanwhile, was laboring harder than ever to torment Amazon, with a motive that was no secret: vengeance for coverage by *The Washington Post*, or what he liked to call "The Amazon Post."

A year earlier, on January 9, 2019, Bezos and his wife, MacKenzie, announced that they were getting divorced after a period of trial separation. "We feel incredibly lucky to have found each other and deeply grateful for every one of the years we have been married to each other," declared a joint statement tweeted by Bezos. A Washington divorce lawyer consulted by *The Post* said its amicable tone signaled a determination to avoid "public spectacle." But the spectacle arrived in a hurry.

One day after the divorce disclosure, the *National Enquirer* delivered to supermarket racks and posted online what it called the "biggest investigation in *Enquirer* history"—disclosing that Bezos, fifty-four, had been involved in a long-running extramarital relationship with Lauren Sánchez, forty-nine, a former entertainment reporter and news anchor whose husband was a prominent talent agent. The *Enquirer* reported that Bezos had been sending Sánchez steamy messages—and "X-rated selfies" including a "d*ck pic" that was "too explicit to describe in detail"—as far back as April 2018.

Trump, though on his third marriage and not known for marital fidelity, wasn't one to miss an opportunity for mockery. He had first sarcastically wished Bezos "luck" on his divorce, saying, "It's going to be a beauty." Then, riffing on the latest in the *Enquirer's* series of online posts, Trump on January 13 resorted to his signature infantilism. "So sorry to hear the news about Jeff Bozo being taken down by a competitor whose reporting, I understand, is far more accurate than the reporting in his lobbyist newspaper, the Amazon Washington Post," Trump gloated on Twitter. It was as if a third grader were in the White House. "Hopefully the paper will soon be placed in better & more responsible hands!"

Bezos had said from the day he first met with *Post* employees that we were free to cover him as we would any other executive. The year 2019 presented the biggest test to date of whether he would honor that pledge. He did. But the conundrum for us now was that *The Post* didn't customarily investigate, or even dwell on, executives' private lives. Though the *Enquirer* said it had pursued Bezos and Sánchez "across five states and 40,000 miles"—watching them go from jets to limos to "five-star hotel hideaways"—we didn't habitually chase after salacious scoops by the *National Enquirer*. Plus, we didn't possess, and couldn't verify, the texts that the *Enquirer* claimed to have.

So while *The Post* had reported immediately on the Bezos divorce and potential consequences for Amazon, some weeks passed before we poured reporting resources into news of Bezos's affair. The *Columbia Journalism Review*, routinely suspicious that we treated Bezos and Amazon with kid gloves (despite abundant evidence to the contrary), interpreted this as *The Post's* "reticence at covering a sex scandal involving its owner." But we ramped up on this story at the same pace as the news departments of other papers with our standards, *The New York Times* and *The Wall Street Journal*, and our overall coverage of the story's fiery developments was roughly equivalent to those publications' in volume and character. In time, though, *The Journal* and *The Times* scored some investigative scoops, and we were left to confirm them.

The story took on larger dimensions with a January 30 disclosure in the *Daily Beast* that Bezos had commissioned private investigators to unearth how the *Enquirer* secured his personal communications. Gavin de Becker, who heads a security company serving celebrities and executives who included Bezos (as well as, by then, *The Post* itself), was tasked with leading the probe. De Becker focused from the start on Lauren Sánchez's brother, Michael Sanchez, a talent manager—harboring suspicions that the leak was politically motivated. Michael had close relationships with Trump-world figures as well as a pattern of tweeting against the "fake news" that was critical of Trump.

At *The Post*, a team of reporters were assigned to dig, as usual without restriction. The headline on our first story, dated February 5, asked, "Was Tabloid Exposé of Bezos Affair Just Juicy Gossip or a Political Hit Job?" The story offered multiple options: "Depending on whom you believe, the *Enquirer*'s exposé on Bezos's affair was a political hit inspired by President Trump's allies, an inside job by people seeking to protect Bezos's marriage, or no conspiracy at all, simply a juicy gossip story." De Becker told *The Post* he "would be blind" if he "didn't register the fact" that Michael Sanchez was an "associate" of certain Trump allies.

The reasons for suspicion didn't stop there. The *Enquirer* had a history of strong ties with the president who loathed Bezos—supporting his candidacy and even paying hush money before the 2016 election to suppress a woman's allegations that she had an affair with Trump. Publisher David Pecker had long been a loyal Trump pal. I, for one, couldn't help but wonder whether the entire love affair might be a setup to humiliate Bezos. *The Post* was not attached to any theory. Until we knew more, all we had was a bizarre, head-shaking moment. How could Bezos be so careless? Why was he even in close proximity to someone like Michael Sanchez?

Michael Sanchez denied any involvement to *The Post*, pointing the finger wildly at the *Enquirer* for wanting to do "a takedown to make Trump happy," "deep state" actors in the U.S. government, Israel's Mossad spy agency, other foreign intelligence agencies, competitive tech companies, and de Becker himself "to sabotage Mr. Bezos and Ms. Sánchez's love affair." For its part, the *Enquirer*'s owner, American Media Inc. (AMI), told *The Post* it "emphatically" rejected "any assertion that its reporting was instigated, dictated or influenced in any manner by external forces, political or otherwise. End of speculation—and story." Personalities in Trump's orbit denied involvement, too.

Bezos and Lauren Sánchez had received separate emails from the *Enquirer* on January 7, 2019, requesting "an interview with you about your love affair." When Jeff and MacKenzie Bezos two days later announced their divorce, *The Post* reported, the *Enquirer*'s top editor was furious that Bezos had preempted his scoop. The *Enquirer* then rushed the story into print a week ahead of schedule.

Bezos promptly made his voice heard in a way that broke all traditions for PR. On February 7, he authored a post on the digital platform Medium to air extraordinary allegations: The *National Enquirer* and parent American Media were engaged in an attempt at "extortion and blackmail," threatening to post "intimate photos" of him unless he made "the specific false public statement to the press that 'we have no knowledge or basis for suggesting AMI's coverage was politically motivated or influenced by political forces.'"

"If in my position I can't stand up to this extortion," Bezos declared in the blog post that he spent five hours writing on his own, "how many people can? . . . Of course I don't want personal photos published, but I also won't participate in their well-known practice of blackmail, political favors, political attacks, and corruption. I prefer to stand up, roll this log over, and see what crawls out." With his counterattack, Bezos was hitting an especially sensitive nerve at AMI. The company had only recently signed a nonprosecution agreement with the Department of Justice over its "catch and kill" deal on behalf of Trump to purchase a negative story about his alleged affair with a former *Playboy* model for the purpose of ensuring it never saw the light of day. The agreement subjected AMI to prosecution if it later committed "any crimes."

Bezos's post on Medium surmised that vengeance for *The Post*'s coverage was at the heart of this intrusion into his personal life. "My ownership of *The Post* is a complexifier for me. It's unavoidable that certain powerful people who experience *Washington Post* news coverage will wrongly conclude I am their enemy. President Trump is one of those people, obvious by his many tweets. Also *The Post*'s essential and unrelenting coverage of the murder of its columnist Jamal Khashoggi is undoubtedly unpopular in certain circles." And he added parenthetically: "Even though *The Post* is a complexifier for me, I do not at all regret my investment. *The Post* is a critical institution with a critical mission. My stewardship of *The Post* and my support of its mission, which will remain unswerving, is something I will be most proud of when I'm 90 and reviewing my life, if I'm lucky enough to live that long, regardless of any complexities it creates for me."

None of us knew what to conclude from this jarring turn in the life of *The Post*'s owner. The lurid publicity threatened to saddle him with an image radically at odds with what we had become accustomed to and with a reputation for gravity that *The Post* aimed to cultivate for itself. But Bezos's astonishing Medium post offered reassurance, too, signaling that he wouldn't be intimidated—not by the *Enquirer*, not by Trump, and not by the Saudis whom he was now suggesting, also without evidence, might also be involved. Bezos liked to call *The Post* "badass." His public retort to the *Enquirer* was pretty badass itself.

As a journalist, I was obligated to keep professional distance from those we covered. My varied interactions with Bezos were different, though, and at times difficult to reconcile. By necessity, he and I worked together on many matters. News coverage was the exception, where I was given full independence. However, I had long ago concluded that my job didn't require me to sacrifice my humanity. I tried to keep in mind that the people we covered—no matter how rich or powerful or prominent—are human beings with emotions like any one of us.

So I felt the need to send Bezos a personal note. I was saddened to see his quarter-century marriage disintegrate. In my few encounters with MacKenzie, I always found her friendly and down-to-earth. The salacious tabloid coverage had to be misery for both. "I want to say how sorry I am for what you're going through," I emailed Bezos. "I wish our work at *The Post* had not so disrupted your life. That you chose to express your commitment to *The Post* and its mission amid all this left me deeply moved. Thank you for your strength and resolve. I trust that better days are ahead." He didn't respond. I didn't expect him to. Sending the note was to satisfy a need of mine.

Bezos was not a natural object of sympathy. He was too stupendously rich and powerful for that. Too many people doubted his own empathy for others, particularly the Amazon workforce. The political left and right found ample reasons to detest him. And his current indignity was a study in self-harm. How could someone so disciplined in other endeavors have been so reckless? How could someone so deeply informed about privacy risks leave himself so vulnerable? Yet Bezos's post on Medium elicited some notable support. "I never expected to see Jeff Bezos emerge as a hero of democracy. But he has. A profile in moral courage," tweeted economist and *New York Times* columnist Paul Krugman. "Today, I hereby nominate Jeff Bezos for the '2019 Pulitzer Prize for Public Service.' His willingness to take on and expose the *National Enquirer* is an enormously important act of civic journalism. Thank you Jeff," tweeted *Times* columnist Tom Friedman.

Solace was slight from the right-wing op-ed page of *The Wall Street Journal*, however. Holman W. Jenkins Jr. dismissed the idea that Trump or the Saudis had any hand in exposing Bezos—or that much more was involved than the *Enquirer*'s characteristically ravenous appetite for "juicy" stories. "It is easy to sympathize with Mr. Bezos in his horror at finding his private text messages and selfies in the hands of a scurrilous publication like the *Enquirer*," Jenkins wrote. "But I suspect he also thinks it would be really, really convenient to turn the story into a Trump political scandal rather than a Bezos sexting and infidelity scandal."

Bezos had the capacity to compartmentalize better than anyone else I'd known. In the aftermath of the *Enquirer*'s report, he was proving his skill. At an Amazon employee meeting in early March, he found a way to briefly raise the subject of his personal life without dwelling on it. "If you don't mind, just raise your hand, if maybe— just maybe—you've had a better start to your 2019 than I have. Anybody?" Bezos quipped, according to CNBC, which listened to a recording. "I noticed that a couple hands didn't come up—I'm sorry for you guys." According to Brad Stone, author of the 2021 book *Amazon Unbound*, Bezos also dismissed the idea that MacKenzie and their four kids were reeling from the revelations. "Just to set the record straight, I did have a relationship with this woman. But the story is completely wrong and out of order," Stone reported Bezos as saying. "MacKenzie and I have had good, healthy adult conversations about it. She is fine. The kids are fine. The media is having a field day. All of this is very distracting, so thank you for being focused on the business."

At *The Post*, the only disruption in business activities was cancellation of a regularly scheduled teleconference for January 9, the day when Bezos's divorce was announced. Bezos made light of his predicament when the meeting was eventually held. "I am trying to stay out of the news and totally failing. Do you have any suggestions?" No sexting, I thought to myself, though not one of us dared utter a word.

For all the drama, this chapter in Bezos's life ended with a whimper. Bezos's speculation that Trump or the Saudis might be involved in the *Enquirer* story was never backed up with any evidence. Bezos has had none to offer. As early as February 10, 2019, the *Daily Beast* reported that Michael Sanchez had provided the Bezos texts to the *Enquirer*. In March, *The Wall Street Journal* revealed that Michael was paid $200,000 up front, the most the *Enquirer* had ever paid for a story. *The New York Times* weighed in with a story in January 2020 that it had reviewed a contract, signed on October 18, 2018, between Michael and American Media "concerning certain information, photographs and text messages documenting an affair between Jeff Bezos and Lauren Sanchez."

Next up was *The Journal* again, disclosing that federal prosecutors in Manhattan had evidence that Lauren Sánchez herself had shared the Bezos texts with her brother. By the end of 2021—nearly two years after the *Enquirer* first published its story—*The Journal* reported that the FBI had concluded its investigation of possible extortion by the *Enquirer*. No charges were forthcoming.

As for Saudi Arabia, there were well-documented connections to the *Enquirer*. Its parent company had held talks with the Saudis for financing or other business deals that would help lift the company out of a crushing debt burden. Not long before Crown Prince Mohammed bin Salman visited the United States in early 2018, AMI published a glossy magazine titled *The New Kingdom* with gushing coverage of the country and the crown prince. By the looks of it, the company was ingratiating itself with Saudi royalty.

De Becker, in an opinion column in the *Daily Beast*, early on accused the Saudis of gaining "access to Bezos's phone" and extracting "private information." A United Nations report issued in January 2020 assessed that an account belonging to the crown prince sent Bezos a WhatsApp message containing a video file with malicious code that allowed it to vacuum up data over many months. UN human rights investigators said the hack suggested "possible involvement of the Crown Prince in surveillance of Mr. Bezos, in an effort to influence, if not silence, *The Washington Post*'s reporting on Saudi Arabia," a claim the Saudis dismissed as "absurd." However, the UN did not connect any Saudi intrusion to publication of the *Enquirer*'s story about Bezos's affair.

In his book, Brad Stone suggested that Bezos's post on Medium was a strategic ploy from the start, a "public relations master stroke" intended to divert attention from his affair and sexting while seeming to bravely stand up to the *Enquirer*, Trump, and the Saudis. And as an aside, Stone wrote that Michael Sanchez never actually had a Bezos "d*ck pic." Sanchez told the FBI that the photo displayed on a FaceTime conversation with his *Enquirer* contacts had been pulled from a male escort site.

Count me skeptical of Stone's hypothesis. Ever since his #sendDonaldtospace tweet in December 2015, Bezos had assiduously avoided saying anything that might directly provoke Trump. The commercial stakes for him in attacking the president now were far higher than a few ephemeral PR points for himself personally. Nor was his highly public denunciation of the *Enquirer* likely to tamp down attention to his affair.

After his Medium polemic, Bezos had warned *The Post* to double down on its own digital security. And on February 25, 2019, Bezos sent a note to *The Post*'s most senior executives attaching a piece in the *Daily Beast* written by Iyad El-Baghdadi, a vocal critic of the Saudi regime under asylum protection in Norway. "This is a long read but as leaders of *The Post*, it's something you should all be aware of if you're not already." The article traced rising Saudi animosity toward Bezos, a four-month social media campaign targeting him, and calls within the kingdom for a boycott of Amazon. It cited one graphic with Bezos's picture captioned "This is the hateful filth." Another was captioned "The Jew: Jeff Bezos," although he isn't Jewish. "There's mounting evidence that the de facto ruler of the kingdom has been trying to punish Bezos for the fierce coverage by his newspaper, *The Washington Post*, of the murder of Saudi journalist Jamal Khashoggi," El-Baghdadi wrote. That was the only time I received any direct communication from Bezos during our entire coverage of this story.

Lauren Sánchez condemned her brother's actions as a "deep and unforgivable betrayal," and Bezos has fully acknowledged that Michael funneled texts to the *Enquirer*. But I'm told that he still wonders whether the Saudis—having, he is convinced, hacked his phone—tipped off the paper and spurred them to contact Michael Sanchez. And, also without evidence, he hasn't discounted the possibility that Trump played some role. With the Trump-Saudi-*Enquirer* nexus so tight, suspicions still nag at him. He hasn't backed off from his broadside on Medium.

Wall Street Journal columnist Holman Jenkins suggested that the insinuations and accusations emanating from Bezos and his team rendered him "unfit" to own a newspaper. "Here Mr. Bezos is a newspaper owner who *himself* manufactured a false story in his own interest," Jenkins wrote in May 2021. Disqualifying Bezos as a proper media owner was pretty rich: Jenkins's own newspaper was controlled by Rupert Murdoch, who also reigned over Fox News, where crackpot conspiracy theories and promoting Trump's lies were daily staples.

Even if Trump's pique over *Washington Post* coverage had nothing to do with the *National Enquirer*'s exposé on Bezos's private life, it was the motive for more costly attacks on Bezos's business interests. Arguably no non-media company and its chief executive were assailed by Trump more frequently or savagely than Amazon and Bezos.

Trump's list of *Post*-inspired grievances against Amazon was already lengthy, dating back to his presidential campaign: It pays too little in taxes. It's skirting antitrust rules. It's wreaking havoc on small retailers. As president, he obsessed over Amazon's deal with the U.S. Postal Service. Stewing over *Washington Post* coverage, Trump declared in December 2017 that Amazon was leaving the mail service "dumber and poorer." The Postal Service, he said, "should be charging MUCH MORE!" At the end of March 2018, he tweeted that Amazon used "our Postal System as their Delivery Boy (causing tremendous loss to the U.S.)." He quickly amped up the rhetoric, calling Amazon a "Post Office scam" that cost taxpayers $1.50 on every package.

There's no question that Amazon wouldn't be what it is today without the Postal Service. From the company's first days, Bezos depended on it for deliveries. "I didn't have to build a transportation network to deliver the packages," he told CBS's Norah O'Donnell in July 2019. "It existed: It was called the post office." As it grew and matured, Amazon developed its own delivery network of planes, trucks, and depots. And yet the company still relied heavily on the Postal Service for the last leg of a package's journey to its final destination.

A few analysts joined some competitors in arguing that the Postal Service was charging Amazon too little, effectively subsidizing it. But most, including USPS itself, concluded that the business with Amazon—and similar shippers—was actually propping up the agency rather than dragging it down. The Postal Service's $2.7 billion net loss was due, by most accounts, to other factors—a precipitous yearslong drop in the volume of first-class and marketing mail as well as a congressional requirement that the agency fund its employees' retirement health benefits in advance.

As early as January 2018, *The Post* reported, Trump was leaning on Postmaster General Megan Brennan to double what Amazon was charged. In those meetings, none of which appeared on Trump's public schedule, Brennan put up strong resistance. The relationship with Amazon was governed by contracts. Rates required review by a regulatory commission.

That April, claiming that Amazon was costing taxpayers "many billions of dollars," Trump took the first concrete step beyond grousing on Twitter. With an executive order, he mandated a review of the Postal Service's finances. While the order didn't mention Amazon specifically, it clearly covered the company's shipping arrangements. In December, the Trump-appointed task force headed by Treasury Secretary Steven Mnuchin recommended a reevaluation of the pricing for e-commerce packages. Amazon entered 2019 facing the prospect that the Postal Service would significantly raise its costs. Tense negotiations between the Postal Service and its largest commercial customer lay ahead.

On March 7, 2018, Pentagon leaders officially kicked off the competition for a gargantuan $10 billion cloud computing contract. The contract, known as Joint Enterprise Defense Infrastructure (JEDI), was intended to dramatically modernize the Defense Department's technology infrastructure, leading to enhanced use of artificial intelligence. The victor in the bidding would get the entire ten-year contract and be ideally positioned to secure the lion's share of the department's cloud computing expenditures many years into the future.

The Pentagon's decision to award JEDI to one company set off a rancorous battle among leading technology companies, including Microsoft, Oracle, IBM, and Amazon. All but one of them protested the military's decision not to divvy up the cloud computing work among more than one company. The outlier: Amazon, which was widely seen as a favorite to win because of its previous work for the CIA, its top-notch certification for handling classified data, and its dominance in the commercial cloud computing field that it pioneered. In the eyes of Amazon's competitors, the process was rigged.

On April 2, *Vanity Fair* reported that Trump's advisers were already encouraging him to obstruct Amazon's bid to win the JEDI contract. "He gets obsessed with something, and now he's obsessed with Bezos," a source told writer Gabriel Sherman. "Trump is like, how can I fuck with him?" Trump, a former White House official told Sherman, figured Bezos could control *The Post* the way *National Enquirer* publisher David Pecker could control that publication: "When Bezos says he has no involvement, Trump doesn't believe him. His experience is with the David Peckers of the world. Whether it's right or wrong, he knows it can be done."

The White House offered assurances to the press that Trump wasn't interfering in the bidding. "The president is not involved in the process," press secretary Sarah Huckabee Sanders declared on April 4. The Defense Department, she said, "runs a competitive bidding process." By July 2019, Trump was expressly interfering. Citing complaints about alleged unfairness, Trump directed aides to investigate the military contract. "His involvement," *The Post* reported at the time, "would be an unusual Oval Office intervention in a process normally handled by military officials trained to follow complicated procurement laws and regulations."

Normal was not Trump's way. "I'm getting tremendous complaints about the contract with the Pentagon and with Amazon . . . They're saying it wasn't competitively bid," Trump said. "Some of the greatest companies in the world are complaining about it, having to do with Amazon and the Department of Defense, and I will be asking them to look at it very closely to see what's going on." Trump cited complaints from "companies like Microsoft, Oracle and IBM." There was no doubt about what Trump was trying to do: That same week he retweeted a Fox News segment on JEDI called "The Bezos Bailout." Host Steve Hilton said, "It's not just appropriate, but vital that the President kills this contract . . . Mr. President, if you want to keep draining the swamp, don't let the Bezos bailout fill it back up."

Only two weeks later, *The Post* reported, Trump upended the process by ordering new defense secretary Mark Esper, in his first week on the job, to reexamine it "because of concerns that the deal would go to Amazon." Competitors' protests had failed, and the Pentagon had designated Microsoft and Amazon as finalists. A decision was expected to be announced shortly.

Trump's intervention came after particularly furious lobbying by Oracle, exploiting the president's grievances against both Amazon and former defense secretary Jim Mattis, who submitted his resignation in December 2018 (and then was pushed out two months early) after clashing with the president over troop withdrawals in Syria and Afghanistan. Aides presented Trump a colorful flowchart labeled "A Conspiracy to Create a Ten-Year DoD Cloud Monopoly" that connected Mattis, Obama's defense secretary Ashton Carter, and Amazon executives. It was identical to a chart in the office of Oracle's top representative in Washington. "With images of dollar signs, arrows, and a heart linking the various figures, the chart leaves the overall impression of corruption and conflicted interests," CNN reported. "But while the chart is heavy on graphics and innuendo, there is no specific charge of wrongdoing."

In October 2019, a retired Navy commander and former fighter pilot who had been Mattis's communications director, Guy Snodgrass, published a book alleging that Trump had told Mattis in the summer of 2018 to "screw Amazon." When Mattis relayed the president's phone call to aides, he reportedly said, "We're not going to do that. This will be done by the book, both legally and ethically." Mattis neither confirmed nor denied the story, leaving a spokesperson to accuse the former aide of "surreptitiously taking notes without authorization" (which suggested confirmation).

Defense Secretary Esper ended up recusing himself that month from any decisions about JEDI, citing his son's employment at IBM (which was no longer even in the running to win it). Days later, the Defense Department awarded the contract to Microsoft, dealing a huge blow to Amazon. In the media universe, a joke quickly made the rounds: *The Washington Post* didn't cost Bezos $250 million. It cost him $10,250,000,000.

The Pentagon's decision set the stage for full-scale war. Bezos and his executive team would no longer contain their fury. When Amazon filed a protest in November 2019 of the DoD's contract decision, its language was stunningly caustic. "The question is whether the President of the United States should be allowed to use the budget of DoD to pursue his own personal and political ends," Amazon wrote. "President Trump's animosity toward Mr. Bezos, Amazon, and the *Washington Post* is well known, and it originates at least in part from his dissatisfaction with the *Washington Post*'s coverage of him from before he assumed office," Amazon added. In calling for the president and the secretary of defense to sit for depositions, the company drew a line from Trump's impeachment over Ukraine to his posture toward Amazon. "This protest," it declared in one brief, "occurs against the background of impeachment . . . which is grounded in the president's repeated refusal to separate his personal interests from the national interest." Microsoft called Amazon's complaint "sensationalist and politicized rhetoric." For its part, the Pentagon rejected the allegation of improper influence from the White House.

Amazon executives knew well that a decision to directly condemn the president would mark a point of no return in their relationship with Trump and his administration. Bezos, Amazon general counsel David Zapolsky, associate general counsel Andrew DeVore, and global corporate affairs chief Jay Carney had hashed out the pros and cons. On the one hand, they felt Trump's intervention was so preposterous, and costly, that Amazon needed to confront it as an abuse of power. Bezos, for one, felt strongly that Trump needed to answer for his behavior. On the other hand, Amazon would be burning any prospect of normal relations with his government. Despite Trump's yearslong attacks on Bezos and Amazon, the company had still been able to work reasonably well with top officials on various matters. Attacking Trump would likely end any constructive ties. Sure enough, Amazon became radioactive among senior officials. Communications largely dried up.

JEDI continued through a tortuous path of continued litigation, a contract halt, DoD reaffirmation of the award to Microsoft, and ultimately a decision to cancel the entire $10 billion program and start over. In November 2021, with Trump out of office, the Pentagon announced that it was taking bids for a new, and newly named, $9 billion cloud computing contract that would no longer be winner-take-all. Amazon, Microsoft, Google, and Oracle were invited to bid. Finally, in December 2022, the Defense Department announced that all four would get a piece of that contract, though it didn't specify who would get how much. Perhaps buying *The Post* hadn't really cost Bezos all of $10,250,000,000. But the financial hit may not end up a whole lot less.

Before restarting the bidding—in April 2020—the office of the Pentagon's inspector general gave its blessing to the process. The IG's review found that the contract award was not tarnished by pressure from higher-level officials "who may have communicated with the White House." But the inspector general's report included quite the caveat on that point. The president had asserted executive privilege, forbidding senior White House and Pentagon officials from being interviewed. Communications among them regarding the mammoth JEDI contract remained secret. "We could not definitively determine the full extent or nature of interactions that administration officials had, or may have had, with senior DOD officials regarding the procurement," the report said. The defensive maneuver by the White House was strikingly familiar: Whenever there was the scent of wrongdoing on his part, Trump pulled executive privilege out of his presidential pocket, ordering people with firsthand knowledge not to talk. It was not the behavior of someone who had nothing to hide.

"Essentially what we learned from the IG report is that while there was no successful effort to influence the award, it appears that they tried given the fact that they invoked the privilege," said Danielle Brian, executive director of the Project on Government Oversight. "And that's not okay. There's no place for the president's personal vendettas in a contracting decision."

In April 2020, Trump saw an opportunity to add even more pressure on the U.S. Postal Service to raise rates for Amazon's package delivery. Two years earlier, he had hectored the postmaster general to double prices charged the company. Now, he said, rates needed to be "four or five times" higher. Obviously, he made up these numbers on the spot. This time Trump was threatening to withhold $10 billion in a pandemic-related line of credit for the Postal Service that Congress had approved. "If they don't raise the price, I'm not signing anything." As *Post* columnist Catherine Rampell wryly observed in a column headlined "We're All Zelensky Now": "Do us a favor though: Before we rescue the U.S. Postal Service, raise postage prices on the president's perceived political enemies."

Doing the president's bidding, Treasury Secretary Steven Mnuchin sought operating control of the agency in exchange for the loan USPS desperately needed. While the administration backed off that idea, it did force the Postal Service to turn over proprietary information about its ten largest private-sector contracts, including those with FedEx, UPS, and, of course, Amazon. In negotiations with USPS, Amazon expressed concerns about the direction of the mail service's rates and its reliability as a partner. Amazon had alternatives, even if imperfect ones: both the Postal Service's competitors and a sprawling logistics operation of its own. Already the company was close to delivering two-thirds of its own packages, and that was expected to escalate rapidly. Exactly what happened with Amazon's rates isn't publicly known. The Postal Service keeps rates for its biggest shippers confidential. But one thing is clear: Amazon did not "crumble like a paper bag," as Trump once fantasized when he began attacking Bezos personally in December 2015, initially over its taxes. When Trump launched his first strike, the overall value of the company's stock was $144 billion. It would sail to $1.7 trillion by the end of 2021. Bezos's wealth would skyrocket in tandem, from $45 billion at the end of 2015 to $171 billion by 2021—notwithstanding a divorce agreement that yielded ex-wife MacKenzie a quarter of their Amazon stock, worth $36 billion at the time.

Bezos's ability to prosper despite Trump's attacks, however, was not what made this chapter in U.S. history so consequential. In some ways, Bezos's resilience blurred the horror of what had just happened. A president of the United States had sought to marshal the full power of the federal government to sabotage the business of a man he perceived as an enemy.

Much of Trump's spitefulness played out in public view but not all: Trump's second White House chief of staff, John Kelly, told *The New York Times* in 2022 that Trump advocated having the IRS and Justice Department investigate Bezos, although there was no follow-up. (A Trump spokeswoman called it "total fiction created by a psycho.") And at one point, I've been reliably informed, Trump went so far as to broach the zany idea of raising taxes only on Amazon and Bezos—until advisers told him that government couldn't devise a tax policy that would apply solely to one company and one individual.

Had Bezos's jaw-dropping wealth not elicited so much antipathy, Trump's venal behavior might have stirred more outrage. Although politicians and the press knew full well that Trump was pressuring Bezos over coverage by *The Washington Post*, the reaction was restrained when measured against the gravity of the offense and what it foreshadowed for democracy. Trump's vengeful acts were the real scandal of those years, not Bezos's more avidly covered private life, which he was entitled to live as he wished.

There were exceptions to the muted response among the press. Perhaps the most eloquent and spot-on was Jonathan Chait of *New York* magazine. "Trump's Retribution Against the *Washington Post* Owner Is His Gravest Abuse of Power," read a headline on his column in November 2019 amid the president's JEDI interference. "The story here," Chait wrote, "is almost certainly a massive scandal, probably more significant than the Ukraine scandal that spurred impeachment proceedings. Trump improperly used government policy to punish the owner of an independent newspaper as retribution for critical coverage. It resembles the Ukraine scandal because it is a flagrant abuse of power, and has been hiding in plain sight for months (as the Ukraine scandal did, until a whistle-blower report leaked in September). The scale of the abuse, though, is far more serious, because it is a concrete manifestation of Trump's authoritarian ambitions . . . He has turned the power of the state into a weapon of intimidation against the free press."

Similarly, during the presidential campaign, Trump had pledged to block the merger of AT&T and Time Warner, which owned CNN, another of Trump's favorite targets. The proposed merger, he said at an October 2016 rally, was "a deal we will not approve in my administration." A campaign press statement against the deal invoked the "wildly anti-Trump CNN." As later reported in *The New Yorker*, the president in 2017 leaned on national economic adviser Gary Cohn and chief of staff John Kelly to instruct the Justice Department to fight the merger. Cohn, according to the report, counseled Kelly not to do as Trump requested. The Justice Department's antitrust division did end up suing to block the merger. After the litigation failed in June 2018, the merger was completed, with Time Warner still bitterly complaining that the lawsuit was "political in its motivation." The DOJ denied that Trump interfered in the AT&T–

Time Warner deal. But when two congressional committees sought to investigate after the *New Yorker* article in March 2019, the White House invoked—what else?—executive privilege.

Trump's campaign to punish Amazon and Bezos carried implications beyond press freedom. It signaled an ominous direction for the GOP. Taking their cue from Trump's worst instincts, Republicans who once carried the banner for free markets now believed it was within their rights to bludgeon companies into supporting the party and its policies by threatening to deploy federal and state governments against them.

House Minority Leader Kevin McCarthy, in August 2021, warned that telecommunications companies would be punished if they complied with entirely lawful subpoenas issued by the House subcommittee investigating the mob attack on the Capitol on January 6, 2021. Solely because Disney assailed a new law that clamped down on classroom discussion of gender identity and sexual orientation, Florida's governor, Ron DeSantis, and Republican legislators in April 2022 revoked the special status that the company had long ago been granted to govern the vast territory it owned, overseeing roads, land use, and municipal services. For companies advocating a range of policies that Republicans find objectionable, "everything will be on the table," Fox News anchor Laura Ingraham said. "Your copyright, trademark protection. Your special status within certain states. And even your corporate structure itself."

Catherine Rampell, the *Washington Post* columnist, put the meaning of these threats succinctly: "In today's Republican Party, the primary economic role of the state is not to get out of the way. It is, instead, to reward friends and crush political enemies." Trump's method was plain to see, with Ukraine and also with Bezos and Amazon: With power comes the right to abuse it. It was the authoritarian way.

15

THE POWERS THAT BE

I should not have been surprised, but I still marveled at just how little it took to get under the skin of President Trump and his allies. In February 2019, *The Post* aired a one-minute Super Bowl ad, with a voice-over by actor Tom Hanks, championing the role of a free press, commemorating journalists killed and captured, and concluding with *The Post*'s logo and the message "Democracy Dies in Darkness." The ad highlighted strong and often courageous work by journalists at *The Post* and elsewhere—including Fox News' Bret Baier, as we strove to signal that this wasn't just about us and wasn't a political statement.

"There's someone to gather the facts," Hanks intoned. "To bring you the story. No matter the cost. Because knowing empowers us. Knowing helps us decide. Knowing keeps us free." Even that simple, foundational idea of democracy was a step too far for the Trump clan. The president's son Donald Trump Jr. couldn't contain himself. "You know how MSM journalists could avoid having to spend millions on a #superbowl comercial [*sic*] to gain some undeserved credibility?" he tweeted with typical two-bit belligerence. "How about report the news and not their leftist BS for a change."

The Post had never advertised during a Super Bowl before, and we had not planned to start. Advertising that costly—with an estimated value of at least $10 million—was beyond our means. But one week before the deadline for submitting a commercial to CBS, Jeff Bezos offered us a Super Bowl advertising slot if we wanted it. Publisher Fred Ryan jumped at the opportunity. I was told that the spot originally had been Blue Origin's, but I had no idea why Bezos's space company was giving it up. The *New York Post* attributed its cancellation to publicity surrounding Bezos's affair with Lauren Sánchez. A helicopter pilot, she and her company had been shooting aerial footage of Blue Origin rocket launches.

Normally, a Super Bowl commercial would take many months to make. We were staring at a submission deadline only a week away. Fred moved nimbly to line up Hanks, who had recently starred in Steven Spielberg's movie *The Post*, about late publisher Katharine Graham and the Pentagon Papers. But coming up with the words for Hanks to read was proving a struggle. I was called at a holiday party one night to help with the script and before midnight emailed what, after shortening and refining by the ad agency, became the commercial's text.

While Fredrick Kunkle, leader of *The Post*'s union, ended up complaining about the cost of the ad—and how it could have been spent on better employee health benefits—the truth was that Bezos and Blue Origin had prepaid for the spot. As a matter of accounting, it may have showed up on our financial statements. But the only real cost to *The Post* was the toll on our nerves from such a ridiculously rushed production schedule. The plus for us was the assertive statement it implicitly made about *The Post*: We had a vital mission. We were here to stay. We were bigger than ever. We were a force to be reckoned with.

That had to annoy the Trump crowd. Three days before kicking off his reelection campaign on June 19, Trump himself offered up a counternarrative on Twitter. He predicted that two media outlets he hated most, *The New York Times* and *The Washington Post*—"these horrible papers"—would "quickly go out of business & be forever gone" once his presumed second term ended. In the real world, just the opposite was happening. Both news organizations were prospering. Americans who saw *The Post* and *The Times* as essential checks on his ravenous authoritarian appetite and Trump-aligned misinformation were purchasing subscriptions at an astonishing pace. While the danger of a president attacking the press is a serious long-term threat, in the short run Trump's attacks on us were better than any sales pitch we could have come up with ourselves. Definitely better than a Super Bowl commercial.

In managing our business day to day, some worries overshadowed even the power of a president. High among them was the power of the world's technology behemoths: Google, Facebook, and Apple. In my field, those companies had come to be known as "frenemies"— friends because they could disseminate our journalism to so many more people, enemies because they were siphoning off advertising dollars that historically kept newspapers in the black. In the internet era, it was impossible to live without them. And living with them was a frustration of its own.

New subscribers had been our salvation. If we were to get many more subscribers, however, people needed first to find our stories. For much of the public, Google's search engine, Facebook's social network, and Apple's phones and apps were the first stop in reading news. Whether people noticed our journalism and whether they subscribed depended, in large part, on the companies' algorithms that governed the visibility of stories and their rules on how much of our work had to be offered for free. Theirs was just the sort of dominance that Bezos's Amazon wielded in the retail field. Smaller sellers often complained that Amazon was ungenerous in treatment, even to the point of being abusive. *The Post* was similarly dependent on the other technology behemoths, and at times no less aggrieved.

In our periodic pilgrimages to Silicon Valley, Google's Sundar Pichai, Apple's Tim Cook, and Facebook's Mark Zuckerberg and

Sheryl Sandberg were invariably gracious hosts. Fred Ryan's line to each of the top tech executives was that we wanted to be their "best partners," and yet in reality we were supplicants in a world where they were sovereign. Bezos wanted us liberated from the grip of the giants.

Almost nine out of ten searches worldwide for information on the internet went through Google, making news organizations' digital traffic (and commercial success) heavily dependent on its search results. Even showing up on the first results page was not enough to draw many readers' notice. News organizations strove to decode Google's secret algorithms, taking steps they hoped would land them at the top of its story list.

For almost two decades the public could read pretty much whatever it wished for free on Google. Arguing for a good "user experience," Google had insisted that, in order to show up in its search results, news organizations had to make their journalism available without charge to search-engine users. That allowed people to easily circumvent digital subscription requirements they encountered when going directly to media websites. Over time, under pressure from news outlets, Google began to allow newspapers and magazines more control over how many stories were available without cost when accessed through searches. And yet Google still had rules on how many articles needed to be free. At one point, in late 2009, it was five articles per user per day; in 2015 it was lowered to three. News organizations wanted no rules whatsoever, without being penalized by Google with less prominence in search results.

There was scarcely a meeting with Bezos when he didn't lean on us to "tighten the paywall," making it ever harder for people to read stories unless they purchased a subscription. When presented with Google's argument that the experience for its users was better when they didn't hit a paywall, Bezos interjected, "Well, tough!" Google, he said in May 2017, would be foolish to penalize *The Wall Street Journal, The New York Times, The Washington Post,* and others by relegating them to inferior positions in search results simply because they gave away fewer free articles. In an era of widespread misinformation, he added, "Google should be helping news-gathering organizations get subscriptions." When one *Post* executive seemed a little too sympathetic to Google's position, Bezos declared, "That's just Stockholm syndrome!"—invoking a psychological condition where hostages begin to identify with their captors and their demands. In October that year, Google dispensed with its old rules, yielding to publishers' ever more insistent complaints and letting them decide for themselves how many free clicks users would get, with no consequences for search results. That represented a big boost to our business.

Bezos felt we were getting the shaft from Facebook, too. Facebook had become a huge source of digital traffic for *The Post* and other media outlets. Many users stumbled across our stories on Facebook's platform rather than on our own website. Zuckerberg at first brushed off our complaints that few people would hit our subscription wall if he kept insisting that ten articles per month had to be free to Facebook users. Even when Bezos pressed him directly at an annual Sun Valley conference of media, tech, and finance executives in 2017, Zuckerberg wouldn't back down, dismissing the argument that the free market should determine the number. As Facebook began to deemphasize news in favor of interactions between family and friends, *Post* executives grew more irritated, no one more so than Bezos. "We're a pimple on the rear-end of a giant elephant," he said that June. After some quick back-of-the-envelope arithmetic on the loss of potential subscription revenue for us, Bezos said, "This isn't just a little bad for us. It's a disaster." Facebook ultimately relented, allowing news outlets to set whatever limits they wished on free access to stories.

Throughout the summer of 2017, Bezos continued to press for tightening the paywall. "We've gone through a twenty-year period where this industry has trained people to think that news was free." Now, he said, we were in the "awkward, painful period where we say,

'We were just kidding about that.'" No question, the new strategy was effective. "Paywalls work," wrote one reader on Twitter. "Shortly after bumping against my 2,648th blocked @washingtonpost link on Twitter last night, I got a digital subscription."

In the spring of 2018, Apple announced that it was acquiring what came to be known as a "Hulu for Magazines," a joint venture of several publishing companies that offered a single subscription providing access to all the stories their publications had to offer. The publishers earned revenue based on how many of their stories were read. The publishers' original joint venture proved to be a dud, but Apple bought it with the idea of building something bigger and better—and called it Apple News+. Apple's goal was to have hundreds of publications sign up to make their journalism available, dangling the prospect of a huge audience: 900 million iPhone users worldwide. The plan was to charge readers $10 a month. Early on, Apple was eager to sign up prestige national publications such as *The Washington Post*, *The New York Times*, and *The Wall Street Journal*. Eddy Cue, one of Apple's most senior executives, made the pitch in person to *Post* management.

The Times, we knew, was taking a pass. Its strategy was to move away from reliance on Big Tech's platforms and lure readers directly to its website or app. Cue told us that if we signed on to Apple News+, *The Post* could well catapult to becoming the most-read newspaper in the world and "annihilate" *The Times*. It was a notion that he conspicuously relished. Apple's massive worldwide reach held obvious appeal, but the pitfalls were equally apparent. Apple, and not *The Post*, would maintain the relationship with readers. We wouldn't even know their names or how to contact them. And Apple would get 50 percent of the revenue earned through sales of its subscriptions, with publishers on Apple News+ battling among themselves for the rest. Bezos was adamantly opposed to getting on board with Apple, seeing how its venture might hobble our growth, and even cannibalize our surging base of subscribers. Even if we gained

millions of new readers through Apple, Bezos said, "I don't count
these people as subscribers. They are, but they are Apple subscribers.
They're not *Washington Post* subscribers."

Then-CEO of *The New York Times* Mark Thompson warned
other publishers against participating in Apple News+, telling
the Reuters news service in March 2019, "If I was an American
broadcast network, I would have thought twice about giving all of
my library to Netflix," he said. "Even if Netflix offered you quite
a lot of money," he continued, "does it really make sense to help
Netflix build a gigantic base of subscribers to the point where they
could actually spend $9 billion a year making their own content
and will pay me less and less for my library?" Hollywood studios
had done exactly that with Netflix, and ultimately sold themselves
to bigger companies while watching Netflix emerge as a direct
competitor.

Bezos sent us a link to Thompson's remarks with a brief message
that served as an unmistakable directive for what *The Post* should tell
Apple: "I agree with him." *The Wall Street Journal* ended up joining
Apple in its new venture. *The Post* did not. Bezos continued to envision lining up ten million *Post* subscribers on our own—and then
many more: "I want us to be in control of our own destiny, even if
that takes ten years."

As Bezos worried about the power imbalance between *The Post* and
Google, Facebook, and Apple, smaller sellers harbored the same
fears about Amazon itself. The company Bezos built from nothing
now possessed fearsome power. Small businesses, and even major
brands, relied heavily on Amazon's convenient, easy-to-use, and
highly effective platform to reach consumers. And yet Amazon held
immense clout over their fate. It controlled their prominence on its
site, could closely monitor buyer behavior to serve its own commercial aspirations, and all along was developing merchandise under its

own brand that could compete with its "partners." Concerns escalated among politicians and regulators at both the state and federal level that Amazon was abusively throwing its weight around. *The Post*'s newsroom was duty-bound to cover the impact of Amazon's immense power in the retail marketplace with energy and full independence. Trump incessantly claimed that *The Post* was Amazon's "lobbyist." The coverage showed that we were anything but.

Press critics, particularly on the left, felt we should have been tougher on Amazon, a prototypical corporate villain. At times, the text of our articles was microscopically examined for presumed censorship by Bezos. When detractors couldn't demonstrate interference (because there was none), there were insinuations of "self-censorship." It was the easiest charge to make: Nothing had to be proved. Everything could be assumed. The potshots were as irritating as they were inevitable.

"Did *The Washington Post* pull its punches on Amazon and USPS?" the *Columbia Journalism Review* asked in a December 2018 headline as it examined a single story about the company and the Postal Service. Suggesting we soft-pedaled a task force's recommendations about postal rates, the *CJR* concluded: "Is there any evidence to suggest that the *Post*'s coverage of the postal service story was deliberately more favorable to Amazon? No. But a newspaper's ownership can influence coverage in more subtle ways than outright calls for censorship, including self-censorship and the pulling of punches. And the price of being owned by one of the world's richest men is that some will inevitably see bias even where it might not exist." A once-influential magazine intended to serve as a watchdog of journalism ethics was engaging in the ethically dubious practice of casting suspicion when it had nothing to offer beyond conjecture.

We didn't set out to try to appease the critics. We were no tougher on Amazon because some wanted us to be, no easier on the company because we feared blowback from Bezos. Difficult as it might be for detractors to believe, our policy was to report on Amazon as we would any other company. Yet it was not until late in 2017 and into 2018 that we acquired the resources to cover Amazon and other tech giants with the scrutiny and tenacity their swollen power deserved. As *The Post* delivered profits and aimed to accelerate growth, we began to expand beyond what had been the biggest pillars of our journalism: politics, investigations, wide-ranging opinion, distinctive narratives, and projects. They had attracted the most traffic and subscriptions. Settling on technology as a new priority for investment, we began to build a muscular journalistic team on the West Coast. There was much to examine: Big Tech's capacity to mold the competitive marketplace to its own advantage; how the companies treated hundreds of thousands of employees and contractors; how they ingested and exploited vast data on private individuals; the companies' influence on political discourse.

In late 2017 *The Post* announced the hiring of a tech columnist and editor in San Francisco, and in October 2018 added another eleven tech journalists. More would be brought aboard later. The first expansion budget called for a tech reporter in Seattle, with Amazon "at the center of this beat." I worked through our budget with publisher Fred Ryan, but Bezos had the final say. I never sensed any hesitation or heard the slightest cautionary word.

I tended to leave assignments regarding Amazon to other editors, letting them direct coverage as they felt appropriate but not making suggestions of my own for stories to pursue. My contacts with Bezos on business matters were too regular. Deep involvement in coverage would have been too awkward. Some on staff would have speculated that I was a vehicle for Bezos to influence what we published. I was satisfied that the coverage was aggressive as well as fair, and was work that I could defend to anyone. If there was bias in our coverage of Amazon, it was toward subjecting the company to extra scrutiny. Journalists at *The Post* almost certainly felt they had something to prove: They weren't the owner's flunkies. Everyone knew our work would be closely studied.

Our technology columnist, Geoffrey Fowler, recruited from *The Wall Street Journal*, rarely had a kind word for Amazon's products. For Amazon Prime: "What are we giving up when we can, and do, buy almost anything imaginable from a single online store? In the worst case, a Prime membership acts like blinders: It steers not only what we buy but also how we behave as consumers—and even which companies get to compete for our dollars." For Alexa: "Would you let a stranger eavesdrop in your home and keep the recordings? For most people, the answer is, 'Are you crazy?' Yet that's essentially what Amazon has been doing to millions of us with its assistant Alexa in microphone-equipped Echo speakers . . . Any personal data that's collected can and will be used against us. An obvious place to begin: Alexa, stop recording us." For Alexa-enabled glasses: "What do you call it when there's a little voice in your head only you can hear? A hallucination? Amazon calls it progress." When Amazon introduced a set of new products in the fall of 2020—including a Ring security camera attached to a flying drone—Geoff seemed to throw up his hands in exasperation: "Amazon appears undeterred by its emerging reputation in consumer technology: creep."

I can only imagine what Bezos thought of our technology critic trashing one new product of Amazon's after the next—and in ever more biting terms. Bezos never told me, and I wasn't going to ask. When candidates for tech reporting jobs inquired about the owner's potential interference, Geoff's columns offered ready proof that there was none. "I review all tech with the same critical eye," Geoff routinely wrote, noting Bezos's ownership of *The Post*.

It was essential, of course, to cast a critical eye on Amazon for more than its new products. Our newly formed technology team focused heavily on privacy intrusions, lobbying in Washington, worker safety, the plight of small sellers on Amazon's dominant online platform, and the company's role in surveillance policing. All of these stories spoke to Amazon's immense power in the marketplace, in people's lives, and in influencing public policy.

Amazon's facial recognition technology was one area of intense coverage. In May 2018, *The Post*'s Elizabeth Dwoskin highlighted the serious civil rights concerns that arose from selling that technology—after initially giving it away—to local law enforcement agencies. Washington County, Oregon, became "ground zero" for the unregulated growth of policing via facial recognition, as staffer Drew Harwell reported in 2019. The sheriff's department had enthusiastically embraced Amazon's Rekognition technology, but artificial intelligence researchers and civil rights advocates worried that mistaken identifications could lead to wrongful arrests and even life-threatening encounters between police and ordinary citizens. Amazon's Ring doorbells also were being used heavily by law enforcement, with the company disclosing in 2019 that it was collaborating with four hundred police departments. The program, as *The Post* reported, was causing alarm among legal experts and civil rights advocates "about the company's eyes-everywhere ambitions and increasingly close relationship with police." A few months later, Drew revealed that Amazon had told a U.S. senator that police departments could keep the Ring videos "forever" and "share them with whomever they'd like without providing evidence of a crime."

After Jay Greene was hired from *The Wall Street Journal* into our Seattle job, where Amazon would be his top priority, he concentrated on the e-commerce giant's fraught relationship with smaller sellers—showing in 2019 how the company gave preference to its own interests over those of its "partners." "In dozens of product searches by *The Washington Post*," he wrote, "offers for a 'Similar item to consider' featuring Amazon brands appeared just above the spot where shoppers click to add an item to their cart. Those boxes touted a lower price for Amazon's versions of items such as Glad trash bags, Dr. Scholl's gel insoles, Energizer batteries, and Nicorette gum."

With the company under pressure on multiple fronts and the government policy stakes so high, Amazon invested heavily in lobbying. *The Post* sought to examine the company's political tactics. Reporter Tony Romm reported on how Amazon and its Big Tech counterparts were helping to fund polling and purportedly independent political groups to combat the escalating threats from Washington politicians and regulators who were calling for stricter antitrust regulation. "The tech industry also has sought to funnel dollars to a wide array of conservative groups in recent years, hoping to earn more favor among Republicans in power at the White House and in Congress," Tony wrote in June 2020. "That includes the National Taxpayers Union, a right-leaning outfit that typically targets government spending it secs as wasteful."

In January 2020, Bezos for the first time testified before Congress on Amazon's practices, finally agreeing to appear after the House Judiciary Committee threatened to legally compel him. Questioned via videoconference along with Cook of Apple, Pichai of Google, and Zuckerberg of Facebook, he mounted a defense that minimized the company's market power. Members of the committee were unpersuaded. That October, the committee staff produced a blistering 450-page report accusing the tech companies of anticompetitive, monopolistic behavior. "To put it simply, companies that once were scrappy, underdog startups that challenged the status quo have become the kinds of monopolies we last saw in the era of oil barons and railroad tycoons," the committee wrote. "Although these firms have delivered clear benefits to society, the dominance of Amazon, Apple, Facebook, and Google has come at a price. These firms typically run the marketplace while also competing in it—a position that enables them to write one set of rules for others, while they play by another, or to engage in a form of their own private quasi regulation that is unaccountable to anyone but themselves." By March 2022, a bipartisan group of Judiciary Committee leaders told the Justice Department that Amazon had engaged in "potential criminal conduct" by misleading the committee when it denied using data from independent sellers to compete with them—an accusation that Amazon vehemently disputed.

When Bezos appeared before that committee, he anticipated questions that veered beyond Amazon's business practices and into his own personal finances. He had every reason to expect a battering about the disconnect between his ballooning wealth and what he paid in taxes (sometimes zero). If asked, I learned, he was prepared to say that he was taxed too little. He wasn't asked.

The 2020 presidential election was well underway by the summer of 2019. Vermont's senator Bernie Sanders was agitated over *The Post's* coverage of his campaign. So Sanders aimed his considerable fire at *The Post*. It wasn't enough, though, for Sanders to slam *The Post's* reporting. He also implied that *The Post's* stories were a direct result of his attacks on Amazon for its labor practices and low tax bills. Ownership by Bezos, as he put it, was to blame.

At a mid-August town hall in Wolfeboro, New Hampshire, Sanders called out to the crowd: "Anybody here know how much Amazon paid in taxes last year?" "Nothing," some replied. And then Sanders took his swipe at *The Post*: "See, I talk about that all of the time. And then I wonder why *The Washington Post*—which is owned by Jeff Bezos, who owns Amazon—doesn't write particularly good articles about me. I don't know why. But I guess maybe there's a connection."

A leading candidate for the Democratic nomination for president was talking a lot like Trump. And I wasn't the only one to think so. "Sanders has long accused the 'corporate media' of putting the interests of the elite above those of the majority of Americans. But Sanders's swipe on Monday went a step beyond his usual media critique in suggesting a news organization covered him unfairly because of its owner," wrote Michael Calderone in *Politico*. "His comments echoed those of President Donald Trump, who has blamed Bezos for unflattering coverage in the paper, calling the *Post* 'the Amazon Washington Post' in tweets."

I wasn't inclined to let Sanders get away with smearing us. Trump's reckless rhetoric was bad enough, but baseless insinuations targeting *The Post* didn't deserve to become common political currency. Asked to respond to Sanders's attack, I delivered one to *The Post*'s public relations department: "Sen. Sanders is a member of a large club of politicians—of every ideology—who complain about their coverage. Contrary to the conspiracy theory the senator seems to favor, Jeff Bezos allows our newsroom to operate with full independence, as our reporters and editors can attest." I threw "conspiracy theory" into the draft statement not only because that's exactly what Sanders was peddling but because the Trumpian flavor of his remarks warranted attention. I expected our PR staff, which routinely shaved the edges off statements I proposed, to delete the phrase. To my surprise, they let this one through. They must have been distracted.

A day later, Sanders toned things down, backpedaling from his innuendo. "I think my criticism of the corporate media is not that they are anti-Bernie, that they wake up, you know, in the morning and say, 'What could we do to hurt Bernie Sanders?'—that's not the case, that Jeff Bezos gets on the phone to *The Washington Post*," he told CNN. "There is a framework of what we can discuss and what we cannot discuss, and that's a serious problem." I also appreciated his defense that day of an independent press. "Donald Trump thinks that media in America is the enemy of the people. And to me, that is a disgusting remark which undermines American democracy," he said. "We need a free media to be there to analyze what's going on, and to criticize, you know, candidates. That's what a free media is about." Sanders's view of the press—and *The Post*, in particular—wasn't Trump's. Something to be thankful for.

I didn't happen to agree with Sanders's critique of what he calls "corporate media." And over an entire career I had yet to see a media ownership model that checked all the boxes that would keep all critics satisfied. Control by a wealthy individual was seen as serving the owner's financial interests. Ownership by a shareholder-owned company was pilloried for seeking short-term profits over long-term investment in its newsrooms. Nonprofits relied heavily on money from rich benefactors with their own agendas and big foundations controlled by trustees from the so-called elite. Media outlets that receive taxpayer money—public radio and TV—regularly faced the threat of having their funding cut off by disgruntled politicians, and only episodically were they a source of groundbreaking investigative journalism. The money for investing in journalism needed to come from somewhere, and I had yet to see small voluntary donations from ordinary citizens give rise to media outlets that had the resources to regularly hold the most powerful to account.

The Post had been pulled out of bankruptcy in 1933 by Eugene Meyer, a supremely wealthy man whose daughter, Katharine Graham, took over the company thirty years later and ran it during the Watergate era and into the early 1990s. During the family's stewardship over eight decades, *The Post* regularly scrutinized entrenched political and commercial interests while standing firm against acts of intimidation. Jeff Bezos acquired *The Post* in 2013, lifting it out of a downward spiral and giving it the wherewithal to report aggressively on a president with authoritarian impulses. For all the attacks on "corporate media," most of what the public knew about Trump and his administration came from those very news organizations.

As the country in 2019 and 2020 considered whether to keep or oust its president, *The Post*'s journalism surely deserved to be judged on its own merits. Bernie Sanders, Donald Trump, other political leaders, and the public itself had every right to challenge us when they felt our reporting went awry. And we weren't perfect, by any means. It was way past time, however, for politicians (Republican and Democratic) and some in the press (from right to left) to stop accusing us of dishonorable motives, falsely imagining that we did our jobs with the interests of the owner as our wretched compass.

For years, *Politico* media critic Jack Shafer, like many other journalists, had been searching for evidence that *The Post* went easy on its owner and Amazon. Finally, in May 2022, he offered a decisive verdict: "Ever since he bought the paper in 2013, I've been on the hunt for examples of the paper pulling Bezos punches, but to my disappointment, I've struck out. The *Post* has reported as thoroughly on Amazon's union battles, its privacy issues, its products, and Bezos' other interests as it would have when the previous regime—the Graham family—owned it. If anything, the paper has been more aggressive on Amazon stories, often beating competitors to the punch."

16

ACCUSER AND ACCUSED

Former vice president Joe Biden was expected to announce soon that he was running for president. The #MeToo movement caught up with him. On March 29, 2019, a Nevada politician and lawyer, Lucy Flores, penned an essay in *New York* magazine's "The Cut" section headlined "An Awkward Kiss Changed How I Saw Joe Biden." Her allegations, and similar ones from more women in the weeks that followed, shifted how others saw Biden, too. His decades-long practice of kissing, hugging, nuzzling, massaging, hand-holding, and patting women was now viewed in a radically different light. What was once seen as the physicality of his politicking—"tactile," "touchy feely," "empathetic"—was now widely described as inappropriate, an invasion of privacy, creepy, and cringeworthy. (He was known for regularly hugging men, too.)

Flores described what happened as she was about to take the stage in 2014 during her run to become the state's lieutenant governor: "As I was taking deep breaths and preparing myself to make my case to the crowd, I felt two hands on my shoulders. I froze. 'Why is the vice-president of the United States touching me?' I felt him get closer to me from behind. He leaned further in and inhaled my hair. I was mortified . . . He proceeded to plant a big slow kiss on the back of my head . . . Even if his behavior wasn't violent or sexual, it was demeaning and disrespectful." And yet, she concluded, "I did what most women do, and moved on with my life and my work."

Flores was no longer moving on. As the #MeToo movement took off after the scandals implicating movie executive Harvey Weinstein, many women were no longer moving on. It was an overdue reckoning with ages of inappropriate behavior and outright abuse. But covering allegations that emerged presented some of the most difficult decisions of my career. Harassers and assailants deserved to be held accountable. Some behavior warranted criminal prosecution. In many instances, if not most, the impact of predatory acts was lifelong trauma, layered on top of wreckage done to women's professional aspirations.

The accused had to be treated fairly, however. I felt strongly about that, too. If published allegations proved untrue, we would inflict unjustified, potentially irreparable damage to their reputations. Under certain circumstances, we could face punishing libel suits without a strong line of defense. And there would be consequences for women, too, if accusations collapsed under closer scrutiny. Credible accounts of abuse would be subjected to undue suspicion.

Striking the balance between fairness and accountability was something everyone involved in this coverage struggled with. Ultimately, though, the call on whether to publish was mine to make. Regardless of my decision, I could be certain that my judgment would be questioned—by friends of the accused, by friends of the accuser, by the public at large, and from within our own newsroom.

In some cases, reporting made a clear case for publication: Women accusers were on the record, and there was supporting evidence in documents or from other individuals. But in many of these investigations, it was a closer call. What did we not know? We were typically investigating an alleged encounter between two people in private, with no one else present. "Believe women" was the dictum of the era. But the phrase was insufficient to the task of journalism. Our obligation was to verify accusations.

Women friends of mine have told me of severe harassment they faced over the course of their careers, of sexual overtures from bosses, of a simple and firm "no" that put in jeopardy their professional ambitions. Simply recalling those episodes brought forth strong emotions. We absolutely owed women a full and empathetic hearing as well as a serious and sustained investigation. Still, publication required corroboration. There had to be sufficient overall evidence to establish that allegations were credible and deserved to be aired publicly. Uncomfortable questions would have to be asked of both accused and accuser.

Mishandling a story would be disastrous. I was keenly aware of notorious cases of false allegations. Charges were dropped in 2007 against three former Duke lacrosse players who had been accused of rape by a woman hired to strip at the team's spring break party. The media, particularly *The New York Times*, were sharply criticized for a rush to judgment in that case. *Rolling Stone* in 2015 retracted a nine-thousand-word article in which a woman claimed she was gang-raped three years earlier by seven men at a University of Virginia fraternity. The magazine ultimately settled multiple defamation lawsuits. An investigation in 2014 by *The Washington Post* itself played a key role in dismantling the story when reporter T. Rees Shapiro revealed severe flaws in *Rolling Stone*'s reporting.

After Lucy Flores published her piece about Biden, the press went looking for other women offended by Biden's immoderate touching. They weren't hard to find. Many came forward on their own. Nor was any of this a new subject. The online site *Gawker* declared in one 2015 headline: "Joe Biden, We Need to Talk About the Way You Touch Women." The Twitter commentariat had gone wild in February that year when Biden left his hands on the shoulders of

Stephanie Carter for ten seconds as her husband, Ash Carter, was sworn in as the new secretary of defense, also whispering closely in her ear. The *New York Post* called it a "move straight out of the stalker handbook."

But as the photo of that handsy moment circulated anew in 2019 with Biden's presidential race in the offing, Stephanie Carter posted an essay on the Medium publishing platform to repudiate the widespread interpretation that Biden's gesture was peculiar and unwelcome. What all the commenters saw was not what she felt. Eyewitness observation, she noted, has its limits. Biden had been offering support as her husband took on a job that likely would disrupt their lives, she wrote. She was also unnerved by a fall she had just taken on ice at the Pentagon. As for the whispering, "he leaned in to tell me 'thank you for letting him do this.'"

"The Joe Biden in *my picture* is a close friend helping someone get through a big day, for which I will always be grateful. So, as the sole owner of my story, it is high time that I reclaim it—from strangers, Twitter, the pundits and the late-night hosts."

Carter's essay underlined the tricky nature of the #MeToo movement for the press, the public, and politicians. As *The Post* story at the time put it, "The gulf between her new account and the breathless reaction to the 2015 image points to the difficulty of recalibrating expectations of acceptable decorum in the #MeToo era, when virality is easily mistaken for certainty." In this new era, what exactly are the new boundaries of acceptable behavior? What is the appropriate response when a gesture that one individual asserts was intended to be warm and genial is seen by the recipient as offensively intimate and intrusive? Does everyone understand the rulebook? What price should be paid for violating it? How do we judge behavior of the past when mores were different, even if they shouldn't have been? How can we be fair to both accuser and accused?

As more women accused Biden of unwanted touching, the prospective presidential candidate recorded a video in April 2019 promising to alter his behavior but without apologizing for gestures in the past that he said were intended "to make a human connection." But Biden's reckoning with the #MeToo movement would only become more troublesome nearly a year later when a California woman named Tara Reade accused him of sexually assaulting her in 1993 when she was a twenty-nine-year-old staff assistant in his Senate office. The allegation, made on a podcast with journalist Katie Halper, set off a crisis in Biden's campaign.

Reade's first account of an inappropriate encounter with Biden came on April 3, when she told *The Union* newspaper of Nevada County, California, that Biden had touched her inappropriately in 1993 when she worked as a twenty-nine-year-old staff assistant in his Senate office. "He used to put his hand on my shoulder and run his finger up my neck," Reade said. She also said her responsibilities in the office were reduced when she refused to serve drinks at an event as Biden requested, purportedly because he liked her legs. She recounted how, feeling pushed out of the office, she left after about nine months.

In the early months of 2020, Reade turned to social media to support the campaign of Bernie Sanders. By March, she was signaling on Twitter that she had a lot more to disclose about Biden's behavior. She tweeted on March 5 that he was a "misogynist pred" (short for predator). "Tell Bernie to stay in!" she tweeted on March 22, adding "voters deserve to hear my silenced history w Biden." Two days later, *The Intercept*'s Ryan Grim reported that Reade had approached Time's Up, an organization established amid the #MeToo movement to assist women who had been harassed and assaulted. The organization referred her to outside lawyers but offered no funds for legal or public relations assistance, arguing that its non-profit status precluded it from involvement in cases against political candidates. But a note the organization planned to send lawyers on her behalf said, according to *The Intercept*, "There is more to the story of the harassment that she did not feel safe sharing at that time." Then came the podcast where Reade made explicit her allegations—that in a semiprivate area of Congress he had pinned her against the wall, put his hand up her skirt, and penetrated her with his fingers. The Biden campaign immediately denied the allegation.

The Post and *The New York Times* did not publish stories on Reade's sexual assault allegations until three weeks later. Other than Fox News, the major cable and broadcast networks also had not offered to put her on the air. Many Sanders supporters were furious at what they saw as the press protecting Biden, who was then closing in on the Democratic presidential nomination. Republicans, too, leveled charges of a media double standard—silence on Biden in contrast to unhesitating coverage of sexual assault allegations against Trump. "I literally think they will just put their heads in the sand and make sure that no one possibly hears about these things because that's the feeling and sentiment I get from today's media," Donald Trump Jr. told *Breitbart News*' Sirius XM Patriot Channel on April 25, 2020. "And they don't 'believe all women.' They only believe women if they're accusing conservatives."

That probably sounded spot-on to the president's supporters, but it was entirely false. Reporters at *The Times* and *The Post* were hard at work investigating Reade's allegations. Real investigations take time. And there were substantial differences between accusations against Trump and Biden. Trump, of course, had notoriously boasted in the *Access Hollywood* tape of forcing himself on women and groping them, as *The Post* first reported in early October 2016. The public could hear his depraved remarks for themselves. By the time Reade came forward, a total of seventeen women had accused Trump of sexual misconduct, frequently assault. While many women felt Biden's touching had been highly inappropriate, none but Tara Reade described sexual assault.

Important parts of Reade's story were corroborated, others were disputed, and the evidence was inconclusive with still others. Publishing information that raised questions about Reade's account alongside information that was corroborative didn't sit well with some of the most ardent advocates of "Believe Women." *The Post's* first story was lambasted by actress Rose McGowan, an original accuser of Hollywood producer Harvey Weinstein, who had become a women's advocate. "This is a hit piece. You've sunk to a new low in slanted journalism and victim shaming @WashingtonPost," McGowan wrote in a tweet that was given full news coverage on the Fox News website. A single line in *The Post* story mentioning the police report Reade filed in April 2020 proved to be a Rorschach test for readers: "Filing a false report is a crime punishable by up to 30 days in jail." We heard from Reade supporters who saw those words as casting unfair doubt on her account. But we also heard from Biden supporters who saw them as giving her claim unwarranted credibility.

The Post conducted the same sort of thorough, time-consuming investigation of Reade's accusations as it had with Christine Blasey Ford when she brought allegations of assault against Supreme Court nominee Brett Kavanaugh. Both men deserved scrutiny. Both were under consideration for positions of enormous power. Both women had come forward with their names, and both deserved a hearing that would allow the press and the public to evaluate their accounts. Both also needed to be asked hard, uncomfortable questions because that's what good journalism requires. As Helen Lewis wrote in *The Atlantic*, "Believe Women" as a declaration "makes the job of journalists more difficult. It has made necessary skepticism look like hostility. Sources should know that reporters are only asking hard questions because *everyone else will* . . . The damage of publishing a story that unravels is huge, not just to the individuals involved, but to the issue of sexual assault as a whole."

The Post published its first story on Reade when we completed all the reporting considered necessary, and we followed up as new evidence emerged. Again, some evidence was supportive and other evidence raised doubts. By the end of May, her lawyer had dropped her as a client (while saying it was no reflection on her claims), and California defense lawyers said they would seek to overturn convictions based on testimony she gave when called as an expert on domestic violence. Her truthfulness had been brought into question: Reade said she had received a bachelor's degree from Antioch University and later worked as an "online visiting professor." The university said neither was true. She told the court she had worked as a legislative assistant to Biden, but she had only been a staff assistant, a very junior position. A résumé provided for court proceedings said she worked in Biden's office three years; in fact, she worked there about nine months. The Tara Reade story faded fast. And the facts about her life have remained in dispute: Reade and her lawyer have repudiated a statement in November 2020 by the district attorney of Monterey County, California, that she provided "false testimony" regarding her educational background and have contested other questions about her employment history.

We were never going to resolve with certainty the veracity of her claims. The American people would be left to weigh the evidence on their own. As Dean Baquet, editor of *The New York Times*, said of their own coverage: "Here's everything we know and you have to make your own judgment . . . I think in this case, that's the best we could offer."

By the time Tara Reade's accusations against Biden surfaced, *The Post* had published many #McToo stories. There were a large number of sexual assault allegations in 2014 against comedian Bill Cosby, which *The Post* thoroughly compiled, investigated, and published. There were the allegations that came to light in 2017 against Alabama Republican Senate candidate Roy Moore, which almost certainly led to his electoral loss. That year *The Post* revealed that hundreds of women who worked at Sterling Jewelers, the multibillion-dollar owner of Kay and Jared Jewelers, alleged that they were "routinely groped, demeaned and urged to sexually cater to their bosses to stay employed" amid a culture of discrimination and sexual harassment that extended to the company's most senior executives. (In 2022, Sterling settled the discrimination suit, where women had filed sworn statements with their harassment accusations, for $175 million.) Also in 2017, *The Post* found fifteen women, including former clerks, who accused powerful federal appeals court judge Alex Kozinski of making sexual comments, inappropriate touching, and showing them pornography. (He denied wrongdoing even as he apologized for making women feel "uncomfortable" and then retired while under judicial investigation.) In 2018, reporters dug up allegations of sexual misconduct against leading figures in classical music, including Cleveland Orchestra concertmaster William Preucil (who was then fired) and the Royal Concertgebouw Orchestra chief conductor Daniele Gatti (who was fired from his post in Amsterdam). Preucil admitted to several acts of wrongdoing but denied other allegations. Gatti went on to conduct elsewhere after reaching a settlement. He denied the accusations against him but apologized and pledged to "focus much more on my behaviors and actions with all women."

In April 2018, *The Post* and *Variety* magazine also disclosed allegations by former NBC News correspondent Linda Vester against legendary anchor Tom Brokaw that he sexually harassed her on two occasions, one time in New York and another in London. Brokaw sent an extraordinary 1,035-word email to NBC News colleagues protesting how we had treated him, repudiating his accuser, and asserting his innocence. "It is 4:00 am on the first day of my new life as an accused predator in the universe of American journalism. I was ambushed and then perp walked across the pages of *The Washington Post* and *Variety* as an avatar of male misogyny, taken to the guillotine and stripped of any honor and achievement I had earned in more than a half century of journalism and citizenship." Of his accuser, he said, "she became a character assassin." Vester, through her lawyer, stood by her story. She had told *The Post*, "I am speaking out now because NBC has failed to hire outside counsel to investigate a genuine, long-standing problem of sexual misconduct in the news division."

Brokaw called me, simultaneously indignant and civil, to complain of the harm we had done to a reputation built up over decades. I told him that I understood his view but that, while I could make no judgment about the conflicting accounts, the accuser's story had met our threshold for publication: She was willing to be publicly identified, unlike many others. There were contemporaneous notes in a diary that our reporter reviewed. She pointed us to friends in whom she confided at the time, and they attested to what she had told them. Naturally, that didn't satisfy Brokaw. Nor did our standards satisfy his many friends, colleagues, and supporters. A petition in support of Brokaw, signed by sixty-five women who had worked with him, declared, "Tom has treated each of us with fairness and respect. He has given each of us opportunities for advancement and championed our successes throughout our careers." One prominent NBC News correspondent took me aside at a party days afterward to berate me for allowing the story to see the light of day. There wasn't much for me to say. I had been an admirer of Brokaw over decades, like so many among the American public. Still, I couldn't make an exception to our standards because I'd been among his fans.

Only several months earlier, Brokaw himself seemed in search of the right parameters for defining misconduct and reporting on allegations. "My issue," he told MSNBC, "is that we've got to decide as an institution of governing and an institution of justice and as a culture about where are the lines about all of this . . . It's not easy to arrive at these conclusions because so many of them are subjective. It's in the minds of the violator or the recipient or even the people who are on the left and the right. But I do think we need to have a healthier, well-defined dialogue, if you will. And I'm not quite sure how we launch into it."

Having accusers identify themselves was a critical step toward publishing allegations of harassment and abuse. At *The Post*, our guidelines required that at least one accuser consent to being identified. I considered that reasonable when a career could well be obliterated by a single anonymous-source story of alleged misconduct. And our policy coincided with what was required at many other news organizations. In their book *She Said* about their 2017 investigation of Hollywood mogul Harvey Weinstein, *New York Times* reporters Jodi Kantor and Megan Twohey repeatedly emphasized their institution's insistence on having at least some named accusers. "What is your strategy for getting these women on the record?" their editor Rebecca Corbett asked every few days. In their first blockbuster story, they ended up with several who agreed to be identified.

When in November 2017 *The Post* published what was arguably its most impactful and most praised #MeToo story—about venerated television interviewer Charlie Rose—the reporters had gotten several women to go on the record. That strengthened the piece immeasurably. A year later, when I was rebuked for declining to publish allegations—this time against Jeff Fager, the powerful executive producer of CBS's *60 Minutes*—no accusers were willing to have their names used. That impaired a prospective story considerably, and it was central to our decision not to publish.

Both the Rose and Fager stories had their roots in the work of reporter Irin Carmon. In 2010, while a reporter for the feminist website *Jezebel*, Irin began hearing about Charlie Rose's sexual misconduct. She contacted some of the women who had been subjected to his behavior, but they were reluctant to speak out, fearful of reprisals and damage to their careers. Her job at a digital start-up, where reporters had to crank out stories at a rapid clip, also didn't allow sufficient time for thorough, uninterrupted investigations.

Things changed, however, as the #MeToo movement took off in late 2017. Women were more willing to come forward. "It took the kind of reporting that was happening in the fall of 2017 in *The New York Times*, in *The Washington Post*, about Harvey Weinstein and then about Roy Moore—that was a piece that was really influential to our process—that actually showed how to frame a story as about an abuse of power as opposed to 'look at this creepy old man,'" Irin told the Longform podcast. As Irin began recontacting women, they were ready to talk on the record. When her original source picked up the phone, she said, "I've been waiting for you to call me." Irin told the *Quartz* online site, "It also helped that these women had a few more years of professional and personal distance from Rose . . . But I think the fact that they wouldn't be alone meant everything."

Upon becoming a freelancer with more flexibility in how she spent her time, Irin could dedicate herself to thoroughly investigating the allegations against Rose. She approached *The Post* as an outlet for publication. We were immediately enthusiastic about the story's potential, putting her on contract and assigning Amy Brittain from our investigative staff to work with her. It proved to be an immensely fruitful collaboration between two talented, deeply committed reporters.

"Eight women," the story began, "have told *The Washington Post* that longtime television host Charlie Rose made unwanted sexual advances toward them, including lewd phone calls, walking around naked in their presence, or groping their breasts, buttocks or genital areas. The women were employees or aspired to work for Rose at the 'Charlie Rose' show from the late 1990s to as recently as 2011. They ranged in age from 21 to 37 at the time of the alleged encounters . . . There are striking commonalities in the accounts of the women, each of whom described their interactions with Rose in multiple interviews with *The Post*. For all of the women, reporters interviewed friends, colleagues or family members who said the women had confided in them about aspects of the incidents. Three of the eight spoke on the record. Five of the women spoke on the condition of anonymity out of fear of Rose's stature in the industry, his power over their careers or what they described as his volatile temper."

The November 2017 story easily met all our requirements for publication: Accusers who had allowed their names to be used. Strong corroboration from family and friends. Multiple women describing similar behavior by Rose—a well-documented pattern of behavior that served as reinforcement for the accuracy of each woman's individual account. They had nailed the story. I made some small editing suggestions with the aim of accentuating its strength. And when it was published, its impact was immediate. Rose, then seventy-five, apologized for his "inappropriate behavior," although his statement was carefully crafted to question some accusers' accounts and suggest that he had endeavored over the years to do right by women. "I always felt that I was pursuing shared feelings, even though I now realize I was mistaken," Rose said.

In the days after *The Post*'s story was published online in November, Rose's stellar career unraveled. CBS suspended him as a cohost of *CBS This Morning* and a contributing correspondent for *60 Minutes*. Distribution of his show was suspended by PBS and *Bloomberg*. Next came outright dismissal of Rose by CBS and cancellation of his shows by PBS and *Bloomberg*. The following morning, his now-former co-host Norah O'Donnell declared, "This is a moment that demands a frank and honest assessment about where we stand and more generally the safety of women."

Irin and Amy stayed on top of the Charlie Rose story. There was more to find out. At issue was institutional accountability: What had CBS, PBS, and *Bloomberg* known about allegations against

Rose? And if they had learned of alleged misconduct, what did they do about it? The news outlets said they had not received reports of wrongdoing. But as Amy and Irin looked deeper into CBS, they discovered that some immediate supervisors were, in fact, told. The reporters worked on the story full-time, and after five months *The Post* published a story under their bylines.

"Incidents of sexual misconduct by Charlie Rose were far more numerous than previously known, according to a new investigation by *The Washington Post*, which also found three occasions over a period of 30 years in which CBS managers were warned of his conduct toward women at the network," the May 3, 2018, story began. "An additional 27 women—14 CBS News employees and 13 who worked with him elsewhere—said Rose sexually harassed them. Concerns about Rose's behavior were flagged to managers at the network as early as 1986 and as recently as April 2017, when Rose was co-anchor of *CBS This Morning*, according to multiple people with firsthand knowledge of the conversations."

Numerous additional women went on the record with their names to level accusations against Rose—and against the network for managers' failure to take action. They told others of their experiences contemporaneously, and those individuals confirmed the women's accounts. Rose himself responded via email with one sentence: "Your story is unfair and inaccurate." Their investigation hit the network hard. President David Rhodes told staff that CBS had retained an outside law firm to help with its investigation of Rose's behavior and the news division's internal culture.

As powerful as the story was, however, it was not at all the one Irin and Amy wished to publish. During their reporting on CBS, they unearthed allegations of sexual misconduct by Jeff Fager, only the second person in a half century to oversee *60 Minutes*. Working privately from a small glass "huddle room," the pair pursued the story with admirable determination. Fager had enormous power over the careers of young journalists. If we could document wrongdoing, our intention was to hold him accountable. With the full support of *Post* editors, Amy and Irin were given the time to investigate without interruption. To avoid a potential conflict of interest, *The Post* also discontinued participation in a joint project with *60 Minutes*.

Irin and Amy's direct editor had even pointed them to an additional accuser when he became aware of her allegation against Fager. And yet, frustratingly, neither that accuser nor a previous one who had been speaking with the reporters was willing to be identified. When I joined Irin and Amy at a meeting with their editors to discuss the investigation, they mentioned that Fager and his accuser had signed a nondisclosure agreement but that they had been unable to procure it. I saw the NDA as a way to circumvent our requirement that at least one accuser be named. Instead, we would have solid evidence of wrongdoing. I urged them to try again to get a copy. Amy and Irin ultimately did obtain it, but it proved to be a letdown. The document included no accusations of misconduct against any specific person, nor did it describe any particular incident. Multiple senior CBS executives, including Fager, were signatories to a document in which the employee made general allegations of both age and sex discrimination.

Fager, whom I had met briefly once before, called me to complain about our investigation. I simply listened and, to be fully transparent about my own interaction with the subject of a *Post* investigation, forwarded my notes of the conversation to the reporters and their editors. Also, two women associates of Fager—one a stellar and strong-willed former colleague of mine—called to tell me that they had never witnessed, or heard of, wrongdoing on his part. I sent the reporters notes of those conversations as well, urging that the women be called. When the reporters followed up, neither of those Fager colleagues agreed to speak on the record.

By then Fager had retained a law firm, Clare Locke, that was notoriously aggressive in threatening libel suits against us and many other media outlets. Its latest batch of hostile letters now suggested it might sue *The Post* on Fager's behalf. The law firm also eventually shared copies of emails the first accuser sent Fager after an alleged incident of grave wrongdoing on his part. Their tone was warm and friendly. "You are wonderful," said one note in thanking him for flowers. "Miss you," said another that wished him and his family a nice Thanksgiving.

Seeing a dozen emails of that sort—and still unable to get an accuser on the record—editors directly involved in the story came to my office to share their unanimous conclusion: The story should not be published. It did not meet our standard for publication. I agreed. The reporters, to say the least, vehemently disagreed. Irin later described their follow-up story on CBS as having been "gutted" because allegations against Fager were not included.

The New Yorker weighed in on the matter in July 2018. Deep into a forceful story about a half dozen allegations of harassment by CBS Corporation's CEO, Les Moonves, and a culture of "harassment and intimidation" against women that he fostered—accusations that led to Moonves's ouster—writer Ronan Farrow also surfaced some allegations against Fager: "Six former employees told me that Fager, while inebriated at company parties, would touch employees in ways that made them uncomfortable. One former '60 Minutes' producer told me, 'It was always "Let's go say hello to Jeff,"'cause you have to pay homage to him, but let's do it early in the evening, before he starts getting really handsy.'" In one incident, at which several employees were present, Fager allegedly made drunken advances to an associate producer, commenting on her breasts and becoming belligerent when she rebuffed him. No accuser was named. Fager denied the allegations, saying "they never happened."

The *New Yorker* story also pointed an accusatory finger at *The Post*, suggesting that, in choosing not to publish allegations against Fager, we had been weak-kneed in the face of a lawsuit threat and baseless attacks on the reporters' professionalism. I helped craft a bare-bones statement that was provided to *The New Yorker*: "The reporting throughout was vigorous and sustained and fully supported by *Post* editors. Nothing that met our long-standing standards for publication was left out. Nor did outside pressures, legal or otherwise, determine what was published." That was all true. And it was also predictably ineffective in averting a wave of criticism. The *New Yorker* piece instantly subjected me to denunciation on social media and elsewhere as cowardly and intimidated by threatened litigation. *The Post* reacted as it typically does—riding out criticism, calculating that this, too, would pass. It didn't.

Prior to the *New Yorker* story, Irin had signaled obliquely that the allegations against Fager would find an outlet. In June 2018, while she and Amy accepted an award for the investigation into Charlie Rose, Irin remarked: "The stories that we have been doing are actually about a system. The system has lawyers and a good reputation. It has publicists. It has a perfectly reasonable explanation about what happened. It has powerful friends who will ask, 'Is this really worth ruining the career of a good man?' . . . Indeed, the system is sitting in this room . . . The system is still powerful men getting stories killed that I believe will someday see the light of day."

I was in that room that day. Fager was seated in the audience, too, to accept an award on behalf of *60 Minutes*. I knew the remarks were directed at Fager, but I sensed (accurately) that I was a target as well. Fager and I never crossed paths that evening. I wasn't his friend; I barely knew him. And I'd never said or thought anything like "Is this really worth ruining the career of a good man?"

In April 2019, Irin, no longer on contract with *The Post*, published a 4,700-word article in *New York* titled "What Was the *Washington Post* Afraid Of?" asserting that we were on the cusp of publishing the Fager story but backed off because we were fearful of a libel suit; were overly swayed by women who spoke up on Fager's behalf;

were deterred by "a dozen obsequious, even affectionate, emails" one accuser had sent Fager after alleged misconduct; failed to pay sufficient heed to the nondisclosure agreement; became unreasonably concerned with the fact that none of the accusers were willing to be named; were influenced by a journalistic partnership with *60 Minutes*; and might have been suffering from #MeToo fatigue. On top of that, she wrote, "I did think it was easier for even the most well-meaning editor to empathize with a newsroom leader, a fellow boss with potentially discontented underlings. It's easier for a lot of us to believe that a man's career matters more than the hypothetical losses of the women he might have harmed."

That stung. There was, of course, room for genuine disagreement about the evidentiary threshold necessary for publishing challenging stories of this sort. I firmly believed in our standards, considering them fair to both accuser and accused. They had often delivered accountability while keeping us on solid ground journalistically. They were in line with established practice at other major news organizations. While I could appreciate that some might question my judgment and my decisions, I could not understand why others would question my motives (and those of my fellow editors). I was confident of my own record on stories about allegations of sexual abuse, both at *The Post* and previously.

At *The Boston Globe*, I had launched the investigation that finally gave survivors of sexual abuse by priests the hearing they deserved and held to account Cardinal Bernard Law, the Archdiocese of Boston, and the entire Catholic Church for a decades-long cover-up. That story, beginning in January 2002, has had an enduring impact all the way up to the Vatican and had a profound influence on how institutions of every sort responded to allegations of sexual misconduct—and how the press dug into them. Writing in *America*, a Jesuit publication, after my retirement, a Lehman College journalism professor argued that disclosures about the Church by the *Globe*'s Spotlight investigative team reached "far beyond Catholicism.

It made possible revelations of sexual abuse in institutions as varied as the Boy Scouts of America, the Penn State football program and the U.S. Olympic Women's Gymnastics team. All of these—as well as the #MeToo movement—flowed from the space for truth-telling about sexual abuse that Mr. Baron blew open."

Emily Steel of *The New York Times* spoke of that investigation's influence on her and reporting colleague Michael Schmidt when in 2017 they broke their Pulitzer-winning stories on sexual harassment by Fox News host Bill O'Reilly. With sources at first unwilling to go on the record, they reviewed the *Globe*'s coverage of clergy sex abuse for ideas on how to move their investigation forward. "We pulled up all of those stories and we actually watched that movie *Spotlight*," the Academy Award winner that portrayed the *Globe*'s investigation, she told the Canadian Broadcasting Corporation.

Globe colleagues and I received many expressions of gratitude from survivors of abuse by clerics; from parishioners and even clergy, too. One priest, Father Thomas P. Doyle, who had waged a solitary, yearslong battle on behalf of survivors, wrote a note that meant the world to me: "As one who has been deeply involved in fighting for justice for the victims and survivors for many years, I thank you with every part of my being. I assure you that what you and *The Globe* have done for the victims, the church and society cannot be adequately measured. It is momentous and its good effects will reverberate for decades." I kept his letter on my desk in Boston to serve as an ever-present reminder of my purpose in journalism.

Over time, we learned more about Fager. And ultimately he faced a reckoning. In September 2018, he was fired for sending a threatening text to a CBS reporter covering the sexual harassment allegations against the company and him. By December 2018, *The New York Times* reported, an investigation by two outside law firms concluded that Fager had "engaged in some type of sexually inappropriate conduct" with CBS colleagues. The draft report said that one woman alleged that Fager tried to kiss her with an open mouth six years earlier. As for the nondisclosure agreement, CBS CEO Moonves confirmed to investigators who were also digging into his own behavior that the company had paid $950,000 to settle a woman's allegations of age and sex discrimination and accusations of sexual misconduct by Fager. The woman declined to participate in the investigation, leaving the outside lawyers CBS retained unable to interview her. "While they could not rule it out," *The Times* reported, investigators "found 'no credible evidence' to confirm her account of misconduct." The report concluded that Fager's overall misconduct "should not have been tolerated, but we find that it was not as severe as the media accounts."

In response to Irin Carmon's piece in *New York* magazine, *The Post* delivered a short statement defending ourselves similar to what we had provided *The New Yorker*. Stewing a day later over Irin's accusations against us, my fellow editors and I drafted a long letter contesting Irin's account. But *The Post*'s public relations department, which always preferred to move on rather than risk ginning things up, urged us not to send it. The letter never left my computer. However, three sentences from that draft letter are worth mentioning here: "Carmon casts this entire episode as a matter of believing women who make allegations of egregious behavior regarding assault and harassment. It's one thing to believe people. At issue here is the evidence required in order to publish such allegations."

In January 2019, Amy Brittain and *Post* colleague Maura Judkis published a powerful story of sexual assault followed by breathtaking leniency from a District of Columbia judge who sentenced the assailant. A twenty-seven-year-old hairstylist had been attacked while jogging in her neighborhood. The attacker was a rising local chef. He put one hand over her mouth and the other between her legs.

The woman fought him off, scratching his face, and he responded by punching her, grabbing her phone, and running off. He was caught within minutes by local police, easily identified by his facial injuries. The assailant later admitted his offense, also acknowledging attacks on five other women. Prosecutors filed only misdemeanor charges, and the judge in the case, Truman Morrison III of D.C. Superior Court, handed down a sentence of only ten days in jail, served on weekends, to suit the attacker's work schedule: eighty days in a half-way house and five years of probation. The process left the attacker entirely off the registry of sex offenders. *The Post* reporters' story told of the woman's pursuit of justice she felt had been denied her.

A fifty-nine-year-old baker in Birmingham, Alabama, who read Amy and Maura's story had a story of her own to tell. The woman told Amy that the judge had himself assaulted her when he was thirty-two years old and she was only sixteen. She had fallen asleep on a deck at a rural Virginia property owned by his family, the woman recounted, but awakened to discover Morrison penetrating her vagina with his fingers. She described subsequent groping incidents by Morrison over the years. Well before Amy heard those allegations, Morrison had become a highly respected judge with a sterling reputation. He led programs to train judges to take the bench. Appointed by President Jimmy Carter in 1979, he had become a national advocate of criminal justice reform.

The allegations against Morrison motivated Amy and her newsroom colleagues to develop *The Post*'s first investigative podcast. They worked on it exclusively for many months. As *Post* editors later wrote, "The podcast shows what it takes to come forward with a claim of sexual assault, how journalists work to corroborate such an account, and why that reporting matters."

When *The Post*'s reporters confronted Morrison with the allegations of sexual assault against a teenager, Morrison initially acknowledged "sexual touching," declaring that he had expressed "deep regret" to her family decades earlier. He later denied touching her while she was asleep as well as any unwanted sexual encounters on later occasions. He declined to describe the nature of the sexual touching. "I certainly did not think that I ever forced myself on her, but the truth remains that it was wrongheaded of me to initiate any sexual contact given her age and our age difference," he told *The Post* in a statement. "Whether or not I thought my contacts were welcome is completely irrelevant. I certainly appreciate that sexual touching of any kind without clear permission is not acceptable at any age."

Before the podcast was released, Amy received pushback from Morrison's friends, and their voices were included in the podcast. A former *New York Times* journalist provided a statement arguing that publication "risks making the Me Too movement look less about justice and more about revenge." She added, "This respected judge spent his entire public life trying to improve a flawed and unfair judicial system for men and women alike."

I, too, had heard from a friend of the judge, a former senior editor of *The Post* who strongly advised me to kill the project outright. "A package of stories about such an old and ambiguous episode would, I fear, destroy the remaining years of a 75-year-old man's life after a long career of admirable public service," he wrote. "This prospect seemed to me inconsistent with the *Washington Post* values I learned and propagated in my 50 years at the paper."

I couldn't help but reflect on the turn of events. In the spring of 2019, I was publicly excoriated by a reporter for having declined to publish allegations of sexual misconduct. Now, in the fall of 2020, I was being admonished by a former high-ranking editor for green-lighting publication of another allegation of that sort.

The story about Judge Morrison may have conflicted with *The Post*'s values of the past, but it did not conflict with our values in the present. In the #MeToo era, old values were being challenged.

They had failed women. Amy's October 2020 podcast had met all our standards for publication. The women accusers were named. The episode was serious. The offender held a position of great authority. The allegations were entirely relevant to his work.

Upon receiving Amy's inquiries, Morrison retired after four decades as a judge. The podcast earned Amy and her *Post* colleagues journalistic honors. "This raw storytelling," wrote the judges for one award, "shone a light on the investigative reporting process and offered a transparent example of how sexual assault stories can be responsibly and respectfully reported."

17

TWITTER STORMS

When Twitter was founded in 2006, I was leading *The Boston Globe*'s news staff. Few of us could envision then what the social media platform would mean for our profession. In almost no time at all Twitter became central to news and the daily lives of journalists. The most alert and adaptable journalists quickly saw how Twitter could aid their reporting, boost readership, and offer them a direct, more personal connection to readers.

At *The Boston Globe* in 2011, I was urged to put someone in charge of our efforts to use social media. Adrienne Lavidor-Berman became the paper's first—and, for years, only—social media editor. Central to her mission was evangelizing for Twitter's possibilities, educating staff on how to use it, encouraging them to be active users, and developing their own social media personality. I became one of her early students—"intimidating but willing," as she remembers me. Although only a sporadic tweeter myself, I encouraged our newsroom to make full use of Twitter.

We could no longer count on readers picking up the newspaper or even going directly to our website. Increasingly, they spent time on Twitter and Facebook, regularly getting their news there and on other social media networks. We had to get our stories onto those platforms where they would be seen. "You saying we had to do this was a big deal," Adrienne recalls. Less than a decade later, while I was leading the newsroom of *The Washington Post*, my message to staff took a sharp turn, not entirely reversing course but moving in that direction: Be more careful with what you say on social media. You don't have to post there. If you do, don't violate our standards.

Official discipline at *The Post* for unacceptable behavior on Twitter was rare. Formal warning letters averaged only one a year. But our limited measures to enforce standards in one instance were enough to provoke a full-scale staff revolt. Hundreds signed a petition protesting a single enforcement action of mine, leading to a broader uprising against our social media rules. In twenty years running a newsroom, I'd experienced nothing like it.

I remain unrepentant, more convinced of the need for strict guidelines. Over the years, Twitter had moved to the center of civic discourse. It allowed journalists to promote themselves and their insights on a gigantic public stage. It drew public attention to the work of news institutions like ours. Yet too often it became a venue for personal opinions, advocacy, anger, snark, sniping, failed humor, virtue signaling, personal animus, and a rush to judgment—never more so than during the Trump years, when newsroom values of inclusiveness, tolerance, equitable treatment, and an independent press were under attack.

For my entire career, reporters and others on news staffs had been expected to keep their personal views to themselves under any circumstance where they might be seen as representing their organizations. They could provide analysis of news events but were to refrain from pure opinion, which was the province of editorial writers and certain columnists. They were to keep in mind at all times that, whenever they spoke publicly, their remarks would likely reflect on the institution that employed them. That called for care and restraint. Traditional media companies, after all, hadn't hired them to make a public show of their opinions. They were hired for their ability to cover the news. Their stories—published only after review by editors to ensure that institutional standards were met—were to do most of the talking. Those age-old principles were established policy at *The Post* when I signed up to be its executive editor. Rules crafted before I arrived there governed what was permitted on social media and what wasn't. New employees were briefed on *The Post*'s expectations for proper behavior.

Social media platforms like Twitter, however, made it nearly impossible to exercise effective supervision over reporters' public remarks. At *The Post*, hundreds of journalists were tweeting multiple times per day and at all hours. Prepublication vetting of all of those postings would have required a sizable full-time team; monitoring afterward, the same. The vast majority of *Post* journalists had no problem abiding by our standards. They were cautious and showed sound judgment. But others—dozens—pushed the boundaries of what was allowed, periodically busting right through them out of impulsiveness, thoughtlessness, recklessness, and, at times, a heartfelt repudiation of the idea that journalists should be prohibited from speaking their minds. There were many hundreds of journalists in our newsroom, but the actions of a relative few begat needless controversy and, at times, outsized damage to the reputation that *The Post* wanted for itself.

A rising generation of young journalists had grown up on social media. Speaking out on Twitter and elsewhere figured in how they defined themselves. They saw it as an extension, and expression, of their own identity. They didn't accept that when they came to work they had to be a "different person" than the one they were at home or out with friends. We were headed for a clash of values: the traditional ones I had absorbed and embraced throughout my career versus an ascendant view that journalists should not be barred from bringing their "whole selves" into the workplace and shouldn't "hide" who they really were and how they really felt.

In January 2014, only one year after I became *The Post*'s executive editor, we hired Wesley Lowery to join a political team covering

Congress. Wes was only twenty-three. I had known Wes from his time as a college intern at *The Boston Globe* while I was its editor. His work demonstrated impressive talent and energy. *The Globe* later lured Wes back to Boston after a year he spent reporting for the *Los Angeles Times*. At *The Post*, where we were seeking gifted journalists, greater staff diversity, and reporters who were savvy about the latest digital-era ways of reporting, I urged managing editor Kevin Merida to explore Wes's interest in employment at *The Post*. *The Post* had already been tracking Wes as a job prospect since his college years. Having expressed a wish to become a national political reporter, he was a natural for our newsroom.

Even in his first weeks as a full-timer at *The Globe*, Wes had excelled in covering the Boston Marathon bombing in April 2013, volunteering for a twenty-four-hour cycle of reporting from Watertown and Cambridge as police chased the two suspects. In one of his interviews with editors at *The Post*, Wes recounted how he live-tweeted from the scene to keep readers up-to-the-minute and then relied on his tweets as notes for the story he wrote for *The Globe*'s website and the next morning's newspaper. He exemplified the speed, agility, digital smarts, and resourcefulness we were looking for in new hires. Jennifer Peter, *The Globe*'s deputy managing editor overseeing local coverage, informed her newsroom of Wes's departure "with a heavy heart" and "no shortage of ill-will for our former editor" who had engineered his move to *The Post* only nine months after his return to Boston.

Wes spent several months on his congressional beat at *The Post* but in August 2014 was dispatched to help cover civil unrest in Ferguson, Missouri, after the fatal shooting of unarmed Black teen Michael Brown by a white police officer. The violent clashes between law enforcement and protesters raised the profile of the Black Lives Matter movement and helped animate the cause of racial justice that intensified amid fatal police shootings of Black citizens in the years that followed. For Wes, a Black journalist, the coverage was a defining moment as well. His national profile rose dramatically, and much of his later coverage at *The Post* was inspired by what he observed while on the ground courageously reporting from Ferguson.

The harsh tactics of the police were felt by Wes personally. Along with reporter Ryan Reilly of the *Huffington Post*, he was arrested by St. Louis County police officers while working out of a McDonald's where he had gone to charge his mobile phone. Police entered the McDonald's even though it was a peaceful retreat from the unrest on the streets, ordering the restaurant shut and people to leave. Wes used his phone to shoot video of the encounter, an entirely legal (and sensible) act of journalism, but it angered the cops. As he tried to gather his belongings, police moved to arrest him, falsely accusing him of resisting, slamming him against a soda dispenser, and then handcuffing him in plastic ties. He was taken with Reilly—who suffered similar mistreatment—to a Ferguson Police Department holding cell. Though released after a half hour, charges of trespassing and interfering with a police officer were filed a year later.

Immediately after the arrest, a reader emailed Jeff Bezos a question: "Will you SUE for FALSE ARREST and protect your reporters?" Bezos, always remarkably attentive to reasonable emails from customers, forwarded the message to me, inquiring whether the facts would support such a case. We needed time to see whether anything would come of the arrest. Once formal charges were filed and as the case dragged on, the reader's suggestion made ever more sense. I recommended to our lawyers that we threaten a lawsuit for wrongful arrest. A draft complaint was emailed to the county in the middle of settlement negotiations, and in May 2016 the charges were dropped. Under terms of the settlement, the two reporters agreed not to sue. The charges constituted, as I said at the time, "contemptible overreaching by prosecutors."

With Wes's vivid coverage of what unfolded on the streets of Ferguson and his deft use of social media to tell the story in real time, his Twitter following exploded. A journalist still in his early twenties, who had only recently arrived at *The Post* with eighteen thousand followers, began to acquire them in the hundreds of thousands. His high profile during an intensely polarizing news event also made him a natural target. Not only did Wes have to endure tear gas and rubber bullets while witnessing protesters' injury and grief, he endured invective on social media, on air, and from right-wing critics intent on tormenting him and disparaging *The Post*. It would have been a lot for anyone to handle; more so for someone at the start of his career. *Post* journalists are expected to take a lot of shit, mostly suppressing their emotions and continuing with their work. That was not Wes's approach. To his nastiest critics, he responded in kind, provoking more attacks. He didn't handle it according to our standards.

Twitter fights were one piece of the overall picture. Perhaps nothing received as much notice as his reaction to Joe Scarborough when the host of MSNBC's *Morning Joe* suggested that Wes bore blame for his arrest because he failed to "move along" as instructed by police. "I don't sit there and have the debate and film the police officer," Scarborough said, "unless I want to get on TV and have people talk about me the next day." It was a callous and ill-informed thing to say, and Scarborough later admitted, "I should have kept my mouth shut." Wes, immersed in covering a story of high emotions, didn't respond with the composure we expected of staff. "I would invite Joe Scarborough to come down to Ferguson and get out of 30 Rock where he's sitting sipping his Starbucks, smugly," Wes told CNN. "Let me be clear about this—I have little patience for talking heads," he added. "This is too important. This is a community, a community in the United States of America, where things are on fire. This community is on edge. There's so much happening here, and instead of putting more reporters on the ground we have people like Joe Scarborough running their mouth and have no idea what they're talking about." Wes's combative instincts were understandable. They were also unhelpful. At *The Post*, where we wanted readers to focus on what we were covering rather than ourselves, Wes himself became a story.

Editors on our national staff urged Wes to exercise restraint, as did managing editor Kevin Merida. Supervisors encouraged him to use his rapidly rising Twitter following as a tool to acquire sources for stories rather than as a platform for pointed, unnecessary, and counterproductive public combat with his critics. For a while, it looked as if he had taken the message to heart. On January 1, 2015, Wes posted to the Tumblr and Instagram platforms a set of goals for the new year. The first: "More writing, less Twitter." The second: "Assume the good in people. (No social media fights.)"

Yet over time, the issue recurred, followed by more conversations between editors and Wes about controlling his social media impulses. By the summer of 2015, *Washingtonian* magazine published a story headlined "Why Does Everyone Want Wesley Lowery to Shut Up?" profiling a "*Washington Post* rising star" who was a "terrific reporter" but who also was "pretty good at driving his critics crazy." The piece rightly noted that Wes had "become a parachuter par excellence: establishing deep sources, writing colorful solo pieces, and contributing to team coverage." And the *Washingtonian* also took note of tweets that were "ill-advised, even ill-tempered." In one, he said, "black ppl don't work for @politico." Another, *Washingtonian* noted, called "a detractor a crude name."

By then, Wes had been given a new, high-visibility beat: "the interactions between law enforcement officials and their communities." It was an ideal match of reporter and subject. As Wes investigated the circumstances around the shooting of Michael Brown in Ferguson, he was astonished to discover that data on fatal police shootings was scarce. He proposed to make that the focus of his reporting and urged our newsroom to log every police shooting in 2015. It was a smart idea, and *The Post* responded with the resources it deserved. The project became what was then the largest in *The Post*'s history, involving about seventy journalists, including reporters from multiple departments, researchers, database experts, photographers, and graphics specialists. The reporting yielded essential insights into the circumstances around some 990 fatal police shootings across the country in 2015, and it earned Wes and his *Post* colleagues a Pulitzer Prize for national reporting.

As a central figure of a Pulitzer-winning team, Wes saw his public profile once again rise. He continued to do superb work. He also became more outspoken, and no less rash. Over the years, editors delivered Wes the same sorts of cautions that he received during his coverage of Ferguson. *The Post* wanted Wes's journalism. We had put unprecedented institutional support behind it. And we wanted the journalism to speak for itself.

The issue came to a head in 2019 after a series of caustic Twitter blasts and other commentary by Wes left editors exasperated. He was defying our counsel. On July 14, a day after Trump lambasted four progressive congresswomen of color and called on them to "go back" to the "totally broken and crime infested places from which they came," Wes used his Twitter account to accuse the media of being "cowardly" for not immediately using the term "racist" to describe Trump's remarks. He slammed those "calling the shots in MSM [mainstream media] newsrooms" and the "people writing the articles." Among editors at *The Post*, the tweet seemed aimed not just at the press in general but also *The Post* in particular. We hadn't used the term "racist" immediately. *The Post*'s practice wasn't to apply categorical labels like that without considerable discussion, even when we found comments detestable, as Trump's were. Our guidelines for language were primarily within the purview of our copy desk chief, who happened to be Black. Within a day, managing editor Cameron Barr assembled a diverse group to thoroughly discuss whether to label Trump's comments "racist." We made the decision to do so.

Deliberativeness isn't cowardice; it's a guardrail against the perils of impulsiveness. Nor was there unanimity within journalism about the wisdom of sticking the "racist" label on Trump. Keith

Woods, NPR's chief diversity officer, who is Black, argued against his own organization's decision to apply the term to Trump's remarks. His commentary—headlined "Report on Racism, but Ditch the Labels"—wondered where labeling of Trump's offensive comments on a variety of subjects might lead over time: "Weren't some misogynistic? Vulgar? Homophobic? Sexist?" Such judgments, he wrote, "belong in the space reserved for opinions."

When Trump later that month denigrated the city of Baltimore as a place where "no human being would want to live," Wes turned to Twitter again. "Black & brown ears can hear the racism clearly while our white colleagues engage in fruitless, if earnest, pedantic games." An article in *Politico* said Lowery "hoped decision-makers in his newsroom and others got his message."

Wes subsequently turned to Twitter to criticize a *New York Times* story examining a decade of the Tea Party movement: "How do you write a 10 years later piece on the Tea Party and not mention—not once, not even in passing—the fact that it was essentially a hysterical grassroots tantrum about the fact that a black guy was president. Journalistic malpractice." In the same time period, he mocked *New York Times* columnist Maureen Dowd for hosting a book party attended by House Speaker Nancy Pelosi and for a column she'd written dismissing criticism that she and her co-author were "decadent aristocrats." Wes tweeted: "look, if you're a 25-year New York Times political columnist who pals around with the Speaker of the House you are, in fact, a 'decadent aristocrat.' If you don't have the self awareness then I'm not sure what to tell you."

Editors lost their patience. All the warnings over five years were being ignored. Maybe a formal disciplinary letter would do the trick. I didn't write it, but I volunteered to deliver it in hopes that he'd at long last take our social media policies seriously.

The final version of *The Post*'s letter, given to him by my deputies, laid out our concerns plainly: "The issue here is where and how to provide your perspective on issues facing the media, including coverage of race. You should not use social media to send messages to your colleagues in the newsroom. You should not use social media to criticize competitors for their coverage. You should not use social media as a forum to express what, by any reasonable reading, would be viewed as your political opinions. You should not use social media in a way that jeopardizes your own ability to cover certain public figures and groups or the ability of *The Post* to cover those same public figures and groups. Above all, what we ask of you is restraint. You may appear in public forums to speak generally about media issues, including coverage of race. That is a valuable contribution to our profession. However, you need to be careful not to step into the role of an opinion journalist. As with any other reporter, your reporting, subject to the customary editing process, should do most of the talking—illuminating important and sensitive issues."

First, though, came a confrontational meeting in my office. Wes rejected the idea that he had done anything improper, asserted that he wasn't expressing political views (just facts), declared that *The Post* didn't "own" him, and advised me that my own "behavior" was what deserved rebuke. I advised him that his job was as a news reporter, not a commentator, activist, or advocate. As the meeting quickly deteriorated, I cut it short as "not constructive," telling him that he was being "insolent" and instructing him to abide by our policies. The letter itself concluded with boilerplate legal language included in every *Post* disciplinary letter (and that is common in the corporate world): "Failure to address this issue will result in increased disciplinary action, up to and including the termination of your employment." In Wes's later telling, I had threatened to fire him, a high-drama overstatement of the disciplinary process at such an early stage. I knew of no one at *The Post* who had ever been fired for social media violations, despite receiving letters like his. In advance of my meeting with Wes, I had asked our legal department to remove the "termination" language but was rebuffed. To my regret, our dispute was exacerbated by some factual errors in an original version of the letter. Understandably, Wes seized on the mistakes in his letter of response.

Wes's letter began by acknowledging his "past conversations with editors about our social media policies." And he added, "It is clear now that top Post editors are more upset than had previously been made clear." Our enforcement of the "sweeping social media policies," he said, was inconsistent. And he claimed that his championing of diversity in hiring and coverage "appears to increasingly run afoul" of *The Post*'s expectations for reporters' behavior. "Generations of black journalists, including here at *The Washington Post*," he wrote senior managers, "have served as the conscience not only of their publications but of our entire industry: their authority derived from the experience navigating this world while cloaked in black skin; their expertise earned through their own daily journalism. Often those journalists have done so by leveling public criticism of both their competitors and their own employers. News organizations often respond to such internal and external pressure."

We had no intention to "muzzle" Wes, as he later characterized it. But we weren't going to back off standards that governed how *The Post*'s journalists handled themselves in public settings. Their individual behavior—on air, on social media, in speaking engagements, wherever—influenced the public's image of *The Post* overall. *The Post* then employed 850 news department reporters and editors. If each of them acted both as newsperson and commentator, it would be a cacophonous, unprofessional mess.

We wanted Wes to keep working at *The Post*. Our view of him as a talented journalist was not at all diminished. But in January 2020, several months after receiving the first and lightest variant of formal discipline, an aggrieved Wes informed us that he would be quitting in a few weeks to take another job. There was widespread lament in the profession that we were losing a journalist of his abilities, and I was sorry our dispute had ended this way. I was the one who had identified him as someone we should hire. We had previously taken measures to keep him from jumping ship to another media outlet. And he had done superb work with our full institutional backing. But the decision to leave was his, not ours. I also expected that, had he stayed, it would not be long before we had the same social media conversations, probably again in vain.

New York Times media columnist Ben Smith promptly championed Wes's outspokenness as placing him at the vanguard of a younger, more diverse generation of journalists challenging the profession's archaic, failed notions of neutrality and objectivity—and supposedly old-school, outmoded editors like me. In Wes's words, news organizations' "core value needs to be the truth, not the perception of objectivity."

No one, though, was aiming for the *perception* of objectivity. The goal was the *reality* of objectivity—which means thoroughly, open-mindedly, and honestly looking at all the evidence and then unhesitatingly publishing what we learn to be true (while acknowledging what we don't yet know). Seeking answers rather than supposing we possess them from the start is at the heart of good reporting. No one had abandoned the idea of truth as was cartoonishly portrayed. The first of *The Post*'s core principles, dating to 1935, declares, "The first mission of a newspaper is to tell the truth as nearly as the truth may be ascertained." That principle, affixed to a wall facing *Post* journalists as they enter the newsroom, affirms that truth exists but recognizes that its pursuit is a process, requiring not only hard work but some humility and often more time and thought than might be first imagined.

The intemperate manner in which Wes expressed himself on social media was in conflict with the identity *The Post* desired for itself. Institutions have as much right as individuals to define themselves. Over many decades *The Post* overwhelmingly chose to express its own identity with sober, independent, and energetic news coverage, expecting that its public image would not be undermined by random, unbridled commentary from any single member of its staff.

President Donald Trump hosted technology executives at the White House on June 19, 2017. Among the guests were Apple CEO Tim Cook, left, and Microsoft CEO Satya Nadella and Amazon CEO Jeff Bezos, right. (Photo by Chip Somodevilla / Getty Images)

Deputy managing editor Scott Vance and I conducted a news meeting in June 2017. Local editor Mike Semel (foreground) made a presentation, with universal news desk editor Kenisha Malcolm and managing editor Emilio Garcia-Ruiz seated beside him. Publisher Fred Ryan sat along the glass wall. Seated with him, at left, were Sunday editor Tim Curran, design editor Emily Chow, and senior video producer Deirdra O'Regan. At right was video planning editor Rhonda Colvin. (Photo by Franco Pagetti / VII via Redux)

Reporter Stephanie McCrummen, left, interviewed Jaime Phillips, who made false accusations against Roy Moore, Alabama's Republican candidate for Senate, in 2017. Phillips, who was recorded by *Post* videographers nearby, was working for Project Veritas as part of a sting operation that aimed to embarrass the news outlet. (Still image captured from video shot by Dalton Bennett and Thomas LeGro / *The Washington Post*)

Bezos shared a laugh with publisher Fred Ryan during a September 2018 ribbon-cutting ceremony to mark the expansion of *The Post*'s headquarters. Chief information officer Shailesh Prakash is at left, and I am behind Ryan. (Photo by Bill O'Leary / *The Washington Post*)

Washington Post opinion writer Jamal Khashoggi was murdered at the Saudi Arabian consulate in Istanbul, Turkey, on October 2, 2018. Advertisements in *The Post* drew attention to his assassination and the assault on free expression, seeking to hold Saudi leadership accountable. (Photo by *The Washington Post*)

Bezos joined Hatice Cengiz, fiancée of murdered Saudi journalist Jamal Khashoggi, at a ceremony in Istanbul on the one-year anniversary of the *Post* opinion columnist's killing. (Photo by Arif Hudaverdi Yaman / Anadolu Agency via Getty Images)

Bezos and Lauren Sánchez together attended an Amazon Prime Video event in Mumbai, India, in early January 2020. (Photo by Francis Mascarenhas / Reuters via Alamy)

President Donald Trump holds up a copy of *The Washington Post* on February 6, 2020, one day after he was acquitted on two articles of impeachment regarding his dealings with Ukraine. (Photo by Drew Angerer / Getty Images)

Journalist Irin Carmon, right, and *Post* investigative reporter Amy Brittain accepted an award in June 2018 for revealing a pattern of sexual harassment by television host Charlie Rose. They were aggrieved when *The Post* decided not to publish allegations against Jeff Fager, executive producer of CBS's *60 Minutes*. (Photo courtesy of Syracuse University)

Police officers wearing riot gear pushed back demonstrators near the White House on June 1, 2020. Protests were held across the country in the aftermath of the May 25 police killing of George Floyd, an unarmed Black man, in Minneapolis. (Photo by Chandan Khanna / AFP via Getty Images)

Rioters harassed journalists and destroyed television equipment during the January 6, 2021, assault on the U.S. Capitol. A mob stormed into the building to block the certification of Joe Biden's presidential victory. (Photo by Jose Luis Magana / AP)

As *The Post*'s executive editor, I celebrated with staff after the Pulitzer Prizes were announced in April 2014. Eli Saslow, right, won a Pulitzer for explanatory reporting on the prevalence of food stamps and hunger. (Photo by Katherine Frey / *The Washington Post*)

For decades that is how *The Post* operated, holding the powerful to account to great effect. Well-reported, well-edited stories were more powerful than any impulsive tweet. *The Post* was entitled to hold on to its reputation and the standards that gave rise to it. My responsibility as executive editor was to make sure it did.

Social media headaches were a constant. A day after the House voted on December 18, 2019, to impeach Trump for pressuring Ukraine for political favors, political reporter Rachael Bade tweeted a photo of *Post* staffers cheerfully enjoying a round of beers with the line "Merry Impeachmas from the WaPo team!" It was a joke. Both Republicans and Democrats were using the line on Capitol Hill. But the public wasn't in on the humor. Outrage followed. The Trump campaign, predictably, jumped to discredit *The Post*. "Ladies & gentlemen, your fair and objective press corps in action! What a joke," Trump's 2020 campaign manager Brad Parscale tweeted. Rachael received the usual informal warning from managers and responded with a note of mature remorse. "No excuses," she emailed her bosses. She deleted the tweet with a note to followers: "To be absolutely clear, we at the *Post* are merely glad we are getting a break for the holidays after a long 3 months."

Another talented *Post* political reporter, David Weigel, in early 2020 responded to a Twitter user who encouraged New Yorkers to beat the deadline for registering as a Democrat so they could vote for Bernie Sanders in the Democratic primaries. For whatever reason, Dave felt compelled to offer this tweet in reply: "tfw [that feeling when] you change your party registration," attaching an image showing what appeared to be male sexual torture. The image, readers relayed to me, had previously been used in a homophobic attack on Democratic presidential candidate Pete Buttigieg. Understandably, the public reacted with disgust. Dave deleted the tweet and apologized, but it didn't mollify critics. "I could not in good conscience subscribe to WaPo again if there can't be consequences for this type of behavior," one reader wrote me. Dave was officially warned about his social media misbehavior. It was hardly the first time. Notoriously, Dave in late 2017 had tweeted out a photo that left a false impression of a small crowd at a Trump rally in Pensacola, Florida. The photo, he quickly learned, was taken before the venue filled up. Trump went on the attack, demanding his dismissal. Dave had promptly deleted his tweet when alerted to his error, and he then apologized to the president on Twitter. But the damage to *The Post*'s reputation was done. Trump would repeatedly point to the tweet as deliberate "fake news." Once again, we had hand-delivered Trump ammunition to fire at us.

Well after I'd left *The Post*, in June 2022, Dave committed another social media blunder, retweeting a sexist joke. Again, *The Post*'s PR department tried to clean up the mess, offering assurances that "reprehensible and demeaning language or actions like that will not be tolerated." The episode kicked off days of mortifying public feuding on Twitter among *Post* staffers. Dave was suspended for a month without pay, a penalty that may have reflected a yearslong accumulation of disciplinary warnings. When I was at *The Post*, our worries over his social media behavior once caused us to take drastic action: An editor was required to review every tweet of his before he could post it. In the fall of 2022, a few months after his most recent Twitter dustup, Dave left *The Post* for news start-up *Semafor*.

Day after day, Twitter seemed to bring out reporters' worst, most unthinking impulses. It was hard to fathom why smart people couldn't exercise more self-control. Most of the time, staffers were merely told to delete an offending tweet and be more prudent. Most of the time, they expressed regret, committed to observing the rules, and sought to move on. And then there was our most notable exception: Felicia Sonmez, who ultimately opted to file a lawsuit against *The Post* and six top editors, including me, citing restrictions on what she could cover because of her nonstop social media commentary.

Typically, I interviewed every finalist for an open news position at
The Post. A single hire could make a big difference for the better, or
for the worse. For some reason I was not available when Felicia came
through our newsroom for interviews in May 2018. But *The Post*
was eager to fill an opening on our breaking-news desk for politics,
and national editors vouched for Felicia. She had worked at *The Post*
previously. She had gone on to report from Beijing, working first for
the wire service Agence France-Presse and then for *The Wall Street
Journal.* So I gave my go-ahead, and she started in mid-June.

The Post knew when editors interviewed Felicia this time that she
had identified herself as a survivor of sexual misconduct. Her allegations against the *Los Angeles Times* bureau chief in Beijing, Jonathan
Kaiman, had been publicly disclosed, including on her Twitter account. Before visiting *The Post*, she had sent a letter containing her
allegations to the Foreign Correspondents Club of China, with a
copy to the *Los Angeles Times*, which then suspended its reporter and
initiated an investigation. She accused Kaiman of sexual misconduct
after she drove him home on her scooter following a correspondents
club party the previous summer. In her account, some of the evening
was consensual, some not, and other memories were lost to the blur
of too much alcohol consumption.

"Even though parts of the evening were consensual, while on the
way, Jon escalated things in a way that crossed the line," her letter
said. She made allegations of digital penetration on a public street
without her consent and asserted that she repeatedly told him no.
She also said she subsequently walked up the six flights of steps to
his apartment. "I don't remember what was going through my head
as I went upstairs, whether I wanted to take a nap or get some water
or maybe make out." By her account, she had "unprotected sex" with
him, and then added, "I am devastated by the fact that I was not
more sober so that I could say with absolute certainty whether what

happened that night was rape." Felicia told a Hong Kong news site that she made no report to Beijing police: "It was over the course of months, from September 2017 to January 2018, that I realized what happened to me was wrong. By the time it had fully sunk in, I was back in the U.S. for a long visit and had already decided to leave Beijing. So, it didn't seem like going to the Beijing police was a viable option."

Felicia came forward with her allegations after she read a January 2018 post on the Medium publishing platform from another woman who claimed "sexual misconduct" by Kaiman. In that post, the woman described how the two had returned to her Beijing apartment, flopped down on the bed, and "began making out and undressing." After a few minutes, she said, she changed her mind, got up from the bed, and insisted she no longer wished to continue. She wrote: "I clearly remember feeling confused and dismayed that he wasn't leaving, or even moving, and that he didn't seem to believe that I knew what I wanted. The back and forth continued for several minutes, and he began to whine. I remember that he made me feel very pressured and very awkward, like it was too late to back out . . . I am still so upset that I concluded the easiest, least confrontational way forward was to place male satisfaction above my own desire and to go back to the bed . . . We had sex, and I felt gross for all of it. He left immediately after." She described what transpired as "being pressured into sex by an opportunistic friend," and had come to the conclusion that "this was not my fault . . . and I do not share the blame." She publicly disclosed the encounter on Medium, she said, "to add my voice to the broader outcry against sexual misconduct."

After the *Los Angeles Times* conducted its investigation, it sent Kaiman an email declaring that his "treatment of women brought undue negative publicity on your news organization." He was given the choice of resigning or being fired, choosing the former in August 2018. Kaiman returned to the United States without a job. The *Los Angeles Times* kept the results of its investigation confidential as a personnel matter, but several weeks later *The New York Times* and other media outlets learned of Kaiman's resignation and published stories. Felicia provided a statement, at once thanking the *Los Angeles Times* for "taking my allegation seriously" and chiding the publication for not doing enough. "In the case of the *L.A. Times'* handling of this situation," she wrote, "several questions remain unanswered. The newspaper has not been transparent about the results of its investigation. It has not made clear whether Mr. Kaiman was fired or resigned voluntarily. And it has not addressed questions about the extent of its knowledge of Mr. Kaiman's actions in January and its decision not to further investigate at the time." She added that she stood "in solidarity" with the other Kaiman accuser "who took the brave step of speaking out first, paving the way for others to follow."

Early on Kaiman had said his perception and Felicia's of the encounter "differ greatly" and "all of the acts we engaged in were mutually consensual." After resigning, Kaiman described a devastating toll from the accusations against him. While "the allegations against me involved no violence, threats, coercion, or power imbalance of any kind," he said, they "irrevocably destroyed my reputation, my professional network, my nine-year career in journalism, and any hope for a rewarding career in the future; they have branded me with a scarlet letter for life, and driven me to the brink of suicide."

In August 2019, *Reason* magazine published an eight-thousand-word examination of the allegations against Kaiman. Author Emily Yoffe forcefully challenged the idea that either of the two publicized sexual encounters that had felled Kaiman, including the one with Felicia, constituted sexual misconduct. "The entire feminist enterprise is undermined if society comes to the conclusion that women bear no responsibility for their choices in the sexual realm," she wrote. From Yoffe's perspective, Kaiman had been unjustly accused. "We are now in a time," she wrote, "when a sexual encounter can be recast in a malevolent light, no matter whether the participants all appeared to consider it consensual at the time and no matter how long ago it took place." Yoffe's skepticism elicited a furious reaction from Felicia, who penned a six-page letter to *Reason* that labeled it "misleading and error-laden." She then appended the letter to a series of eighteen tweets one day, followed by a series of thirteen tweets a couple of days later. *Reason* responded with three minor corrections.

Five weeks later, Felicia took to Twitter again to criticize another reporter's comments that she felt were directed at her and suggest her employer "reconsider its association" with that journalist. In another long series of tweets, she also positioned herself as speaking for women accusers in general, with other women "watching and taking notice."

All of this played out publicly on social media. Felicia not only accused other journalists of shoddy work, she effectively called for firing one of them. She had expressed "solidarity" with a previous Kaiman accuser whose allegations had never been adjudicated and most likely never would be. She criticized Kaiman's employer, the *Los Angeles Times*, for what she considered an inadequate response to her allegations. She portrayed herself as carrying the torch for other women accusers. All of this involved her personal life, and yet she pinned one of her tweets about it to the top of the Twitter account she used in her professional capacity at *The Post*, mixing personal and business matters. Despite newsroom managers' requests, she declined for weeks to remove the tweet.

None of this was normal behavior for *Post* journalists, regardless of the trauma or injustice they experienced in their personal lives. It also ran counter to our code of standards and ethics that called on reporters to "remain in the audience . . . to report the news, not to make the news." And her unrelenting advocacy on Twitter raised concerns among her managers about whether she could be seen as impartially covering the subject of sexual assault and harassment. *The Post*'s ethics code barred "conflict of interest or the appearance of conflict of interest wherever and whenever possible." Standards of that sort have been common at all five news organizations where I have worked over four and a half decades. Life experience informed our journalism, but commingling our personal lives and professional endeavors was a step too far. Public advocacy was strictly prohibited, as was anything that could be perceived that way.

When Felicia was hired, *The Post* placed no restrictions whatsoever on any subjects she could cover, knowing full well about her accusations against Kaiman. For several days in September 2018 she was among the *Washington Post* reporters covering Christine Blasey Ford's sexual assault allegations against Supreme Court nominee Brett Kavanaugh. But with the release of her statement about Kaiman's exit from the *Los Angeles Times*, her immediate supervisors and our standards editor concluded that she could not simultaneously engage in that sort of public advocacy while also covering the nation's most high-profile dispute over sexual assault allegations—or anything similar. Our coverage was being closely scrutinized, above all for fairness.

Months later, after a lull in Felicia's social media commentary about her own case, *The Post* allowed her to resume covering stories about sexual abuse and harassment. But the stream of Twitter postings that followed the August 2019 publication of the *Reason* magazine story led us to impose the prohibition once again. Her dozens of tweets, in the view of senior editors, collided with our policy on conflicts of interest as well as involvement in partisan causes. Her attacks ran counter to another policy that barred using Twitter accounts associated with *The Post* to criticize other journalists and their news organizations. A disciplinary letter in October called for the "immediate cessation" of such activities. Felicia, with the support of the newsroom's union, filed a grievance and complained of unfair treatment even as she continued to cover a wide range of other breaking news in the realm of national politics.

A month after I retired from *The Post* in February 2021, six senior newsroom managers, yielding to pressure from newsroom staff, allowed Felicia to once again resume covering stories of sexual assault and harassment. Weeks later, again to placate staff, they also acceded to her public insistence on an apology, expressing remorse "for the way we have handled your situation. We imposed limitations on the scope of your work that we've concluded are unnecessary. We see the ways in which we should have supported you more than we did." Having retired, I didn't participate in the decision to write that letter. It wasn't one I would have sent. We had enforced traditional journalistic standards to safeguard *The Post*'s reputation. That's not something I would ever apologize for.

My former colleagues, however, hoped to put the long-running conflict with Felicia and her newsroom allies behind them. I knew it wouldn't, and sure enough it didn't. Felicia wrote back, calling upon two superb editors who were candidates to succeed me to withdraw from consideration. "I view your actions in my situation as disqualifying," she said, "and I do not think either of you should be elevated to a role where you will potentially be leading this newsroom for the next ten years . . . Your actions are an outrage, and all *Post* employees deserve better." (Neither got the position, but both were later promoted by my successor, deservedly so.)

The next step came in July 2021 when Felicia filed a lawsuit against six top editors individually, including me, as well as *The Post* for "unlawful discrimination and a hostile work environment based on her gender and her protected status as a victim of a sexual offense." The lawsuit was widely covered, and much of the coverage credulously took as fact Felicia's core allegation that we had banned her from covering sexual misconduct cases simply because she was a sexual assault survivor. But that was fiction, as a District of Columbia Superior Court judge made evident in dismissing her claims eight months later.

News organizations, Judge Anthony C. Epstein wrote, "have the right to adopt policies that protect not only the fact but also the appearance of impartiality." The facts of the case, even as Felicia alleged them, made it "affirmatively implausible that her victim status or gender was a reason for the *Post*'s decisions concerning her assignments." Felicia's appeal of that decision was pending as this was written.

After the solid lower-court victory, *The Post* made no public comment. But I wasn't going to let the moment pass without saying something on my own behalf. Felicia had been speaking freely. As a defendant, I was hamstrung. The only wise course had been to keep my mouth shut until the judge ruled. However, news coverage of the case had dismayed me. It was gullible, agenda-driven, unfair, and nasty, in many instances depicting *The Post*, my colleagues, and me as insensitive, if not cruel, toward a sexual assault survivor. Now, with one dry sentence, I hoped to make a point: Fact, law, and reason had finally prevailed in court, even if they hadn't in the press. "I am grateful," I said, "for a legal process that allowed the claims in this lawsuit to be evaluated objectively." At least a judge understood the rationale behind ethics standards, even if too many journalists in *The Post*'s newsroom and elsewhere didn't.

I skipped over one notable episode because it deserves a discussion all its own. It began on January 26, 2020, with news that basketball legend Kobe Bryant died at age forty-one in a helicopter crash on a hillside near Calabasas, California. His thirteen-year-old daughter, Gianna, and seven others, including the pilot, were also killed. I was in Madrid at the time, and the shock and grief there ran deep, as it did around the world.

Close to midnight, I received an urgent call from *Post* editors. A tweet by Felicia had ignited a furor on social media. Seventy-eight minutes after Bryant's death was first reported by the TMZ news outlet and thirty-eight minutes after the Associated Press provided confirmation of that report—as calculated for the 2022 edition of *The Ethical Journalist* textbook—Felicia had tweeted a story from the *Daily Beast* news site headlined "Kobe Bryant's Disturbing Rape Case: The DNA Evidence, the Accuser's Story, and the Half-Confession." Pieces of the aircraft were still smoldering, and many people were just learning the news of the crash. Public outrage over Felicia's perceived insensitivity, and *The Post's*, was immediate. She and *The Post* were targeted with hate, seen as heartless and tasteless.

Felicia responded to the public furor with yet more tweets. "Well, THAT was eye-opening. To the 10,000 people (literally) who have commented and emailed me with abuse and death threats, please take a moment and read the story—which was written 3+ years ago, and not by me. Any public figure is worth remembering in their totality even if that public figure is beloved and that totality unsettling. That folks are responding with rage & threats toward me (someone who didn't even write the piece but found it well-reported) speaks volumes about the pressure people come under to stay silent in these cases."

Other senior editors and I were livid. Her tweets threatened to become the face of *The Post's* coverage in lieu of the stories written by the reporters actually assigned to write about Kobe Bryant's death. She needlessly stirred up animosity toward *The Post* when people were grieving and in shock, many having just learned the news. She had injected herself crassly into a story that no one at *The Post* had asked her to cover or comment upon. She had seized on Kobe Bryant's death to press a cause close to her heart. To me, her tweet was atrociously timed and conceived.

Felicia and her supporters argued that she was merely tweeting an accurate story—what could possibly be wrong with that?—and that the rape allegations against Bryant were being, as she put it, "erased." Accuracy is, of course, central to high-quality journalism, but journalists thankfully have long respected other standards, too. Tone and timing also matter. In the case of deaths, the public expects from us sensitivity, empathy, and humanity. Felicia's tweets showed none of that. By my reading and much of the public's, there was an implicit but inescapable message in her simple posting of the *Daily Beast*'s rape story so soon after Bryant's death: The man you're mourning was a monster.

Nor were the rape allegations against Bryant being erased. *The Post* and other media, of course, would write about them. Even in obituaries about the most accomplished and admired individuals, *The Post* had never shied from revisiting chapters of dishonor. In Bryant's case, a nineteen-year-old hotel employee in Colorado had accused him of sexual assault in 2003. He was arrested, but prosecutors dropped the case in 2005 shortly before a scheduled trial because the accuser declined to testify, despite strong evidence against Bryant. "Although I truly believe this encounter between us was consensual," Bryant said at the time, "I recognize now that she did not and does not view this incident the same way I did." He and his accuser agreed on a confidential settlement. *The Post* had written in depth about the sexual assault allegations against Bryant, most recently in November 2018, in what was essentially a psychological portrait of the athlete. So probing was reporter Kent Babb on the subject that, before publication, Bryant's representative emailed me to accuse *The Post* of "deceitful tactics in order to create a sensationalist story about Kobe in the #MeToo era." In polite but firm terms, I told her to pound sand.

If Felicia felt that, seventy-eight minutes after the deaths of Bryant and his daughter were first reported (and thirty-eight minutes after confirmation), we were overdue for turning a spotlight on the rape allegations, she had avenues other than Twitter to make known her concerns: She could have directly emailed, called, or walked over to *Post* reporters and editors responsible for the coverage. From my hotel room in Madrid, I wrote, "Felicia, A real lack of judgment to tweet this. Please stop. You're hurting this institution by doing this." When I look back today at that message, my opinion hasn't changed a bit, despite the torrent of criticism I received when my email was disseminated to other media.

Felicia was advised to delete what she had already said on Twitter and to stop posting more tweets. Our security team had consistently counseled journalists not to respond to abuse and threats online. Retorts from our journalists only made matters worse, increasing safety risks. Managing editor Tracy Grant, who had the thankless task of enforcing newsroom standards, gave that advice to Felicia. It was urgent that her social media posts not continue to stir things up. On the evening of her first tweet about Kobe Bryant, noting that her home address had been posted online, Felicia inquired about personal security. Tracy advised her to go to a hotel or a friend's home for her safety. *The Post*'s security team was then contacted. However, that team is tiny. When necessary, it arranges with outside firms to provide full-time protection for an employee. Dispatching guards can take time. When I needed them (twice) at my own residence, about twenty-four hours passed before they arrived. In Felicia's case, she remained in the hotel for three days, with *The Post* paying the cost. A *Post* security officer accompanied her daily from the hotel to the office and back. After that, security was at her residence for ten days.

The Post's security consultants also engaged in a weeks-long effort to identify individuals who had harassed and threatened Felicia in emails and tweets, all the while expressing exasperation that her irrepressible Twitter activity was merely drawing additional threats. In her public comments and subsequent lawsuit, Felicia suggested *The Post* was unconcerned about her safety and treated male reporters' security more seriously than women's. The facts, I am confident, show *The Post* responded appropriately.

My management colleagues and I could have ignored her tweet about Kobe Bryant, sparing ourselves internal conflict, but my view was that her behavior was reckless and offensive. *Post* policies urged respect for "taste and decency." They called for employees to reflect on the impact that social media posts might have on the institution's reputation. *The Post* put Felicia on administrative leave, with full pay, as we investigated whether her Twitter behavior violated our social media guidelines. Members of the union that represented *Post* news staffers, on the other hand, saw no wrongdoing on her part, only on the part of management. A petition signed by several hundred *Post* journalists listed one grievance after the next: Felicia had received "insufficient guidance" on how to protect herself. *The Post* was failing to provide her adequate security. We should have issued a statement of support for her when "articles attacking her" on the Kaiman matter were published elsewhere. Managers had shown "utter disregard for best practices in supporting survivors of sexual violence." The social media policies were "arbitrary and over-broad." And Felicia's administrative leave amounted to "being censured for making a statement of fact."

To my astonishment, a writer for the *Columbia Journalism Review*, which is associated with Columbia University and purports to be an advocate of high standards, weighed in with the opinion that social media rules were a form of "tyranny"—nothing but a "tool of management control"—while ludicrously labeling this whole episode "Sonmezgate." Another *CJR* writer, designated by the publication to be the "public editor" critiquing our work, advised getting rid of all social media standards, and mocked our policy that forbade posting anything "that could objectively be perceived as reflecting political, racial, sexist, religious or other bias or favoritism." The *CJR* columnist suggested such judgments were beyond our intellectual capacity, and we should stop trying: "Maybe God is up to that job, but Marty Baron is not." A column in Harvard's *Nieman Reports*, associated with a prestigious journalism fellowship, accused me of "tradition bias" and then pronounced my actions "a chilling message to sexual assault survivors: if the man is powerful and popular enough, even journalists will turn a blind eye to the harm he's caused, and we will do it even in the era of #MeToo."

All of this commentary was nonsense. We didn't use the social media policy as a "tool of management control," nor did I or anyone in senior management believe that we should turn a "blind eye" to sexual assault by powerful and revered men. Plenty of journalism under my direction stood as proof to the contrary. Still, *The Post*'s senior management hoped to quiet an uprising among the staff. As I was flying back to the United States from Spain, my colleagues in senior management were hoping to put the matter behind us. The social media policy posed an obstacle, too: No policy could cover every circumstance, and ours contained no specific provision about tweeting out an accurate story, regardless of how disruptive, insensitive, and abominably timed. So Felicia was reinstated after a day, and a statement was issued under Tracy's name that declared her tweets "ill-timed" but not in "clear and direct violation" of our written policy.

The differences I had with some *Post* journalists on standards seemed at that moment like a chasm. I couldn't agree with what I was hearing. I had strong convictions on how journalists at a news organization like *The Post* should carry themselves: Reporters and editors, in my view, should not use social media platforms afforded them by jobs at *The Post* to inject themselves into stories they weren't responsible for covering—substituting their judgment for how coverage should be conducted over the editors'. One person's desire for self-expression should not take priority over the institution's right to protect its reputation by setting limits. Journalists in the news department should not use Twitter accounts associated with *The Post* to advocate for causes close to their heart, no matter how meritorious.

I didn't consider our standards too strict, too broad, too vague, or arbitrarily enforced when the spirit of the standards—exercise care and restraint—seemed obvious from any plain reading and when formal discipline was demonstrably rare. I didn't think *The Post* should rush to its staffers' defense when they got into Twitter fights that had nothing to do with their employer. I couldn't abide absolving journalists of personal responsibility when their thoughtless behavior on social media provoked an entirely understandable, and predictable, public furor. And none of us, I firmly believed, should be dismissive of the public's sensitivities when there is a tragic death, as if we lived by a unique moral code that can't find room for both accuracy and empathy.

I also had to wonder: Did the staff really believe I and my fellow senior managers were so coldhearted, so uncaring about sexual assault survivors and cavalier about the safety of the staff? If so, there wasn't merely a chasm between my views and theirs. There was a chasm between their views and reality. And if this was how the staff genuinely felt—after all *The Post*'s hard-won accomplishments and after all they knew of me—why would I choose to make this my professional home any longer?

I was especially appalled by the attacks on Tracy, whose responsibilities covered a vast territory beyond standards to recruiting, hiring, training, and budgets. No one in *Post* management pushed harder for greater diversity, better employee benefits, staff security, and special accommodations when staffers suffered personal tragedies. She also believed in our guidelines for proper employee behavior, and that without enforcement they were rendered meaningless. She did all this while raising two boys as a single mom after the 2007 death of her husband and serving as the primary caregiver for her mother. I feared she would quit. And if she did, I would, too, in protest against how shabbily she had been treated by a segment of the staff. I drafted a resignation note. "This turn of events has revealed something about our newsroom that had been unfamiliar to me," I wrote.

"I had always taken pride in our collegiality and the collaboration that led to our best journalism. Now what I see is that, in justifiably seeking equity and justice for all people, some people are willing to commit a grave injustice against a single good individual. I can't abide a newsroom that would do that, and so I am letting you know that I, too, will be leaving *The Post* immediately."

Reading my emotions must have been easy. Even journalists who felt my enforcement of social media rules had been too quick and heavy-handed tried to buck me up and discourage any thought of quitting. "We know your intent: to defend and strengthen *The Post* institution and brand that you have made synonymous with accuracy, excellence and public service above reproach," wrote one who felt I had acted wrongly. Another emailed: "I know it must feel like much of the newsroom is against you, but I want to assure you that it is not. The great majority of people, of course, did not sign that letter and every day brings more who regret doing so . . . I am sure right now you are having a pretty epic 'who needs this?' moment— and who could blame you? But I hope it won't last." A third wrote: "I know it's been a rough week but please know that you have the support of so many people. Yes there is a vocal minority. It's temporary. Don't let it color your feelings about the newsroom or the relationships you've built over the years."

Tracy didn't quit, and I concluded I shouldn't either. I couldn't let this episode define my tenure at *The Post*. But I also concluded I shouldn't stay beyond another year. Meantime, I was obligated to say something to the staff. I was seething inside, but I had to keep my emotions in check. I wrote a note that began to outline my views:

"*The Post* is more than a collection of individuals who wish to express themselves. It is an institution with a common set of values and principles and a history of appropriate practices. When we cover stories, editors together with reporters and other colleagues agree on an approach that aims to uphold our institutional reputation. We seek and honor the truth always. We also strive to be fair and furnish context. Routinely our journalism requires sensitivity, empathy and humanity . . . We count on staffers to be attuned to how their social media activity will be perceived, bearing in mind that time, place and manner really matter."

Shortly afterward, we announced three one-hour sessions where we would hear staff concerns about the social media policy. At the first session, I was determined to only listen closely and take notes. So I did just that, staying quiet and suppressing any temptation to dissent. But maintaining my silence just earned me further criticism. What I heard at that session and the others that followed, where I spoke up, only served to trouble me more. I couldn't accept an assessment that our judgments on activism, objectivity, and perception of political bias were almost entirely subjective. I heard an ardor for sharing views on social media platforms, with such expression framed as an extension of staffers' "humanity," "identity," and even "soul." *The Post*, some contended, needed to somehow "extricate" its institutional reputation from the individual speech of its journalists. I didn't see how that was possible.

Younger journalists were the ones who spoke up most, and there was consensus among them. I knew from private comments that many veteran staffers who were raised on traditional standards had a view more in sync with my own. To my disappointment, they kept quiet, skittish about finding themselves in conflict with newsroom colleagues.

After I left the last of those meetings on February 14, I jotted down my own reaction to all that I had heard: "Never have I felt more distant from my fellow journalists . . . The staff's feelings about social media, to me, valued individual expression over the interests of the institution. The emphasis was on I, me, my—not we, us, our . . . The whole thing was depressing, and I was more convinced than ever that this was a good time to leave daily journalism. I love the profession, but it now seemed to be going astray. I could not explain the behavior of some of my colleagues on social media. I couldn't justify it. I didn't want to defend it. Because to defend it would be to embrace it on behalf of the institution."

We had promised that we would begin rewriting our social media policy. But I couldn't bring myself to try. The task seemed impossible. What I heard in those meetings was a staff seeking to evade accountability for their own wreckage. In the final weeks before I retired in February 2021, publisher Fred Ryan asked me to quickly issue a revised policy so that my successor wouldn't inherit the thankless task. His own views, I was confident, were in line with mine. We had discussed the subject from time to time. I also knew I had the backing of Bezos. In the throes of the social media controversy in February 2020, he sent me a reassuring note: "I hope you can feel the support from afar. You've done so much for this institution as a whole, this newsroom in particular, and indeed the whole field of quality journalism everywhere, which . . . to me feels more like an endangered species all the time."

Despite the support, I refused Fred's request to complete a social media policy rewrite before retiring. We had promised the staff full involvement in crafting new standards, and my deliberate delay had left no time for that. There were other reasons for that delay: The epic year of 2020 was not a time to take our eyes off news coverage as we struggled to resolve internal, and possibly irreconcilable, differences. The divide between my views and much of the staff's seemed unbridgeable. Their sentiments on acceptable journalistic behavior were not mine. I didn't want to defend what I thought was indefensible, nor be held responsible for what I thought was irresponsible. Let a new editor find a way forward.

Over time, I have felt the tide turning a tiny bit in the direction of my traditionalist (and, in another era, entirely conventional) views. The BBC, under instructions from a new director general, issued strict new guidelines in October 2020. "If your work requires you to maintain your impartiality, don't express a personal opinion on matters of public policy, politics, or 'controversial subjects,'" the policy read. "Avoid 'virtue signaling'—retweets, likes or joining online campaigns to indicate a personal view, no matter how apparently worthy the cause," read another provision.

In April 2022, *New York Times* editor Dean Baquet issued a memo calling for a "reset" on Twitter. After calling for *Times* journalists to "meaningfully reduce how much time you're spending on the platform, tweeting or scrolling, in relation to other parts of your job," Baquet said he wanted to "emphasize that your work on social media needs to reflect the values of *The Times* and be consistent with our editorial standards, social media guidelines and behavioral norms. In particular, tweets or subtweets that attack, criticize or undermine the work of your colleagues are not allowed."

Tougher standards like the BBC's and reminders like *The Times'* were overdue. By June *The Washington Post* had become a mortifying case study in anarchic social media behavior. Its journalists were feuding openly with each other on Twitter instead of having face-to-face conversations among themselves about disagreements, as expected in any typical workplace. This latest episode began with Felicia Sonmez posting tweets that reproached her colleague David Weigel and *The Post* for his foul sex joke on Twitter. Soon, others on staff came under her Twitter fire.

My successor as executive editor, Sally Buzbee, ultimately invoked *The Post's* standards and promised a crackdown on "colleagues attacking colleagues." When Felicia persisted, she was fired "for misconduct that includes insubordination, maligning your co-workers online and violating *The Post's* standards on workplace collegiality and inclusivity." While many journalists covet more freedom on social media, the embarrassing Twitter storm at *The Post* added to a mountain of evidence that they should be granted less.

Later that year, the newsroom settled on an updated social media policy. Though better written than the one I inherited, it was not materially different. The paramount issue now for *The Post* and other news organizations will not be how their ethics and social media policies are written but whether they are meaningfully enforced. The public has ample reason to wonder whether these are standards in name only.

18

UPRISINGS

The nation exploded in rage after the May 25, 2020, police killing of George Floyd on a Minneapolis street corner. Video captured Officer Derek Chauvin driving his knee into Floyd's neck. He kept at it for about nine minutes as Floyd was handcuffed and gasping for breath—and even for nearly four minutes after Floyd had taken his last one.

Perhaps no single image in American history has had such an immediate and profound impact, due to cell phone video taken by seventeen-year-old bystander Darnella Frazier that was disseminated through social media. The footage was, as Harvard's Nieman Foundation for Journalism curator Ann Marie Lipinski said, "one of the most important civil rights documents in a generation."

We all became eyewitnesses to police brutality that left a Black man dead, and this time it set off the largest movement for racial justice since the 1960s. Weeks of protests were predominantly peaceful but also descended into violence, destruction, and theft. Police and National Guard troops responded with massive and often brute force. On May 29, President Trump tweeted, "When the looting starts, the shooting starts." Blood was spilled on America's streets. The country's divisions deepened.

Washington Post reporters, photographers, and videographers were deployed across the country—in the midst of a pandemic that had already killed a hundred thousand Americans—to investigate Floyd's killing, explore the bitter emotions it ignited, and document the explosive street unrest that continued unabated for weeks. In Washington, D.C., thousands marched to Lafayette Park, at the northern edge of the White House grounds, for days of demonstrations and confrontations with police. So nervous was the Secret Service on May 29 that it moved Trump into a secure bunker under the White House, humiliating a president who liked to project strength when it was disclosed only two days later by *The New York Times*. On June 1, shortly after Trump called for "total domination" of protesters and a half hour before a seven p.m. curfew, law enforcement and military forces moved aggressively to empty the park, firing gas canisters and tossing grenades that contained rubber pellets. Protesters were chased by police on horseback. It was a shocking scene. In front of the White House, a wide array of federal forces, many with shields that said "military police," were on the attack against fellow American citizens who had protested peacefully.

With the path cleared, Trump—having just proclaimed himself "your president of law and order" and promising to send "thousands and thousands" of heavily armed soldiers to Washington, D.C.— walked one block to St. John's Church, which had been partially burned by a group of rioters. He was accompanied on the walk by Attorney General William Barr, National Security Advisor Robert O'Brien, Defense Secretary Mark Esper, Chairman of the Joint Chiefs of Staff Mark Milley, and Chief of Staff Mark Meadows. In front of the church, he grimly held up a Bible for a few seconds, all for a photo op. It would be weeks before the nation returned to a veneer of calm. Yet the anger remained as intense as ever, boiling beneath the surface—aimed not only at police brutality but at a society that had failed to eradicate its deep-rooted racial disparities.

I was proud of *The Post's* staff. Over the previous months, our journalists had reported on a worldwide pandemic and resulting economic calamity, the impeachment of a president, and an accel-

erating presidential campaign that would be among the most contentious and consequential in memory. Now—with George Floyd's
killing, masses expressing outrage, and fierce clashes with police—
they were covering a story that tested their stamina and threatened
their safety. Members of the news media were regularly assaulted
by police—manhandled, pepper-sprayed, and hit by rubber bullets.
Post journalists had performed "brilliantly, with courage and dedication and resourcefulness," I wrote in a message to the newsroom.
"Our entire staff has been mobilized to cover this story and all the
others unfolding at the same time. There seems to be no limit to the
tests you've been required to face—and no limit to your capacity to
rise to the occasion."

The note reflected my genuine gratitude. I quickly learned,
though, that it was not well received. I had written of the racial
justice protests as if they were just another huge story, failing to recognize that they were far more than that. I had omitted any mention
of the deep pain felt by our Black journalists. The killing of George
Floyd represented more than an act of police brutality. It was em-
blematic of the injustices, indignities, and inequities they themselves
had experienced in their own lives. To them, this story was personal.
And my failure to grasp and reflect that was, in their view, symptom-
atic of what was missing in our own newsroom: No Black journalists
among three managing editors and two deputy managing editors.
Too few among department heads. Too few overall in our newsroom. Coverage that failed to adequately communicate the Black
experience. Not enough leaders who were able to see the world from
a Black perspective. Leadership that had not done nearly enough to
set things right.

They were tired of waiting, they said, their patience exhausted.
They were furious, with *The Post* and with me. This was not a moment when they would ask for change. They demanded it.

By the time *The Post* held a virtual town hall with employees in early June 2020, its senior management had been challenged with questions by a staff insistent on unequivocal answers: "Will *The Washington Post* make a statement in regards to George Floyd's death at the hands of police?" "What does *The Post* plan on doing to support its Black employees during this trying time?" "What specifically is *The Post* doing to prioritize hiring more people of color?" "Other large organizations have persons and leadership positions dedicated to promoting diversity and facilitating tough conversations and change. What structural/management changes is *The Post* making to do the same?" "Are donations to Black-centered charities such as Black Lives Matter allowed under company policy? If not, can a policy change be revisited?"

The Post's most senior executives endeavored to show sensitivity to the staff's heartache. Publisher Fred Ryan emphasized that our company stood against racism but, as a news organization, we did that through our journalism, where we revealed injustices and held the powerful to account. He spoke of *The Post*'s commitment to not only hiring and promoting people of color but also of supporting them in difficult times.

In my own remarks, I expressed my very real empathy. "The death in Minneapolis—on top of previous horrifying events—has had a deeply personal and devastating impact on so many of our journalists, particularly our Black journalists and other journalists of color," I said. "For them, a pattern of racial and ethnic inequities, indignities and discrimination is not a distant abstraction. They have lived it, as have their family and friends. So, in a stressful news environment, the stress becomes compounded through yet another infuriating and sorrowful reminder, as if one were needed, of how our society fails them. As journalists, we can give voice to that anguish through our reporting among communities that are feeling so much pain. As colleagues, we want to be as comforting and supportive as we can."

I lamented my failure to recognize their pain while acknowledging the need for "deeper discussions about issues of race and inclusion that are now front and center." But staff members remained dissatisfied; some, angry. They wanted firm commitments to immediate change, and admittedly my response was well short of that. In increasing our staff at that point from 580 people when I arrived to almost 1,000 by then, I noted, we had "opened up opportunities at *The Post* for journalists of color from around the country. We've done a lot of hiring." When it came to greater diversity in leadership, I was seen as offering excuses in lieu of action. "There is no question that we have not done well enough. We need to do better," I said. "The challenge has been that these senior leadership positions don't open up frequently and we can't just move people out of their jobs when they're performing well in order to make room for others. We also don't want to have an excessive number of managers. When we've expanded our staff, we tried to hire more people for frontline work."

My remarks came across as defensive and detached. They provoked a response I should have anticipated. And yet what I told the staff was true. Throughout my tenure under Bezos's ownership and with Fred Ryan as publisher, getting approval for new editing jobs—especially those with fancy titles and higher salaries—had been borderline impossible. Early in his ownership, Bezos had sought to place employees in two categories—those who had a "direct" impact on readers and the rest who had an "indirect" impact. Within the newsroom, reporters were among those who obviously fell in the first category. Editors, however, were generally seen by those in charge of *The Post*'s business operations as "indirect." The classification system was a misreading of how newsrooms worked, and I forcefully said so. Still, the direct/indirect philosophy hovered over all budgeting for new staff positions, making extra editor positions hard to come by.

There was a logic behind it: Ever since Bezos bought *The Post*, the single-minded goal of management was to pull us out of the deep, and ominous, hole we were in financially and strategically.

Our hiring centered on what could most immediately accomplish a turnaround and then propel growth over the long run. The layer of newsroom managers was to stay lean—and get even leaner, if possible. Contrary to public perception, Bezos wasn't spending with abandon. His investments in *The Post* were selective, strategic, and disciplined. Nor was *The Post* his charity. Every proposal for a new position had to be justified and required approval by my own bosses. As we began the town hall meeting in June 2020, I had no idea whether I would be authorized to hire more senior-level managers in our newsroom. My experience to date suggested I wouldn't.

How was I to effectively explain that to the staff? I couldn't. One Black reporter let me have it. "I was disappointed, maybe even offended, at your comments during the townhall last week about why we can't improve diversity among the top level of managers in the newsroom," she wrote me in an email. "Suggesting that the only way to address this concern is for our white colleagues to lose their jobs 'to make room' for journalists of color is unfair and unnecessarily antagonistic . . . And your other argument—that you don't want to have 'an excessive number of managers'—is unconvincing and insulting. Like it would be a ceremonial appointment just to appease a special interest group."

She continued, "I love you've brought a great deal of journalistic vision, purpose and integrity back to our newsroom. We got our swagger back!" But the praise was a two-sentence exception in a long message of admonishment: "The lack of African Americans, and other journalists of color, who are readily associated with *The Post*'s brand makes people inside and outside the newsroom wonder how much we value diversity." It didn't help that all the senior executives who spoke at the town hall were white.

One reporter, Jessica Contrera, said that she had "decided to reach out to my colleagues and former colleagues of color, asking them to share their stories with me, through a Google submission form." She was now forwarding their accounts in the form of a thirty-two-page compilation of their experiences over a long period with *The Post*, including ones that preceded my editorship. "Certainly," she wrote us, "I have heard stories and snippets of discrimination or racism in our company that made me shudder. But I hoped—as perhaps you have—that those situations were rare. They are not."

The stories made for difficult reading: "Yes, we have one of the most diverse newsrooms in America, but that diversity is superficial when people of color who come through these doors feel ignored, slighted and unvalued." "Speaking out honestly about anything but especially about a possible racially biased headline, caption, photo or paragraph or calling out a racial blind spot would be met with some form of punishment." "How can we feel safe and equal and valued when our own criticisms are ignored—or fall on deaf ears?" "It feels like I'm told to stifle my identity, like only some parts are okay to express. It makes me question how long I can be at the *Post*." "Colleagues constantly comment on our hair and clothing choices, but do not take the time to look at our work and give productive feedback." *The Post* and I were falling grievously short in making journalists of color feel respected, fully consulted on coverage, and equitably treated in promotions and reassignments.

The Washington Post Guild, the union that represents employees in the newsroom and in certain commercial operations, sent its own "11 evidence-based, actionable solutions ... to address discrimination and inequality at *The Post*." Employees, said its letter signed by 450 employees, "deserve leaders who are clear-eyed about the reality of racism and take ownership of the systemic bias that exists in our company."

Less than seven years earlier, only a month after I joined *The Post* as executive editor, I appointed Kevin Merida, fifty-six, as managing editor overseeing all news and features departments—that is, the vast majority of reporters. A twenty-year veteran of *The Post*, Kevin was a hugely popular figure. He was also a keen listener and a judicious manager of people, with an instinctive sense for good stories. An elegant writer himself, he could coach others in how to tell them. He was also the first Black managing editor in *The Post*'s history. Journalists of color at *The Post* had longed for such a moment.

Kevin had covered the White House and national affairs and overseen *The Post*'s coverage of some of its biggest stories: the killing of Osama bin Laden, the BP oil spill in the Gulf of Mexico, the 2012 presidential campaign, mass shootings in Fort Hood, Texas; Aurora, Colorado; and Newtown, Connecticut. He had coordinated a penetrating series titled "Being a Black Man." His roots in the region ran deep. As a tenth grader, in 1973, he was among the first class of students bused to schools outside their neighborhoods to achieve racial integration in public education in Prince George's County, Maryland. In a nuanced and reflective *Post* essay in 1998, he recounted the experience of being yanked from his neighborhood Central High School and bused twelve and a half miles to Crossland High School, which until then was only 5 percent Black:

"Occasionally," Kevin wrote, "when I pause to assess my life—and consider that my job has enabled me to survey the crumbled Berlin Wall, jog with a president, and shoot jumpers with a top NBA draft choice—I wonder whether busing was the linchpin to so many rich and varied adventures. My mother assures me that if I had stayed at Central and strayed at Central, she and my dad would have steered me back on course, found ways to keep me motivated. I believe her. But it is also easy to see myself evolving mostly as an athlete at Central, never working for the school newspaper, never being encouraged to develop my writing talent, accepting a basketball scholarship at some small college. And from there, who's to say?"

Kevin's experience was radically different from my own: a Jew born in Tampa, Florida, to parents who had immigrated from Israel, by way of France, only three months earlier. I had attended public school through sixth grade but then was placed in a small nearby prep school of only 250 students in grades seven through twelve. Its affiliation with the Episcopal Church meant that I sat through years of Communions. Unlike Kevin, I had manifested no athletic talents. As early as junior high school, I had imagined becoming a journalist. My only connection to busing was through an editorial I wrote as editor of the high school paper in 1971. "Although the headmaster has annually stressed that we are desegrated," I wrote, a Black person at the upper and middle division was "nonexistent," and in the lower division "not in the least a common one." I went on to endorse busing, which had no impact on students at a private school: "Those obstinate parents who race . . . to the suburb should no longer have the opportunity to envenom their children with the racial suspicions that result from segregation."

Kevin's appointment gave the staff a lift and early hope that *The Post* might be correcting course on multiple fronts, well beyond diversity. A practitioner of the art of gentle persuasion, Kevin could tell me what I didn't know or fully appreciate about subjects of varied sorts. Staffers confided in him, particularly journalists of color. He and I developed a strong, trusting, and highly productive relationship. So, like legions in the newsroom, I was heartbroken when he informed me in October 2015 that he was leaving to take a high-paying job as senior vice president of ESPN and editor in chief of The Undefeated, its digital site centered on the intersection of sports, race, and culture. I had done everything possible to keep him. We had raised our compensation offer as high as possible. And then I privately told Kevin that I was willing to retire early—in two years—if he stayed, with the goal of him becoming my successor. I suggested he use those years to build relationships with the publisher and hone digital and business skills that would make him the preferred candidate.

Kevin's departure was a blow not only to me but also to the morale of Black journalists on our staff, made worse by his move to recruit a half dozen of them to his new employer (at substantially higher salaries). His replacement, Cameron Barr, was an exceptionally talented and deeply experienced newsman. That didn't reassure journalists who were mourning the loss of a Black editor of Kevin's plentiful talents from such a powerful leadership position. Black staffers at *The Post* then grew upset that, after Kevin's departure, no Black journalist held one of the newsroom's most senior positions.

In April 2016, Black journalists asked to meet with Tracy Grant, then a deputy managing editor, and me about what they perceived as our failure to adequately address diversity in the newsroom, particularly in the upper ranks. A top priority of the group was adding a senior-level editor to oversee diversity and inclusion. At the same time, they advocated for a set of "policies, programs and strategies to advance diversity."

That year at *The Post*, two and a half years after Bezos's purchase, we were still early in the effort to achieve a turnaround. Every newsroom department was pleading for more staff. They needed the resources if we were to ever challenge our most formidable competitors. There were signs that we were on the right course—our digital readership and subscription numbers were rising—but we had a long way to go. The painful truth was, if we didn't succeed, there wouldn't be much hiring of any sort.

So, I was reluctant to add another senior-level manager and a set of costly programs when funding was sorely needed for additional reporters, graphic artists, social media experts, and an array of other frontline positions that seemed most likely to boost our immediate commercial performance. And when I discussed the staff's diversity demands with the publisher, he was no more enthusiastic than I about shifting resources to pay for another high-priced newsroom executive. It all made financial sense at the time, but the staff's frustrations are also understandable.

The posture toward extra editors would change shortly after I retired in February 2021, after Black Lives Matter protests and mounting pressure to diversify the newsroom's leadership. Seven months later, *The Post* announced it would add forty-one editors, including two for senior-level positions. That was welcome news. But there was zero chance anything like that would have happened in 2016—or for years afterward.

I had always believed that a newsroom composed of people with varied backgrounds and life experiences—from race, ethnicity, and gender to class, education, military service, and religious beliefs— was essential for understanding and covering our communities and the country in all their complexity. I could see that from my first job at the *Miami Herald* in the late 1970s, when South Florida was already experiencing rapid demographic change due to immigration from Cuba and Haiti. I later spent years learning to speak Spanish fluently (though not perfectly) so that I was more able to connect directly to the community where I worked. When I returned to Miami as the *Herald*'s editor in 2000, the city was sharply split over whether young Elián González should be returned to his father in Cuba or allowed to stay in the United States. I was gratified when my publisher at the time, Alberto Ibargüen, said twenty years later that I had "a good sense for the town and what was happening and how [racially] divided the town was. It was really a divided place, and so was the newsroom . . . Marty didn't shy away from those discussions."

Varied perspectives on newsroom staffs meant deeper insights, more illuminating stories, and a more thorough realization of our mission. By 2016 we had significantly boosted overall staff diversity at *The Post* above the level when I was hired, putting us well ahead of *The New York Times* and keeping us among the most diverse major newsrooms in the country.

None of that ultimately mattered. I had not been the good listener I regularly urge others to be. Black journalists at *The Post* were telling me we had not done nearly enough—that their voices weren't being heard at senior levels and that our diversity efforts needed to go deeper than a top-level appointment or overall numbers. I should have assessed our newsroom with a wider lens. Our immediate growth needs were existentially pressing, but other needs should not have been ignored. Whether I expected to be successful or not, I should have advocated for a top-level editor who could lead our diversity efforts, not just for purposes of hiring but also to strengthen our coverage of long-standing, unresolved issues of race, ethnicity, and identity. Success at getting the resources might have eluded me, but failing to try was regrettably the most serious error of my tenure at *The Post*.

In the aftermath of the town hall meeting in 2020, as my standing with Black journalists and others on the staff suffered, it was imperative to name a managing editor to ensure we made significant, consistent progress on diversity and inclusiveness in everything we did: coverage of race, ethnicity, and identity as well as improved recruitment, retention, and career advancement for journalists of color. After a national search, I named Krissah Thompson, an accomplished writer in our own features department, to that position. In the meantime, managing editor Cameron Barr had been listening closely to staff concerns and proposed that we do far more—add almost a dozen positions to focus on race, ethnicity, and identity in a variety of ways, from the administration of justice to environmental and health inequities. It was the right idea but a big budget request. I presented it to Fred Ryan as publisher with my strong endorsement. The world had changed, and within days it was approved. The hiring was an important signal that *The Post* would take concrete steps.

Even so, I felt that some on staff were still aiming to portray me as grossly insensitive on matters of race. It was painful then, and remains painful now. I feared that my professional reputation, more than four decades in the making, was about to be unjustly shredded. I also had grown weary of well-meaning but moralistic young journalists—and their forever enabling union—lecturing me on best management practices when precious few had ever managed anyone, had any experience with budget constraints, had ever been tasked to compete in hiring and retaining diverse talent, had ever worked for bosses as demanding as my own, or had any appreciation for the difficult task of meeting ambitious growth goals that bestowed benefits on all of them.

I had never led a staff with the express goal of being liked. Too many newsroom managers did, in my estimation. I saw it as a serious flaw when our industry's survival demanded tough, inevitably upsetting, decisions. I only cared to be respected for journalistic and commercial achievement in an environment that was humane, fair, professional, collegial, and civil. Not everyone's wish could be fulfilled, even if the union seemed to regard that as my obligation. I had become hardened over many years to being attacked by powerful figures who received press scrutiny, but the invective leveled against me by colleagues—whose skill and bravery I admired and whose news organization I had busted my butt for eight years to turn around—was tougher to take. Nothing was more hurtful.

I was also feeling physically vulnerable and drained. I suffered from a steadily worsening genetic bleeding disorder called hereditary hemorrhagic telangiectasia (HHT) that can cause sudden, severe, and seemingly unstoppable nosebleeds, often multiple times a day. Twice over the previous year, but unknown to all but a few colleagues, I had lost so much blood that I rushed myself in the early-morning hours to the emergency room at George Washington University Hospital. Once I had to receive two units of blood. There were days, before the pandemic had us working from home, when bleeding was so severe and unsightly that I had to leave my glass office and go home. I reflected on how my father died of the same condition twenty-four years earlier at age seventy-four, his bleeding having eventually manifested in the gastrointestinal tract. I was sixty-five, and I was losing the emotional desire and physical strength to continue working at a job that demanded so much of me—almost every waking hour—but was now yielding such a dispiriting level of censure. My bonds with the staff, I feared, were frayed beyond repair. My desire to continue working at *The Post* was disintegrating.

In a mood of despondency in June 2020, I offered publisher Fred Ryan my resignation. There was an excellent natural successor internally in Cameron Barr, managing editor for news. I had fought in 2015 for his promotion from national editor, threatening to quit if Fred didn't let up on resistance that I found unfathomable and his demand for a formal national search that I considered unnecessary. But the moment called for someone different. Working alone from home during the pandemic, I suggested to Fred that he lure Kevin Merida back from ESPN and name him as my replacement. Kevin, I emailed him, was "better equipped than I to lead this newsroom through the fraught period we are in."

I went on: "This moment of anguish, anxiety and anger, by the way, is not going to dissipate anytime in the near future. For a variety of reasons, I don't believe getting through this plays to my strengths. And, with the inevitable and unceasing rancor, it's not really how I wish to end my career. I'd like to end it doing something constructive for *The Post*. Being an editor of a major news organization right now brings almost unbearable burdens. The pressures mount by the day, along with the volume of work. The pleasures are real and at times thrilling, but they are fewer. Some of the pressures, including those brought to the surface by the protests of our time, defy quick or easy resolution. The painfully slow progress brings more frustration on the part of the staff. A lot of that gets directed at me. I get angry at becoming a target when I feel it's undeserved and when I feel our remarkable achievements are unappreciated or taken for granted. That leaves me in a dark mood, which is where I am right now. It is not a good place for me or for our organization."

Fred refused my resignation offer, declaring it good for neither me nor for *The Post*. He expressed the hope that I would stay years longer. I did stay, but my plan was to not stay for long. A year and a half earlier, I had told Fred I expected to retire sometime after the presidential election. Now I told him we needed to set a specific date. I offered him three: immediately after the November election, at year's end, or shortly after the inauguration on January 20, 2021. He picked the last of the three options but said we'd revisit the subject to see if I changed my mind. Within days, I had. I wanted to go back to leaving by year's end. "I've done my duty here," I told Fred. "I never expected it to be reciprocated this way. But it is what it is. I can think of better ways to spend my time." Fred asked me to reconsider. "You have served *The Post* and American journalism with honesty and integrity. You've devoted your life to that," he wrote back. "I just hope we can get past the heat of the moment and make a reasoned and thoughtful plan that gives you the dignity you deserve, whenever you depart, and positions *The Post* to build on your enormous achievements." His judgment was more levelheaded than mine, and I relented. Fred checked on my intentions from time to time, and again in early January 2021. I was ready to go. I'd had enough. I would leave at the end of February.

My suspicion that the attacks wouldn't subside was confirmed when *New York Times* media critic Ben Smith published a column in late June 2020 about how I was "grappling with a moment of cultural reckoning." That was true. I was. But the "previously untold stories" he promised readers left the noxious impression that I, as the "ultimate old-school" editor, had presided over, if not tolerated, a cesspool of racial discrimination even while helping to engineer "perhaps the greatest news business success story of the past decade."

Smith's "previously untold stories" were uniformly detached from reality. One suggested that a Black video editor was required to ask for permission to go to the bathroom while white colleagues were not. It was defamatory nonsense. As Smith was told, all video editors on a breaking-news team had to have someone cover for them when they expected to be away for extended periods. I had no involvement in setting the policy (nor did I have any interactions with the video editor), but it represented customary practice in journalism. News-rooms can't afford delay in covering unanticipated news. Smith also implicitly tied me to *The Post*'s decision not to include a Black edi-torial writer's pieces in a staff submission for a Pulitzer Prize, even though the opinion pages were outside my area of oversight and the decision wasn't mine to make.

A third staffer, who held one of the most coveted investigative reporting jobs in the country, expressed irritation on Twitter over not being named an investigations editor, seeing it as a slight and a strike against diversity. Her job was one of two in the investigative unit that I had saved in 2014 when foundation funding for them was cut off and I refused the publisher's order to eliminate the positions because they were unbudgeted. I understood her grievance and re-gretted her disappointment. But she also happened to be someone who had good things to say about me and her time at *The Post*. She later solicited, and received, my advice shortly after she took on an important editing position elsewhere. Placing me "at the top of the list" among "the great role models I've been fortunate to have," she emailed, "I am grateful for my time at the *Post*, which prepared me for this next step; and for the wisdom I received from you and all the excellent people I worked with."

The Post had ample work to do to advance diversity in all its forms, and as the top editor I was rightly held accountable for the ways we fell short. But Smith's column was a prejudicial caricature. *The Post*, especially during recent years of fast growth, had also pro-vided abundant opportunities to many journalists of color. Hon-esty and objectivity required acknowledging both realities. There was a broader context, too, even if it yielded me—or the staff as a whole—no comfort. America's racial reckoning was unfolding in just about every institution. Though *The Post* and I were getting dispro-portionate attention, few major media organizations were exempt.

The top editor of *The Philadelphia Inquirer*, Stan Wischnowski, resigned that June after dozens of staff members walked out when the paper ran the headline "Buildings Matter, Too" over a piece by the architecture critic about damage to structures from civil disorder. Dozens of journalists of color signed a letter of protest to management. "We're tired of shouldering the burden of dragging this 200-year-old institution kicking and screaming into a more equitable age," they wrote. "We're tired of being told of the progress the company has made and being served platitudes about 'diversity and inclusion' when we raise our concerns. We're tired of seeing our words and photos twisted to fit a narrative that does not reflect our reality. We're tired of being told to show both sides of issues there are no two sides of." *The Inquirer* published an apology for the headline.

At the *Los Angeles Times*, a newly formed Black Caucus of its newsroom's union that June wrote an open letter to owner Patrick Soon-Shiong that Black journalists there were "often ignored, marginalized, under-valued and left to drift along career paths that leave little opportunity for advancement. Meanwhile, we're hearing the same empty promises and foot-dragging from management." In July, the Latino Caucus wrote Soon-Shiong that the organization had failed "in its staffing and coverage, to reflect a region where nearly one of every two residents is Latino . . . For decades, we've asked management to hire more of us, promote us and make us editors. But those calls have largely gone unanswered." In November, the *Los Angeles Times* and its previous owner, Tribune Publishing, agreed to pay $3 million to settle a class-action lawsuit by journalists of color who alleged they were paid less than white male counterparts.

A group of *Wall Street Journal* staff members that July dispatched a letter to editor in chief Matt Murray calling for changes in coverage of race, policing, and business overall. "In part because *WSJ*'s coverage has focused historically on industries and leadership ranks dominated by White men, many of our newsroom practices are inadequate for the present moment," the letter said. It called for "more muscular reporting about race and social inequities," more journalists to cover "race, ethnicity and equality," more diversity in newsroom leadership, and a study that would evaluate whether *The Journal*'s reporting resources were deployed sufficiently to cover people who weren't white men. The following month, *The Journal* announced that it was establishing the new position of senior vice president of inclusion and people management and conducting "a comprehensive review of diversity, equity and inclusion across our business."

That summer, James Bennet, the editorial page editor of *The New York Times*, resigned after staffers expressed outrage over an op-ed authored by Republican senator Tom Cotton. Headlined "Send in the Troops," it called for "an overwhelming show of force to disperse, detain and ultimately deter lawbreakers" during protests against police brutality and racial inequities. Reporters tweeted some version of "Running this puts Black @nytimes staff in danger." *New York Times* reporter Jazmine Hughes tweeted, "as if it weren't already hard enough to be a black employee of the *New York Times*." And Pulitzer winner Nikole Hannah-Jones took to Twitter to say, "As a black woman, as a journalist, I am deeply ashamed that we ran this." *New York Times* publisher A. G. Sulzberger and Bennet initially offered a defense for publishing the piece, then backed off with an editor's note saying the essay "fell short of our standards and should not have been published." In February 2021, *The Times* released an internal report that found, "The Times is too often a difficult place to work for people of all backgrounds—particularly colleagues of color, and especially Black and Latino colleagues. It calls for us to transform our culture." And a letter to staff signed by the publisher, CEO, and top editor promised to pursue "a bold plan for building a more diverse, equitable and inclusive *New York Times*."

By mid-July, *The New York Times* was writing about largely identical tensions within ESPN, where more than a dozen current and former employees "described a company that projected a diverse outward face, but did not have enough Black executives, especially ones with real decision-making power. They said the company did not provide meaningful career paths for Black employees behind the camera and made decisions based on assumptions that its average viewer is an older white man, in spite of its audience trends."

The demand for greater diversity was accompanied by an effort by many journalists to overturn traditional standards that set boundaries on their public activities. Some newsroom staff wanted to donate to Black Lives Matter and other advocacy organizations. Some wanted to join in the Black Lives Matter protests sweeping the country. Neither was permitted under long-standing rules at *The Post* and most other mainstream media organizations.

One Black staff member at *The Post*, a rising talent, made an impassioned argument that foreshadowed an emerging assault among many journalists on the very idea that we should strive for "objectivity" in our work: "I have remained publicly 'objective' during overt displays of violence, prejudice and hatred. I was objective about Nazi rallies and black children being killed and women being assaulted. All the while knowing that the definition of objective followed by our entire industry is the objective truth of white men. It cannot be bias to stand up against a societal structure based on the systemic oppression of entire groups of people . . . I urge you to consider making space for the objective truth of a good number of your news staff, none of whom are really in power and many of whom never will be in the way that you are. Can we protest? Can we donate funds to humanitarian groups that can help empower people? Can we say Black Lives Matter? Can we be honest about who we are and what experiences shape our worldview?" Later that year, she left *The Post*. Her new employer was *The New York Times*, with a history, ethic, and rulebook largely identical to our own.

The Post's long-standing guidelines were brief, clear, and absolute: "We avoid active involvement in any partisan cause—politics, community affairs, social action, demonstrations—that could compromise or seem to compromise our ability to report and edit fairly." But a segment of the news staff was arguing for what would represent a drastic revision of our ethics code to accommodate protesting, donating, and petition-signing. At *The Post's* town hall that June, I was asked whether I would consider permitting that. My answer was a firm no. "We don't allow donations to activist, advocacy and political groups, and we don't allow participation in marches and protests. When we lose the perception and reality of independence, we give the public a reason to question our authority as well," I said. "They will see us as activists or partisans. As journalists, our role should be to observe, inquire, investigate, document and effectively communicate. That's core to the profession we chose to pursue. Every profession comes with some constraints, and we have ours."

Every place I had ever worked in journalism had a policy of that sort, and historically the policies were strictly enforced. Journalists were to accurately and fairly cover the news, not be participants in the very events we were covering. In 2020, however, what had been foundational principles in our profession were being challenged as antiquated and inadequate to a fraught moment in history. "There is a new generation in this field who want to take journalism at *The Post*, the *NYT* and other organizations in an activist direction," I wrote a former boss that summer after he encouraged me to stick to my guns. "I'm adamantly opposed. Rigorous journalism held to high standards should do the talking." With principles under siege, however, ethics policies were giving way to all sorts of exceptions. Pressed by staff, editors felt the need to demonstrate their wholehearted commitment to the cause of racial justice.

In June, a week after the killing of George Floyd, the head of *Axios* announced in a companywide email that the news site would allow its staff members to participate in public protests. Responding to an anonymous question, co-founder Jim VandeHei wrote that "we proudly support and encourage you to exercise your rights to free speech, press, and protest." And then his email added that the company would cover bail if staff members were arrested and would pay medical bills if they were harmed. "As a company we condemn police brutality and racism," he wrote. And he added, "We'd be proud if you wanted to wear *Axios* gear while exercising your rights." VandeHei told me later that he had heard from staff about "how devastated and tormented and sad they were, and you're looking for a response to show your solidarity."

The June 2020 email about protests seemed to conflict in spirit with a stern warning only two years earlier from VandeHei regarding self-expression by staff, at that time on social media: "News organizations should ban their reporters from doing anything on social media—especially Twitter—beyond sharing stories. Snark, jokes and blatant opinion are showing your hand, and it always seems to be the left one. This makes it impossible to win back the skeptics." But VandeHei told me he viewed the racial justice protests, at least initially, as different and not in violation of *Axios* rules against political activity or, as its ethics policy states, anything that might give the public "reason to doubt our trustworthiness or impartiality."

VandeHei allows that the protests over George Floyd's killing quickly became a partisan political issue, but he argues that there was a "fleeting moment" when they weren't. "There was a moment—and it only lasted let's say a week—where it wasn't really a political topic . . . There was this moment where you had national solidarity: Something needs to be done." Although VandeHei subsequently told his staff that it was always clear that they couldn't do anything "overtly political" during the protests, his email was silent on the subject, didn't suggest that permission to protest might expire under certain circumstances, and set no boundaries on what could be protested. It only called upon staff to "use the same sound judgment you always have when representing Axios and keep our higher calling top of mind."

Journalists seeking to blow up the old, stricter ethics policies typically said they were looking for greater clarity. For the most part, however, what they were really seeking was permission, a green light to express themselves as they wished. Even if the new policies wouldn't give staff carte blanche, they could still be drafted with so much nuance and so many loopholes that accountability became impossible. Journalists who proudly sought to hold public officials, business executives, and an array of others to account for violating rules and regulations were lobbying for gauzy ethics codes that made accountability ever less likely for themselves. Rules were being rendered largely unenforceable (not that editors showed much will to strictly apply them anyway).

One argument among journalists was that under the old rules they could not bring their "full selves" to work, forcing them to be one version at home and another in the office. But that sort of thinking wasn't something they'd likely tolerate from certain other professions—judges or police, for example. Or, for that matter, from colleagues who might embrace ideas that most in the newsroom would find objectionable. Or from their own newsroom supervisors. I can only imagine the reaction among staff if I, as executive editor of *The Post*, had chosen to march for a cause that ran counter to the views of many in our newsroom.

The profession's traditional ethics standards had been fashioned with one overriding idea: How can news organizations earn the public's trust? As revisions were cobbled together in 2020 and beyond, another idea took hold: How can news organizations placate a restive staff? The two ideas aren't axiomatically compatible. Satisfying the wishes of a staff isn't the same as winning confidence from the public. They might well be in conflict. As time passed, it was encouraging to see at least some editors reminding their staffs that public trust had to take precedence over their desire for self-expression, no matter how strongly individual staffers felt or how worthy the cause.

Recruiting and retaining a more diverse staff would help news organizations like *The Post* deliver better journalism. Staffers who have lived very different lives could help us see the world from perspectives that had been missing, ignored, or only casually and clumsily addressed in our newsrooms for too long. Their experiences could better inform conversations among ourselves about race, ethnicity, gender, identity, sexuality, and spirituality, inspiring more sophisticated, sensitive, and trailblazing coverage.

One goal of greater diversity had to be inclusiveness: Allowing all Americans to see themselves, their concerns, and their aspirations more accurately and fully reflected in our stories. Another had to be understanding: Giving Americans the means to see the world from the vantage point of others whose background and experiences were very different from their own.

However, participation by journalists in the very events our news organizations covered—whether through marches or donations or social media—risked undermining public confidence in the independence and professionalism of our work. The cause of public understanding would not be well served if our journalists were seen as indistinguishable from activists. Within the news department at *The Post*, our mission was to inform, not to advocate. Good journalism would have to do the talking, as it had for decades. For us, there was no more effective form of speech.

19

PLAGUE OF DECEIT

On the afternoon of March 10, 2020, *Washington Post* publisher Fred Ryan advised all employees of new measures the company was taking to "serve our readers and assure the well-being of our employees." The United States and the world were confronting a pandemic threatening to cause millions of deaths. All employees were encouraged, though not mandated, to work from home if practical to do so. A hard mandate soon followed.

With advances in technology, I could do my job from home. Others could, too. But certainly not all. A news organization like ours needed reporters, photographers, and videographers out in the community and on the road, never more so than during a crisis that was overwhelming hospitals while devastating businesses and livelihoods everywhere. Those journalists faced ever-present risks to their health.

And yet the greatest challenge of the pandemic for *The Post*, and the mainstream American press overall, proved to be something else: It was the uncontainable mendacity of the president.

One of our tasks was to accurately communicate to the public the severity of the coronavirus threat and how people could protect themselves. Another was to assess how well, or poorly, the U.S. government was doing in its efforts to contain the spread of disease. Throughout the year, Donald Trump proved hostile to the truth about both. Never before had his contempt for facts carried such dire consequences. His lying was now a matter of life and death.

As the rapid spread of the coronavirus pointed to a global plague, I thought the press would have a rare opportunity to earn renewed confidence from the public. Journalists specializing in public health would be turning to the world's most respected scientists and doctors, reporting what they knew and were still learning. The best available knowledge would be in high demand.

Early signs were that the vast majority of Americans saw us as a venue for solid information. But when the science didn't serve Trump's political interests, he fell into a familiar pattern: He went on the attack. The very experts we relied upon as authoritative sources became his latest target. Leading doctors and researchers were dismissed and demeaned. Their motives were questioned, even their expertise. They suffered a loss of trust; so did we. Their job was made infinitely harder; so was ours.

Trump's deceit began late in January 2020 after the Centers for Disease Control and Prevention confirmed the first U.S. coronavirus case in Washington State. "We have it totally under control," Trump told CNBC from Davos, Switzerland. "It's one person coming in from China, and we have it under control. It's going to be just fine." Hours after the World Health Organization on January 30 declared a global health emergency—by which point five cases were confirmed in the United States—Trump told a Michigan audience, "We have very little problem in this country at this moment—five—and those people are all recuperating successfully. But we're working very closely with China and other countries, and we think it's going to have a very good ending for us . . . that I can assure you." By February 10, Trump was declaring that "a lot of people" expected that "as the heat comes in" the virus would vanish. "Typically, that will go away in April. We're in great shape though. We have 12 cases—11 cases, and many of them are in good shape now." Two weeks later, he said, "We have it very much under control in this country." By month's end, it was: "Because of all we've done, the risk to the American people remains very low." "It's going to disappear. One day, it's like a miracle, it will disappear." "We are working on cures and we're getting some very good results." "Now the Democrats are politicizing the coronavirus . . . And this is their new hoax."

Some hoax: On March 11, the World Health Organization declared a global pandemic. Trump would later admit to Bob Woodward for his book *Rage* that the virus was more dire than he had acknowledged to the American public. As revealed upon the book's publication in September 2020, Trump told Bob in a February 7 call, "You just breathe the air and that's how it's passed. And so that's a very tricky one. That's a very delicate one. It's also more deadly than even your strenuous flus . . . This is deadly stuff." And in a March 19 interview with Bob, Trump avowed that he had deliberately minimized the risks to the American public: "I wanted to always play it down. I still like playing it down, because I don't want to create a panic." And play it down he did, for months on end, choosing instead to berate the press when it was telling the public the truth.

Trump's family, aides, and allies also chimed in with sunny scenarios, laced with the usual slams against the press. Mick Mulvaney, the acting White House chief of staff, told conservative activists in late February that the media "think this will bring down the president, that's what this is all about." Kellyanne Conway, a senior adviser to the president, said of the virus a week later, "It's being contained." It wasn't contained, not even close.

For a while Trump changed his tune. Suddenly, the country was in a "war" against the pandemic, and he was, by his own description, a "wartime president." On March 18, he invoked wartime powers under which he could order companies to produce desperately needed medical equipment. By then, there were 7,800 confirmed cases and 115 deaths nationwide. The economy was cratering, and the stock market had erased nearly all its gains since Trump's inauguration. A study by Imperial College London was projecting that 2.2 million Americans could die of COVID-19 if nothing was done by government and individuals and the pandemic remained out of control.

A president deserves to be evaluated by the press and the public on how he performs, never more so than in wartime. Deep reporting by *The Post*'s journalists led to a withering assessment of the pandemic war effort. White House correspondents Philip Rucker and Ashley Parker wrote of Trump on March 20 that the previous "seven days at the helm of the coronavirus effort illuminated his mercurial nature and underscored his difficulty overseeing the national response to a global catastrophe largely out of his—or any other leader's—control." He had been "lapsing into his self-destructive ways even when aides stress the importance of steady leadership during a national emergency."

Trump that day, based on "just a feeling," was championing hydroxychloroquine as a coronavirus treatment. The antimalarial drug was not then considered to be effective, and since then it has been proved not to be. (Trump dismissed one of those studies as a "Trump-enemy statement.") When asked by an NBC News reporter what message he had for Americans who were worried, Trump lashed out. "I say that you're a terrible reporter. That's what I say." And his messaging was all over the place, once claiming, "I felt it was a pandemic long before it was a pandemic," days after having advised, "Just stay calm. It will go away." By March 31, Trump was surmising the outbreak might only last another month. And by April, he was pooh-poohing the idea of a resurgence that was being forecast, accurately as it turned out, by many public health professionals.

The press briefings of the White House coronavirus task force, once led by Vice President Mike Pence, were taken over by Trump, snatching for himself the attention he always covets. Standing at the podium, Trump could once again be the star of his own show—"playing the role of the ringmaster, the marketer and the brander, and the self-professed expert," as Michael Kruse put it in *Politico*. A single episode of the show could go on for two hours or more. Length, though, was the least of their failings.

Years earlier, I had barred live video on our website of the Trump administration's so-called briefings for the press. Although in every presidency daily briefings had been chock-full of spin, they had also routinely produced real information. But it was evident from the Trump administration's first one, as press secretary Sean Spicer badgered the media over the size of the inauguration crowd, that these "briefings" would mostly be a forum for misinformation and political spectacle. For an administration eager to portray the press as Public Enemy No. 1, they also were deliciously tempting opportunities for him to wage attacks against journalists on live television.

A worldwide pandemic seemed the right occasion for an exception to my long-standing prohibition on live feeds. The public deserved to hear from the government's leading health authorities and the president himself. Months into the crisis, however, I had lost any expectation that the "briefings" might prove useful to the American public. I ordered a halt to live feeds in mid-April. "These aren't briefings any longer," I wrote our video and website chiefs. "They're campaign events—2½ hours turned over to the president, which he uses for political purposes. The information component has all but vanished."

His press "briefing" on March 19 was of typically low caliber. Naturally, he attacked the media, this time adding *The Wall Street Journal* to his target list. "It amazes me when I read the things that I read," he said. "It amazes me when I read the *Wall Street Journal*, which is always so negative. It amazes me when I read—the *New York Times* is not even—I barely read it. You know, we don't distribute it in the White House anymore, and the same thing with the

Washington Post." And then the president slipped into habitual conspiracy mode: "They are siding with China. They are doing things
that they shouldn't be doing. They're siding with many others; China
is the least of it. So why are they doing this? You'll have to ask them."
(Not one for consistency, Trump only a few days earlier had said, "I
really think the media has been very fair." He also seemed to confirm
that Jeff Bezos and Amazon had been in contact with the White
House about providing some sort of assistance.)

What the press owed the public in that moment was not a platform for the president's cascade of falsehoods. We had a duty instead
to deliver thorough and energetic journalism that held the president
to account.

The pandemic posed major challenges for a news operation that
relied heavily on its journalists being out and about, meeting people
face-to-face, and covering stories firsthand. Many had experienced
danger in their jobs, from reporting on violence in America's streets
to covering brutal conflicts overseas. A few had chronicled the mid-
decade Ebola virus epidemic in West Africa. For everyone else, however, the coronavirus was a menace unlike any they had experienced
before. The danger was unseen. It could be anywhere. Potentially it
was everywhere. And it could well prove fatal.

The newsroom itself emptied out. Only a few dozen editors remained after the publisher's first work-from-home advisory, physically separating themselves from each other by at least several desks.
But the news department was making contingency plans to evacuate
the main office altogether in the event of contamination. A single
positive test would likely lead to an immediate, complete shutdown
of our headquarters. We needed to prepare for the possibility.

Over the course of ten days, a facilities team, technology specialists, and newsroom leaders worked to set up a satellite operation out of a company-owned facility in Laurel, Maryland. Twenty

workstations were set up for a core newsroom team. The space was fully scrubbed; it was also fumigated to excise the residual odor from what had only recently been a printing facility. Editors tested the operation for two days to ensure we could effectively regroup there. The preparations were for naught. In short order, all employees were instructed to work from home, without exception. Even gathering as a small group in our headquarters, or in our pop-up satellite facility, was considered too risky.

The Post's wide-open newsroom had long facilitated minute-by-minute, in-person communication and collaboration. Now all of us had to learn on the fly how to cover the news twenty-four hours a day, and instantly, when we were no longer working side by side. Younger journalists who shared apartments with roommates were sleeping and working every day in the same small room. Journalists with families were struggling to do their jobs even as they attended to restless kids who were attempting virtual school at home. The print newspaper still needed to be published and delivered on time every day. Our website, apps, news alerts, social media presence, and email newsletters had to be operated without interruption.

Post reporters, videographers, and photographers were courageous while reporting from the field, risking infection merely by doing their jobs. And yet some were understandably reluctant to take on unseen, incalculable risks that could leave them or their families ill, incapacitated, or even struggling for life. As coronavirus "hot spots" multiplied, we were finding ourselves without enough journalists to report on the pandemic from locations that had been hit hardest.

When Michigan experienced a sharp increase in cases—prompting Governor Gretchen Whitmer to issue a stay-at-home order and close the schools—*The Post* was caught short-handed, with no one on the ground in Detroit, where the case count was escalating rapidly. A regular freelancer was "unwilling to go out because of safety concerns," one editor warned. And while one reporter was working on an unrelated story in the vicinity, the editor expressed concern for the risks he would be asked to assume if diverted to cover a wave of coronavirus cases. "I would be uneasy asking him to go to downtown Detroit."

Mandated quarantines also put a severe squeeze on the number of staffers available for assignments outside their homes. When reporters returned from active outbreak zones, they were typically required to isolate at home and stop traveling for fourteen days, per the government's guidance at the time. As a number of our journalists fell ill, *The Post* was having to weigh the imperative of covering the news—which the public expected of us—with the need to keep staff safe. We weren't going to send individual journalists to places where they feared to go. Still, we needed a lot of staffers to willingly go to a lot of places. With the pandemic's impact felt across the world and in every field—from restaurants and retailers to sports, the arts, and workplaces of all varieties—a massive deployment of staff was required.

The Post's correspondent in Italy, Chico Harlan, was at the epicenter of the crisis in its early months, living in central Rome with his wife and infant son. His experience was a case study in how reportorial resourcefulness could yield vivid coverage while also keeping himself and his family healthy. Chico previously had concentrated on the Vatican and immigration. He was now covering a country under nationwide lockdown. Italy would foretell what was in store for the United States and the rest of the world.

Chico was no stranger to extraordinary health risks. He had reported from Japan when in 2011 the Fukushima Daiichi nuclear plant was hit by tsunami waves, damaging backup generators and triggering a partial meltdown of fuel rods and the release of radiation. Nearly 232 square miles around the reactor were evacuated. "That was, in a way, similar—this sort of invisible danger," Chico told *Vanity Fair* in mid-March 2020. "And yet the difference there was, I didn't have a family at the time. And if you get sick from radiation, or if you get hurt in the field covering violence, that is something that's gonna affect your family. But you're not going to bring the risk home."

In Italy, Chico had to rely heavily on the telephone in lieu of on-the-ground reporting. To document the scale of deaths in Bergamo province, he and colleague Stefano Pitrelli printed out local newspaper obituaries, checked names against phone directories, and made a list of forty phone numbers to call. They called twenty, and four families were willing to talk.

"In the part of Italy hit hardest by the coronavirus, the crematorium has started operating 24 hours a day," they wrote in mid-March. "Coffins have filled up two hospital morgues, and then a cemetery morgue, and are now being lined up inside a cemetery church. The local newspaper's daily obituary section has grown from two or three pages to 10, sometimes listing more than 150 names, in what the top editor likens to 'war bulletins.' By death toll alone, the coronavirus has landed in the northern province of Bergamo with the force of a historic disaster. But its alarming power goes even further, all but ensuring that death and mourning happen in isolation—a trauma in which everybody must keep to themselves."

The Post's health journalists needed to be in hospitals, serving as witnesses to the devastation caused by a virus that was on the move. Reporter Lenny Bernstein and video journalist Jon Gerberg volunteered to report in March from inside Brooklyn's Maimonides Medical Center, which by then was almost entirely filled with COVID-19 patients. "Health reporter is a nice, safe job. Usually quite uneventful," Lenny later told his *Post* colleagues, "but if you cover hospitals in a pandemic, the story is inside the hospital, and the best way to get it is by going there . . . Once inside, we saw real bravery. While we dropped in for a day or two, the doctors, nurses and other staff we met were risking their health and their lives, shift after shift, day after day, for weeks—then months—at a time."

Post staffers also experienced the pandemic in the most personal, sorrowful way. For example, Lena Sun, who helped lead the coverage of the coronavirus from the moment it was first reported in China, mourned the loss of her own mother that spring. Yu Lihua, renowned author of more than two dozen novels and short-story collections that illuminated the immigrant Chinese experience, died of respiratory failure due to COVID-19.

Given the ubiquitous health risks, along with work disruptions and the peril to household income, it was infuriating to hear Trump and his allies suggest that the mainstream media were rooting for him to fail. When declaring in March that he wanted to reopen businesses by Easter—a timeline widely viewed as overly optimistic—Trump accused the media of joining Democrats in yearning for the economy's collapse. "The media would like to see me do poorly in the election," he said at a White House briefing.

Depicting journalists as callous, hoping for human and economic carnage, was no doubt an easy sell to the Trump followers who swallowed whatever loathsome nonsense the president dished out. Many had bought into his trademark vilification of the media as the most contemptible species on earth. But no one in the media, of course, wished for Trump's defeat in the election over their own health and that of their family and friends. Or over their own livelihoods, for that matter: The pandemic was inflicting havoc on an already struggling news business.

Although public anxiety had supercharged readership—*The Post* netted fifty-six thousand new subscriptions in the first two weeks of March alone, propelling us past two million digital subscribers—advertising was vanishing. Many companies forbade their ads from appearing next to any stories about the pandemic, as if their products and services would be poisoned by the adjacency. Because the story dominated domestic and international news coverage, advertisements on digital news sites were being canceled in huge volumes overnight. *BuzzFeed News* reported that in the first three weeks of March, one unidentified major global brand had prohibited two million ads from appearing on the sites of *The Washington Post*, *The New York Times*, CNN, and *USA Today*. More than three thousand advertisers were said to be blocking ads from appearing next to stories containing the word "coronavirus." The prospect of an economic crash made matters far worse. Companies were calling an abrupt halt to advertising campaigns. You don't advertise when people are unlikely to buy and their shopping destinations are being shuttered.

Local news organizations suffered the greatest. Most were already in a state of severe financial distress, having yet to discover a sustainable business model for the digital age. Suddenly they were being drained of the diminished revenue that remained. The *Tampa Bay Times*, for one, cited the coronavirus in scaling back publication of its print edition to a mere two days per week, Sundays and Wednesdays. The newspaper also placed some staff on furlough for eight weeks and reduced working hours for others. With retail outlets closed, community events suspended, and overall economic activity paralyzed, the newspaper industry's ad revenue declined by 25 percent in 2020. By the end of 2021, the nonprofit Poynter Institute reported, at least a hundred local newsrooms had closed during the pandemic, largely as a result of its merciless financial impact.

The Post was not immune. Our advertising was drying up fast, too. And yet members of our news staff and other journalists were pressing me to have the site made free to everyone. During an urgent health crisis, their argument went, accurate information needed to be made available without charge. Bezos, in their view, should personally absorb the cost; his bank account could handle the hit. Or, as one seasoned journalist sneeringly wrote me: "Jeff Bezos should see that rising to this occasion would help him. I know every nickel has to be pried from him. Pry."

The decision on when, whether, and what to charge for subscriptions wasn't mine—I didn't oversee business operations—but the "give it all away for free" reasoning, however well-meaning, wasn't convincing to me. I had zero desire to argue that case to the publisher or the owner. We could make a lot of pandemic coverage available for free—and we did—but people would still have to pay if they wanted access to everything.

The Post had struggled for years to claw our way back into profitability. No one at the top of the organization could stomach the idea of dipping back into the red. There was no future in that. "We're run as a business, not a charity," I wrote one journalist. "Regardless of Bezos's wealth or what anyone thinks of him, we have to stand on our own two feet." Finally, I added, "No one else is giving away their work for free: not mask or ventilator makers, not medical professionals, not the makers of Purell, not the federal government, which still requires us to pay taxes. Why should our profession be the only one? If we keep giving away our work for free, no one will ever think it carries enough value to pay for."

Readers bought subscriptions to *The Post* with the expectation that we would hold the government to account, and rightly so. That's what we aimed to do during the pandemic. *The Post* reported in March 2020 that U.S. intelligence agencies "were issuing ominous, classified warnings in January and February about the global danger posed by the coronavirus" even as Trump played down the threat and failed to take effective action. "Donald Trump may not have been expecting this, but a lot of other people in the government were—they just couldn't get him to do anything about it," one official told *Post* reporters. The president lashed out: "I saw the story. I think it's a disgrace, but it's *The Washington Post*, and I guess we have to live with it."

In early April, as the health crisis worsened, *The Post* published a retrospective on the administration's performance. Noting that Trump was first alerted on January 3 to the outbreak of the coronavirus in

China, *Post* reporters wrote, "And yet, it took 70 days from that initial notification for Trump to treat the coronavirus not as a distant threat or harmless flu strain well under control, but as a lethal force that had outflanked America's defenses and was poised to kill tens of thousands of citizens. That more-than-two-month stretch now stands as critical time that was squandered."

Government health officials and their agencies also did damage to themselves, particularly with confusing reversals in their recommendations. Most notoriously, guidance on wearing masks belatedly went from no, don't wear them, to yes, you absolutely should. Advice to "follow the science," though sensible, meant following it through sharp turns and even flips as researchers learned more. There were outright flops, too.

The Post dug deep into the disastrous failure by the Centers for Disease Control to deliver an effective coronavirus test of its own. The agency was slow to enlist the aid of experts from outside its own staff. "In their private communications," *Post* journalists wrote on April 3, "scientists at academic, hospital and public health labs—one layer removed from federal agency operations—expressed dismay at the failure to move more quickly and frustration at bureaucratic demands that delayed their attempts to develop alternatives to the CDC test." *The Post* revealed two weeks later that the CDC's failure was "triggered by a glaring scientific breakdown" at its central laboratory facilities in Atlanta that "violated sound manufacturing practices, resulting in contamination of one of the three test components used in the highly sensitive detection process."

Trump's image suffered immeasurably when on April 23 he mused that ingesting disinfectants might help kill the coronavirus. "I see the disinfectant that knocks it out in a minute, one minute," Trump said. "And is there a way we can do something like that by injection inside, or almost a cleaning? Because you see it gets inside the lungs and it does a tremendous number on the lungs, so it would be interesting to check that." The maker of the Lysol disinfectant spray and cleaner rushed to warn that "under no circumstance should our disinfectant products be administered into the human body (through injection, ingestion or any other route)." Trump later implausibly claimed he was just being sarcastic, though that was not at all his tone.

When White House bureau chief Phil Rucker asked Trump at that April 23 briefing whether, given severe outbreaks in Florida and Singapore, it was wise for him to suggest that people set aside quarantining at home and go outside in the heat and sun, Trump excoriated him. Trump had cited a "very nice rumor" about how light and heat could kill viruses. "But respectfully, sir," Phil followed up, "you're the president and people tuning in to these briefings—they want to get information and guidance and want to know what to do. They're not looking for a rumor." Trump's response could not have been more foul or infantile. "Hey Phil, I'm the president and you're fake news. And you know what else I'll say to you? I'll say it very nicely . . . I know what he writes. He's a total faker."

As usual, Phil handled the president's attack and its amplification on Fox News with composure. "I'm fine," he told me when I checked with him. "Some of my incoming messages are ugly, but it's not the first time and probably won't be the last." (Once out of office and away from performing for the public on the White House podium for the TV audience, Trump welcomed "total faker" Phil Rucker and colleague Carol Leonnig to Mar-a-Lago, where they interviewed him for their book, *I Alone Can Fix It*.)

The next evening Trump was calling *The Post* "one of the worst in the 'news' business. Total slime balls." That followed an analysis led by reporters Philip Bump and Ashley Parker that dissected how Trump used his "briefings" during the pandemic: "Trump has spoken for more than 28 hours in the 35 briefings held since March 16, eating up 60 percent of the time that officials spoke . . . Over the past three weeks, the tally comes to more than 13 hours of Trump—including two hours spent on attacks and 45 minutes praising himself and his administration, but just 4½ minutes expressing condolences for coronavirus victims . . . Trump has attacked someone in 113 out of 346 questions he has answered—or a third of his responses. He has offered false or misleading information in nearly 25 percent of his remarks."

Less than a week after Trump was castigated and mocked for speculating about disinfectant, the near-daily late-afternoon coronavirus press briefings came to a halt at the urging of aides who worried that they were hurting Trump's poll numbers. "What is the purpose of having White House News Conferences," Trump tweeted on April 25, "when the Lamestream Media asks nothing but hostile questions, & then refuses to report the truth or facts accurately. They get record ratings, & the American people get nothing but Fake News. Not worth the time & effort!" Trump would make a reappearance shortly afterward, but the "briefings" then went on hiatus for three months. Not until July 21 did Trump return, this time hoping to attract a large audience and lift his poll numbers. A *Washington Post*–ABC News poll showed that six in ten Americans disapproved of his handling of the pandemic and that Democratic nominee Joe Biden's lead in the presidential race had risen to fifteen percentage points among registered voters.

Trump was fed up with restrictions that depressed the economy, sank the stock market, and propelled the unemployment rate to the highest level since the Great Depression. As other countries opened up with hopes of putting the pandemic behind them, he was itching to do the same, despite rising cases and deaths and the likelihood of a new surge. The self-proclaimed wartime president was now launching a very different war, this one against measures to contain the virus, the doctors and political leaders who advocated for them, and even the data that showed the virus still out of control.

An easy way to deny facts is to not go looking for them. While the press aims to dig up facts, Trump regularly aimed to keep them hidden, substituting his own "alternative facts." That spring he began defining the COVID problem as too much testing—"If we didn't do any testing, we would have very few cases." Uncomfortable forecasts were attacked, and rosy ones embraced, no matter their flaws.

When a draft Centers for Disease Control report emerged in early May predicting daily COVID-related deaths would surpass 3,000 by month's end, the White House assailed the forecast, offering up instead a farcical model from the Council of Economic Advisers that showed deaths plunging to zero by midmonth. The CDC distanced itself from its own draft report, declaring that it was still working on the projections. Daily COVID-related deaths that May ranged between 556 and 2,732, totaling close to 40,000 for the month. They subsided somewhat in the five months that followed, only to rise sharply again through the winter.

That spring, Trump moved to sideline Anthony Fauci, the government's leading expert on infectious diseases, keeping him out of the Oval Office only to put him squarely in the White House's crosshairs. When *The Post* in July documented the deteriorating relationship between Trump and Fauci, including how the White House had canceled his media appearances, there was no denial from the administration. Just the opposite: Officials capitalized on *The Post*'s queries to tarnish Fauci's reputation, volunteering a statement of concern about "the number of times Dr. Fauci has been wrong on things." Fauci wouldn't talk at the time about his treatment by the president. Instead, he aired his views through outlets other than the White House press briefing room, finding fault with the U.S. pandemic response.

Next among health leaders to be disparaged by Trump was White House coronavirus response coordinator Deborah Birx, whom he called "pathetic" after she said in early August that the virus remained "extraordinarily widespread," affecting "both rural and urban" areas, and correctly predicted as many as three hundred thousand deaths by year's end.

Cherry-picking coronavirus data, Trump tried to make the pandemic appear less menacing than it was. In a late-July interview with *Axios*'s Jonathan Swan for HBO, he pointed to charts that showed the United States with a trend toward lower deaths as a percent of total cases. That disguised the fact that the total number of new COVID-related deaths remained at a high level—about a thousand per day, Swan pointed out. As a percent of population, new U.S. COVID-related deaths at the time were running well above the European Union, England, and Japan. "They are dying, that's true," Trump responded when pressed by Swan. "And you have—it is what it is. But that doesn't mean we aren't doing everything we can. It's under control as much as you can control it." As *Post* reporters Yasmeen Abutaleb and Damian Paletta observed in *Nightmare Scenario*, their 2021 book about the Trump administration's pandemic response, "It was one of the most startling admissions yet that Trump had thrown up his hands and somehow found a way to justify the high death count—or even declare victory—just as the virus was surging again."

Nothing sent a stronger message to Americans that they could ignore science and scientists than Trump's own behavior. He wouldn't wear a mask himself and frowned on others wearing one in his presence, seeing it as a sign of weakness. At crowded White House gatherings, attendees typically went maskless; at his political rallies, with thousands packed together, the same. After he himself got sick with COVID-19 and was airlifted to Walter Reed National Military Medical Center—more gravely ill than he ever admitted—he told Americans, "Don't be afraid of COVID. Don't let it dominate your life." It was "magical thinking," as *The Post* editorial board noted. By then, Trump had recovered and was safely back at the White House, the beneficiary of urgent advanced medical care unavailable to all but the president of the United States.

In the final stretch of his campaign, Trump signaled that COVID-19 was yesterday's news. The pandemic was "rounding the corner," he said at an October campaign rally in Gastonia, North Carolina. "All you hear is COVID, COVID, COVID, COVID, COVID, COVID, COVID, COVID, COVID, COVID. That's all they put on, because they want to scare the hell out of everyone." To Trump, getting reelected was what mattered most. But the country could not afford to be as cavalier as its president. COVID was on a long and deadly march. By mid-May 2022, COVID-19 deaths exceeded one million in the United States. Worldwide, an estimated 6.3 million people had died.

Scientific knowledge about COVID had evolved, but Trump was denying science outright. His motive was the usual one: his own political interests. Yet millions believed him, no matter the evidence in bodies buried. It was dismaying for me to see so many Americans deny reality when the human cost was so tragically high and when *The Post* and other media, consulting with the world's most renowned scientists, had kept them informed as facts became known. Our efforts never seemed more futile, the truth never more endangered. Yet we couldn't allow ourselves to be defeatist. Telling the truth often must be its own reward.

20

THE PLOT AGAINST DEMOCRACY

The *Post*'s truth-telling mission found its ultimate test in the presidential election of 2020 and in its terrifying aftermath.

Three reporters who constituted *The Post*'s Fact Checker team had been tracking every false or misleading statement Donald Trump made since he was sworn in as president. By October 2020, the deceptions were coming so rapidly that the team told readers it was unable to keep up. In the final stretch of the campaign, Trump's untrue claims were running at more than 50 per day. On August 11, they hit a one-day record of 189. In the first year of his presidency, he averaged 6 false claims a day; then 16 in 2018, 22 in 2019, and 27 daily in 2020 up until two months shy of the election. During the pandemic, when Trump found additional reasons to deceive, he added 1,400 falsehoods to his inglorious list in just six months. By the end of his four years as president, the lies and deceptions added up to 30,573.

That number alone, no matter how astounding, could not adequately capture all that was at stake. A nation needs fact as its anchor. Trump was cutting the anchor loose. "The power of his lies is not merely in their tally but in the escalating demands they make on us," as *The Post*'s Carlos Lozada argued in his 2020 book, *What Were We Thinking*. "First, we are asked to believe specific lies. Then, to bend the truth to our preferred politics. Next, to accept only what the president certifies as true, no matter the subject or how often his positions shift. After that, to hold that there is really no knowable, agreed-upon truth. Finally, to conclude that even if there is a truth, it is inconsequential. Lies don't matter, only the man uttering them does."

Cataloging Trump's deceit was a noble effort—a service to citizens, history, and truth. His lies had accumulated into a cancerous threat to American democracy. But if any of our fact-checking resonated with Trump's hard-core base, I didn't detect it. Trump had labored for years to inoculate himself from the truth. He would fabricate his own, and then have his detractors labeled as liars themselves.

The pattern was a dismayingly familiar one. Throughout history, leaders who aspired to authoritarian power had done the same. The ranks of strongmen worldwide were now swelling again—in Hungary, Turkey, Brazil, the Philippines, and elsewhere, where the press proved a convenient enemy, vulnerable target, and unsteady counterweight. I worried that the mainstream American press faced the same fate amid Trump's grievance-propelled populism. Given our inability to get Trump loyalists to reject his smaller lies—or persuade them even to give a damn—how could we gain their trust in 2020 when his lies ranked as the most sinister and colossal in modern American presidential history?

There were journalism pundits aplenty who offered advice: Use stronger language (unequivocally say more often, and more forcefully, that politicians "lie"). Refuse to publish what Trump says, especially if he's just repeating his lies. Refuse to give a platform to politicians and their operatives who made a practice of joining in his most dangerous lies. Write and broadcast stories that vividly demonstrate that the United States is in a life-or-death struggle for truth and democracy. Set up teams of journalists to report doggedly on the threat to democracy at every level of government.

Major news outlets were justifiably doing much or all of that.

Trump's dishonesty, along with the hazard he posed to democracy, received relentless coverage for years. It was comprehensive, thoroughly documented, and increasingly blunt.

Trump's most devoted supporters, however, weren't reading or listening to media outlets like mine. To the extent they paid attention, they saw us as not delivering facts so much as animus. And as *Politico* media columnist Jack Shafer noted in late 2022, the facts weren't what concerned them most anyway. "The most horrifying thing about Trump's constant lies," he wrote, "is not that he convinces his supporters to accept them but that his supporters don't care that much about whether he's telling the truth as they do about his positions or affectations about the culture war, race, immigration, abortion, grievance, police, trade, guns and political elites."

And yet I still had confidence that enough Americans were open to genuine evidence, that a majority were interested in separating fact from fiction, that enough didn't truly believe journalists for the most renowned media institutions just made stuff up, and that the country as a whole was not prepared to cut the cord with objective reality and its democratic heritage. It was more than faith on my part: There were millions of Trump voters who didn't just blindly support him. As president, he had never achieved more than 50 percent approval from the American public, and his approval rating had fallen as low as 37 percent. For most of his presidency, Gallup polls showed, Americans rating him "honest and trustworthy" fell in the miserable range of 33 to 37 percent.

Trump's most unwavering loyalists would repudiate what we published, but not all his voters would. My hope was that, as our reporting was validated over time, skeptics would look past partisan rhetoric, acknowledge verifiable reality, and recognize the calamitous risks of denying it. It was hope based on a long history of our country's most effective journalism, even when it was under sustained attack. Trump had made our task harder, but I was not prepared to concede that he had made it impossible.

I also knew that this was a story I very much wanted to be a part of. Overseeing coverage of Trump's assault on facts and American democracy would constitute the final chapter of my career, and arguably its most important. Though my disposition had darkened in 2020 due to internal controversies, now was a time to focus single-mindedly on actual journalism. Nothing mattered to me more. Nothing was more meaningful. The mission of journalism is what drew me full-time to the field in 1976 and now it would carry me through to retirement, when I could leave our newsroom divisions behind.

As we neared the election, I was grateful to still be leading the news staff of *The Washington Post*. I was relieved that my offer to resign had been rejected. I found myself newly energized, able to beat back physical exhaustion and the gloomy mood that had overtaken me. There was no place I would rather have been than at *The Post* at that perilous moment in history. For all its episodic fractiousness, the gifted staff always pulled together when urgent news demanded unity of effort and purpose. We needed that now. It became obvious we also would need it from election day until January 20 and most likely well beyond.

I was increasingly convinced that Trump, if he lost the election, would not willingly leave the White House and that he would do whatever he could to retain power. The man who had always loved money and attention clearly came to love power above all else. He could never tolerate the idea of losing. It became increasingly evident that he would simply deny he had lost. Facts were nothing to him. Democracy and his oath to "preserve, protect, and defend" the Constitution were no dearer to him, either. He enjoyed fighting. He would fight to the end, and fight dirty. At *The Post*, we were prepared for that.

Anyone familiar with Trump's political history could sense the gathering storm. Trump had a record of making false accusations of fraudulent elections. When Barack Obama in 2012 defeated Mitt Romney, whom he supported, Trump called the election a "total sham and a travesty." At the time, Trump was grumbling that Obama's victory was based on the Electoral College, when it initially appeared that Romney might lead in overall votes. (Obama ultimately won the popular vote, too, and by a sizable margin.)

In February 2016, Trump claimed that he hadn't actually lost the Iowa caucuses, which kicked off the Republican primary contests. "Ted Cruz didn't win Iowa, he stole it," Trump tweeted, adding: "Based on the fraud committed by Senator Ted Cruz during the Iowa caucus, either a new election should take place or Cruz results nullified."

Before the presidential election in 2016, Trump said he'd accept the election results "if I win." Trump didn't give up on unfounded accusations of fraud even after winning. He had prevailed in the Electoral College but won nearly three million fewer overall votes than Hillary Clinton, capturing the presidency because of an Electoral College system he had decried only four years earlier as a "disaster for democracy." Shortly after the election, however, he declared on Twitter that he "won the popular vote if you deduct the millions of people who voted illegally."

Thousands of Massachusetts residents were bused into New Hampshire to vote illegally, he claimed, costing him a victory in the state. There was, of course, never any evidence of that. He made claims of "serious voter fraud" in Virginia and California in the 2016 presidential election as well; again, no evidence. A few months after taking office, Trump set up a commission purportedly to investigate voter fraud. The commission was disbanded less than a year later without substantiating any wrongdoing, though the White House continued to insist that fraud had occurred.

So Trump's latest iteration of stolen-election claims, in 2020, was straight out of a well-worn playbook. The lies just became more extravagant, the repercussions more serious. In May, he denounced

Michigan for sending out absentee ballots to "7.7 million people," suggesting the state was going down a "Voter Fraud path!"—even though the secretary of state had merely sent out applications for ballots, just as Republican counterparts in other states had done. Trump threatened to withhold federal funds to Michigan, and then did the same with Nevada, claiming it was distributing "illegal vote by mail ballots" and warning "you must not cheat in elections." In early July, Trump tweeted that "Mail-In Ballots will lead to massive electoral fraud and a rigged 2020 Election."

Ultimately, *The Post* calculated, 84 percent of American voters were eligible to cast ballots by mail. Thirty-four states and the District of Columbia allowed anyone to vote with an absentee ballot. Many states, aiming to ensure access to voting during a pandemic, were making it easier by either mailing ballots or applications for ballots to voters. The anticipated surge in voting by mail didn't foreshadow an increase in fraud—Trump would never prove it had—but it did mean that counting the vote would take a lot longer than in the past. Critically, it also meant that an early lead reported for Trump on election night could be overwhelmed by mail ballots that were yet to be tallied. Due to their greater concerns about COVID, Democrats appeared more likely to vote by mail, which of course was the reason for Trump's complaints.

With the prevalence of absentee ballots, *The Post* sought to prepare the public—in stories, in graphics, in any way we could—for how vote totals probably would evolve on election night. Published vote counts then were likely to be misleading. Trump might surge ahead in early counts, but then fall behind when mail ballots were included. Recording the absentee vote would take longer. National reporter Amy Gardner, who was working full-time on voting issues, noted that the rise in mail balloting and resulting slow vote tallies in state elections that summer were "a stark preview of what's coming on Nov. 3—or, more accurately, what may not be coming: an election night result in the race for the White House." Election officials, she wrote, were cautioning that results in battleground states "could take days, even weeks, to resolve."

Post readers were repeatedly alerted to how far Trump might go to retain power. As early as July, reporters Elise Viebeck and Robert Costa ran through possibilities: "Trump could claim victory before the vote in key states is fully counted—a process that could take days or even weeks this year because of the expected avalanche of absentee ballots. He could also spend weeks refusing to concede amid a legal war over which votes are valid and should be included in the tally . . . Or he could simply refuse to leave on Jan. 20—a possibility Biden has discussed publicly."

Trump was no more willing in September than he had been in the summer to commit to a peaceful transfer of power. "We're going to have to see what happens," he said when directly asked at a news conference. *The Post*'s Dan Balz wrote presciently that the president's comments were "aimed at rallying his own army of supporters, prepping them to respond, if necessary, with protests or perhaps worse if he challenges vote tabulations—and therefore the results—in the days after the election."

The worst seemed increasingly likely. Contributing to that concern was Trump's refusal to condemn militant groups that he counted among his political base. He had condoned, even encouraged, violence among his supporters who showed up at his rallies during the 2016 presidential race. And in a 2020 debate at the end of September, he refused to denounce white supremacists and other heavily armed right-wing extremists. When pressed by moderator Chris Wallace of Fox News during a debate with Joe Biden, Trump responded, "Proud Boys, stand back and stand by." Trump's comments sparked excitement within the Proud Boys, a group that openly endorsed violence. Members called the president's remarks "historic," seeing an endorsement of their mission and methods. The

Proud Boys would, in fact, stand by until they answered Trump's call to go to Washington on January 6, 2021, to "stop the steal" of an election he lost.

Winks and nods to armed groups were part of Trump's old playbook, too. Exactly a year before the September debate, Trump outlined the most apocalyptic and violent scenario for what might happen if he were removed from office through impeachment, tweeting a quote that it might "cause a Civil War like fracture in this Nation from which our Country will never heal." The leader of the militant Oath Keepers immediately followed up with a tweet of his own: "This is where we are. We ARE on the verge of a HOT civil war. Like in 1859." Earlier, in March 2019, Trump suggested in an interview with *Breitbart* that people would play "tough" on his behalf if they reached a breaking point. "I can tell you I have the support of the police, the support of the military, the support of the Bikers for Trump—I have the tough people, but they don't play it tough— until they go to a certain point, and then it would be very bad, very bad," he said. Trump was unhesitating in his approval of people who were "angry" on his behalf and admiring of their capacity to rough people up.

By the end of October, *The Post* was sounding the alarm that the election could lead to mayhem. Reporter Marc Fisher wrote, "The signals are disturbing: A sharp increase in gun sales. A spike in chatter about civil war in online forums where right-wing extremists gather. An embrace of violent language by President Trump and other leaders. And surveys showing an increased willingness by some Americans to see violence as an acceptable tool against political opponents."

Trump's own words provided clear evidence that the country was most likely headed for a constitutional crisis. Bruising battles in the courts were one thing, but signs also pointed to possible fighting in the streets. *Axios* reported, just days before election day, that Trump had told confidants he would declare victory on election night if the count showed him ahead, not waiting for the entirely legitimate mail-in ballots to be tallied. "We're going to go in the night of, as soon as that election is over, we're going in with our lawyers," Trump told reporters in Charlotte, North Carolina, on November 1.

One day before the election, a *Post* news story advised readers to anticipate "a stretch of uncertainty and chaos as a purge of top officials, legal challenges to election results and potential resistance to a normal transition cloud the prospects for an orderly post-election period no matter who wins." *The Post*'s journalists were ready: for recounts, for litigation, and for violence. Nine reporters were assigned to chase down any voting irregularities after immersing themselves in the laws in eleven potentially decisive states: Wisconsin, Florida, Georgia, Michigan, Arizona, Nevada, Ohio, Pennsylvania, Texas, Minnesota, and Nebraska. Seventy reporters on staff and in our network of freelancers were deployed on the ground in thirty-seven states to cover the voting but also "potential unrest."

As with so much about Trump, his behavior on election night was shocking but not surprising. He attacked the integrity of the elections, anointing himself the winner even though all the votes had yet to be counted. "This is a fraud on the American public," Trump declared before 150 supporters at 2:20 a.m. the morning after the election from the East Room of the White House. "We were getting ready to win this election. Frankly, we did win this election."

Dan Balz, a wise and careful analyst of politics throughout his decades-long tenure at the paper, wrote an assessment of Trump that was more blistering than anything I'd ever seen him publish:

> *For four years, President Trump has sought to undermine the institutions of a democratic society, but never so blatantly as in the early morning hours of Wednesday. His attempt to falsely claim victory and to subvert the election itself by calling for a halt to vote-counting represents the gravest of threats to the stability of*

the country . . . A president who respected the Constitution would let things play out. But Trump has shown once again he cares not about the Constitution or the stability and well-being of the country or anything like that. He cares only about himself and retaining the powers he now holds.

After the vote tallies began to show a Biden victory, I was inundated with emails and voice mails from Trump supporters spewing the hostility he had fomented for years against *The Post* and the press overall. Some threatened harm—and a few of those, research by our security team showed, were sent by people with criminal records: "Your [*sic*] nothing but democratic douches and I curse all you mother fuckers and hope you and your families die a horrible death. You just killed our country ya ignorant bastards." "When the masses come for you to hang you from the nearest tree I'll tell your grandkids you were a traitor to the country that made you rich. Should not have worshipped Satan you freak." "You son of a bitch, Trump is the best president this country has or will ever see . . . we true american patriots will hunt every one of you pieces of shit and exterminate you lowlife anti-america communist dogs." "I pray for your tabloid to burn and hope President Trump gives a coup with the support of the military and shuts up you and all the fake news poison up."

More astonishing to me than the threats was an email I received from the former top official of a major public agency in Massachusetts whom I had gotten to know when I was leading the newsroom of *The Boston Globe*. He had gone on to become chief executive of two sizable companies. We had stayed in touch over the years, occasionally meeting for lunch in Washington, D.C., and I knew he leaned conservative. After all major networks, including Fox News, on November 7 called the presidential election for Joe Biden, I received an email from him expressing indignation:

"I've re-read *1984*. Who in the media or the Democrat Party is now Big Brother or in charge of the Ministry of Truth?" he wrote. "Where do I turn myself into the Thought Police to be re-educated? Fox News has been brought into line so now the media call elections and are in total control of all truth. No differences of opinions are tolerated . . . Gore took 32 days to concede after the Supreme Court rule. The First Amendment is now irrelevant under the current stream of political correctness. Who's going to bring us together? The hypocrisy, the arrogance, and the hubris is breathtaking." He signed it, "Your despicable, deplorable friend."

I was stunned at the vitriol from someone who had always been so amiable. He had been an honorable, effective public servant in a state that was no stranger to government corruption, cronyism, and incompetence. I considered him a good person and still do. But it was unsettling firsthand evidence that Trump's latest and most despicable act of guile had cast a dark spell on even the most traditional Republicans. Offended that he would associate me with Hillary Clinton's obnoxiously dismissive "basket of deplorables" comment in 2016, I told him, "I'd really appreciate it if you didn't impute to me, even sarcastically, beliefs that I don't hold." I was particularly appalled that he would equate Trump's voter fraud claims with the disputed race between George W. Bush and Al Gore in 2000. I had been editor of the *Miami Herald* during that election, and there was a yawning difference between 2000 and 2020. Gore had merely requested a recount, following the ordinary legal process and never alleging fraud. Whoever won Florida would win the election, and Gore was said to have lost the state of Florida by a mere 537 votes. When the U.S. Supreme Court halted a recount, Gore graciously conceded: "This is America, and we put country before party; we will stand together behind our new president."

In the *Miami Herald* newsroom, that 2000 ruling by the Supreme Court in *Bush v. Gore* gave us cause and inspiration to do more work.

The public was entitled to know who had really won the presidency. And we had a way of finding out. Florida's expansive public records laws permitted us to examine every ballot cast. So we embarked on a recount of our own, also hiring a major accounting firm to inspect the ballots independently in all sixty-seven Florida counties, running up about $1 million in total costs. The *Herald* reporters and the accounting firm came to the same conclusion: Bush most likely would have still won if the Supreme Court had not denied the recount.

Twenty years later, at *The Washington Post*, we were again laser-focused on the evidence in a disputed election. Having monitored the election closely with staff around the country, we had seen no evidence of significant fraud. Now we were waiting to see if Donald Trump and his legal team could produce any. They didn't. The election had not been rigged, but Trump was now trying mightily himself to rig the outcome.

A bit more than a week after the election, reporters David Fahrenthold, Rosalind Helderman, and Tom Hamburger showed just how flimsy Trump's claims were. Examining the affidavits of Republican poll watchers, they found anything but the "shocking" misconduct that Trump had promised the American public, despite Republicans' offers of cash rewards for evidence of fraud. In Michigan, where Biden led by 154,000 votes and Trump asked a federal judge to block the state from certifying the election, the president's lawyers promised 230 pages of sworn statements from a hundred people who observed ballot-counting problems. What they delivered was inconsequential. One complained, for example, about the public address system; another that a poll worker was wearing a Black Lives Matter T-shirt; and another that military ballots weren't trending Republican as he expected.

The Post dug aggressively into the pressures that Republicans put on Georgia secretary of state Brad Raffensperger, including by Senator Lindsey Graham, whom Raffensperger accused of proposing ways to throw out legally cast ballots. (Graham denied that.) No one brought greater pressure, though, than Trump himself. *The Post*'s Amy Gardner delivered one of the most explosive stories of the post-election period when she revealed that Raffensperger had received a call from the president urging him to "find" enough votes to reverse Biden's narrow victory in Georgia. "So look," Trump told Raffensperger, according to a recording of the phone call that Amy obtained. "All I want to do is this. I just want to find 11,780 votes, which is one more than we have. Because we won the state." And Trump, as the recording showed, threatened Raffensperger and his general counsel with potential criminal liability if they didn't bend to his will. Fulton County's district attorney later opened an investigation into whether Trump illegally interfered in the election, with Trump's phone call to Raffensperger at the heart of the case. The investigation was ongoing as this was written.

We owed it to the public not to mince words about what Trump had inflicted on the country. "The result was an election aftermath without precedent in U.S. history," *Post* reporters wrote in a story titled "20 Days of Fantasy and Failure" that reconstructed the three weeks since election day. "With his denial of the outcome, despite a string of courtroom defeats, Trump endangered America's democracy, threatened to undermine national security and public health, and duped millions of his supporters into believing, perhaps permanently, that Biden was elected illegitimately." Reporting by our political correspondents found a president who, in the weeks since the election, was "brooding," "rageful," and "at times delirious."

The Post outlined for the public in mid-December how at least eighty-six judges at every level, even those Trump himself had appointed, repudiated the president's fraud claims and his plea to throw out millions of legally cast votes. The U.S. Supreme Court, where Trump's appointments had cemented a 6–3 conservative majority, dismissed a lawsuit by Texas seeking to overturn election results in four other states. "The Supreme Court really let us down.

No Wisdom, No Courage!" Trump tweeted. Overall at that point, Trump and his allies had lost more than fifty lawsuits, winning only one on a minor matter. "Free, fair elections are the lifeblood of democracy. Charges of unfairness are serious. But calling an election unfair does not make it so," wrote federal appeals court judge Stephanos Bibas, who was appointed by Trump, in rejecting his attempt to throw out Pennsylvania's votes for Biden. "Charges require specific allegations and then proof. We have neither here."

Polls showed that Trump supporters weren't taking their cue from the courts any more than they were from the press. They got their "facts" only from Trump and media that parroted his falsehoods. A Fox News poll that December showed that 68 percent of Republicans believed the election was stolen while 77 percent of Trump voters believed that. Thirty-six percent of Americans believed that Biden was not legitimately elected as president. The numbers barely budged over time. And by the fall of 2022, *The Post* calculated, a majority of Republican nominees for House, Senate, and key statewide offices either outright rejected the legitimacy of the 2020 election or questioned the results.

Perhaps Trump's true believers could never be persuaded of anything other than what he told them, particularly when the media he demonized was the source. But our job was to provide verifiable facts. The democracy we had all taken for granted was at risk, sabotaged by the president himself. Sharp political differences were a feature of our system. But how could democracy survive if Americans couldn't agree on the most basic facts—couldn't agree on how to establish something as fact, even when it came to an election?

I asked our staff in December 2020 to assemble all allegations of election misconduct leveled by Trump and his allies and explain how they had been addressed by the courts, election officials, and federal agencies. *The Post* systematically went through every issue, posting on its website key documents so readers could review them for themselves: Was voting software from Dominion Voting Systems' machines compromised, as Trump supporters claimed? "There is no evidence that any voting systems were compromised, according to the Cybersecurity and Infrastructure Security Agency." Has the federal government investigated or found any evidence of voting fraud? "Attorney General William P. Barr said Dec. 1 that FBI agents and U.S. attorneys have been investigating complaints but 'to date, we have not seen fraud on a scale that could have effected a different outcome in the election.'" Did election officials manipulate signature-verification machinery in Clark County, Nevada? "After a nine-hour evidentiary hearing that focused in large part on the signature-verification machine, a Carson City judge found no evidence that the use of the so-called Agilis machine was illegal, error-prone or had led to the county of fraudulent votes." And on the story went, through one allegation after the next, first the Trump claim and then reality.

It was telling that after onetime Trump attorney Sidney Powell was sued for defamation by Dominion Voting Systems over her emphatic claims that its election equipment was deployed in a conspiracy to rig the election, her defense in March 2021 was that "no reasonable person would conclude that the statements were truly statements of fact."

Trump, in a tweet on December 19, summoned his supporters to a rally in the nation's capital on January 6, 2021: "Big protest in D.C. on January 6th. Be there, will be wild!" Armed extremist groups, other thugs, and hundreds of enraged Trump followers immediately understood it as a battle cry, undoubtedly as he intended. "We are going to only be saved by millions of Americans moving to Washington, occupying the entire area, if necessary, storming right into the Capitol," one right-wing commentator said in a video that was promptly posted.

Covering Trump and his followers that day, along with possible counterprotesters, would require special precautions: *Post* editors reminded staff of security best practices. Kevlar bulletproof vests, helmets, and goggles were made available. *The Post*'s security team positioned additional personnel at headquarters, and a reconnaissance vehicle was situated as close to the Trump protests as possible to extract staff if necessary.

This is what Trump had wrought. The press was now required to physically protect itself from fellow American citizens inflamed by the president of the United States. Trump's unrelenting rhetoric condemning the press as the enemy had made this moment inevitable. Time and again the president had been warned that his incendiary language could get people hurt. He didn't let up. He doubled down. So what if it led to tragedy?

Local editor Mike Semel's memo for deploying his reporters to five different rallies on January 6 emphasized that their own eyewitness observations of violence would ensure the greatest accuracy. "Ideally, we won't have to rely on he said/he said accounts, police reports or snippets of video. We would like to be able to say definitively what happened." And yet reporters would have to do that without endangering themselves. "Don't put yourself in harm's way," Mike cautioned. "No story is worth your health, safety and peace of mind."

Mike advised his staff that chatter on right-leaning social media sites popular with Trump supporters suggested protests could become something far worse: "Proud Boys will be in town. We do not know what their numbers will be. Wednesday has the added element of finality. If you believe posts on Parler, there are people coming to make the last stand. They are coming armed."

Violence against an independent press that had been foreseen for so long erupted in front of the Capitol. A large crowd descended on a media staging area set up outside the northeast corner of the Capitol grounds, forcing journalists to flee. Rioters cursed at, spat at, and shoved reporters, photographers, and videographers, including many of *The Post*'s. An Illinois man picked up media equipment and tossed it, then tackled a cameraman. A Massachusetts man who claimed to be a documentarian was recorded stomping on equipment. A Virginia man, later arrested, boasted to a friend, "We attacked the CNN reporters and the fake news and destroyed tens of thousands of dollars of their video and television equipment; here's a picture behind me of the pile we made out of it." CNN was a particular focus of harassment and attack. "CNN sucks!" they shouted. "Fuck CNN!"

A group of men who had broken through police lines to storm into the Capitol approached a photographer in the building demanding to know whom she worked for. When she declined to answer, they reached into her vest and grabbed her press credentials. Discovering that she was a *New York Times* photographer, they threw her to the floor and snatched her camera. When she stood up and sought to recover her equipment, they pushed her away. "Get her out, mace her," yelled one rioter who was later arrested. Outside the Capitol, an Associated Press photographer, accused of being a member of the left-wing "antifa" movement despite his visible press pass, was grabbed by his backpack, pulled down a flight of stairs, and tossed over a ledge as someone screamed, "We'll fucking kill you."

Amanda Andrade-Rhoades, a freelance photographer on assignment for *The Washington Post*, reported that three individuals threatened to shoot her, although she didn't see whether they were armed. One leaned over and warned her, "I'm coming back with a gun tomorrow, and I'm coming for you." *Post* videojournalist Kate Woodsome was surrounded by about ten rioters at the Capitol steps, shortly after the shooting inside of thirty-five-year-old intruder Ashli Babbitt by a twenty-eight-year veteran of the Capitol Police. When asked to disclose her affiliation, she said she worked for *The Post*. "Yeah, get the fuck out of here," one shouted at her. "All the lies you've told all this time, that's what made this happen." She stayed calm, stayed put, and continued to do her job, just like other *Post* journalists that day.

Though *Post* editors had foreseen possible violence, we were as stunned and horrified as anyone when Trump loyalists launched a vicious, hate-filled assault on the seat of American democracy, breaching security barriers, pummeling Capitol police, and sending members of Congress—and Vice President Mike Pence—fleeing for their lives. Over decades as an editor, I had stayed unemotional, if not clinical, in overseeing coverage of heart-wrenching stories, from the slaughtering of innocents in an epidemic of mass shootings to the human devastation of natural disasters. Like cops, I thought, journalists need emotional armor to do our jobs, and I was inherently stoic anyway.

There were occasional exceptions when I was personally shaken by news events. One was 9/11, when thousands were killed in a barbarous terrorist attack and the United States felt alarmingly vulnerable. Another was May 9, 2003, when I learned that a brilliant and courageous *Boston Globe* reporter, Elizabeth Neuffer, was killed in an auto accident while covering the aftermath of war in Iraq. I called the *Globe* newsroom together to announce that we had lost a beloved colleague. With so many reporters in conflict zones, I prayed ever since that I never had to make such an announcement again. On January 6, 2021, emotions surged once more. One bitter, deceitful, and self-absorbed man, born to great privilege and yet always playing the victim, had put America's entire constitutional system at death's door for the sole purpose of holding on to power that voters no longer wished to grant him. I felt rage and sadness, and I feared what the insurrection foreshadowed for the country's future.

Video journalist Rhonda Colvin was in the Capitol Rotunda for *The Post*'s scheduled live show of the joint session of Congress where Vice President Pence was to count electoral votes and confirm the result of the presidential election. Behind her, a Capitol Police officer was barking, "Evacuate now! Evacuate now!" She and videographer Lindsey Sitz were directed down three flights of stairs to the

Capitol basement. "We were told to just keep moving, keep moving," she recounted on a *Post* video two days later. From an officer's radio, she could hear shots fired.

Rhonda watched video of the mob storming the Capitol, viciously attacking police. "You're not sure how far these people will be able to get, and if they'll be able to get to you," Rhonda recalled with remarkable understatement. "There is a fear of what would have happened if I alone would have been walking in those hallways and run into these men who, we know, many of them are from nationalist groups and the Proud Boys and white supremacists. I mean, I would have stuck out like a sore thumb . . . Seeing me wearing a *Washington Post* badge—and I'm Black—that could bring some attention that I don't want." Rioters were not at all subtle about their hatred: "Murder the Media" was etched on a door inside the Capitol.

Ultimately, after the lockdown was lifted, Rhonda and Lindsey were picked up by two *Post* security personnel in a reconnaissance van at the Longworth House Office Building, adjacent to the Capitol grounds, delayed only by reports of an explosive on their route. During the attack on the Capitol, as Rhonda and Lindsey sought safety, they kept reporting and maintained contact with the live show's anchor, Libby Casey. "President Trump is staying silent on this. He's not calling for people to stand down," Libby said, momentarily breaking down emotionally over the danger faced by her colleague. "I'm sorry," she continued. "Rhonda, talk about the role the president's playing right now."

Remaining composed, Rhonda articulated what the rioters, members of Congress, journalists, and the American public were all thinking. "Uh, well, the fact that he is being silent and not decrying the activities that are happening in the U.S. Capitol right now, that sort of speaks volumes." It sure did. He approved. These were his people. They were fighting for him. They were doing what he wanted them to do.

At 12:17 p.m., in his speech at the rally near the White House,

Trump told protesters they should march toward the Capitol—"and I'll be there with you"—because "you'll never take back our country with weakness." Shortly before 1:00 p.m., as the joint session of Congress was convened, a mob overwhelmed police at barricades around the Capitol. At 1:02 p.m., Vice President Pence issued a statement that he wouldn't stop the counting of electoral ballots as Trump had insisted. At 1:10 p.m., concluding his speech and again directing the crowd to head to the Capitol, Trump said, "And we fight. We fight like hell. And if you don't fight like hell, you're not going to have a country anymore." Trump used the word "fight" twenty times in his remarks.

At 2:12 p.m., rioters burst into the Capitol. The Senate was called into recess; then the House. At 2:13 p.m., security agents evacuated the vice president from the Senate chamber. At about 2:15 p.m., the mob outside the Capitol began chanting "Hang Mike Pence." At 2:24 p.m., Trump tweeted, "Mike Pence didn't have the courage to do what should have been done to protect our Country and our Constitution." It was not until 4:17 p.m. that Trump called upon the insurrectionist mob to leave the Capitol with the words "We love you. You're very special." At 6:00 p.m., he tweeted, "These are the things that happen when a sacred landslide victory is so unceremoniously and viciously stripped away from great patriots who have been badly & unfairly treated for so long . . . Remember this day forever!"

The rampage didn't happen on its own. Trump made it happen—and, untroubled, let it continue for hours—after plotting desperately but unsuccessfully to get states and the vice president to overturn a fair election. Additional reporting over time would reveal the extreme, lawless measures he took to defy the will of the voters. The House's select committee to investigate the January 6 attack would in 2022 deliver a mountain of testimony and documentary evidence that, to any observer interested in the facts, should serve as overwhelming proof of his culpability.

As the riot at the Capitol was unfolding, *Post* journalists had some instant decisions to make about the language we would use to describe what happened on January 6. What to call the people who attacked the Capitol? "Mob," I decided. Should we say the president incited them? Yes. It was clear from his words that he had. *The Post's* story was blunt in its account of what happened that afternoon. It was "an attempted coup" by a "mob" that was "incited" by the president who told his supporters that they "should never accept defeat." Police were overrun in a "monumental security failure." And within the week *Post* journalists had investigated Trump's sickening inaction while police were attacked, the Capitol was ransacked, members of Congress and the vice president were hunted, journalists were assaulted, and the democratic process came frighteningly close to being demolished.

And what was Trump doing while all this happened? *The Post's* journalists reported that, after he returned to the White House, Trump watched the violence escalate on live TV. "Even as he did so," *The Post* revealed on January 11, as part of its determined yearlong coverage that ended up earning a Pulitzer Prize for public service, "Trump did not move to act. And the message from those around him—that he needed to call off the angry mob he had egged on just hours earlier, or lives could be lost—was one to which he was not initially receptive." It was a portrait of a president who had "failed to perform even the basic duties of his job." White House reporters Ashley Parker, Josh Dawsey, and Philip Rucker wrote, "The man who vowed to be a president of law and order failed to enforce the law or restore order. The man who has always seen himself as the protector of uniformed police sat idly by as Capitol Police officers were outnumbered, outmaneuvered, trampled on—and in one case, killed. And the man who had long craved the power of the presidency abdicated many of the responsibilities of the commander in chief." In 2022, hearings held by the House committee investigating January 6 would confirm every word of their account.

One week after the attack, Trump was impeached, for a second time, with a 232–197 vote of the House of Representatives. The resolution, charging "incitement of insurrection," declared that Trump had "gravely endangered the security of the United States and its institutions of Government. He threatened the integrity of the democratic system, interfered with the peaceful transition of power, and imperiled a coequal branch of Government." Only ten House Republicans supported impeachment. On February 13, with the inauguration of Joe Biden now history and the former president resettled into his lavish Mar-a-Lago resort in Palm Beach, Florida, Trump was acquitted by the Senate. Two-thirds of the senators were required to convict. But the vote fell short, with fifty-seven voting in favor and forty-three against. Only seven Republican senators voted to find Trump guilty.

Trump was rescued by a Republican Party that had been brought under his complete control. "Real power is—I don't even want to use the word—fear," Trump had famously told Bob Woodward and Robert Costa of *The Washington Post* in early April 2016 when he was still battling for his party's nomination. Trump could not have been more satisfied now, years later, to have been proved so right. Fear of Trump's retribution predetermined how nearly all Republicans in Congress would vote on impeachment. Political careers would be in jeopardy if they withheld their support. Even those who had immediately denounced Trump as responsible for the January 6 attack lacked the spine or integrity to hold him to account. Trump "bears responsibility for Wednesday's attack on Congress by mob rioters," said House Minority Leader Kevin McCarthy, who went on to vote against impeachment and later assign blame instead to House Speaker Nancy Pelosi. Trump was "practically and morally responsible for provoking the events of the day," in the words of Senate Minority Leader Mitch McConnell, although he had just voted against conviction.

In short order Republicans resorted to what had routinely proved

so easy, useful, and effective for Trump himself: Deny objective reality. Invent conspiracies. Offer up phony "alternative facts." Just as
Trump had lied about the election, they lied about the election aftermath: The attackers were really antifa members disguised as Trump
supporters. The "deep state" FBI had orchestrated the attack. The
intruders carried themselves as if they were on a "normal tourist
visit." The events that day were "nothing," just "patriots standing up."
The rioters arrested were "political prisoners of war." The Republican
National Committee in February 2022 put the party's official stamp
on all the dishonesty when it described the attack and the events
leading to it as "legitimate political discourse."

Trump had the Republican Party in his grip and doing his bidding. If he lied, they would lie, too. If he invented conspiracies, they
would treat them as truth, adding conspiracies of their own wild
imaginations. Trump's behavior became theirs. Whatever his wrongdoing, they would find words and means to excuse it.

Voters, however, get to exercise their independence. They had
chosen to evict him from the White House based on what they
had learned about all he had done with the power of his office and
who he was as a human being. Trump's conviction that he could retain the presidency with a minority of voters—just 47 percent, as he
boasted when *The Post*'s owner, publisher, editorial page editor, and
I had dined with him at the White House in 2017—proved mis-
placed: Key states had shifted against him, denying him the Electoral College victory that was his in 2016.

A reality-based press had resisted Trump's ugly bullying and his followers' violent threats to give American citizens the information
they were entitled to know. Unlike weak-kneed politicians among
the GOP, self-respecting journalists don't buckle easily and cravenly.
That's the value of a free and strong press. It should be cause for

Americans to reflect on how democracy would crumble if this country ever loses its independent media.

Journalism rooted in facts clearly had suffered an accelerating loss of trust and influence during the Trump years. Trump counted that as one of his greatest achievements. His ritual denunciations of "fake news" and "enemy of the people" had delivered results. He wanted us perceived as the "opposition party," and among tens of millions of Trump supporters we were. But his ploy hadn't worked as well as he'd wished. Authentic journalism had not lost all its impact. Facts still mattered—in elections, in the courts, and even (somewhat) in a polarized Congress. Maybe, I reasoned, the country was less immune to truth than I had feared. It appeared, as I'd hoped and believed, that most Americans were independent-minded, respectful of facts, and concerned for the future of our democracy.

I wasn't being Pollyannaish. There was ample cause for worry. On the eve of Joe Biden's inauguration as the nation's forty-sixth president, a *Washington Post* poll showed that seven in ten Republicans still believed he was not legitimately elected. But there was also reason to reject despair: Overall, among Americans, six in ten believed Biden was legitimately elected. Independents believed that by the same margin. And an NBC News poll as of October 2022 showed that independents' belief in the election's legitimacy had risen since January 2021 to 74 percent from 62 percent.

It remains alarming that so many Americans still believe the 2020 election was stolen. By contrast, when George W. Bush was inaugurated as president in 2001, eight of ten Americans accepted the legitimacy of his presidency despite the sharply contested outcome of the 2000 presidential election. Stubborn denial of results for a presidential election twenty years later is a warning of possibly even greater danger ahead. And yet for now, facts can claim a victory: Despite Trump never letting up on his bogus fraud claims, most Americans are convinced he truly lost.

Getting the facts, publishing them forthrightly, and defying intimidation still proved a powerful formula. I was satisfied that our journalism had made a positive difference. History, I was certain, would judge it well. My colleagues in the newsroom needed to know that.

"This news staff," I wrote in announcing my imminent retirement, "has delivered the finest journalism, shedding light where it was much needed and holding to account the powerful, especially those entrusted to govern this country . . . You stood up time and again against vilification and vile threats. You stood firm against cynical, never-ending assaults on objective fact."

Fifty-three days after the January 6 assault on the Capitol, as I removed the last of my possessions from a newsroom that the pandemic had emptied out, I felt confident that a reinvigorated *Washington Post* had fulfilled its duty to the American people and a fragile democracy. A president had waged war against us, but we kept at our work. Never had the work been more urgent.

The Post had grown and strengthened under a new owner who remained firmly committed to its mission in a democracy, even as he was relentlessly attacked and his other business interests threatened. Its journalistic resources had nearly doubled since his acquisition in 2013. *The Post*'s capacity to gather information and keep a watchful eye on those who run and influence our government is today greater than at any time in its history.

The Post can continue that work because of the freedoms granted the press under the Constitution. This democracy of ours rightly demands much from the press as well. We are called upon to dig for the truth fearlessly and share what we learn clearly, completely, honestly, and directly. What happens after that depends on what the American people do with the facts available to them. The fate of the country and its democracy rests overwhelmingly in their hands.

EPILOGUE

For eight years I have observed Donald Trump upend American politics. Faced with the challenge he has posed to democracy, I find my conviction about the need to hold powerful leaders accountable is as strong as ever. So, too, are my convictions about the standards that journalists should meet as they endeavor to do that.

I staked out a position in the early days of Trump as president. One day into his presidency, he declared himself to be in a "running war with the media." My response, when asked shortly afterward, was straightforward: "We are not at war . . . We are at work."

Many fellow journalists enthusiastically embraced the idea that we should not think of ourselves as warriors but instead as professionals merely doing our job to keep the public informed. Many others, though, came to view that posture as naive. One critic went so far as to label my statement an "atrocity" when, after my retirement, publisher Fred Ryan had my quote mounted on the wall overlooking *The Post*'s national desk. Like it or not, in the view of some, journalists are in a war for truth, decency, and democracy, and the only proper response is to be more fiercely and unashamedly bellicose ourselves.

I agree that responsible journalists should be guided by fundamental principles. Among them: We must support and defend democracy. Citizens have a right to self-governance. Without democracy, there will be no independent press, and without an independent press, there can be no democracy. We must work hard and honestly to discover the truth, and we should tell the public unflinchingly what we learn. We should support the right of all citizens to participate in the electoral process without impediment. We should endorse free speech and understand that vigorous debate over policy is essential to democracy. We should favor equitable treatment for everyone, under the law and out of moral obligation, and abundant opportunity for all to attain what they hope for themselves and their families. We owe special attention to the least fortunate in our society, and have a duty to give voice to those who otherwise would not be heard. We must oppose intolerance and hate, and stand against violence, repression, and abuse of power.

I believe journalists can best honor those ideals by adhering to traditional professional principles. The press will do itself and our democracy no favors if it abandons what have long been bedrock standards. Too many norms of civic discourse have been trampled. We should uphold ours.

For the press to hold power to account today, we will have to commit to what constitutes our moral core. But more belongs on our agenda. A few thoughts: We as a profession will need strong, principled, and innovative leadership. We will need to build and maintain institutions whose finances are as sturdy as our values, with the capacity to ensure our commercial future and withstand the persistent, malevolent attacks against us. We must devote far more resources to legal strategy, regularly seeking access to documents that those in power seek to hide, and should more aggressively defend our reputations in court, finally going on the offensive against those who defame us. We must invest far more resources in investigative reporting and acquire new tools that can help us do that work more effectively.

At all times, we will have to hold fast to standards that demonstrate that we are practicing our craft honorably, thoroughly, fairly, with an open mind and with a reverence for evidence over our own opinions. In short, we should practice objective journalism.

In championing "objectivity" in our work, I am swimming against what has become, lamentably, a mighty tide in my profession. No word seems more unpopular today among mainstream journalists. A report in January 2023 by a previous executive editor at *The Washington Post* and a former CBS News president argued that objectivity in journalism is outmoded. "Objectivity has got to go," a former close colleague of mine told them.

Objectivity, in my view, has to stay. Maintaining that standard does not guarantee the public's confidence. But I firmly believe it increases the odds that we will earn it.

The principle of objectivity has been under siege for years, but perhaps never more ferociously than during Trump's presidency and its aftermath. Several primary arguments are leveled against it by my fellow journalists: None of us can honestly claim to be objective, and we shouldn't profess to be. We all have our opinions. Objectivity also is seen as just another word for neutrality, balance, and so-called both-sidesism or "on the one hand, on the other hand" journalism. It pretends, according to this view, that all assertions deserve equal weight, even when the evidence shows they don't.

Finally, critics argue that objectivity historically excluded the perspectives of those who have long been among the most marginalized in society (and media): women, Black people, Latinos, Asian Americans, Indigenous Americans, the LGBTQ+ community, and others.

Genuine objectivity, however, does not mean any of that. This is what it really means: As journalists, we can never stop obsessing over how to get at the truth—or, to use a less lofty term, "objective reality." Doing that requires an open mind and rigorous method. We must be more impressed with what we don't know than with what we know, or think we know. We should not start our work by imagining we have the answers; we need to seek them out. We must be generous listeners and eager learners. We should be fair. And by that, I include being fair to the public: Report directly and fearlessly what we find to be fact.

The idea of objective journalism has uncertain origins. But it can be traced to the early twentieth century in the aftermath of World War I, when democracy seemed imperiled and propaganda was developed into a polished instrument for manipulating public opinion and the press during warfare—and, in the United States, for deepening suspicions about marginalized people who were then widely regarded as not fully American.

Renowned journalist and thinker Walter Lippmann helped give currency to the term when he wrote *Liberty and the News*, published in 1920. In that slim volume, he described a time that sounds remarkably similar to the United States of today. "There is everywhere an increasingly angry disillusionment about the press, a growing sense of being baffled and misled," he wrote. The onslaught of news was "helter-skelter, in inconceivable confusion." The public suffered from "no rules of evidence." He worried over democratic institutions being pushed off their foundations by the media environment of his time.

Lippmann made no assumption that journalists could be freed of their own opinions. He assumed, in fact, just the opposite: They were as subject to biases as anyone else. He proposed an "objective" method for moving beyond them: Journalists should pursue "as impartial an investigation of the facts as is humanly possible."

That idea of objectivity doesn't preclude the lie-detector role for the press; it argues for it. It is not an idea that fosters prejudice; it labors against it. "I am convinced," he wrote, in a line that mirrors my own thinking, "that we shall accomplish more by fighting for truth than by fighting for our theories."

Journalists routinely expect objectivity from others. Like everyone else, we want objective judges. We want objective juries. We want frontline police officers to be objective when they make arrests and detectives to be objective in assessing evidence. We want prosecutors to evaluate cases objectively, with no prejudice or preexisting agendas. Without objectivity, there can be no equity in law enforcement, as abhorrent abuses have demonstrated all too often.

We want doctors to be objective in diagnosing the medical conditions of their patients, uncontaminated by bigotry or baseless hunches. We want medical researchers and regulators to be objective in determining whether new drugs might work and can be safely consumed. We want scientists to be objective in evaluating the impact of chemicals in the soil, air, and water. Objectivity among science and medical professionals is at the very heart of our faith in the food we eat, the water we drink, the air we breathe, and the medicines we take.

In business, we want objectivity, too. Applicants for bank loans and credit cards should be evaluated on valid criteria, not on biases about race or ethnicity or other factors that are similarly irrelevant.

Objectivity in all these fields, and others, gets no argument from journalists. We accept it, even insist on it by seeking to expose transgressions. Journalists should insist on it for ourselves as well. The public expects that of us. It has every right to. If we hope to effectively hold the powerful to account, we will have to show that we are objective in how we go about our work.

The lightning-fast spread of misinformation, disinformation, and crackpot conspiracy theories of today makes the pursuit of truth more essential, and more difficult. Efforts to deceive are more numerous and sophisticated, resources dedicated to deception more abundant. The field of journalism must respond by becoming more investigative in nature.

Investigative reporting has been a ripe target for cost-cutting in an industry where resources are scarce. It is expensive, takes a lot of time, cannot guarantee results (or even a story), and may not quicken the digital traffic that is prized currency in the internet era. When journalists abdicate their role as watchdogs, however, unscrupulous behavior is encouraged. Readers have demonstrated, with the purchase of subscriptions, that they want wrongdoing brought to light.

News organizations will need adequate staff, greater technical prowess, and state-of-the-art technological tools to penetrate the dark arts now increasingly deployed to instantly spread lies and baseless suspicions with the aim of political and commercial gain. They will have to collaborate more effectively among themselves and with independent specialists who possess expertise in artificial intelligence and the manipulation of social networks. Fabrications of every sort, including visual images, inevitably will become more frequent, dangerous, and challenging to detect and disprove.

Early in this millennium, as the business model of most legacy news organizations suffered under the crushing impact of the internet, many newspapers cut back on the sort of investigative journalism that had been heavily inspired by *The Washington Post*'s Watergate reporting in the early 1970s. Investigative reporting, however, underwent a renaissance after the 2015 release of the film *Spotlight*, which portrayed *The Boston Globe*'s investigation into the decades-long cover-up of clergy sexual abuse within the Boston Archdiocese. Almost fourteen years after the investigation itself, the movie rekindled a commitment among owners, publishers, and editors to investigative reporting. The movie highlighted for the public why we need investigative journalism, and the difficulty of doing it correctly. News leaders were also reminded that we have a civic duty to hold power to account.

Shortly after *Spotlight*'s release, the publisher of the *San Francisco Chronicle*, Jeffrey Johnson, stepped into the office of the paper's editor in chief, Audrey Cooper. He mentioned that he had just been to a screening of the movie, and he wondered how much it might cost to build the investigative unit she had long proposed. "Are you kidding me? You want to start an I-team after watching a movie?" Cooper asked.

The *Chronicle* had previously boasted a powerful investigative unit. But advertising revenue had dried up, and by the end of 2009 the last member of that team left the paper. With the team rebuilt post-*Spotlight*, it delivered high-impact results within a year. "I always meant to email Marty Baron and say, 'you probably hear this all the time, but it inspired our newsroom to start an I-team,'" Cooper told the Poynter news organization in late 2016. "What a great legacy for that movie."

While investigative reporting is thriving in some corners of journalism, particularly at the national level, it is being starved to death in others. Local news outlets continue to see their primary sources of revenue dry up, leaving them poorly resourced to fund ambitious journalism of any type. Too many local newspapers have been taken over by private equity firms and hedge funds. Those owners seem determined to milk their properties for every last penny they can cough up, without regard for the public interest. Investigative journalism at the local level is threatened anew.

The future of local investigative reporting may depend heavily on whether new journalism nonprofits receive adequate support from readers and philanthropists as well as on collaborations between national news organizations and local ones. The national investigative nonprofit ProPublica has established investigative reporting hubs around the country and joined forces with local newsrooms on accountability journalism, with impressive results. *The Washington Post* in February 2023 worked with the *Las Vegas Review-Journal* on an investigation that was left incomplete when highly accomplished reporter Jeff German was assassinated outside his home. *The New*

York Times announced in April 2022 that its former top editor, Dean Baquet, would head a fellowship program to promote local investigative reporting, with projects offered without charge to local print, digital, and broadcast outlets.

"The decline of local investigative reporting is a national tragedy," Times publisher A. G. Sulzberger aptly put it at the time. "It means that fewer and fewer people across the country have access to essential information about their communities—too often there is no one to track school board meetings; comb through court documents; or reveal the significance of everyday developments in towns, cities and states. No watchdog to keep local governments honest . . . As a result, it's almost certain that corruption, injustice and wrongdoing go unnoticed."

Financial concerns are destined to remain a plague for the entire media industry. Any threat to economic strength jeopardizes the ability of the press to fulfill its watchdog role. Those who aim to cripple us will exploit perceived weakness. Everyone at a news organization— from chief executives to union chiefs—has a duty to help ensure its sustainability. The business, perpetually disruptive, punishes stasis. No one should be surprised if strategy has to shift, sometimes painfully, every few years.

As I was completing this book at the end of 2022, questions were being raised about The Post's own future. It was recording heavy losses, setting off skepticism about its leadership and doubts about its strategy. A financial recovery in the years since Bezos's acquisition in 2013 had endowed The Post with the resources to keep close watch on a bullying and capricious president. Now, red ink tarnished an image The Post had built for itself as a powerhouse capable of meeting any commercial, journalistic, or political challenge.

Adversity underlined how suddenly and radically fortunes could shift in the media business. Leadership at The Post could take pride in previous achievements but not comfort. Losses exposed severe shortcomings in how *The Post* was positioned for a predictable post-Trump readership drop-off and against a savvy, well-resourced, acquisitive rival in *The New York Times*.

At *The Post*, six years of profitability had underwritten an increase of dozens of journalists every year, given life to a wide variety of new initiatives, and boosted its investigative reporting capacity. Earnings in 2021 were the highest since Bezos took possession of *The Post*, bringing cumulative profits to a level that fully covered his $250 million purchase price. The profits were plowed back into the business.

The year 2022 saw further expansion of *The Post*'s newsroom—"the biggest investment year in our history," publisher Fred Ryan told me—but the extra costs were incurred as the country threatened to tumble into a recession. Digital advertising for media and tech companies tanked. After Fred used a town hall just before Christmas to announce imminent layoffs, angry *Post* journalists stood to pepper him with questions. They got no answers. Fred walked out, only pausing a few seconds to say that he would not turn the town hall into a union "grievance session." Video of his dreadful retreat went viral.

Troubles for *The Post* had been building for some time. Subscriptions had fallen by nearly 500,000 from a peak of 3 million, and monthly digital traffic plunged to 58 million users by the end of 2022 from 139 million in March 2020. At one level, less-committed readers who had bought subscriptions at sharply discounted introductory rates were not sticking with *The Post* when required to pay full price. But the business challenge was far bigger than that: Donald Trump was out of the White House, easing fears of many readers about his threat to democracy. Public interest in politics, the beating heart of *The Post*'s coverage, sagged. The "Trump bump" became the "Trump slump."

A report in *Axios* that former New York mayor Mike Bloomberg was "interested in acquiring" *The Washington Post* or *The Wall Street*

Journal's parent company, Dow Jones, set off speculation that Bezos had lost interest and might sell. *The Post*, however, wasn't for sale. Bezos, in my assessment, is firmly committed to its long-term success.

It was stunning to observe in late 2022 and early 2023 how easily *The Post*'s remarkable commercial turnaround in prior years was forgotten, among media pundits and even among staff who had witnessed far worse times. Only ten years earlier, when I joined *The Post*, its woeful condition was common conversation in Washington and in media more broadly. *The Post*'s stature as a news heavyweight was in question. Dozens of its journalists were losing their jobs every year. *The Post*'s inability to extract itself from a financial sinkhole was why the paper was sold in the first place.

When Fred Ryan took over as publisher in 2014, the preexisting five-year forecast showed losses escalating to terrifying levels. With massive perpetual losses unacceptable to Bezos, Fred committed to getting *The Post* to the breakeven point in his second full year, I've since learned, and into profitability after that. With innovative digitally oriented initiatives, improved technology, and Trump's engrossing dominance of the political landscape, that is what happened.

At the moment of Bezos's purchase, *The Post* was unnervingly far behind its archcompetitor. *The New York Times*, having already made itself a national newspaper, launched digital subscriptions in 2011, more than two years ahead of *The Post*. By the time of Bezos's purchase, *The Times* already had 727,000 digital-only subscribers; *The Post* had hardly any.

The Post's digital traffic soared in the following years, at one point topping *The Times*'s, and digital subscriptions took off as well. The turnaround explains why Bezos placed so much confidence in Fred as publisher. Fred was the only one at *The Post* to meet one-on-one with Bezos, and my understanding is that almost never have they had a serious disagreement.

In my final few years at *The Post*, however, it was becoming obvious that the paper faced a seemingly insurmountable competitive gap with *The Times*. The previous September Ryan announced that paid digital-only subscriptions had passed a million. But that was still far behind *The Times*, which had 2.5 million. *The Times* was already making big bets on ways other than news to lure subscribers. It had invested heavily in developing a stellar cooking app (launched in 2014, with digital subscriptions introduced in 2017) and built a successful subscription model for its long-famous crossword puzzle that was a precursor to a broad portfolio of digital word games like Wordle (acquired in January 2022). It was on the hunt for acquisitions, too. In late 2016, it purchased the Wirecutter product-recommendation service. *The Times* was, as its then-CEO Mark Thompson said, "creating products that are an indispensable part of our readers' lives."

By 2018, I was making the case to Bezos and Fred that *The Post* needed to significantly broaden its coverage. In a teleconference that fall, the newsroom proposed a major boost to our technology coverage. Eleven tech reporters, editors, and videographers were approved. Far more was invested in subsequent years, giving *The Post* a muscular reporting presence in technology. When we also asked for support to build up our popular cooking offerings, though, Bezos was unenthusiastic. How would we differentiate ourselves from the many competitors such as *Epicurious*, *Bon Appetit*, and, now, *The New York Times*? Other lifestyle proposals—for expanded wellness coverage, for example—received paltry budget appropriations until, nineteen months after my retirement, major initiatives were announced.

In late 2019, *The Post* invested heavily in a travel initiative and, only hesitatingly, in a section on video games and e-sports. Meanwhile, we were given approval to add foreign correspondents, building their ranks to the highest level in *The Post*'s history. By any measure, Bezos was staking substantial sums on *The Post*'s future. It was immensely gratifying. And yet it was not nearly enough. *The Post* had not made big strategic bets. No active efforts were made to identify potential acquisitions, though we entertained pitches from struggling digital sites. Importantly, unlike *The Times*, we had not insinuated ourselves into people's daily, non-news routines.

Several times over my final two years at *The Post*, I implored Fred to pull Bezos into a thorough, long-term strategy conversation. There was an urgent competitive threat, and we needed his counsel. And whatever we settled on doing, we needed his bank account. To my frustration, that meeting was never proposed to Bezos. In early January 2023, I asked Fred why. He didn't give me a direct answer, only saying: "Whenever we have Jeff's time, I've never missed the opportunity to take it."

The Post, however, remains a journalistic dynamo. Its staffing is among the most robust of any news organization in the world. It continues to break agenda-setting stories one after the next. It boasts a deep reservoir of extraordinary talent, and rightly continues to be a magnet for top journalists. Few news organizations can claim to be as innovative. *The Post* also has a historic record of resilience, having transformed itself in a few short years from a regionally focused news outlet of deflated ambitions to a trailblazer in technology and journalism. And it has the backing of one of the world's richest and smartest entrepreneurs.

When Bezos stepped down as CEO of Amazon in July 2021 to become executive chair of the board, he signaled he'd be devoting more "time and energy" to *The Post*, Blue Origin, and his charitable endeavors. Blue Origin and philanthropy got the extra attention. *The Post* did not, even as it badly needed it. I suspect *The Post* is getting it now. In one-on-one meetings with key staffers, he has been apprised of deep internal discontent.

Few news organizations in American history have played as important a role as *The Post* in holding power to account. The country needs a healthy, growing, and confident *Washington Post*. I feel sure it will have one.

The mainstream media's legal strategy deserves a rethink, too. Libel suits increasingly have been used as a blunt weapon against media outlets. They cost time, money, and mental well-being, just the sort of pain Donald Trump openly hoped for as he proposed to "open up" the libel laws. Most recently, Florida governor Ron DeSantis has advocated making libel suits easier, even floating the idea of legislation requiring courts to treat the statements of anonymous sources as false.

Legacy media have always vigorously defended against libel suits. Rarely have they brought defamation lawsuits of their own. What good could come of pursuing the sort of litigation we deplored? However, those who smear us find comfort in the expectation that, while we might complain, we're unlikely to sue. We have rendered ourselves sitting ducks for slander.

I don't want mainstream journalists to behave like warriors in the practice of their craft, but neither do I want us to suffer attacks on our character without fighting back. Winning in the court of public opinion may require, at times, going to court. If DeSantis, and copycat governors, make it easier for defamation plaintiffs to prevail, perhaps we should make some of those victories our own.

I was intrigued in 2022 by a legal maneuver of *The New York Times*. A year after my retirement, a lawyer representing *Times* reporter Charlie Savage, a Pulitzer-winning former colleague of mine at *The Boston Globe* and *The Miami Herald*, implicitly threatened a libel suit against the *Washington Examiner* while demanding corrections to "knowingly false statements."

The lawyer's February letter to the *Washington Examiner* objected to an opinion column headlined "Charlie Savage Is the Reason No One Trusts Journalists." The piece was a rebuke to Charlie's story a day earlier about a recent court filing by special counsel John H. Durham, who was digging into the origins of the Russia-related investigation of Trump's 2016 campaign. The motion by Durham, Charlie wrote, had "set off a furor among right-wing outlets about purported spying on former President Donald J. Trump. But the entire narrative appeared to be mostly wrong or old news—the latest example of the challenge created by a barrage of similar conspiracy theories from Mr. Trump and his allies." *The Examiner*'s commentary editor accused Charlie, whom I know to be scrupulously honest and honorable, of doing "everything in his journalistic power to bury this story from readers and obfuscate the truth."

The letter from Charlie's lawyer, who was actually compensated by *The Times*, contained all the standard language that implies a potential libel suit: "defamatory statement . . . defamatory conclusion," "immediately take steps to retain and preserve all documents," and "I hereby demand." The *Washington Examiner* made one correction, after failing to do so when first alerted to the error, and declined to make others, arguing they constituted opinion.

In the scheme of things, the letter was small potatoes. But the saber-rattling was a worthy experiment that carried greater symbolic import. The *Examiner* had to spend money on a lawyer, just the sort of penalty Trump and his political allies had sought to inflict on less Trump-friendly news organizations, and it felt pressure to correct an error. I'll be curious to see if *The Times* tries the maneuver again. I hope it does, and that other news outlets go on the offensive, too.

I had raised with *The Post*'s lawyers for several years whether the time hadn't arrived to bring libel suits against our organization's most shameless, reckless, and loathsome accusers. Why should we unilaterally disarm? The lawyers would chuckle, seeming to humor me. But one, James McLaughlin, deputy general counsel, began to draw me out on the subject when I made annual guest appearances at his Georgetown University law school class. Typically, I was invited a week or two after Jim's students had heard from one of the name partners for the aggressive defamation litigators Clare Locke, which proudly boasts on its website of facing off against major media companies like *The Washington Post*.

And when news organizations prevail in defending against litigation brought by powerful individuals for no purpose other than harassment, they should consider seeking sanctions against the plaintiffs. A $1 million fine imposed by a federal judge in January 2023 against Trump and his lawyer Alina Habba for a frivolous lawsuit represents just the sort of retribution that may well be necessary. "Mr. Trump is a prolific and sophisticated litigant who is repeatedly using the courts to seek revenge on political adversaries," wrote U.S. District Judge Donald M. Middlebrooks in explaining the sanctions he ordered. "He is the mastermind of strategic abuse of the judicial process."

As I was writing this epilogue, I traveled to Bogotá to spend time with journalists of Central and South America. Their countries are among the most dangerous places to work for people in my profession, and serve as a warning of how government-imposed press restrictions and politicians' intimidation tactics against media can expedite the erosion of democracy.

I went to Colombia in January 2023 to help with a training program for editors that was organized by Carlos Eduardo Huertas, a top-notch investigative journalist whom I had befriended when he was a Nieman Fellow at Harvard University in 2011 and 2012 and I was editor of *The Boston Globe*. Carlos Eduardo was then building Connectas, a nonprofit network for journalists across Latin America and a platform for in-depth and investigative journalism. The training program was later created to assist editors with the innumerable challenges they face—from adapting to the digital era to managing their teams of reporters and contending with the expectations of owners and publishers. The young participants eagerly aspired to become better leaders and to elevate the quality of journalism in their countries, even as they struggled with precious few resources.

One afternoon, we packed into a few vans and headed to the mountain of Monserrate, which towers above Bogotá. Outside the sanctuary that stands at its peak, I was touched when the journalists proposed to have their photos taken with me. The first photo was with the editors from Venezuela. Second were the editors from Nicaragua. "*Próxima dictadura!*" someone then shouted, setting off howls of laughter. Next dictatorship! Then came the editors from El Salvador, Honduras, Guatemala, Bolivia, Mexico, and Brazil, the last of which had just survived a coup attempt by supporters of Jair Bolsonaro, the far-right former president who refused to concede his recent election loss.

The dark humor was telling. Authoritarianism is once again on the march in Latin America. Some of the editors' countries have sunk into dictatorship. Other nations are moving fast in that direction. And, among the rest, leaders have exhibited authoritarian behavior, subjecting editors, reporters, photographers, and videographers to daily attacks as fake news and enemies. Journalists in all these countries are targets of harassment, surveillance, or violence by police, the military, government's powerful allies, and ordinary citizens responding to their leaders' repeated incitements. Across much of the region, as in so much of the world, journalism is being criminalized.

In Venezuela, President Nicolás Maduro is reinforcing the media-suppression policies of his predecessor, Hugo Chávez. Newspapers long ago were denied the paper and other supplies required to publish. Broadcast licenses were withheld. Media outlets were taken over by government allies. News outlets practicing genuine journalism are now blocked from access to internet providers.

In Nicaragua, President Daniel Ortega has waged a war of brutal repression against independent journalists, forcing most to flee the country. Some now run digital sites that seek to cover Nicaragua from their homes in exile. Honduras is described by Reporters Without Borders as "one of the most dangerously murderous" countries in the Americas for journalists. Charges of defamation have led to imprisonment, and journalists are frequently assaulted and threatened with death by the military police and the army. Organized crime poses an additional, and mortal, threat.

In Guatemala, the government of President Alejandro Giammattei in July 2022 arrested illustrious journalist José Rubén Zamora on bogus charges of money laundering, influence peddling, and blackmail. His outlet, *elPeriódico*, had courageously focused on corruption at the highest levels of government—practicing the sort of journalism that had been its hallmark for twenty-six years, despite being subjected to defamation campaigns, kidnappings, an assassination attempt, and, most recently, a government-imposed commercial boycott that denied it access to advertising. Under unrelenting legal pressure, the paper shut down in May 2023.

Just south, in El Salvador, media pioneer Carlos Dada and other journalists at his digital news site *El Faro* have gone into exile after their phones were hacked with the notorious Pegasus spyware, allowing their communications and physical movements to be surveilled. Under the country's president, Nayib Bukele, journalists have been routinely assailed and threatened.

"Why do we do what we do?" Dada reflected in late 2022. "This is a serious question to ask in the middle of the crisis a lot of our colleagues are going through all around the world. But we need to defend our reasons for doing journalism, and that means each one of us needs to look deep inside and around, and find those reasons. We all have the right to decide not to do journalism anymore, since the price for doing it is getting higher. It may actually be the sane, healthy decision to make.

"But if you decide to go on, you must know that silence is not an option. Our word is our power, our contribution to our communities, and our fate. And we must use our word to break the monologues of power. We cannot renounce the search for truth."

The work of the young journalists I joined in Bogotá is informed by a simple idea: Citizens are entitled to know what is happening in their community, country, and government. Merely for committing themselves to that task, those journalists and their colleagues have faced perils that are unimaginable to most of us in the United States. And yet they persevere, with inspiring enthusiasm, dedication, hope, and even humor.

In assessing how journalists can best hold powerful individuals and institutions to account, I doubt I will identify anything more essential than what I found in the young Latin American editors I met in Colombia: an indomitable spirit. Idealism, determination, and courage like theirs are what we are likely to need most.

ACKNOWLEDGMENTS

Much of this book relies on what I experienced directly. With Jeff Bezos's acquisition of *The Washington Post* in 2013 and as Donald Trump burst onto the political landscape in 2015, I became both observer and participant in an epochal period for the United States and a legendary news organization. One day, I thought, I might wish to tell this story from my perspective as executive editor. History deserved an account.

Still, there were significant gaps in my knowledge, and for this book I turned frequently to former *Post* colleagues to help fill them. Many generously shared their recollections with me, even as I pried at times into subjects that caused discomfort. It was odd for them to be interviewed by me, their former boss. It was odd for me to be asking the questions. The conversations, however, were crucial to reconstructing events as fully and fairly as possible. I am enormously grateful for the cooperation.

Speaking with *Post* journalists reinforced how fortunate I had been to work with individuals of such remarkable talent and dedication. Journalism is not for the faint of heart. Reporters, editors, photographers, videographers, and others at *The Post* withstood regular attacks on their integrity, most notably from the president of the United States, and faced physical danger abroad and at home. I remain in awe of their fortitude and tenacity.

During my eight-plus years as *The Post*'s executive editor, there were several highly publicized instances of internal discord, with my decisions and convictions at the center of controversy. I discuss those conflicts, and my point of view, in this book. Never, however, has there been a rupture in my admiration for the news staff's commitment to its journalistic mission and their courage in carrying it out.

New to writing a book, I was in particular need of an exceptional editor. I was thankful to have one in Zachary Wagman at Flatiron Press. His enthusiasm, easy disposition, collaborative style, and sound counsel gave me needed reassurance at recurring moments of struggle and doubt. In covering journalism, business strategy, and politics, this book grapples with overlapping storylines. A lot happened concurrently at *The Post*. Zack's advice on organizing episodes and selecting from among their many elements proved critical throughout the writing process.

I greatly appreciate, too, the advocacy, attention, and craftsmanship the book has received from Zack's colleagues: Flatiron president Bob Miller, publisher Megan Lynch, associate publisher Malati Chavali, publicity director Marlena Bittner, marketing director Nancy Trypuc, cover designer Keith Hayes, copy editor Sarajane Herman, production editor Frances Sayers, assistant editor Maxine Charles, and Don Weisberg, who backed it wholeheartedly when he was CEO of Macmillan Publishers. Thanks are due as well to Henry R. Kaufman for his careful legal review.

There would have been no book without the urging and astute guidance of my agent and good friend Todd Shuster of Aevitas Creative Management, who also proposed and smartly shepherded major books at *The Boston Globe* and *The Washington Post* when I led those newsrooms. Todd and his Aevitas colleagues David Kuhn, Daniella Cohen, and Allison Warren were a source of uncommon wisdom from the project's inception.

In the final stages of the manuscript, I turned to several individuals to read it closely as complete outsiders. John Felton, an editor with decades of experience overseeing and reviewing sensitive news coverage at NPR and *Congressional Quarterly*, fact-checked the text and made hundreds of thoughtful editing recommendations that I incorporated. My dear friends Laura Bailyn and Nicholas Diamand devoted weeks of their scarce time to an exacting assessment of, well, every word. Neither chose editing as a career, but they would have been good—and tough—ones. Their judgments, on everything from tone to clarity, were a welcome and invaluable contribution. Thankfully, too, I was referred to a dream photo editor, Crary Pullen, who took on the arduous task of pulling together a marvelous package of images, and received the invaluable assistance of *The Post*'s director of photography, MaryAnne Golon.

I was incredibly lucky to work for almost half a century with America's best journalists at five of the country's most distinguished newspapers. *The Washington Post* was my final professional stop, but before that I found daily inspiration in two additional newsrooms I led, *The Boston Globe* and *The Miami Herald*, and in the others where I was entrusted with senior positions, *The New York Times* and the *Los Angeles Times*.

Over the years, I have benefited from the confidence placed in me by numerous leaders in the journalism profession. I was hired out of college into my first full-time job by Pete Weitzel at *The Miami Herald*, assigned at first to cover a town of only twelve thousand people and its county of fifty thousand. A few years later, Paul Steiger and John Lawrence gave me the opportunity to work at the *Los Angeles Times*, where I spent seventeen rewarding years. Paul, who went on to become the highly accomplished top editor of *The Wall Street Journal* and founder of the pioneering ProPublica investigative nonprofit, has been a mentor, role model, and friend. John bravely named me business editor of the *Los Angeles Times* at the age of twenty-nine. I was promoted into senior positions by executive editor

Shelby Coffey, who allowed me to edit its prestigious front-page feature called Column One and then to take charge of its fiercely competitive 165-person edition in Orange County.

Joseph Lelyveld, while executive editor of *The New York Times*, took the rare and bold step of going outside the ranks of the paper's longtime editors when he chose me to oversee its nighttime news operations. Joe's deeply principled leadership of *The Times*, which I was privileged to witness up close, had a profound influence on my own thinking about the role of a top editor.

As publisher of *The Miami Herald*, Alberto Ibargüen took a gamble when he selected me for my first position leading a newspaper. South Florida is known as a hotbed for the wildest news, and it lived up to that reputation during my time there. I look back with gratitude on Alberto's unwavering support during a period of intense emotions, both among Miami's populace and within our newsroom. I have treasured his friendship and our work together supporting journalism, the arts, and community-building through the Knight Foundation that he has led with vision and limitless energy.

Arthur Sulzberger Jr. and Janet Robinson—when they were chairman and CEO, respectively, of the New York Times Company—and *Boston Globe* publisher Richard Gilman invited me to run *The Globe's* gifted newsroom that had a defining impact on my career. I remain forever grateful for their confidence, and for that of successor publishers Steven Ainsley and Christopher Mayer. They granted us the independence we needed to hold the region's most powerful individuals and institutions to account. I owe special thanks to members of *The Globe's* Spotlight team and their newsroom colleagues for a groundbreaking investigation into wrongdoing by the Archdiocese of Boston; Boston lawyer Jonathan Albano, a personal hero of mine whose masterful legal work unlocked a long-secret trove of revelatory documents; and to all those involved in making the magnificent film *Spotlight*, which told that story so movingly to people around the world.

Being chosen as executive editor of *The Washington Post* by publisher Katharine Weymouth and Don Graham, the parent company's CEO, was an honor beyond my imagination. Both Katharine and Don were ceaselessly encouraging, trusting, and gracious. President Steve Hills, chief information officer Shailesh Prakash, and lawyers Jay Kennedy, Jim McLaughlin, and Kalea Clark were stalwart partners over my years at *The Post*, helping me navigate the disruptive business landscape and the ever more threatening legal one.

With changes in *Post* ownership and leadership, I became the beneficiary of steadfast support from Jeff Bezos and publisher Fred Ryan. They both endured unrelenting political pressures as a direct result of our newsroom's work. Both safeguarded the integrity of our journalism and advocated eloquently for the safety of our journalists. *The Post* would not be the same potent journalistic force it is today without their intellectual, emotional, and financial investment in its success. They tolerated and respected my dissents, at times impassioned. We were always united in keeping faith with *The Post*'s mission and in efforts to secure a sustainable commercial future.

The individuals who provided me invaluable assistance at *The Post* are too numerous to identify. However, I am especially indebted to *The Post*'s managing editors who absorbed so many of the burdens of newsroom leadership in a turbulent period and were key to achieving our highest ambitions: Kevin Merida, Tracy Grant, Emilio Garcia-Ruiz, Cameron Barr, and, in the homestretch of my tenure there, Krissah Thompson and Kat Downs. Finally, I can't begin to express the full depth of my gratitude to my executive assistants over many high-pressure years. In particular, Joanny McCabe at *The Boston Globe* and Angela Barnes at *The Washington Post* kept me on course every hour of every day with their calm, commitment, forbearance, and superior organizational skills. I was blessed to work among journalism's finest.

NOTES

Prologue

3 *shooter was a Trump hater:* Jose Pagliery, "Suspect in Congressional Shooting Was Bernie Sanders Supporter, Strongly Anti-Trump," CNN, June 15, 2017.

3 *media took particular note:* "This Is What Ivanka Trump Wore to the Congressional Baseball Game," *InStyle,* June 16, 2017.

3 *later cited security reasons:* John T. Bennett, "Trump Will Not Attend Congressional Baseball Game," *Roll Call,* June 15, 2017.

3 *"lowest form of life":* Alexander Burns and Nick Corasaniti, "Donald Trump's Other Campaign Foe: The 'Lowest Form of Life' News Media," *New York Times,* August 12, 2016.

4 *published a report:* Sari Horwitz, Matt Zapotosky, and Adam Entous, "Special Counsel Is Investigating Jared Kushner's Business Dealings," *Washington Post,* June 15, 2017.

4 *on top of a previous one:* Ellen Nakashima, Adam Entous, and Greg Miller, "Russian Ambassador Told Moscow That Kushner Wanted Secret Communications Channel with Kremlin," *Washington Post,* May 26, 2017.

4 *had reported as well that Kushner:* David Filipov, Amy Brittain, Rosalind S. Helderman, and Tom Hamburger, "Explanations for Kushner's Meeting with Head of Kremlin-Linked Bank Don't Match Up," *Washington Post,* June 1, 2017.

4 *client was the "focus":* Matt Zapotosky, Sari Horwitz, Devlin Barrett, and Adam Entous, "Jared Kushner Now a Focus in Russia Investigation," *Washington Post,* May 25, 2017.

5 *denounced the press:* Michael M. Grynbaum, "Trump Calls the News Media the 'Enemy of the American People,'" *New York Times,* February 17, 2017.

6 *April 2017 editorial:* "The Secret Presidency," *Washington Post*, April 15, 2017.

7 *book by Barak Ravid:* David Horovitz, "Trump Quotes Confirm What We Saw: He Never Quite Bought Netanyahu's Palestinian Line," *Times of Israel*, December 12, 2021.

10 *tweeted against* Post *reporters:* Adam Shaw, "Trump Slams 'Nasty' *Washington Post* Reporters; Newspaper Hits Back, Calls Tweet 'Unwarranted and Dangerous,'" Fox News, September 7, 2019.

10 *piled on by saying:* Doug Stanglin, "Trump: 'Washington Post' Should Register as Lobbyist over Amazon's 'Postal Scam,'" *USA Today*, March 31, 2018.

11 *gathered at the White House:* Nancy Scola and Steven Overly, "Tech CEOs Descend on White House to Talk Fixing Federal IT," *Politico*, June 19, 2017.

Chapter 1: "Take the Gift"

13 *helped persuade:* Katharine Graham, "He Loved Me and I Loved Him," *Washington Post*, January 27, 1997.

14 *fallen while horseback riding:* Sheryl Gay Stolberg, "The Next Edition," *New York Times*, August 2, 2013.

15 *most notably the CIA:* Cade Metz, "Amazon's Invasion of the CIA Is a Seismic Shift in Cloud Computing," *Wired*, June 18, 2013.

16 *unless thirteen unions immediately agreed:* Jason Szep and Robert MacMillan, "*New York Times* Threatens to Shut *Boston Globe*," Reuters, April 3, 2009.

16 *shelled out $1.1 billion:* William Glaberson, "Times Co. Acquiring *Boston Globe* for $1.1 Billion," *New York Times*, June 11, 1993.

17 *suffered from budget pressures:* Paul Farhi, "Marcus Brauchli to Step Down as Editor of *The Washington Post*," *Washington Post*, November 13, 2012.

17 *disclosure of* Post *plans:* Michael Calderone and Mike Allen, "*WaPo* Cancels Lobbyist Event," *Politico*, July 2, 2009.

Chapter 2: Top Secrets

32 *practiced rampant patronage:* Scott Allen, Marcella Bombardieri, Andrea Estes, and Thomas Farragher, "Agency Where Patronage Is Job One," *Boston Globe*, October 20, 2011.

32 *drove up health-care costs:* Scott Allen, Marcella Bombardieri, Michael Rezendes, and Thomas Farragher, "A Healthcare System Badly out of Balance," *Boston Globe*, November 16, 2008.

32 *abusive behavior:* Michael Rezendes, Beth Healy, Francie Latour, Heather Allen, and Walter V. Robinson, "No Mercy for Consumers," *Boston Globe*, July 30, 2006.

34 *described by* New York Times *media columnist:* David Carr, "*Washington Post's* Chief Falters Anew," *New York Times*, November 18, 2012.

35 *wrote sneeringly:* Erik Wemple, "Martin Baron on Resources and Revenues: Honest, Depressing," *Washington Post*, November 15, 2012.

37 *prevailing by a mere 537 votes:* Curt Anderson, "Trump Election Challenge Not Same as 2000 Florida Recount," Associated Press, November 10, 2020.

37 *only one more electoral vote:* Michael Levy, "United States Presidential Election of 2000," *Encyclopedia Britannica Online*, last updated December 15, 2022; https://www.britannica.com/event/United-States -presidential-election-of-2000.

39 *colleagues advised:* Barton Gellman, *Dark Mirror: Edward Snowden and the American Surveillance State* (New York: Penguin Press, 2020), 98.

40 *Bart wrote years later:* Gellman, *Dark Mirror*, 104.

42 *later write in his book:* Gellman, *Dark Mirror*, 112.

43 *David wrote in* The Boston Globe: David Filipov, "Nowhere to Hide from Reminders of 9/11," *Boston Globe*, September 11, 2011.

49 *testified over the summer:* Ellen Nakashima and Jerry Markon, "NSA Director Says Dozens of Attacks Were Stopped by Surveillance Programs," *Washington Post*, June 12, 2013.

49 *told a Defense Department blog:* Josh Gerstein, "NSA Chief: Stop Reporters 'Selling' Spy Documents," *Politico*, October 24, 2013.

49 *testimony early the following year: Worldwide Threat Assessment to the Senate Select Committee on Intelligence*, 113th Congress (2014) (Remarks by James R. Clapper, Director of National Intelligence).

49 *drafted a forceful letter:* Craig Timberg, "Major Tech Companies Unite to Call for New Limits on Surveillance," *Washington Post*, December 9, 2013.

50 *acknowledged everyone's point:* Transcript, "Obama's Speech on N.S.A. Phone Surveillance," *New York Times*, January 17, 2014.

53 *member of Amazon's board:* "Snowden Criticizes Amazon for Hiring Former NSA Boss," BBC, September 10, 2020.

53 *raid to seize:* Gellman, *Dark Mirror*, 245.

Chapter 3: Regime Change

54 *home of* The Post's *new owner:* Fang Block, "Where Do the Richest Americans Live?," *Mansion Global.com*, October 4, 2016.

55 *intended as a symbol:* Chaim Gartenberg, "Construction Begins on Jeff Bezos' $42 Million 10,000-Year Clock," *The Verge*, February 20, 2018.

66 *magazine listed: "Fast Company* Names *The Post* the Most Innovative Company of 2015 in Media," *Washington Post*, February 9, 2015.

67 *six-page memos:* Ruth Umoh, "Why Jeff Bezos Makes Amazon Ex-ecs Read 6-Page Memos at the Start of Each Meeting," CNBC, April 23, 2018.

69 *disclosed to* Fortune: Adam Lashinsky, "Bezos Prime," *Fortune*, March 24, 2016.

69 *One outlet suggested:* Jason Abbruzzese, "Jeff Bezos Gets a Little Punchy, Suggests 'Disemvoweling' the *Washington Post*," *Mashable*, March 24, 2016.

70 *asked one news site:* Dillon Baker, "Will *Washington Post*'s Talent Net-work Become the Uber of Freelancing," *MediaShift*, August 25, 2015.

71 *pension maneuver:* Steven Mufson, "*Washington Post* Announces Cuts to Employees' Retirement Benefits," *Washington Post*, September 23, 2014.

74 *additional thought:* Ellen McCarthy, "Katharine Weymouth Reflects on Departure from *The Washington Post*," *Washington Post*, September 2, 2014.

75 *Fred made encouraging statements:* Karen Tumulty, Philip Rucker, and Ben Terris, "New *Post* publisher: Strong Washington Ties and Longtime Interest in the News Business," *Washington Post*, September 2, 2014.

Chapter 4: Badass

77 *conservative commentator:* Charles Kreitz, "Levin Slams *Washing-ton Post* Publisher over Reagan Foundation 'Conflict of Interest,'" Fox News, July 27, 2020.

84 *took their idea elsewhere:* John Harris, "I Led the Revolution Against Journalistic Institutions. Now I Think We Need to Build Them Back Up," *Politico*, January 21, 2022.

84 *declared that* Politico: Lindsey McPherson, "Politico Animal," *Amer-ican Journalism Review*, August/September 2008.

84 *crowning him:* Mark Leibovich, "The Man the White House Wakes Up To," *New York Times*, April 21, 2010.

84 New Republic *magazine:* Editors, "Washington's Most Powerful, Least Famous People," *New Republic*, October 12, 2011.

88 *Scarborough lavished praise: Morning Joe*, aired November 20, 2014, 4:01–4:02 p.m. PST, on MSNBC; https://archive.org/details /MSNBCW_20141120_110000_Morning_Joe/start/3660/end/3720.

88 *Carr declared in his media column:* David Carr, "*The Washington Post* Regains Its Place at the Table," *New York Times*, October 5, 2014.

90 *conviction was overturned:* Robert Barnes, "Supreme Court Over-turns Corruption Conviction of Former Va. Governor McDonnell," *Washington Post*, June 27, 2016.

90 *police around the country:* Michael Sallah, Robert O'Harrow Jr., Steven Rich, and Gabe Silverman, "Stop and Seize," *Washington Post*, September 6, 2014.

90 *catastrophic mismanagement:* Lena H. Sun and Scott Wilson, "Health Insurance Exchange Launched Despite Signs of Serious Problems," *Washington Post*, October 21, 2013.

90 *apparent heart attack:* Matt Schudel, "Michel du Cille, *Post* Photojournalist Who Won Pulitzer Three Times, Dies at 58," *Washington Post*, December 11, 2014.

91 *died at home:* Robert G. Kaiser, "Ben Bradlee, Legendary *Washington Post* Editor, Dies at 93," *Washington Post*, October 21, 2014.

Chapter 5: Showtime

94 *led the first ranking:* Chris Cillizza, Aaron Blake, and Sean Sullivan, "The Fix's First Rankings of the 2016 Republican Presidential Field!," *Washington Post*, February 8, 2013.

94 *ascended to the top:* Chris Cillizza, "Rand Paul, 2016 Republic Front-Runner," *Washington Post*, September 13, 2013.

94 *turned to the rising prospects:* Chris Cillizza, "2013 Has Been a Very Good Year for Chris Christie. And It's Going to Get Better," *Washington Post*, October 23, 2013.

95 *Peter Grier wrote:* Peter Grier, "Donald Trump Says He's 'Serious' About 2016 Bid. Shark Jumped?," *Christian Science Monitor*, February 26, 2015.

95 *Other outlets chose to ignore:* Maggie Haberman (@MaggieNYT), "I made the defendable but ultimately wrong choice in 2015 not to write that he was going to run because there had been too many intentionally false starts. But a presidency later, that feels like wishcasting," Twitter, October 13, 2021, 9:34 p.m.; https://twitter.com/maggieNYT/status/1448462257294348289.

95 *except for a flirtation:* Edward Helmore, "How Trump's Political Playbook Has Evolved Since He First Ran for President in 2000," *Guardian*, February 5, 2017.

95 *whip a gathering:* Annalyn Censky, "Trump: U.S. Is a Laughing Stock," CNN, February 10, 2011.

95 *first joint poll that included:* Washington Post–ABC News Poll, May 28–31, 2015; https://www.washingtonpost.com/politics/poll-2016-repub licans-tightly-bunched-clintons-image-erodes/2015/06/01/9c9c26c6 -0893-11e5-9e39-0db921c47b93_story.html.

96 *reported on the $2 billion:* Rosalind S. Helderman, Tom Hamburger, and Steven Rich, "Clintons' Foundation Has Raised Nearly $2 Billion— and Some Key Questions," *Washington Post*, February 18, 2015.

97 *Millions came from foreign governments:* Rosalind S. Helderman and Tom Hamburger, "Foreign Governments Gave Millions to Foundation While Clinton Was at State Dept.," *Washington Post*, February 25, 2015.

97 *contradicting pledges:* Rosalind S. Helderman and Tom Hamburger, "1,000 Donors to a Canadian Charity Tied to Clinton Foundation Remained Secret," *Washington Post*, April 28, 2015.

97 *power couple's $25 million:* Matea Gold, Rosalind S. Helderman, and Anne Gearan, "Clintons Have Made More Than $25 Million for Speaking Since January 2014," *Washington Post*, May 15, 2015.

97 *Bill Clinton himself earned:* Rosalind S. Helderman and Michelle Ye Hee Lee, "Inside Bill Clinton's Nearly $18 Million Job as 'Honorary Chancellor' of a For-Profit College," *Washington Post*, September 5, 2016.

97 *fund-raising machine:* Matea Gold, Tom Hamburger, and Anu Narayanswamy, "Two Clintons. 41 Years. $3 Billion," *Washington Post*, November 19, 2015.

97 *used a private email server:* Michael S. Schmidt, "Hillary Clinton Used Personal Email Account at State Dept., Possibly Breaking Rules," *New York Times*, March 2, 2015.

98 *stingy three-sentence statement:* Hillary Clinton (@HillaryClinton), "I want the public to see my email. I asked State to release them. They said they will review them for release as soon as possible," Twitter, March 4, 2015, 11:35 p.m.; https://twitter.com/hillaryclinton/status/573340998287413248?lang=en.

98 *attributed her email practices:* Glenn Thrush and Gabriel Debenedetti: "Clinton: I Used Private Email Account for 'Convenience,'" *Politico*, March 10, 2015.

98 *based on a referral:* Karen DeYoung, Sari Horwitz, and Anne Gearan, "Probe Sought into Classified 'Details' in Clinton Private E-Mails," *Washington Post*, July 24, 2015.

98 *delay in her delivery:* Anne Gearan, "Hillary Clinton Apologizes for E-Mail System: 'I Take Responsibility,'" *Washington Post*, September 8, 2015.

98 *practices were not materially worse:* Deirdre Walsh, "Hillary Clinton's Emails with Colin Powell Released," CNN, September 8, 2016.

98 *finally expressed exasperation:* Editorial Board, "The Hillary Clinton Email Story Is Out of Control," *Washington Post*, September 8, 2016.

99 *Clinton's email decisions:* Editorial Board, "Hillary Clinton Had a Duty Higher Than Convenience," *Washington Post*, March 10, 2015.

99 *Fourteen months later:* Editorial Board, "Clinton's Willful, Inexcusable Disregard for the Rules," *Washington Post*, May 25, 2016.

99 *labeling the investigation:* Eric Bradner, "Julian Castro: Clinton E-mails a 'Witch Hunt,'" CNN, May 25, 2015.

99 *pioneer in truth-telling:* Michael Kruse, "The Muckraker Who Tormented Trump," *Politico,* January 20, 2017.

100 *Barrett would later write:* Kruse, "The Muckraker Who Tormented Trump."

100 *Marc Fisher wrote:* Marc Fisher, "Donald Trump, Remade by Reality TV," *Washington Post,* January 27, 2016.

101 *suddenly had the support:* Dan Balz and Peyton M. Craighill, "Poll: Trump Surges to Big Lead in GOP Presidential Race," *Washington Post,* July 20, 2015.

101 *Republicans viewed Trump:* Peyton M. Craighill and Scott Clement, "Trump's Popularity Spikes Among Republicans," *Washington Post,* July 15, 2015.

101 *ban all Muslims:* Ed Pilkington, "Donald Trump: Ban All Muslims Entering US," *Guardian,* December 7, 2015.

101 *campaign manager, Terry Sullivan:* Institute of Politics, Harvard Kennedy School, *Campaign for President: The Managers Look at 2016* (Lanham, MD: Rowman & Littlefield, 2017), 150.

102 *support continued to surge:* Dan Balz and Scott Clement, "In Face of Criticism, Trump Surges to His Biggest Lead over the GOP Field," *Washington Post,* December 15, 2015.

102 *strategist for Rubio's presidential campaign:* Institute of Politics, *Campaign for President: The Managers Look at 2016,* 151.

102 *Trump pollster Tony Fabrizio:* Institute of Politics, *Campaign for President: The Managers Look at 2016,* 144.

102 *one of the most telling stories:* David Weigel, "Attacks on Trump Just Made These Voters Like Him More," *Washington Post,* December 10, 2015.

103 *printout of the co-bylined story:* Philip Rucker and Robert Costa, "Donald Trump: 'We Have to Take Back the Heart of Our Country,'" *Washington Post,* July 11, 2015.

104 *in-flight interview:* Robert Costa, "Listening to Donald Trump Swear and Talk Politics on His Private Plane," *Washington Post,* July 12, 2015.

104 *meet with the candidate:* Robert Costa, Philip Rucker, and Dan Balz, "Donald Trump Plots His Second Act," *Washington Post,* October 7, 2015.

104 *searing editorial declared:* Editorial Board, "Donald Trump Is a Poison Pill for the Republican Party," *Washington Post,* December 5, 2015.

105 *debunking one statement:* Glenn Kessler and Michelle Ye Hee Lee,

"Fact Checking Donald Trump's Presidential Announcement Speech," *Washington Post*, June 17, 2015.

105 *awarded him "Four Pinocchios":* Glenn Kessler, "Trump's Claim That He 'Predicted Osama bin Laden,'" *Washington Post*, December 7, 2015.

105 *said in one of his books:* Dan Merica, "Trump's Love of Getting Even Comes to Washington," CNN, March 31, 2017.

106 *Bezos certainly did:* Jeff Bezos (@JeffBezos), "Finally trashed by @real-DonaldTrump. Will still reserve him a seat on Blue Origin rocket. #sendDonaldtospace," Twitter, December 7, 2015, 6:30 p.m.

106 *explicit that he would punish:* Tim Stenovec, "Donald Trump Just Said If He's Elected President Amazon Will Have Problems," *Insider*, February 26, 2016.

106 *Trump was in our new offices:* Philip Rucker and Robert Costa, "Trump Questions Need for NATO, Noninterventionist Foreign Policy," *Washington Post*, March 21, 2016.

107 *reenacted verbatim: The Daily Show with Trevor Noah*, "Donald Trump Speaks to the *Washington Post*: A Dramatic Reenactment," YouTube, March 24, 2016.

107 *showed up at a Trump rally:* Karen Tumulty and Jenna Johnson, "Why Trump May Be Winning the War on 'Political Correctness,'" *Washington Post*, January 4, 2016.

107 *rarely saw a presidential candidate:* Jenna Johnson, "These Are the Towns That Love Donald Trump," *Washington Post*, January 8, 2016.

108 *dodgy tax schemes:* David Barstow, Susanne Craig, and Russ Buettner, "Trump Engaged in Suspect Tax Schemes as He Reaped Riches from His Father," *New York Times*, October 2, 2018.

108 *promoting the "birther" lie:* Robert Farley, "Trump on Birtherism: Wrong, and Wrong," *FactCheck.org*, September 16, 2016.

108 *sinister connection:* Louis Jacobson and Linda Qiu: "Donald Trump's Pants on Fire Claim Linking Ted Cruz's Father and JFK Assassination," *PolitiFact*, May 3, 2016.

109 *extolled what he called:* Emily Price, "'I Call It Truthful Hyperbole': The Most Popular Quotes from Trump's 'The Art of the Deal,'" *Fast Company*, April 4, 2017.

109 *misrepresented the number:* Vivian Yee, "Donald Trump's Math Takes His Towers to Great Heights," *New York Times*, November 1, 2016.

109 *half dozen corporate bankruptcies:* Linda Qiu, "Yep, Donald Trump's Companies Have Declared Bankruptcy . . . More Than Four Times," *PolitiFact*, June 21, 2016.

109 *pursuit of a Trump Tower:* Devlin Barrett, Matt Zapotosky, and Rosalind S. Helderman, "Michael Cohen, Trump's Former Lawyer, Pleads

Guilty to Lying to Congress About Moscow Project," *Washington Post*, November 29, 2018.

109 Post *reporter Robert O'Harrow noted:* Robert O'Harrow Jr., "Trump Swam in Mob-Infested Waters in Early Years as an NYC Developer," *Washington Post*, October 16, 2015.

109 *failed Trump Mortgage:* Tom Hamburger and Michael Kranish, "Trump Mortgage Failed: Here's What That Says About the GOP Front-Runner," *Washington Post*, February 29, 2016.

109 *demise of Trump University:* "Donald Trump Said 'University' Was All About Education. Actually, Its Goal Was: 'Sell, Sell, Sell!,'" *Washington Post*, June 4, 2016.

109 *use of cheap foreign labor:* Rosalind S. Helderman and Tom Hamburger, "Trump Has Profited from Foreign Labor He Says Is Killing U.S. Jobs," *Washington Post*, March 13, 2016.

110 *stink and stain:* Rosalind S. Helderman and Tom Hamburger, "Former Mafia-Linked Figure Describes Association with Trump," *Washington Post*, May 17, 2016.

110 *Trump's thirty year pursuit:* Tom Hamburger, Rosalind S. Helderman, and Michael Birnbaum, "Inside Trump's Financial Ties to Russia and His Unusual Flattery of Vladimir Putin," *Washington Post*, June 17, 2016.

111 *Marc and Michael recounted in a story:* Marc Fisher and Michael Kranish, "The Trump We Saw: Populist, Frustrating, Naïve, Wise, Forever on the Make," *Washington Post*, August 12, 2016.

112 *reported that celebrated* Post *investigative journalist:* Paul Bedard, "*Washington Post* Assigns Army of 20 to Dig into 'Every Phase' of Trump's Life," *Washington Examiner*, May 11, 2016.

113 *I had to speak up:* Benjamin Mullin, "*Washington Post* Denies Jeff Bezos Sways Coverage," Poynter, May 13, 2016.

113 *took to Fox News' Sean Hannity:* Matt Yglesias, "Donald Trump Threatens Amazon as Payback for *Washington Post* Articles He Doesn't Like," *Vox*, May 13, 2016.

113 *remarks would be the first made:* "Prime Time: A Conversation with Jeff Bezos," *Washington Post*, Video, May 18, 2016; https://www.washingtonpost.com/video/postlive/prime-time-a-conversation-with-jeff-bezos/2016/05/18/3ceb5154-1d55-11e6-82c2-a7dcb313287d_video.html.

114 *administration of Richard Nixon:* "Nixon Friend Seeks TV License of a *Washington Post* Station," Associated Press, January 4, 1973.

114 *heaped praise:* Tal Axelrod, "Trump Praises Jeff Bezos, *Washington Post* in Resurfaced 2013 Interview," *The Hill*, August 10, 2018.

114 *candidate had ducked out:* Jessica Taylor, "Trump Will Skip GOP Debate as Feud with Fox News Boils Over," NPR, January 26, 2016.

115 *Trump held a benefit rally:* Ed O'Keefe and Jenna Johnson, "Trump Ditches Debate for Telethon-Style Rally," *Washington Post*, January 28, 2016.

115 *Lewandowski was asserting:* David A. Fahrenthold, "David Fahrenthold Tells the Behind-the-Scenes Story of His Year Covering Trump," *Washington Post*, December 29, 2016.

115 *shutdown of the Trump Foundation:* David A. Fahrenthold, "Trump Pays $2 Million in Damages Ordered by Judge over Misuse of Charity Funds, According to the NY Attorney General," *Washington Post*, December 10, 2019.

116 *Lewandowski hadn't told the truth:* David A. Fahrenthold, "Four Months After Fundraiser, Trump Says He Gave $1 Million to Veterans Group," *Washington Post*, May 24, 2016.

116 *castigated his media inquisitors:* Eli Stokols and Nolan D. McCaskill, "Trump Taunts Media to Its Face," *Politico*, May 31, 2016.

116 *what White House press briefings would be like:* Maggie Haberman and Ashley Parker, "Trump Lashes Out at Media While Detailing Gifts to Veterans," *New York Times*, May 31, 2016.

116 *announced charitable pledges:* David A. Fahrenthold, "Trump Promised Millions to Charity. We Found Less Than $10,000 over 7 Years," *Washington Post*, June 28, 2016.

117 *portrait of himself:* David A. Fahrenthold, "How a Univision Anchor Found the Missing $10,000 Portrait That Trump Bought with His Charity's Money," *Washington Post*, September 21, 2016.

117 *revoking* The Post's *press credentials:* Paul Farhi, "Trump Revokes Post Press Credentials, Calling the Paper 'Dishonest' and 'Phony,'" *Washington Post*, June 13, 2016.

117 *tie Obama to the massacre:* Jenna Johnson, "Donald Trump Seems to Connect President Obama to Orlando Shooting," *Washington Post*, June 13, 2016.

119 *explicitly call Obama:* Tyler Pager, "Trump: Obama 'Is the Founder of ISIS,'" *Politico*, August 10, 2016.

120 *Comey was on television:* Mark Landler and Eric Lichtblau, "F.B.I. Director James Comey Recommends No Charges for Hillary Clinton on Email," *New York Times*, July 5, 2016.

120 *lifted his vengeful ban:* Paul Farhi, "Trump Lifts Ban That Excluded *The Washington Post* and Other Media," *Washington Post*, September 7, 2016.

Chapter 6: "Don't Worry About Me"

122 *released nearly twenty thousand hacked emails:* Tom Hamburger and Karen Tumulty, "Hacked Emails Are Posted Online as Democrats' Convention Nears," *Washington Post*, July 22, 2016.

122 *purportedly neutral:* Aaron Blake, "Here Are Latest, Most Damaging Things in the DNC's Leaked Emails," *Washington Post*, July 25, 2016.

122 *wanted the press, the public, and politicians:* Amber Phillips, "Clinton Campaign Manager: Russians Leaked Democrats' Emails to Help Donald Trump," *Washington Post*, July 25, 2016.

123 *role of the press:* Institute of Politics, Harvard Kennedy School, *Campaign for President: The Managers Look at 2016* (Lanham, MD: Rowman & Littlefield, 2017), 61–90.

124 *memo to the staff:* Joe Pompeo, "'Connect the Dots': Marty Baron Warns *Washington Post* Staff About Covering Hacked Materials," *Vanity Fair*, September 23, 2020.

124 *breezing past:* Jack Gillum and Shawn Boburg, "'Journalism for Rent': Inside the Secretive Firm Behind the Trump Dossier," *Washington Post*, December 11, 2017.

125 *lines from the top:* Ken Bensinger, Miriam Elder, and Mark Schoofs, "These Reports Allege Trump Has Deep Ties to Russia," *BuzzFeed News*, January 10, 2017.

129 *hesitant to give:* Greg Miller, "Candidates Poised for Classified Briefings Despite Spy Agency Worries over Trump," *Washington Post*, July 28, 2016.

129 *Clapper advised:* Mike Levine, "Top Intel Official Tells Americans to End 'Hyperventilation' over DNC Hack but Calls Breach Potentially 'Serious,'" ABC News, July 28, 2016.

130 *he said matter-of-factly:* David E. Sanger, "U.S. Wrestles with How to Fight Back Against Cyberattacks," *New York Times*, July 30, 2016.

130 *one-hour slot:* Glenn Simpson and Peter Fritsch, *Crime in Progress: Inside the Steele Dossier and the Fusion GPS Investigation of Donald Trump* (New York: Random House, 2019), 110.

131 *lack of privacy:* Tom Hamburger and Rosalind S. Helderman, "Hero or Hired Gun? How a British Former Spy Became a Flash Point in the Russia Investigation," *Washington Post*, February 6, 2018.

132 *released their assessment:* Department of Homeland Security, "Joint Statement from the Department of Homeland Security and Office of the Director of National Intelligence on Election Security," October 7, 2016.

132 *hot-mic recording:* David A. Fahrenthold, "Trump Recorded Having Extremely Lewd Conversation About Women in 2005," *Washington Post*, October 8, 2016.

133 *WikiLeaks almost immediately:* Adolfo Flores and Emma Loop, "WikiLeaks Posts over 2,000 Emails from Clinton's Campaign Chairman," *BuzzFeed News*, October 7, 2016.

133 *open prediction:* Philip Bump, "Timeline: The Roger Stone Indictment Fills in New Details About WikiLeaks and the Trump Campaign," *Washington Post*, January 25, 2019.

133 *emails revealed:* Rosalind S. Helderman and Tom Hamburger, "Hacked Emails Appear to Reveal Excerpts of Speech Transcripts Clinton Refused to Release," *Washington Post*, October 7, 2016.

134 *online magazine* Slate*:* Franklin Foer, "Was a Trump Server Communicating with Russia?," *Slate*, October 31, 2016.

134 New Yorker *would go on:* Dexter Filkins, "Was There a Connection Between a Russian Bank and the Trump Campaign?," *New Yorker*, October 8, 2018.

134 Time *magazine piece:* Eric Lichtblau, "Questions Remain About Putin's Request for a Back Channel to the Trump Transition," *Time*, May 21, 2019.

134 *carried a different flavor:* Franklin Foer, "Trump's Server, Revisited," *Slate*, November 2, 2016.

134 *FBI concluded:* Office of the Inspector General, U.S. Department of Justice, Review of Four FISA Applications and Other Aspects of the FBI's Crossfire Hurricane Investigation, December 2019 (Revised), 119, Footnote 259.

134 *even owned or operated:* Indictment, United States of America v. Michael A. Sussmann, United States District Court for the District of Columbia, September 16, 2021; https://www.justice.gov/sco/press-release/file/1433511/download.

135 *editorial board wrote:* Editorial Board, "Republicans Need to Stand Up to Trump's Bullying," *Washington Post*, November 23, 2015.

135 *before the first presidential debate:* Editorial Board, "It's Beyond Debate That Donald Trump Is Unfit to Be President," *Washington Post*, September 25, 2016.

135 *launched into a series:* Editorial Board, "The Clear and Present Danger of Donald Trump," *Washington Post*, September 30, 2016.

136 *endorsement was published:* Editorial Board, "Hillary Clinton for President," *Washington Post*, October 13, 2016.

137 *lifted a ban:* Paul Farhi, "Trump Lifts Ban That Excluded *The Washington Post* and Other News Media," *Washington Post*, September 7, 2016.

137 *five-sentence press statement:* Jenna Johnson, "Trump Admits Obama Was Born in U.S., but Falsely Blames Clinton for Starting Rumors," *Washington Post*, September 16, 2016.

138 *Despite once declaring:* Jill Disis, "All the Things Donald Trump Has Said About Releasing His Tax Returns," CNN, April 17, 2017.

138 *tax deduction:* David Barstow, Susanne Craig, Russ Buettner, and Megan Twohey, "Donald Trump Tax Records Show He Could Have Avoided Taxes for Nearly Two Decades, *The Times* Found," *New York Times*, October 1, 2016.

138 *source offering:* Paul Farhi, "A Caller Had a Lewd Tape of Donald Trump. Then the Race to Break the Story Was On," *Washington Post*, October 7, 2016.

138 *interrupted Trump:* Maggie Haberman, *Confidence Man: The Making of Donald Trump and the Breaking of America* (New York: Penguin Press, 2022), 252.

139 *apologizing for the first time:* Ted Johnson, "Donald Trump Apologizes for Lewd Remarks: 'I Pledge to Be a Better Man,'" *Variety*, October 7, 2016.

139 *Trump picked up:* Robert Costa, "Amid Growing Calls to Drop Out, Trump Vows to 'Never Withdraw,'" *Washington Post*, October 8, 2016.

140 *decisive blow:* Nate Silver, "The Comey Letter Probably Cost Clinton the Election," *FiveThirtyEight*, May 3, 2017.

Chapter 7: The Russia Riddle

144 *belligerently declared:* Philip Rucker, John Wagner, and Greg Miller, "Trump, in CIA Visit, Attacks Media for Coverage of His Inaugural Crowds," January 21, 2017.

144 *notoriously argued:* Eric Bradner, "Conway: Trump White House Offered 'Alternative Facts' on Crowd Size," CNN, January 23, 2017.

145 *personally called:* Karen Tumulty and Juliet Eilperin, "Trump Pressured Park Service to Find Proof for His Claims About Inauguration Crowd," *Washington Post*, January 26, 2017.

145 *told ABC's David Muir:* Transcript, "ABC News Anchor David Muir Interviews President Trump," ABC News, January 25, 2017.

145 *disclosed in 2018:* Dan Mangan, "President Trump Told Lesley Stahl He Bashes Press 'to Demean You and Discredit You So . . . No One Will Believe' Negative Stories About Him," CNBC, May 22, 2018.

145 *response that caught fire:* Tess Townsend, "*Washington Post*'s Marty Baron: 'We're Not at War with the Administration, We're at Work,'" *Vox*, February 14, 2017.

146 *disclosed the conclusions:* Adam Entous, Ellen Nakashima, and Greg Miller, "Secret CIA Assessment Says Russia Was Trying to Help Trump Win White House," *Washington Post*, December 9, 2016.

146 *told* Time *magazine:* Maya Rhodan, "Donald Trump: If I Lost and

Blamed Russia It Would Be Called a Conspiracy Theory," *Time*, December 12, 2016.

146 *taking a swipe:* John Wagner and Karoun Demirjian, "After Obama Sanctions Russia, Trump Says It's Time to 'Move On to Bigger and Better Things,'" *Washington Post*, December 29, 2016.

147 *unclassified report:* Office of the Director of National Intelligence, "Background to 'Assessing Russian Activities and Intentions in Recent US Elections': The Analytic Process and Cyber Incident Attribution," January 6, 2017; https://www.dni.gov/files/documents/ICA_2017_01.pdf.

147 *revealed in court:* Aleksej Gubarev, XBT Holdings S.A., and Webzilla, Inc. v. BuzzFeed, Inc. and Ben Smith, U.S. District Court, Southern District of Florida, Case No. 17-cv-60426-UU, Non-Party David J. Kramer's Sealed Motion for Protective Order, January 29, 2018.

148 *Fusion gave a copy:* Glenn Simpson and Peter Fritsch, *Crime in Progress: Inside the Steele Dossier and the Fusion GPS Investigation of Donald Trump* (New York: Random House, 2019), 141.

148 *one-hour political talk show:* David Filipov, "This Is What It's Like to Be the Token American Journalist on Russian State TV," *Washington Post*, March 23, 2017.

150 *ended up accepting:* Special Counsel Robert S. Mueller III, U.S. Department of Justice, *Report on the Investigation into Russian Interference in the 2016 Presidential Election*, Volume 2, 139, Footnote 958; https://www.justsecurity.org/wp-content/uploads/2019/04/Muelller-Report-Redacted-Vol-II-Released-04.18.2019-Word-Searchable.-Reduced-Size.pdf.

151 *CNN reported:* Evan Perez, Jim Sciutto, Jake Tapper, and Carl Bernstein, "Intel Chiefs Presented Trump with Claims of Russian Efforts to Compromise Him," Video, CNN, January 12, 2017.

151 *reported a week before:* David Corn, "A Veteran Spy Has Given the FBI Information Alleging a Russian Operation to Cultivate Donald Trump," *Mother Jones*, October 31, 2016.

151 *raced to publish:* Ken Bensinger, Miriam Elder, and Mark Schoofs, "These Reports Allege Trump Has Deep Ties to Russia," *BuzzFeed News*, January 10, 2017.

152 *confirmed CNN's report:* Greg Miller, Rosalind S. Helderman, Tom Hamburger, and Steven Mufson, "Intelligence Chiefs Briefed Trump and Obama on Unconfirmed Claims Russia Has Compromising Information on President-Elect," *Washington Post*, January 10, 2017.

153 *sharing a note:* Ben Smith (@semaforben), "Here's the note I sent to @buzzfeednews staff this evening," Twitter, January 10, 2017, 7:32 p.m.; https://twitter.com/semaforben/status/818978955965464580?ref_src=twsrc%5Etfw.

153 *dismiss criticism:* Ben Smith, "Why *BuzzFeed News* Published the Dossier," *New York Times*, January 23, 2017.

153 *column one year later:* Ben Smith, "I'm Proud We Published the Trump-Russia Dossier," *New York Times*, January 9, 2018.

153 BuzzFeed *declared:* Aleksej Gubarev, XBT Holdings S.A., and Webzilla, Inc. v. BuzzFeed, Inc. and Ben Smith, U.S. District Court, Southern District of Florida, Case No. 17-cv-60426-UU, Defendants' Motion for Summary Judgment and Incorporated Memorandum of Law, October 1, 2018.

153 *Smith testified:* Aleksej Gubarev, XBT Holdings S.A., and Webzilla, Inc. v. BuzzFeed, Inc. and Ben Smith, U.S. District Court, Southern District of Florida, Declaration of Ben Smith in Support of Motion for Summary Judgment, October 1, 2018.

154 *theme park ride:* Aleksej Gubarev, XBT Holdings S.A., and Webzilla, Inc. v. BuzzFeed, Inc. and Ben Smith, U.S. District Court, Southern District of Florida, Declaration of Ken Bensinger in Support of Motion to Dismiss, October 1, 2018.

155 *predominantly hearsay:* Office of the Inspector General, U.S. Department of Justice, Review of Four FISA Applications and Other Aspects of the FBI's Crossfire Hurricane Investigation, December 2019 (Revised), 187.

156 *Among them were MSNBC:* Erik Wemple, "The Steele Dossier Just Sustained Another Body Blow. What Do CNN and MSNBC Have to Say?," *Washington Post*, April 18, 2020.

156 *CNN anchor asserted:* Erik Wemple, "Dear CNN: What Parts of the Steele Dossier Were Corroborated?," *Washington Post*, January 3, 2020.

156 *much of the material:* Office of the Inspector General, Review of Four FISA Applications and Other Aspects of the FBI's Crossfire Hurricane Investigation, 172.

158 *chaotic management style:* Dana Priest and Greg Miller, "He Was One of the Most Respected Intel Officers of His Generation. Now He's Leading 'Lock Her Up' Chants," *Washington Post*, August 15, 2016.

158 *paid more than $45,000:* Rosalind S. Helderman and Tom Hamburger, "Trump Adviser Flynn Paid by Multiple Russia-Related Entities, New Records Show," *Washington Post*, March 16, 2017.

158 *barely talked:* Reuters staff, "Putin's Dinner with Michael Flynn: 'I Didn't Really Even Talk to Him,'" Reuters, June 4, 2017.

158 *column published:* David Ignatius, "Why Did Obama Dawdle on Russia's Hacking?," *Washington Post*, January 12, 2017.

159 *entirely innocent:* Paul Sonne and Shane Harris, "Michael Flynn's

Contact with Russian Ambassador Draws Scrutiny," *Wall Street Journal*, January 13, 2017.

159 *questioned Vice President–elect:* Transcript, *Face the Nation*, CBS News, January 15, 2017.

160 *discussed sanctions:* Greg Miller, *The Apprentice: Trump, Russia and the Subversion of American Democracy* (New York: Custom House, 2018), 251.

161 *clandestine conversations:* Greg Miller, Adam Entous, and Ellen Nakashima, "National Security Adviser Flynn Discussed Sanctions with Russian Ambassador, Despite Denials, Officials Say," *Washington Post*, February 9, 2017.

162 *previously advised the White House:* Adam Entous, Ellen Nakashima, and Philip Rucker, "Justice Department Warned White House That Flynn Could Be Vulnerable to Russian Blackmail, Officials Say," *Washington Post*, February 13, 2017.

162 *instinctively lashed out:* Ashley Parker, "Trump Says Flynn Was Treated Unfairly, a Day After Spicer Said He Was Fired Because of a Lack of Trust," *Washington Post*, February 15, 2017.

162 *following day:* "Trump on Flynn Firing: 'I Asked for His Resignation,'" Video, *Washington Post*, February 16, 2017; https://www.washingtonpost .com/videonational/trump-on-flynn-firing-i-asked-for-his-resignation /2017/02/16/6e09cf38-f476-11e6-9fb1-2d8f3fc9c0ed_video.html.

162 *declared in a speech:* Tara Golshan, "Full Transcript: President Trump's CPAC Speech," *Vox*, February 24, 2017.

162 *railing against:* Parker, "Trump Says Flynn Was Treated Unfairly, a Day After Spicer Said He Was Fired Because of a Lack of Trust."

163 *scoops that shook:* 2018 Pulitzer Prize Winner in National Reporting: Staffs of *The New York Times* and *The Washington Post*; https://www .pulitzer.org/winners/staffs-new-york-times-and-washington-post.

163 *immediate relevance:* Ashley Parker, Carol D. Leonnig, Philip Rucker, and Tom Hamburger, "Trump Dictated Son's Misleading Statement on Meeting with Russian Lawyer," *Washington Post*, July 31, 2017.

164 *gladly accepted:* Jo Becker, Adam Goldman, and Matt Apuzzo, "Russian Dirt on Clinton? 'I Love It,' Donald Trump Jr. Said," *New York Times*, July 11, 2017.

164 *especially strong:* 2018 Pulitzer Prize Winner in National Reporting: Staffs of *The New York Times* and *The Washington Post*.

164 *asked in a headline:* James Warren, "Is *The New York Times* vs. *The Washington Post* vs. Trump the Last Great Newspaper War?," *Vanity Fair*, July 30, 2017.

Chapter 8: Democracy Dies in Darkness

167 *vaulted past:* Brian Stelter, "*Washington Post* Subscriptions Soar Past 1 Million Mark," CNN, September 26, 2017.

169 *quote of mine:* Ken Doctor, "Newsonomics: Marty Baron Shines a New Spotlight on Journalism," NiemanLab, December 3, 2015.

170 *even drew attention: People's Daily*, China (@PDChina), "'Democracy Dies in Darkness' @washingtonpost puts on new slogan, on the same day @realDonaldTrump calls media as the enemy of Americans," Twitter, February 22, 2017, 9:34 a.m.; https://twitter.com/PDChina/status/834410962597847040.

170 *sudden surge:* "'Democracy Dies in Darkness': Lookups for 'Democracy' Spiked After *The Washington Post* Unveiled Its New Slogan," *Merriam-Webster.com*, February 22, 2017.

170 *weighed in:* Will Oremus, "15 Metal Albums Whose Titles Are Less Dark Than *The Washington Post*'s New Motto," *Slate*, February 22, 2017.

170 *twist on a ruling:* Dan Billin, "The Case That Inspired a Newspaper Motto," *Valley News*, March 3, 2017.

172 *Nine days before:* "Donald Trump's News Conference: Full Transcript and Video," *New York Times*, January 11, 2017.

172 *own story noted:* Paul Farhi, "Trump's First News Conference Since Election Blasts a Usual Suspect: The Media," *Washington Post*, January 11, 2017.

172 *something to commend:* Editorial Board, "Five Policies Trump Might Get Right," *Washington Post*, January 18, 2017.

173 *seeking to renege:* Greg Miller and Philip Rucker, "'This Was the Worst Call by Far': Trump Badgered, Bragged and Abruptly Ended Phone Call with Australian Leader,"*Washington Post*, February 2, 2017.

173 *full transcript:* Greg Miller, Julie Vitkovskaya, and Reuben Fischer-Baum, "'This Deal Will Make Me Look Terrible': Full Transcript of Trump's Calls with Mexico and Australia," *Washington Post*, August 3, 2017.

176 *sign nondisclosure agreements:* Ruth Marcus, "Trump Had Senior Staff Sign Nondisclosure Agreements. They're Supposed to Last Beyond His Presidency," *Washington Post*, March 18, 2018.

177 *received access:* Devlin Barrett, "Trump Justice Department Secretly Obtained *Post* Reporters' Phone Records," *Washington Post*, May 7, 2021.

177 *records also revealed:* "Recently Released Unsealed Court Records Shed Light on Why DOJ Targeted *Washington Post* Journalists," *First AmendmentWatch.org*, New York University, July 14, 2021.

178 *case of CNN:* Adam Goldman, "Trump Justice Department Seized

CNN Reporter's Email and Phone Records," *New York Times*, May 20, 2021.

178 *resisted the subpoenas:* Charlie Savage, "*Times* Requests Disclosure of Court Filings Seeking Reporters' Email Data and Gag Order," *New York Times*, June 8, 2021.

178 *our front page:* Ashley Parker and Philip Rucker, "Trump Is Struggling to Stay Calm on Russia, One Morning Call at a Time," *Washington Post*, June 23, 2017.

179 *Staten Island Ferry:* Philip Rucker, "Aboard the Staten Island Ferry, a Snapshot of Donald Trump's New York," *Washington Post*, April 13, 2016.

180 *complaint this time:* Philip Rucker, Robert Costa, and Ashley Parker, "Who's Afraid of Trump? Not Enough Republicans—At Least for Now," *Washington Post*, June 27, 2017.

181 *prepared remarks:* Martin Baron, "*Washington Post* Editor Marty Baron Has a Message to Journalists in the Trump Era," *Vanity Fair*, November 30, 2016.

183 *Darcy disclosed:* Oliver Darcy (@OliverDarcy), "My first contribution to @DylanByers' PACIFIC: Jeff Bezos was spotted last month dining with Dean Baquet, Marty Baron, Arthur and A.G. Sulzberger, Fred Ryan and Mark Thompson at The Ribbon on Manhattan's Upper West Side," Twitter, April 10, 2018, 12:26 p.m.; https://twitter.com/oliverdarcy/status/983743129844113408.

183 *gotten its hands:* Madeline Conway, "Lewandowski: *Times* Editor Dean Baquet 'Should Be in Jail' for Publishing Trump Tax Docs," *Politico*, December 2, 2016.

183 *risk of incarceration:* Chris Isidore, "*N.Y. Times* Editor: I'd Risk Jail to Publish Donald Trump Tax Docs," CNN, September 12, 2016.

184 *John Mitchell barked:* Katharine Graham, *Personal History* (New York: Alfred A. Knopf, 1997), 465.

184 *note to staff:* Jeff Bezos, "Jeff Bezos on *Post* Purchase," *Washington Post*, August 5, 2013.

Chapter 9: Explosions

186 *something favorable:* Sebastian Murdock, "Trump Attacks, Then Says He Relies on Press to Vet Nominees," *HuffPost*, August 2, 2019.

187 *fully assembled:* WashPostPR, "The *Post* Announces Staff for Rapid-Response Investigative Team," *Washington Post*, August 11, 2017.

187 *paid tribute:* "David Finkel: Journalist, Class of 2012," MacArthur Foundation, October 2, 2012.

190 *recalled in one interview:* Libby Casey, "How to Be a Journalist: How Stephanie McCrummen and Beth Reinhard Broke the Roy

Moore Story," Video, *Washington Post*, December 8, 2017; https://www.washingtonpost.com/video/other/how-to-be-a-journalist/how-to-be-a-journalist-how-stephanie-mccrummen-and-beth-reinhard-broke-the-roy-moore-story/2017/12/08/13df3466-dc39-11e7-a241-0848315642d0_video.html.

190 *preemptive story:* Callum Borchers, "Roy Moore Used *Breitbart* to Get in Front of Allegations That He Pursued Teenage Girls," *Washington Post*, November 9, 2017.

190 *suggest a connection:* Aaron Klein, "After Endorsing a Democrat in Alabama, Bezos's *Washington Post* Plans to Hit Roy Moore with Allegations of Inappropriate Relations with Teenagers; Judge Claims Smear Campaign," *Breitbart*, November 9, 2017.

191 *Corfman recounted:* Stephanie McCrummen, Beth Reinhard, and Alice Crites, "Woman Says Roy Moore Initiated Sexual Encounter When She Was 14, He Was 32," *Washington Post*, November 9, 2017.

191 *subsequent defamation suits:* Kirsten Fiscus, "Verdict: Jury Finds Neither Party Defamed Each Other in Roy Moore-Leigh Corfman Lawsuits," *Montgomery Advertiser*, February 2, 2022.

191 *falsely purported:* Marwa Eltagouri and Herman Wong, "He Said He Was a *Washington Post* Reporter Offering a Reward for Dirt on Roy Moore. It Wasn't True," *Washington Post*, November 15, 2017.

191 *frequently trafficked:* Paul Farhi, "What Is Gateway Pundit, the Conspiracy-Hawking Site at the Center of the Bogus Florida 'Crisis Actors' Hype?," *Washington Post*, February 23, 2018.

191 *amplified an allegation:* Jim Hoft, "Report: Alabama Woman Claims Reporter Offered Her $1000s to Accuse Roy Moore of Sexual Abuse?," *Gateway Pundit*, November 10, 2017.

192 *aimed to smear:* Manuela Tobias, "No, the *Washington Post* Roy Moore Reporter Doesn't Have a History of 'Faking,'" *PolitiFact*, November 14, 2017.

192 *astonishing scheme:* Shawn Boburg and Dalton Bennett, "Attorney Says Roy Moore Supporters Offered Him $10,000 to Drop Client Who Accused the Senate Candidate of Sexual Impropriety," *Washington Post*, March 23, 2018.

192 *effort to sabotage:* Shawn Boburg, Aaron C. Davis, and Alice Crites, "A Woman Approached *The Post* with Dramatic—and False—Tale About Roy Moore. She Appears to Be Part of Undercover Sting Operation," *Washington Post*, November 27, 2017.

193 *prior consent:* "Maryland: Reporter's Recording Guide," Reporters Committee for Freedom of the Press, May 2020.

193 *Virginia requires:* "Virginia: Reporter's Recording Guide," Reporters Committee for Freedom of the Press, June 2020.

194 *sit undetected:* "*Post* Reporter Confronts Woman Who Made False Accusations Against Roy Moore," Video, *Washington Post*, November 27, 2017; https://www.washingtonpost.com/video/national/post-reporter -confronts-woman-who-made-false-accusations-against-roy-moore /2017/11/27/272c883a-d3af-11e7-9ad9-ca0619edfa05_video.html.

196 *espionage techniques:* Mark Mazzetti and Adam Goldman, "Erik Prince Recruits Ex-Spies to Help Infiltrate Liberal Groups," *New York Times*, March 7, 2020.

196 *training took place:* Matthew Cole, "The Complete Mercenary," *The Intercept*, May 3, 2019.

197 *actually believed:* Oliver Darcy, "*Breitbart* Went All Out for Roy Moore. Now Its Top Editor Says He Was a 'Weak Candidate,'" CNN, December 20, 2017.

198 *obligation to be fair:* "2018 Toner Prize Ceremony Featuring Sen. Mark Warner of Virginia," Video, Newhouse School of Public Communications, March 30, 2018; https://www.youtube.com/watch?v =bxdsMQHpPWM&t=4595s.

198 *ousted from Project Veritas:* Isaac Stanley-Becker, "Project Veritas Claimed James O'Keefe Risked Group's Nonprofit Status," *Washington Post*, February 21, 2023.

198 *tweeted his congratulations:* Jeff Bezos (@JeffBezos), "Great reporting requires patience, grit and a willingness to follow a story wherever it leads, whether Alabama or Moscow. Proud of @washingtonpost #Pulitzer winners! And big congrats to the @nytimes, as well! #DemocracyDiesInDarkness," Twitter, April 16, 2018, 7 p.m.; https://twitter .com/jeffbezos/status/986016459351515136.

198 *CNBC's interpretation:* Eugene Kim, "Amazon CEO Jeff Bezos Tweaks Trump with Tweet Praising *Washington Post*'s Pulitzer Prize Wins," CNBC, April 16, 2018.

199 *spoke eloquently:* "2018 Toner Prize Ceremony Featuring Sen. Mark Warner of Virginia."

199 *via WhatsApp:* Ruth Marcus, *Supreme Ambition: Brett Kavanaugh and the Conservative Takeover* (New York: Simon & Schuster, 2019), 224.

200 *another message:* Exhibit 3, Memorandum from Senator Chuck Grassley to Senate Republicans, *Senate Judiciary Committee Investigation of Numerous Allegations Against Justice Brett Kavanaugh During Senate Confirmation Hearings*, November 2, 2018; https://www .judiciary.senate.gov/imo/media/doc/2018-11-02%20Kavanaugh%20 Report.pdf.

200 *would be memorialized:* "Kavanaugh Hearing: Transcript," *Washington Post*, September 27, 2018.

201 *sought to make contact:* Marcus, *Supreme Ambition*, 92.

201 *shared her story:* Marcus, *Supreme Ambition*, 226.

202 *reporters revealed:* Jodi Kantor and Megan Twohey, *She Said: Breaking the Sexual Harassment Story That Helped Ignite a Movement* (New York: Penguin Press, 2019), 189–90.

203 *wrote in the prologue:* Emma Brown, *To Raise a Boy* (New York: One Signal Publishers, 2021), 2.

203 *Ford told Emma:* Emma Brown, "California Professor, Writer of Confidential Brett Kavanaugh Letter, Speaks Out About Her Allegation of Sexual Assault," *Washington Post*, September 16, 2018.

204 *Feinstein possessed:* Ryan Grim, "Dianne Feinstein Withholding Brett Kavanaugh Document from Fellow Judiciary Committee Democrats," *The Intercept*, September 12, 2018.

204 *Two days later:* Nicholas Fandos and Michael S. Schmidt, "Letter Claims Attempted Assault by a Teenage Brett Kavanaugh," *New York Times*, September 14, 2018.

204 *disturbing allegations:* Ronan Farrow and Jane Mayer, "A Sexual-Misconduct Allegation Against the Supreme Court Nominee Brett Kavanaugh Stirs Tension Among Democrats in Congress," *New Yorker*, September 14, 2018.

206 *identified individual standing:* Brown, "California Professor, Writer of Confidential Brett Kavanaugh Letter, Speaks Out About Her Allegation of Sexual Assault."

206 *with accounts:* Aaron C. Davis, Emma Brown, and Joe Heim, "Kavanaugh's 'Choir Boy' Image on Fox Interview Rankles Former Yale Classmates," *Washington Post*, September 25, 2018.

206 *excessive drinking:* Mike McIntire and Ben Protess, "At the Center of the Kavanaugh Accusations: Heavy Drinking," *New York Times*, September 26, 2018.

206 *despicable mockery:* Maggie Haberman and Peter Baker, "Trump Taunts Christine Blasey Ford at Rally," *New York Times*, October 2, 2018.

207 *shamefully incomplete:* Bess Levin, "The FBI Confirms Its Brett Kavanaugh Investigation Was a Sham," *Vanity Fair*, August 5, 2022.

208 *began his weekly column:* Ben Smith, "Marty Baron Made *The Post* Great Again. Now the News Is Changing," *New York Times*, June 28, 2020.

Chapter 10: The Owner

212 *told his superiors:* Adam Entous, Ellen Nakashima, and Greg Miller, "Sessions Discussed Campaign-Related Matters with Russian Ambassador, U.S. Intelligence Intercepts Show," July 21, 2017.

212 *fund titan:* Chris Isidore, "Hedge Fund Manager: Trump Asked Me If Amazon Is a Monopoly," CNN, December 8, 2017.

212 *incited the crowd:* Mark Landler and Maggie Haberman, "At Rally, Trump Blames Media for Country's Deepening Divisions," *New York Times*, August 22, 2017.

213 *law professor:* Adam Chodorow, "The One Thing Trump Got Right in His Rant Against the 'Amazon Washington Post,'" *Slate*, July 26, 2017.

213 *complained on Twitter:* Megan Trimble, "Trump: Amazon's Getting Richer and USPS 'Dumber and Poorer,'" *U.S. News & World Report*, December 29, 2017.

213 *unilaterally double:* Damian Paletta and Josh Dawsey, "Trump Personally Pushed Postmaster General to Double Rates on Amazon, Other Firms," *Washington Post*, May 18, 2018.

213 *becoming obvious:* "1 Big Thing . . . Inside the Room: Trump Hates Amazon, not Facebook," *Axios*, March 28, 2018.

214 *Cohn estimated:* Peter Baker and Susan Glasser, *The Divider: Trump in the White House, 2017–2021* (New York: Doubleday, 2022), 57.

214 *wrote Jonathan Chait:* Jonathan Chait, "Trump Is 'Obsessed' with Amazon Because He Wants to Crush the *Washington Post*," *New York*, March 28, 2018.

214 *stock sank:* Mike Allen, "Amazon Shares Tumble on Fear of Trump," *Axios*, March 28, 2018.

215 *further battering:* Sydney Ember, "To Trump, It's the 'Amazon Washington Post.' To Its Editor, That's Baloney," *New York Times*, April 2, 2018.

215 *facing pressure:* Jonathan O'Connell and David A. Fahrenthold, "From Mueller to Stormy to 'Emoluments,' Trump's Business Is Under Siege," *Washington Post*, March 30, 2018.

215 *plenty of lobbying:* "Client Profile: Amazon," *OpenSecrets.org*, 2018; https://www.opensecrets.org/federal-lobbying/clients/summary?cycle=2018&id=D000023883.

215 *described Trump and Bezos:* Edward Helmore, "What Is the Donald Trump v Jeff Bezos Feud Really About?," *Guardian*, April 7, 2018.

215 *had it right:* Matthew Yglesias, "Donald Trump's Twitter Feud with Amazon, Explained," *Vox*, April 4, 2018.

216 *lies about us:* Ember, "To Trump, It's the 'Amazon Washington Post.' To Its Editor, That's Baloney."

216 *unusual directness:* Marc Fisher, "Why Trump Went After Bezos: Two Billionaires Across a Cultural Divide," *Washington Post*, April 5, 2018.

220 *high school girlfriend:* Brad Stone, *The Everything Store: Jeff Bezos and the Age of Amazon* (New York: Little, Brown), 151.

222 *against President Joe Biden's rhetoric:* Jack Shafer, "Why Jeff Bezos' Anti-Biden Tweets Are So Dumb," *Politico*, May 16, 2022.

223 *question-and-answer session:* Steven Overly, "Bezos to Trump: It's 'Dangerous to Demonize the Media,'" *Politico*, September 13, 2018.

223 *best capture:* Jeff Bezos (@JeffBezos), "Too many of our elected officials are still using these techniques," Twitter, May 7, 2022, 10:40 p.m.

223 *tax returns:* Jesse Eisinger, Jeff Ernsthausen, and Paul Kiel, "The Secret IRS Files: Trove of Never-Before-Seen Records Reveal How the Wealthiest Avoid Income Tax," ProPublica, June 8, 2021.

224 *reason for dread:* Brad Stone, *Amazon Unbound: Jeff Bezos and the Invention of a Global Empire* (New York: Simon & Schuster, 2021), 118–19.

224 *expressed regret:* Kelsey Sutton, "Jeff Bezos: Trump's Treatment of the Press 'Erodes Democracy Around the Edges,'" *Politico*, October 20, 2016.

224 *political contributions:* OpenSecrets.org, https://www.opensecrets.org/donor-lookup/results?name=jeffrey+bezos.

225 *split fairly evenly:* OpenSecrets.org, https://www.opensecrets.org/political-action-committees-pacs/amazon-com/C00360354/candidate-recipients/2020.

225 *gay marriage:* Amanda Holpuch, "Amazon CEO Jeff Bezos Pledges $2.5m to Same-Sex Marriage in Washington," *Guardian*, July 27, 2012.

225 *scholarship fund:* Ed O'Keefe and Nick Anderson, "Jeff Bezos Donates $33 Million to Scholarship Fund for 'Dreamers,'" *Washington Post*, January 12, 2018.

225 *scheduled to gather:* David Streitfeld, "'I'm Here to Help,' Trump Tells Tech Executives at Meeting," *New York Times*, December 14, 2016.

226 *sent alone:* Catherine Clifford, "Jeff Bezos Says Dad Emigrated from Cuba Alone at 16: 'His Grit, Determination, Optimism Are Inspiring,'" CNBC, May 16, 2019.

226 *supports veterans:* "Amazon's Jeff Bezos Donates $10m to Back Military Veterans," BBC, September 5, 2018.

226 *their own causes:* Bill Chappell, "Dolly Parton Gets $100 Million from Jeff Bezos to Spend on Charity," NPR, November 14, 2022.

226 *two of those gifts:* Brett Molina, "After Returning from Space Flight, Jeff Bezos Donates $100m Each to Chef José Andrés and Van Jones," *USA Today*, July 21, 2021.

228 *proudly boasting:* "Jeff Bezos on Launching First Fully Reusable Space Rocket," Video, *CBS This Morning*, November 24, 2015; https://www.youtube.com/watch?v=xO6toNtwdyQ.

228 *online monthly readers:* "*Washington Post* Tops *New York Times* Online for First Time Ever," Digiday, November 13, 2015.

228 *brooding instead:* NYT Innovation Report 2014, Scribd, Uploaded by BuzzFeedDocs; https://www.scribd.com/doc/224332847/NYT -Innovation-Report-2014#.

228 *media analyst:* Ken Doctor, "Is *The Washington Post* Closing In on the *Times?*," *Politico*, August 6, 2015.

230 *wrote in* HuffPost: Fredrick Kunkle, "Jeff Bezos Wants to Give More Money to Charity. He Should Pay His Workers First," *HuffPost*, September 1, 2017.

230 *told writer Charles Duhigg:* Charles Duhigg, "Is Amazon Unstoppable?," *New Yorker*, October 10, 2019.

232 *Jason recounted:* Jason Rezaian, *Prisoner: My 544 Days in an Iranian Prison* (New York: Ecco, 2018), 20–21.

234 *made clear:* WashPostPR, "New Statement from Martin Baron Ahead of Jason Rezaian's Trial in Iran," *Washington Post*, May 25, 2015.

235 *truer statement:* Rezaian, *Prisoner*, 298.

236 *disclaimed any responsibility:* Andrew Beaujon, "*Washington Post* Editor Meets with Iranian President," Poynter, September 23, 2014.

238 *prisoner exchange:* Interview with Steve Inskeep, "Speaker of Iran's Parliament Suggests Prisoner Swap for Rezaian, Other Americans," NPR, September 3, 2015.

238 *Swiss plane carried:* Carol Morello, Karen DeYoung, William Branigin, and Joby Warrick, "Plane Leaves Iran with *Post* Reporter, Other Americans in Swap," *Washington Post*, January 17, 2016.

239 *Bezos recalled:* Adam Lashinsky, "Bezos Prime," *Fortune*, March 24, 2016.

240 *his vision:* "'The Future of Newspapers'—Panel 4: Owner's View," Video, *La Stampa*, June 22, 2017; https://www.youtube.com/watch?v =xyiowqNu23s.

242 *subscriptions had climbed:* Brian Stelter, "*Washington Post* Subscriptions Soar Past 1 Million Mark," CNN, September 26, 2017.

Chapter 11: Work, Not War

243 *anti-Semitic imagery:* Daniel Politi, "Is Donald Trump's Closing Campaign Anti-Semitic?," *Slate*, November 6, 2016.

243 *concede the outcome:* Karen Tumulty and Philip Rucker, "At Third Debate, Trump Won't Commit to Accepting Election Results If He Loses," *Washington Post*, October 19, 2016.

243 *praise for strongmen:* Domenico Montanaro, "6 Strongmen Trump Has Praised—and the Conflicts It Presents," NPR, May 2, 2017.

243 *declared to Franklin Foer:* Franklin Foer, "Viktor Orbán's War on Intellect," *The Atlantic,* July 2019.

245 *investigations-oriented news outlet:* Mark Follman, "Trump's 'Enemy of the People' Rhetoric Is Endangering Journalists' Lives," *Mother Jones,* September 13, 2018.

246 *confront Hitler:* James Risen, "Trump Is a Dangerous Demagogue. It's Time for a Crusading Press to Fight Back," *The Intercept,* August 16, 2018.

246 *extraordinary series:* Jay Rosen (@jayrosen_nyu), "'We're not at war, we're at work' is genius. Its genius has limits," Twitter, August 9, 2018, 6:56 p.m.

247 *commentary in* The Atlantic: Todd S. Purdum, "Jim Acosta's Dangerous Brand of Performance Journalism," *The Atlantic,* August 7, 2018.

247 *walked out:* Jim Acosta (@acosta), "I walked out of the end of that briefing because I am totally saddened by what just happened. Sarah Sanders was repeatedly given a chance to say the press is not the enemy and she wouldn't do it. Shameful," Twitter, August 2, 2018, 2:02 p.m.

247 *White House correspondents:* Michael M. Grynbaum, "CNN's Jim Acosta Challenges Sarah Huckabee Sanders, Then Makes a Quick Exit," *New York Times,* August 2, 2018.

249 *nauseating revelry:* Paul Bond, "Leslie Moonves on Donald Trump: 'It May Not Be Good for America, but It's Damn Good for CBS,'" *Hollywood Reporter,* February 29, 2016.

249 *Moonves would later say:* Alex Weprin, "CBS CEO Les Moonves Clarifies Donald Trump 'Good for CBS' Comment," *Politico,* October 19, 2016.

250 *strategist Steve Bannon:* Michael M. Grynbaum, "Trump Strategist Stephen Bannon Says Media Should 'Keep Its Mouth Shut,'" *New York Times,* January 26, 2017.

251 *his 2005 book:* Harry G. Frankfurt, *On Bullshit* (Princeton, NJ: Princeton University Press, 2005), 66.

251 *hush money:* Dan Balz, "Trump and His Attorney Didn't Tell the Truth, if Giuliani Is Right. Will That Change Anything?," *Washington Post,* May 3, 2018.

251 *now-documented fact:* Glenn Kessler, "Not Just Misleading. Not Merely False. A Lie," *Washington Post,* August 22, 2018.

252 *shun the event:* Emily Heil, "White House Staff to Skip Correspondents' Dinner in 'Solidarity' with Trump," *Washington Post,* March 28, 2017.

252 *issued orders:* Emily Heil, "Trump Administration Members to Skip

the White House Correspondents' Dinner, Too," *Washington Post*, April 23, 2019.

252 *some praise:* Julia Manchester, "Read Trump's Remarks at Gridiron Dinner," *The Hill*, March 4, 2018.

253 *encouraged violence:* Associated Press, "Trump Praises Montana Congressman Who Body-Slammed Reporter," CNBC, October 19, 2018.

253 *pipe bombs:* "Man Who Mailed Explosive Devices to CNN, Others Sentenced to 20 Years in Jail," U.S. Press Freedom Tracker, August 5, 2019.

253 *told a federal judge:* Faith Karimi, "Pipe Bomb Suspect Cesar Sayoc Describes Trump Rallies as 'New Found Drug,'" CNN, April 24, 2019.

254 *poll had just found:* Philip Bump, "Trump Points at the Media, 'You're to Blame for Encouraging Violence,'" *Washington Post*, November 2, 2018.

254 *contributor manipulated:* Paul Farhi, "Sarah Sanders Promotes an Altered Video of CNN Reporter, Sparking Allegations of Visual Propaganda," *Washington Post*, November 8, 2018.

254 *signature achievement:* Philip Rucker, "New Book by Trump Advisers Alleges That the President Has 'Embedded Enemies,'" *Washington Post*, November 24, 2018.

255 *envision his attacks:* Donald J. Trump (@realDonaldTrump), "There has never been a time in the history of our Country that the Media is so Fraudulent, Fake, or Corrupt! When the 'Age of Trump' is looked back on many years from now, I only hope that a big part of my legacy will be exposing of massive dishonesty in the Fake News!" Twitter, August 28, 2019, 8:35 p.m.; https://twitter.com/realDonaldTrump/status /1166871882764824577.

255 *denigrated the press:* Stephanie Sugars, "From Fake News to Enemy of the People: An Anatomy of Trump's Tweets," Committee to Protect Journalists, January 30, 2019.

255 *fundraising pitch:* Mike Allen, "Scoop: Trump Allies Raise Money to Target Reporters," *Axios*, September 3, 2019.

255 *Days earlier:* Kenneth P. Vogel and Jeremy W. Peters, "Trump Allies Target Journalists over Coverage Deemed Hostile to White House," *New York Times*, August 25, 2019.

255 *senior staff editor:* Lindsey Ellefson, "*NY Times* Senior Staff Editor Tom Wright-Piersanti Apologizes and Deletes Past 'Offensive' Tweets," *The Wrap*, August 22, 2019.

255 *CNN photo editor:* Caleb Howe, "CNN Photo Editor Resigns from Network over Vicious Anti-Semitic Tweets on Death of 'Jewish Pigs,'" *Mediaite*, July 25, 2019.

255 *antigay slurs:* Ron Dicker, "CNN Reporter Kaitlan Collins Apologizes for Past Gay Slurs on Twitter," *HuffPost*, October 8, 2018.

255 *written as irony:* Jack Shafer, "Why Journalists' Old Tweets Are Fair Game for Trump," *Politico*, August 26, 2019.

256 *Trump's "lost summer":* Philip Rucker and Ashley Parker, "Trump's Lost Summer: Aides Claim Victory, but Others See Incompetence and Intolerance," *Washington Post*, September 1, 2019.

256 *childish mimickry:* Stephanie Grisham and Hogan Gidley, "The *Washington Post*'s Lost Summer," *Washington Examiner*, September 5, 2019.

257 *Sulzberger recounted:* "Statement of A. G. Sulzberger, Publisher, *The New York Times*, in Response to President Trump's Tweet About Their Meeting," New York Times Company, July 29, 2018; https://www.nytco.com/press/statement-of-a-g-sulzberger-publisher-the-new-york-times-in-response-to-president-trumps-tweet-about-their-meeting/.

Chapter 12: Murder in Mind

260 *at his Georgetown home:* Souad Mekhennet and Greg Miller, "Jamal Khashoggi's Final Months as an Exile in the Long Shadow of Saudi Arabia," *Washington Post*, December 22, 2018.

262 *appeared chummy:* Carol Morello, "In Saudi Arabia, Few Signs of a Crisis as Pompeo and Saudi Officials Exchange Pleasantries," *Washington Post*, October 16, 2018.

262 *Pompeo ultimately revealed:* Mike Pompeo, *Never Give an Inch: Fighting for the America I Love* (New York: Broadside Books, 2023), 111.

263 *dissolved in acid:* "Khashoggi Murder: Body 'Dissolved in Acid,'" BBC, November 2, 2018.

263 *outdoor oven:* "Jamal Khashoggi's Body Likely Burned in Large Oven at Saudi Home," Al Jazeera, March 4, 2019.

263 *despite convictions:* "Saudi Arabia: Four Years After Orchestrating the Killing of Jamal Khashoggi, the Crown Prince's Predator in Chief Saud al-Qahtani Remains Protected and Free," Reporters Without Borders, September 30, 2022.

264 *in-your face statement:* WashPostPR, "*Washington Post* Publisher and CEO Fred Ryan Statement on Jamal Khashoggi," *Washington Post*, November 20, 2018.

264 *told Bob Woodward:* Bob Woodward, *Rage* (New York: Simon & Schuster, 2021).

264 *moneymaking opportunity:* Josh Dawsey and Jonathan O'Connell, "Trump in Talks to Host Lucrative Saudi Golf Events," *Washington Post*, February 19, 2022.

264 *private equity fund:* David D. Kirkpatrick and Kate Kelly, "Before

Giving Billions to Jared Kushner, Saudi Investment Fund Had Big Doubts," *New York Times*, April 10, 2022.

265 *citizens were boycotting:* Zahraa Alkhalisi, "'Boycott Amazon' Is Trending in Saudi Arabia," CNN, November 5, 2018.

265 *sudden halt:* Marc Fisher and Jonathan O'Connell, "The Prince, the Billionaire and the Amazon Project That Got Frozen in the Desert," *Washington Post*, October 27, 2019.

266 *hashtag #TheList:* Cooper Fleishman, "#TheList: Alt-Right Donald Trump Trolls Have Found a New Way to Attack Journalists," *Mic*, October 24, 2016.

266 *bullet hole:* "Jewish Reporter Targeted with Anti-Semitic Tweets from Trump Supporter," Jewish Telegraphic Agency, October 18, 2016.

267 *gas chamber:* David French, "The Price I've Paid for Opposing Donald Trump," *National Review*, October 21, 2016.

267 *year covering Trump:* David Fahrenthold, "David Fahrenthold Tells the Behind-the-Scenes Story of His Year Covering Trump," *Washington Post*, December 29, 2016.

268 *anonymous caller:* Amanda Lee Myers (@amandaleeUSAT), formerly with AP, "Call into our newsroom just now: 'At some point we're just going to start shooting you fucking assholes,'" Twitter, August 22, 2018, 5:44 p.m.; https://twitter.com/AmandaLeeUSAT/status /1032382934622253058.

268 *said in one call:* Affidavit of FBI Special Agent Thomas M. Dalton in support of a criminal complaint and arrest warrant, United States of America v. Robert D. Chain, U.S. District Court, District of Massachusetts, August 29, 2018.

268 *FBI SWAT team:* Milton Valencia and John R. Ellement, "Calif. Man Charged with Making Threatening Calls to *Globe*," *Boston Globe*, August 30, 2018.

268 *Boston University student:* Maria Cramer, "Man Who Threatened the *Globe*, Other Papers Sentenced to Four Months in Prison," *Boston Globe*, October 2, 2019.

270 *defendant told the judge:* Paul Duggan, "Coast Guard Lt. Christopher Hasson Sentenced to 13 Years in Alleged Terror Plot," *Washington Post*, January 31, 2020.

270 *hauled to prison:* Daniel Greenfield, "Arrest the Editor of the *Washington Post*," *FrontPage Magazine*, August 16, 2017.

271 *Trump campaign:* Zoe Tillman, "Trump 2020 Campaign Suit Against *Washington Post* Dismissed," *Bloomberg*, February 3, 2023.

271 *legal actions:* Nick Penzenstadler and Susan Page, "Exclusive: Trump's 3,500 Lawsuits Unprecedented for a Presidential Nominee," *USA Today*, June 1, 2016.

272 *libel cases:* James D. Zirin, *Plaintiff in Chief: A Portrait of Donald Trump in 3,500 Lawsuits* (New York: All Points Books, 2019), 8.

272 *deposition by Trump:* David A. Fahrenthold and Robert Harrow Jr., "Trump: A True Story," *Washington Post,* August 10, 2016.

272 *hurt O'Brien:* Michael Kranish and Marc Fisher, *Trump Revealed: An American Journey of Ambition, Ego, Money, and Power* (New York: Scribner, 2016), 304.

272 *similar headaches:* Kranish and Fisher, *Trump Revealed,* 304.

273 *dashed off:* Peter Baker, "After Trump Seeks to Block Book, Publisher Hastens Release," *New York Times,* January 4, 2018.

274 *world's worst:* Richard Fletcher, "Polarisation in the New Media," Digital News Report 2017, Reuters Institute, University of Oxford.

275 *main source:* Elizabeth Grieco, "Americans' Main Sources for Political News Vary by Party and Age," Pew Research Center, April 1, 2020.

275 *protecting immigrants:* Josh Dawsey, "Trump Derides Protection for Immigrants from 'Shithole' Countries," *Washington Post,* January 12, 2018.

276 *defied cautions:* Carol D. Leonnig, David Nakamura, and Josh Dawsey, "Trump's National Security Advisers Warned Him Not to Congratulate Putin. He Did It Anyway," *Washington Post,* March 20, 2018.

276 *interpreter's notes:* Greg Miller, "Trump Has Concealed Details of His Face-to-Face Encounters with Putin from Senior Officials in Administration," *Washington Post,* January 13, 2019.

Chapter 13: Truth and Lies

282 *op-ed for* The Washington Post: Robert S. Mueller III, "Robert Mueller: Roger Stone Remains a Convicted Felon, and Rightly So," *Washington Post,* July 11, 2020.

282 *team delivered:* "Key Findings of the Mueller Report," American Constitution Society; https://www.acslaw.org/projects/the-presidential -investigation-education-project/other-resources/key-findings-of-the -mueller-report/.

282 *federal prosecutors:* "Statement by Former Federal Prosecutors," Medium, May 6, 2019; https://medium.com/@dojalumni/statement-by -former-federal-prosecutors-8ab7691c2aa1.

283 *lied every which way:* Rachel Weiner, "Paul Manafort a 'Hardened' and 'Bold' Criminal, Mueller Prosecutors Tell Judge," *Washington Post,* February 23, 2019.

284 *letter of intent:* Trump Acquisition LLC letter signed by Donald Trump and Andrey Rozov, October 28, 2015, re "Proposed development of a first class, luxury, mixed use to be known as Trump Moscow (or

other such name as mutually agreed upon by the Parties), and located in Moscow City (the "Project"); http://cdn.cnn.com/cnn/2018/images /12/18/attachment.1.pdf.

285 *declaring unequivocally:* Tamara Keith, "Special Counsel Mueller's Office Says 'Buzzfeed' Report Is Not Accurate," NPR, January 18, 2019.

286 *subsequently testified:* Tom Hamburger, Ellen Nakashima, and Karoun Demirjian, "Cohen Told Lawmakers Trump Attorney Jay Sekulow Encouraged Him to Falsely Claim Moscow Project Ended in January 2016," *Washington Post*, May 20, 2019.

286 *regrettable blunder:* Paul Farhi, "*The Washington Post* Corrects, Removes Parts of Two Stories Regarding the Steele Dossier," *Washington Post*, November 12, 2021.

286 *remarkable amount:* Al Tompkins, "Mueller Proves 'Fake News' to Be True," Poynter, April 18, 2019.

286 *under investigation:* Devlin Barrett, Adam Entous, Ellen Nakashima, and Sari Horwitz, "Special Counsel Is Investigating Trump for Possible Obstruction of Justice, Officials Say," *Washington Post*, June 14, 2017.

286 *Trump's demand that Mueller:* Michael S. Schmidt and Maggie Haberman, "Trump Ordered Mueller Fired, but Backed Off When White House Counsel Threatened to Quit," *New York Times*, January 25, 2018.

289 *phone call:* Kenneth P. Vogel and Andrew E. Kramer, "Giuliani Renews Push for Ukraine to Investigate Trump's Political Opponents," *New York Times*, August 21, 2019.

289 *military aid:* Caitlin Emma and Connor O'Brien, "Trump Holds Up Ukraine Military Aid Meant to Confront Russia," *Politico*, August 28, 2019.

289 Washington Post *editorial:* Editorial Board, "Trump Tries to Force Ukraine to Meddle in the 2020 Election," *Washington Post*, September 5, 2019.

290 *flesh out the contents:* Greg Miller, Ellen Nakashima, and Shane Harris, "Trump's Communications with Foreign Leader Are Part of Whistleblower Complaint That Spurred Standoff Between Spy Chief and Congress, Former Officials Say," *Washington Post*, September 18, 2019.

290 *whistleblower complaint:* Ellen Nakashima, Shane Harris, Greg Miller, and Carol D. Leonnig, "Whistleblower Complaint About President Trump Involves Ukraine, According to Two People Familiar with the Matter," *Washington Post*, September 19, 2019.

290 *pressured Zelensky:* Alan Cullison, Rebecca Ballhaus, and Dustin Volz, "Trump Repeatedly Pressed Ukraine President to Investigate Biden's Son," *Wall Street Journal*, September 21, 2019.

291 *No such server exists:* Salvador Rizzo, "President Trump's Alternate Reality on Ukraine," *Washington Post*, October 29, 2019.

292 *broken no laws:* Matt Zapotosky, Josh Dawsey, and Carol D. Leon-nig, "Trump Wanted Barr to Hold News Conference Saying the Pres-ident Broke No Laws in Call to Ukrainian Leader," *Washington Post*, November 6, 2019.

296 *suggested on Fox News:* "Stephanie Grisham: Dems Must Be Held Accountable for 'Corrupt' Impeachment," Video, Fox News, February 6, 2020; https://www.foxnews.com/media/stephanie-grisham-dems-must -be-held-accountable-for-corrupt-impeachment.

299 *ethics principle:* "APA's Goldwater Rule Remains a Guiding Prin-ciple for Physician Members," American Psychiatric Association, Oc-tober 6, 2017; https://www.psychiatry.org/newsroom/news-releases /apa-goldwater-rule-remains-a-guiding-principle-for-physician -members.

301 *ignore the rule:* Sharon Begley, "Psychiatry Group Tells Members They Can Ignore 'Goldwater Rule' and Comment on Trump's Mental Health," *Stat*, July 25, 2017.

301 *narcissistic personality disorder:* Allen Frances, "I Helped Write the Manual for Diagnosing Mental Illness. Donald Trump Doesn't Meet the Criteria," *Stat*, September 6, 2017.

Chapter 14: Scandals

303 *Renovation plans:* Mimi Montgomery, "Here Are the Floor Plans for Jeff Bezos's $23 Million DC Home," *Washingtonian*, April 22, 2018.

304 *extramarital relationship:* Ruth Brown, "Jeff Bezos's Racy Texts to Lauren Sanchez Revealed," *New York Post*, January 10, 2019.

305 *pursued Bezos:* Nik Hatziefstathiou, "Billionaire Jeff Bezos Busted— See the Shocking Cheating Photos That Destroyed His Marriage," *Na-tional Enquirer*, January 22, 2019.

306 *harboring suspicions:* Lachlan Markay and Asawin Suebsaeng, "Bezos Launches Investigation into Leaked Texts with Lauren Sanchez That Killed His Marriage," *Daily Beast*, January 30, 2019.

306 *pattern of tweeting:* Marc Fisher, Manuel Roig-Franzia, and Sarah Ellison, "Was Tabloid Exposé of Bezos Affair Just Juicy Gossip or a Political Hit Job?," *Washington Post*, February 5, 2019.

306 *hush money:* Sarah Ellison and Paul Farhi, "Publisher of the *National Enquirer* Admits to Hush-Money Payments Made on Trump's Behalf," *Washington Post*, December 12, 2018.

310 *listened to a recording:* Eugene Kim, "Jeff Bezos Responds to Em-ployee Concerns About His Personal Life: 'I Still Tap Dance into the Office,'" CNBC, March 11, 2019.

310 *dismissed the idea:* Brad Stone, *Amazon Unbound: Jeff Bezos and the Invention of a Global Empire* (New York: Simon & Schuster, 2021), 318.

311 *paid $200,000 up front:* Michael Rothfeld, Joe Palazzolo, and Alexandra Berzon, "How the *National Enquirer* got Bezos' texts: It Paid $200,000 to His Lover's Brother," *Wall Street Journal,* March 18, 2019.

311 *reviewed a contract:* Jim Rutenberg and Michael Rothfeld, "Jeff Bezos' Hack Inquiry Falls Short of Implicating *National Enquirer*," *New York Times,* January 23, 2020.

311 *texts with her brother:* Joe Palazzolo and Corinne Ramey, "Prosecutors Have Evidence Bezos' Girlfriend Gave Texts to Brother Who Leaked to *National Enquirer*," *Wall Street Journal,* January 24, 2020.

311 *concluded its investigation:* Corinne Ramey, Dustin Volz, and Aruna Viswanatha, "Racy Affair Saga Between Jeff Bezos and *Enquirer* Reaches Final Chapter," *Wall Street Journal,* December 1, 2021.

312 *malicious code:* Marc Fisher, "U.N. Report: Saudi Crown Prince Was Involved in Alleged Hacking of Bezos Phone," *Washington Post,* January 22, 2020.

312 *male escort site:* Stone, *Amazon Unbound,* 333.

312 *vocal critic:* Iyad El-Baghdadi, "How the Saudis Made Jeff Bezos Public Enemy No. 1," *Daily Beast,* February 25, 2019.

313 *her brother's actions:* Christian Berthelsen and Hailey Waller, "Jeff Bezos Sued for Defamation by Girlfriend Lauren Sanchez's Brother," *Bloomberg,* February 1, 2020.

314 *Bezos depended on it:* Mary Hanbury, "Jeff Bezos Risks Angering Trump by Acknowledging the US Postal Service Gave Him a Huge Helping Hand in Building Amazon," *Insider,* July 16, 2019.

315 *strong resistance:* Damian Paletta and Josh Dawsey, "Trump Personally Pushed Postmaster General to Double Rate on Amazon, Other Firms," *Washington Post,* May 18, 2018.

316 *obstruct Amazon's bid:* Gabriel Sherman, "Trump Is Like, 'How Can I F—k with Him?' Trump's War with Amazon (and the *Washington Post*) Is Personal," *Vanity Fair,* April 2, 2018.

316 *segment on JEDI:* "Swamp Watch: Amazon's Shady Dealings in Lobbying and Within the Government," Video, Fox News, YouTube, July 22, 2019; https://www.youtube.com/watch?v=Gz0aYouV3xA&list =PLITLHnxSVuIwe-735fxLKQD_9xzOgcGwW&index=3.

317 *upended the process:* Aaron Gregg and Josh Dawsey, "After Trump Cites Amazon Concerns, Pentagon Reexamines $10 Billion JEDI Cloud Contract Process," *Washington Post,* August 1, 2019.

317 *flowchart:* Michael Warren, Kylie Atwood, and Alex Rogers, "Exclusive: Inside the Effort to Turn Trump Against Amazon's Bid for a $10 Million Contract," CNN, July 27, 2019.

317 *book alleging:* Paul Solzdra, "11 of the Best Bits from the Book James Mattis Doesn't Want You to Read," *Task & Purpose,* October 24, 2019.

320 *mail service's rates:* Jay Greene, "Amazon's Big Holiday Shopping Advantage: An In-House Shipping Network Swollen by Pandemic-Fueled Growth," *Washington Post,* November 27, 2020.

321 *investigate Bezos:* Michael S. Schmidt, "Trump Wanted I.R.S. Investigations of Foes, Top Aide Says," *New York Times,* November 13, 2022.

322 *block the merger:* Jim Rutenberg, "In AT&T Deal, Government Action Catches Up with Trump Rhetoric," *New York Times,* November 8, 2017.

322 *fight the merger:* Jane Mayer, "The Making of the Fox News White House," *New Yorker,* March 4, 2019.

323 *executive privilege:* Congressman David N. Cicilline (@Rep Cicilline), "Chairman Nadler and Cicilline received this letter from the White House on their request for documents related to DOJ's involvement in the AT&T merger. Statement to follow shortly," Twitter, April 16, 2019, 4:03 p.m.; https://twitter.com/RepCicilline/status /1118243416746483712.

323 *Fox News anchor:* "Ingraham: Apple Joins Disney's Political Alliance with the Left," Fox News, April 2, 2022; https://www.youtube.com /watch?v=SNNhb67Yvzc.

Chapter 15: The Powers That Be

325 *attributed its cancellation:* Emily Smith, "Jeff Bezos Yanked $20 Million Super Bowl Ad over Lauren Sanchez Affair," *New York Post,* February 4, 2019.

327 *searches worldwide:* "Worldwide Desktop Market Share of Leading Search Engines from January 2010 to July 2022," Statista, 2022.

327 *five articles:* "Changes in First Click Free," Google Search Central, December 1, 2009.

327 *lowered to three:* "First Click Free Update," Google Search Central, September 29, 2015.

329 *users worldwide:* Dami Lee, "Apple Says There Are 1.4 Billion Active Apple Devices," *The Verge,* January 29, 2019.

329 *battling among themselves:* Peter Kafka, "The Logic Behind Apple's Give-Us-Half-Your-Revenue Pitch to News Publishers," *Vox,* February 13, 2019.

330 *against participating:* Kenneth Li and Helen Coster, "*New York Times* CEO Warns Publishers Ahead of Apple News Launch," Reuters, March 21, 2019.

333 *Amazon Prime:* Geoffrey A. Fowler, "Why You Cannot Quit Amazon Prime—Even If Maybe You Should," *Washington Post,* January 31, 2018.

333 *For Alexa:* Geoffrey A. Fowler, "Alexa Has Been Eavesdropping on You This Whole Time," *Washington Post*, May 6, 2019.

333 *Alexa-enabled glasses:* Geoffrey A. Fowler, "I've Worn Alexa-Enabled Glasses for Two Weeks. They're Driving Me Bananas," *Washington Post*, August 4, 2020.

333 *hands in exasperation:* Geoffrey A. Fowler, "Amazon's New Security Drone Pushes the Boundaries of Surveillance, Again," *Washington Post*, September 24, 2020.

334 *unregulated growth:* Drew Harwell, "Oregon Became a Testing Ground for Amazon's Facial-Recognition Policing. But What If Rekognition Gets It Wrong?," *Washington Post*, April 30, 2019.

334 *police departments:* Drew Harwell, "Doorbell-Camera Firm Ring Has Partnered with 400 Police Forces, Extending Surveillance Concerns," *Washington Post*, August 28, 2019.

334 *keep the Ring videos:* Drew Harwell, "Police Can Keep Ring Camera Video Forever and Share with Whomever They'd Like, Amazon Tells Senator," *Washington Post*, November 19, 2019.

334 *gave preference:* Jay Greene, "Aggressive Amazon Tactic Pushes You to Consider Its Own Brand Before You Click 'Buy,'" *Washington Post* August 28, 2019.

335 *fund polling:* Tony Romm, "Amazon, Facebook and Google Turn to Deep Network of Political Allies to Battle Back Antitrust Probes," *Washington Post*, June 10, 2020.

335 *monopolistic behavior: Investigation of Competition in Digital Markets*, Majority Staff Report and Recommendations, Subcommittee on Antitrust, Commercial and Administrative Law of the Committee on the Judiciary, 2020; https://www.govinfo.gov/content/pkg/CPRT -117HPRT47832/pdf/CPRT-117HPRT47832.pdf.

335 *misleading the committee:* John Wagner and Cat Zakrzewski, "House Panel Flags Amazon and Senior Executives to Justice Department over Potentially Criminal Conduct," *Washington Post*, March 9, 2022.

339 *decisive verdict:* Jack Shafer, "Opinion: Why Jeff Bezos' Anti-Biden Tweets Are So Dumb," *Politico*, May 16, 2022.

Chapter 16: Accuser and Accused

342 *Charges were dropped:* Duff Wilson, "Former Duke Players Cleared of All Charges," *New York Times*, April 11, 2007.

342 *rush to judgment:* Rachel Smolkin, "Justice Delayed," AJR, ajrarchive .org, August/September 2007.

342 *ultimately settled:* Sydney Ember, "*Rolling Stone* to Pay $1.65 Million to Fraternity over Discredited Rape Story," *New York Times*, June 13, 2017.

342 *investigation in 2014:* Erik Wemple, "The Demise of *Rolling Stone*'s Rape Story," *Washington Post*, December 11, 2014.

342 *dismantling the story:* T. Rees Shapiro, "U-Va. Students Challenge *Rolling Stone* Account of Alleged Sexual Assault," *Washington Post*, December 10, 2014.

342 *gone wild:* Natalie O'Neill, "Joe Biden Caught 'Snuggling' with Defense Chief's Wife," *New York Post*, February 17, 2015.

343 *posted an essay:* Stephanie Carter, "The #MeToo Story That Wasn't Me," Medium, March 31, 2019.

344 *podcast with journalist:* Katie Halper (@kthalps), "This is a story that @ReadeAlexandra has been trying to tell since it happened in 1993. It's a story about sexual assault, retaliation and silencing. #meToo," Twitter, March 25, 2020, 1:56 a.m.

344 *first account:* Alan Riquelmy, "Nevada County Woman Says Joe Biden Inappropriately Touched Her While Working in His U.S. Senate Office," *The Union*, April 3, 2019.

344 *Two days later:* Ryan Grim, "Time's Up Said It Could Not Fund a #MeToo Allegation Against Joe Biden, Citing Its Nonprofit Status and His Presidential Run," *The Intercept*, March 24, 2020.

345 *sexual misconduct:* Meghan Keneally, "List of Trump's Accusers and Their Allegations of Sexual Misconduct," ABC News, September 18, 2020.

346 *full news coverage:* Brian Flood, "Rose McGowan Slams *Washington Post* over Story on Joe Biden Accuser," Fox News, April 13, 2020.

346 *single line:* Beth Reinhard, Elise Viebeck, Matt Viser, and Alice Crites, "Sexual Assault Allegation by Former Biden Senate Aide Emerges in Campaign, Draws Denial," *Washington Post*, April 12, 2020.

346 *Helen Lewis wrote:* Helen Lewis, "Why I've Never Believed in 'Believe Women,'" *The Atlantic*, May 14, 2020.

347 *overturn convictions:* Matt Viser and Michael Scherer, "As Her Lawyer Quits, Biden Accuser Tara Reade's Credibility Is Challenged by Lawyers Whose Clients She Testified Against as an Expert Witness," *Washington Post*, May 22, 2020.

347 *repudiated a statement:* Mary Duan, "Prosecutors Decline to File Perjury Charges Against Biden Accuser Who They Say Lied About Her Credentials as an Expert Witness," *Monterey County Weekly*, November 19, 2020.

347 *contested other questions:* Ryan Grim, "A Year Later, Tara Reade Works to Correct the Record," *The Intercept*, March 14, 2021.

347 *their own coverage:* Ben Smith, "The *Times* Took 19 Days to Report

an Accusation Against Biden. Here's Why," *New York Times*, April 13, 2020.

348 *culture of discrimination:* Drew Harwell, "Hundreds Allege Sex Harassment, Discrimination at Kay and Jared Jewelry Company," *Washington Post*, February 27, 2017.

348 *making sexual comments:* Matt Zapotosky, "Nine More Women Say Judge Subjected Them to Inappropriate Behavior, Including Four Who Say He Touched or Kissed Them," *Washington Post*, December 15, 2017.

348 *classical music:* Anne Midgette and Peggy McGlone, "Assaults in Dressing Rooms. Groping During Lessons. Classical Musicians Reveal a Profession Rife with Harassment," *Washington Post*, July 26, 2018.

348 *admitted to several acts of wrongdoing:* Peggy McGlone and Anne Midgette, "Cleveland Orchestra Fires Concertmaster, Top Musician After Sex Harassment Investigation," *Washington Post*, October 24, 2018.

348 *apologized and pledged:* Tom Huizenga, "Top Dutch Orchestra and Ousted Conductor Daniele Gatti Settle Dispute," NPR, April 24, 2019.

348 *legendary anchor:* Sarah Ellison, "NBC News Faces Skepticism in Remedying In-House Sexual Harassment," *Washington Post*, April 26, 2018.

349 *petition in support:* Amanda Arnold, "65 Women in Media Sign Letter in Support of Tom Brokaw," *New York*, April 29, 2018.

349 *right parameters:* "Brokaw on Sexual Misconduct: 'It Will Be the Century of Women,'" Video, MSNBC, December 7, 2017.

350 *every few days:* Jodi Kantor and Megan Twohey, *She Said: Breaking the Sexual Harassment Story That Helped Ignite a Movement* (New York: Penguin Press, 2019), 47.

350 *television interviewer:* Irin Carmon and Amy Brittain, "Eight Women Say Charlie Rose Sexually Harassed Them—with Nudity, Groping and Lewd Calls," *Washington Post*, November 20, 2017.

351 *Longform podcast:* "Longform Podcast #320: Irin Carmon," Audio, November 28, 2018; https://longform.org/posts/longform-podcast-320 -irin-carmon.

351 Quartz *online site:* Alexandra Ossola, "The Journalist Who Took Down Charlie Rose Explains Why It Took Seven Years to Expose His Abuse," *Quartz*, March 12, 2019.

352 *following morning:* CBS Mornings (@CBSMornings): "'This is a moment that demands a frank and honest assessment about where we stand and more generally the safety of women. Let me be very clear. There is no excuse for this alleged behavior. It is systematic and perva-

sive and I've been doing a lot of listening'—@NorahODonnell," Twitter, November 21, 2017, 7:12 a.m.

353 *story full-time:* Amy Brittain and Irin Carmon, "Charlie Rose's Misconduct Was Widespread at CBS and Three Managers Were Warned, Investigation Finds," *Washington Post*, May 3, 2018.

355 *half dozen allegations:* Ronan Farrow, "Les Moonves and CBS Face Allegations of Sexual Misconduct," *New Yorker*, July 27, 2018.

356 *find an outlet:* "2018 Mirror Awards—Irin Carmon," Video, YouTube, June 26, 2018; https://www.youtube.com/watch?v=s4w6BGTVTFs.

356 *magazine titled:* Irin Carmon, "What Was the *Washington Post* Afraid Of?," *New York*, April 1, 2019.

357 *Jesuit publication:* Eileen Markey, "Catholics Owe Marty Baron a Debt of Gratitude. He Told Us the Truth About the Clerical Sex Abuse Crisis," *America: The Jesuit Review*, March 26, 2021.

358 *investigation forward:* Tarannum Kamlani, "How Emily Steel Toppled TV Titan Bill O'Reilly—the Inside Story," CBC News, April 29, 2018.

358 *concluded that Fager:* Rachel Abrams and John Koblin, "At '60 Minutes,' Independence Led to Trouble, Investigators Say," *New York Times*, December 6, 2018.

359 *breathtaking leniency:* Amy Brittain and Maura Judkis, "'The Man Who Attacked Me Works in Your Kitchen': Victim of Serial Groper Took Justice into Her Own Hands," *Washington Post*, January 31, 2019.

360 *investigative podcast:* Amy Brittain, "Canary: *The Washington Post* investigates," Audio, *Washington Post*, October 1, 2020.

362 *wrote the judges:* "2021 Excellence in Audio Digital Storytelling, Limited Series, Winner," Online News Association; https://awards.journalists.org/entries/canary-the-washington-post-investigates/.

Chapter 17: Twitter Storms

364 *Hundreds signed:* Victoria Albert, "Washington Post Guild Defends Reporter Placed on Leave After Tweet About Rape Allegation Against Kobe Bryant," CBS News, January 27, 2020.

367 *he was arrested:* Mark Berman, "*Washington Post* Reporter Arrested in Ferguson," *Washington Post*, August 13, 2014.

367 *trespassing and interfering:* Mark Berman, "*Washington Post* Reporter Charged with Trespassing, Interfering with a Police Officer," *Washington Post*, August 10, 2015.

367 *charges were dropped:* Niraj Chokshi, "Ferguson-Related Charges Dropped Against *Washington Post* and *Huffington Post* Reporters," *Washington Post*, May 19, 2016.

368 *Scarborough later admitted:* Ben Smith, "Inside the Revolts Erupting in America's Big Newsrooms," *New York Times*, June 7, 2020.

368 *Wes told CNN:* Jeff Poor, "*WaPo* Reporter to 'Smugly' Scarborough: Come to Ferguson, Do Some Reporting," *Breitbart*, August 14, 2014.

369 *Instagram platforms:* Wesley Lowery (@wesleylowery), Instagram, January 1, 2015.

369 *story headlined:* Andrew Beaujon, "Why Does Everyone Want Wesley Lowery to Shut Up?," *Washingtonian*, June 2, 2015.

369 *astonished to discover:* Allyson Vasilopulos, "Pulitzer Prize Winner Wesley Lowery Talks About Police Shootings, Data Surprises," *Columbia Missourian*, April 4, 2017.

369 *then the largest:* Paul Farhi, "*Post* Series on Police Shooting Wins Pulitzer Prize for National Reporting," *Washington Post*, April 18, 2016.

371 *wondered where labeling:* Keith Woods, "Opinion: Report on Racism, but Ditch the Labels," NPR, July 27, 2019.

371 *article in* Politico: Michael Calderone, "Black Journalists Push Media to Cover 'Hyper-Racial' Moment in Politics," *Politico*, July 29, 2019.

371 *dismissing criticism:* Maureen Dowd, "Spare Me the Purity Racket," *New York Times*, July 27, 2019.

373 *letter began by acknowledging:* https://int.nyt.com/data /documenthelper/7003-lowery-memo/efc475797987966bdaab /optimized/full.pdf.

373 *later characterized it:* J. Clara Chan, "Wesley Lowery Suggests His *Washington Post* Editors 'Threatened' Him over His Tweets," *The Wrap*, February 3, 2020.

374 *promptly championed:* Smith, "Inside the Revolts Erupting in America's Big Newsrooms."

376 *demanding his dismissal:* Emily Yahr, "President Trump Calls for *Washington Post* Reporter Who Apologized for Inaccurate Tweet to Be Fired," *Washington Post*, December 9, 2017.

376 *sexist joke:* Ariel Zilber, "*Washington Post*'s Felicia Sonmez Blasts Colleague David Weigel for Retweeting Sexist Joke," *New York Post*, June 3, 2022.

377 *suspended its reporter:* Alexandra Stevenson, "*L.A. Times* Suspends Beijing Bureau Chief After Accusation," *New York Times*, May 16, 2018.

377 *accused Kaiman:* Catherine Lai, "Second Allegation of Sexual Misconduct Against *LA Times* Beijing Bureau Chief Jonathan Kaiman Surfaces," *Hong Kong Free Press*, May 15, 2018.

378 *Beijing police:* Lai, "Second Allegation of Sexual Misconduct Against *LA Times* Beijing Bureau Chief Jonathan Kaiman Surfaces."

378 *another woman:* Laura Tucker, "Sharing Something from 2013," Medium, January 10, 2018.

378 *given the choice:* Emily Yoffe, "'I'm Radioactive,'" *Reason*, October 2019.

379 *provided a statement:* Complaint, Felicia M. Sonmez v. WP Company LLC et al., Superior Court of the District of Columbia, Civil Division, July 21, 2021.

379 *his perception:* Stevenson, "*L.A. Times* Suspends Beijing Bureau Chief After Accusations."

379 *devastating toll:* Catherine Lai, "*L.A. Times* Beijing Bureau Chief Jonathan Kaiman Resigns After Investigation into Alleged Sexual Misconduct," *Hong Kong Free Press*, September 19, 2018.

379 *forcefully challenged:* Yoffe, "'I'm Radioactive.'"

380 *suggest her employer:* Felicia Sonmez, "An update: Yesterday, I wrote a letter to Atlantic editors including @JeffreyGoldberg, @AdrienneLaF and @YAppelbaum asking them to address the recent public statements made by Caitlin Flanagan (@CaitlinPacific). Here's a copy of my letter; I have yet to receive a response. 1x," Twitter, October 8, 2019, 9:45 a.m.

382 *dismissing her claims:* Amy Argetsinger, "Judge Dismisses Sonmez Lawsuit Against *The Washington Post*," *Washington Post*, March 25, 2022.

383 *Seventy-eight minutes:* Gene Foreman, Daniel R. Biddle, Emilie Lounsberry, and Richard G. Jones, *The Ethical Journalist: Making Responsible Decisions in the Digital Age*, 3rd ed. (Hoboken, NJ: Wiley-Blackwell, 2022), 227–28.

384 *allegations against Bryant:* Rachel Abrams, "*Washington Post* Suspends a Reporter After Her Tweets on Kobe Bryant," *New York Times*, January 27, 2020.

385 *psychological portrait:* Kent Babb, "The Revisionist," *Washington Post*, November 14, 2018.

387 *petition signed:* "Post Guild Statement in Support of Felicia Sonmez," Google Doc, last updated January 30, 2020; https://docs.google.com/document/d/1ErQ7bN352jQZ0Ka8kCzAW8CWr2zEnUlvms5BG2Kdt1E/edit.

387 *social media rules:* Jon Allsop, "Felicia Sonmez and the Tyranny of Social-Media Policy," *Columbia Journalism Review*, January 29, 2020.

387 *mocked our policy:* Hamilton Nolan, "The *Post*'s Masthead Will Have to Accept That It Is Not God," *Columbia Journalism Review*, February 7, 2020.

387 *pronounced my actions:* Isaac J. Bailey, "Felicia Sonmez, *The Post*, Gayle King, and the Perils of Tradition Bias," *Nieman Reports*, February 7, 2020.

388 *under Tracy's name:* Kristine Koratti Kelly, "New Statement Regarding Post Reporter Felicia Sonmez," Twitter, January 28, 2020, 5:13 p.m.; https://twitter.com/kriscoratti/status/1222281539100250114.

390 *outline my views:* Oliver Darcy (@oliverdarcy), "News: Marty Baron

just sent this email about social media use to The Washington Post newsroom," Twitter, January 30, 2020, 2:20 p.m.

393 *strict new guidelines:* "Guidance: Individual Use of Social Media," BBC, October 2020.

393 *Baquet issued:* Steven Perlberg, "Leaked Memo: *The New York Times* Has Issued a Twitter 'Reset,' Urging Reporters to 'Meaningfully Reduce' How Much Time They Spend on the Platform," *Insider*, April 7, 2022.

393 *feuding openly:* Sarah Rumpf, "*WaPo* Editor Admonishes Staff to 'Treat Each Other with Respect and Kindness' as Numerous Messy Feuds Play Out on Twitter. It Doesn't Work," *Mediaite*, June 5, 2022.

393 *Felicia persisted:* Paul Schwartzman and Jeremy Barr, "Felicia Sonmez Terminated by *The Washington Post* After Twitter Dispute," *Washington Post*, June 9, 2022.

Chapter 18: Uprisings

396 *secure bunker:* Peter Baker and Maggie Haberman, "As Protests and Violence Spill Over, Trump Shrinks Back," *New York Times*, May 31, 2020.

397 *assaulted by police:* Marc Tracy and Rachel Abrams, "Police Target Journalists as Trump Blames 'Lamestream Media' for Protests," *New York Times*, June 1, 2020.

398 *challenged with questions:* Paul Farhi and Sarah Ellison, "Ignited by Public Protests, American Newsrooms Are Having Their Own Racial Reckoning," *Washington Post*, June 13, 2020.

402 *nuanced and reflective:* Kevin Merida, "Where That Bus Ride Took Me," *Washington Post*, September 2, 1998.

404 *add forty-one editors:* WashPostPR, "*The Washington Post* Announces the Addition of 41 Editing Roles, Including 2 Masthead Positions," *Washington Post*, September 20, 2021.

405 *gratified when my publisher:* Christina Pazzanese, "'He Was Fearless,'" *Harvard Gazette*, May 25, 2020.

405 *staff diversity:* "2016 Minority Percentages at Participating News Organizations," News Leaders Association; https://members.newsleaders .org/files/2016%20Summary%20Report%20for%20each%20news%20 organization.pdf.

406 *big budget request:* WashPostPR, "*The Washington Post* Announces More Than a Dozen Newsroom Positions to Be Focused on Race, Including Managing Editor for Diversity and Inclusion," *Washington Post*, June 18, 2020.

409 *wouldn't subside:* Ben Smith, "Marty Baron Made The *Post* Great Again. Now the News Is Changing," *New York Times*, June 28, 2020.

411 *letter of protest:* Hanaa' Tameez, "The *Philadelphia Inquirer*'s Journal-

ists of Color Are Taking a 'Sick and Tired' Day After 'Buildings Matter, Too' Headline," Nieman Lab, June 4, 2020.

411 *letter to owner:* Los Angeles Times Guild, "Letter to Patrick Soon-Shiong from the L.A. Times Guild's Black Caucus," June 23, 2020; https://latguild .com/news/2020/6/23/letter-from-la-times-guild-black-caucus.

411 *organization had failed:* Los Angeles Times Guild, "Latino Journalists at the *L.A. Times* Pen Open Letter for Better Newsroom Representation," July 21, 2020; https://latguild.com/news/2020/7/21/latino -caucus-letter.

411 *changes in coverage:* Marc Tracy and Ben Smith, "*Wall Street Journal* Staff Members Push for Big Changes in News Coverage," *New York Times*, July 10, 2020.

412 *tweeted some version:* Rishika Dugyala, "*NYT* Opinion Editor Resigns After Outrage over Tom Cotton Op-Ed," *Politico*, June 7, 2020.

412 *offered a defense:* Ken Meyer, "*NY Times* Publisher A.G. Sulzberger Writes Internal Memo After Staff Revolt over Cotton Op-Ed: 'Essential' That We Reflect on Criticism," *Mediaite*, June 4, 2020.

412 *internal report:* "A Call to Action: Building a Culture That Works for All of Us," New York Times Company; https://www.nytco.com /company/diversity-and-inclusion/a-call-to-action/?fbclid=IwAR2A YjiYXTdbdGi4HnZUp1lqcpm8Y7n1scfuomIBmnIlAOiHLJ1zFIBo _1Y#intro.

412 *identical tensions:* Kevin Draper, "ESPN Employees Say Racism Endures Behind the Camera," *New York Times*, July 13, 2020.

414 *companywide email:* Edmund Lee and Ben Smith, "*Axios* Allows Its Reporters to Join Protests," *New York Times*, June 8, 2020.

415 *stern warning:* Jim VandeHei, "4 Ways to Fix 'Fake News,'" *Axios*, October 21, 2018.

415 *set no boundaries:* Laura Wagner, "*Axios* to Staff: Our Values Are Cynically Engineered and Incoherent," *Defector*, May 11, 2022.

Chapter 19: Plague of Deceit

419 *loss of trust:* Brian Kennedy, Alec Tyson, and Cary Funk, "Americans' Trust in Scientists, Other Groups Declines," Pew Research Center, February 15, 2022.

420 *more dire:* Robert Costa and Philip Rucker, "Woodward Book: Trump Says He Knew Coronavirus Was 'Deadly' and Worse Than the Flu While Intentionally Misleading Americans," *Washington Post*, September 9, 2020.

420 *conservative activists:* Annie Karni, "Trump Criticized Media for Coverage of Coronavirus," *New York Times*, February 28, 2020.

421 *Americans could die:* William Booth, "A Chilling Scientific Paper

Helped Upend U.S. and U.K. Coronavirus Strategies," *Washington Post*, March 17, 2020.

421 *withering assessment:* Philip Rucker and Ashley Parker, "Seven Days as a 'Wartime President': Trump's Up-and-Down Command of a Pandemic," *Washington Post*, March 20, 2020.

421 *Trump dismissed:* Philip Bump, "Trump Describes Medical Researchers as Enemies Because He Doesn't Like Their Results," *Washington Post*, May 19, 2020.

422 *star of his own show:* Michael Kruse, "Trump Turns a Crisis into His New Nightly TV Show," *Politico*, March 25, 2020.

423 *confirm that Jeff Bezos:* "Trump Credits 'Very Fair' Media and Jeff Bezos' WH Coordination on Coronavirus," Video, MSNBC, March 16, 2020; https://www.msnbc.com/the-beat-with-ari/watch/trump-credits -very-fair-media-and-jeff-bezos-wh-coordination-on-coronavirus -80730181712.

428 *blocking ads:* Craig Silverman, "Coronavirus Ad Blocking Is Starving Some News Sites of Revenue," *BuzzFeed News*, March 26, 2020.

428 *scaling back:* Times staff writer, "*Tampa Bay Times* Adopts Temporary Sunday, Wednesday Print Schedule Due to Coronavirus," *Tampa Bay Times*, March 30, 2020.

428 *ad revenue:* Newspapers Fact Sheet, Pew Research Center, June 29, 2021.

428 *local newsrooms:* Kristen Hare, "More Than 100 Local Newsrooms Closed During the Coronavirus Pandemic," Poynter, December 2, 2021.

429 *published a retrospective:* Yasmeen Abutaleb, Josh Dawsey, Ellen Nakashima, and Greg Miller, "The U.S. Was Beset by Denial and Dysfunction as the Coronavirus Raged," *Washington Post*, April 4, 2020.

430 *CDC's failure:* David Willman, "Contamination at CDC Lab Delayed Rollout of Coronavirus Tests," *Washington Post*, April 18, 2020.

431 *excoriated him:* "President Trump with Coronavirus Task Force Briefing," Video, C-Span, April 23, 2020.

431 *followed an analysis:* Philip Bump and Ashley Parker, "13 Hours of Trump: The President Fills Briefings with Attacks and Boasts, but Little Empathy," *Washington Post*, April 26, 2020.

432 *urging of aides:* Jordyn Phelps, "Poll Numbers Dropping amid the Pandemic, Trump Returns to the Briefing Room Podium," ABC News, July 21, 2020.

432 *Americans disapproved:* Dan Balz and Scott Clement, "Biden Leads by Double Digits as Coronavirus Takes Toll on the President, Post-ABC Poll Finds," *Washington Post*, July 19, 2020.

433 *Daily COVID-related deaths that May:* The Covid Tracking Project at *The Atlantic*; https://covidtracking.com/data/national/deaths.

434 *less menacing:* Philip Bump, "Trump Actually Doesn't Appear to Understand How Bad the Pandemic Is," *Washington Post*, August 4, 2020.

434 *percent of population:* "Coronavirus Tracked: See How Your Country Compares," Updated December 23, 2022, *Financial Times*; https://ig.ft.com/coronavirus-chart/?areas=eur&areas=usa&areas=jpn&areas=grc&areas=nzl&areas=e92000001&areasRegional=usny&areasRegional=usnm&areasRegional=uspr&areasRegional=usaz&areasRegional=usfl&areasRegional=usnd&cumulative=0&logScale=0&per100K=1&startDate=2020-01-01&values=deaths.

434 *their 2021 book:* Yasmeen Abutaleb and Damian Paletta, *Nightmare Scenario: Inside the Trump Administration's Response to the Pandemic That Changed History* (New York: Harper, 2021), 350.

434 *gravely ill:* Noah Weiland, Maggie Haberman, Mark Mazzetti, and Annie Karni, "Trump Was Sicker Than Acknowledged with Covid-19," *New York Times*, February 11, 2021.

Chapter 20: The Plot Against Democracy

436 *lies and deceptions:* Glenn Kessler, Salvador Rizzo, and Meg Kelly, "Trump's False or Misleading Claims Total 30,573 over 4 Years," *Washington Post*, January 24, 2021.

436 *Lozada argued:* Carlos Lozada, *What Were We Thinking: A Brief Intellectual History of the Trump Era* (New York: Simon & Schuster, 2020), 100.

438 *media columnist:* Jack Shafer, "Opinion: Stop Blaming the Press for Trump's Success," *Politico*, October 28, 2022.

438 *never achieved:* "How Popular Is Donald Trump?," Graphic, *FiveThirtyEight*, January 20, 2021; https://projects.fivethirtyeight.com/trump-approval-ratings/.

438 *miserable range:* Megan Brenan, "Americans' Views of Trump's Character Firmly Established," Gallup, June 18, 2020.

440 *called the election:* Adam Kelsey, "Donald Trump's 2012 Election Tweetstorm Resurfaces as Popular and Electoral Vote Appear Divided," ABC News, November 9, 2016.

440 *four years earlier:* Kelsey, "Donald Trump's 2012 Election Tweetstorm Resurfaces as Popular and Electoral Vote Appear Divided."

440 *never any evidence:* Ella Nilsen, "Trump Claims 'Serious Voter Fraud' in New Hampshire," *PolitiFact*, November 28, 2016.

440 *made claims:* Sean Gorman, "Trump's Pants on Fire for Claiming 'Serious Voter Fraud' in Virginia," *PolitiFact*, November 29, 2016.

440 *without substantiating:* John Wagner, "Trump Abolishes Controversial Commission Studying Alleged Voter Fraud," *Washington Post*, January 4, 2018.

441 *eligible to cast:* Kate Rabinowitz and Brittany Renee Mayes, "At Least 84% of American Voters Can Cast Ballots by Mail in the Fall," *Washington Post*, September 25, 2020.

442 *wrote presciently:* Dan Balz, "Facing Possible Defeat, Trump Threatens the Integrity of the Election," *Washington Post*, September 26, 2020.

442 *sparked excitement:* Sheera Frenkel and Annie Karni, "Proud Boys Celebrate Trump's 'Stand By' Remark About Them at the Debate," *New York Times*, September 29, 2020.

443 *leader of the militant:* Laura Thompson, "Trump's Tweet About Civil War Was Just What the Far Right Oath Keepers Wanted to Hear," *Mother Jones*, October 1, 2019.

443 *breaking point:* Alexander Marlow, Matthew Boyle, Amanda House, and Charlie Spiering, "Exclusive—President Donald Trump: Paul Ryan Blocked Subpoenas of Democrats," *Breitbart*, March 13, 2019.

443 *sounding the alarm:* Marc Fisher, "With Election Day Looming, an Anxious Nation Hears Rumblings of Violence," *Washington Post*, October 31, 2020.

443 *told confidants:* Jonathan Swan, "Scoop: Trump's Plan to Declare Premature Victory," *Axios*, November 1, 2020.

444 *more blistering:* Dan Balz, "Trump Has Attacked Democracy's Institutions, but Never So Blatantly as He Did Overnight," *Washington Post*, November 4, 2020.

446 *mere 537 votes:* Michael Levy, "United States Presidential Election of 2000," *Britannica*, last updated December 15, 2022.

447 *accounting firm:* "Media Recount: Bush Won the 2000 Election," PBS, April 3, 2001.

447 *just how flimsy:* David A. Fahrenthold, Rosalind S. Helderman, and Tom Hamburger, "In Poll Watcher Affidavits, Trump Campaign Offers No Evidence of Fraud in Detroit Ballot-Counting," *Washington Post*, November 11, 2020.

447 *dug aggressively:* Amy Gardner, "Ga. Secretary of State Says Fellow Republicans Are Pressuring Him to Find Ways to Exclude Ballots," *Washington Post*, November 16, 2020.

448 *explosive stories:* Amy Gardner, "'I Just Want to Find 11,780 Votes': In Extraordinary Hour-Long Call, Trump Pressures Georgia Secretary of State to Recalculate the Vote in His Favor," *Washington Post*, January 3, 2021.

448 *correspondents found:* Philip Rucker, Ashley Parker, Josh Dawsey, and

Amy Gardner, "20 Days of Fantasy and Failure: Inside Trump's Quest to Overturn the Election," *Washington Post*, November 28, 2020.

448 *repudiated the president's:* "'The Last Wall': How Dozens of Judges Across the Political Spectrum Rejected Trump's Efforts to Overturn the Election," *Washington Post*, December 12, 2020.

449 *voters believed:* Fox News poll, December 6–9, 2020; https://static .foxnews.com/foxnews.com/content/uploads/2020/12/Fox_December -6-9-2020_National_Topline_December-11-Release.pdf.

449 *barely budged:* Jon Greenberg, "Most Republicans Still Falsely Believe Trump's Stolen Election Claims. Here Are Some Reasons Why," Poynter, June 16, 2022.

449 *rejected the legitimacy:* Amy Gardner, "A Majority of GOP Nominees Deny or Question the 2020 Election Results," *Washington Post*, October 12, 2020.

450 *her defense:* Jane C. Timm, "Sidney Powell's Legal Defense: 'Reasonable People' Wouldn't Believe Her Election Fraud Claims," NBC News, March 23, 2021.

450 *right-wing commentator:* Michael S. Schmidt, "Four Takeaways from the Latest Hearing of the Jan. 6 Committee," *New York Times*, June 12, 2022.

452 *tackled a cameraman:* Press release, "Illinois Man Arrested for Assault on Law Enforcement, and First to Be Arrested for Assault on Members of the News Media During Jan. 6 Capitol Breach," United States Attorney's Office, District of Columbia, June 24, 2021; https://www .justice.gov/usao-dc/pr/illinois-man-arrested-assault-law enforcement -and-first-be-arrested-assault-members-news.

452 *stomping on equipment:* United States of America v. Chase Kevin Allen, United States District Court, District of Columbia, filed June 21, 2021; https://www.justice.gov/usao-dc/case-multi defendant/file /1408341/download.

452 *boasted to a friend:* Devlin Barrett, "FBI Launches Flurry of Arrests over Attacks on Journalists During Capitol Riot," *Washington Post*, July 3, 2021.

452 *focus of harassment:* "January: Journalists Harassed, Threatened While Reporting from DC Riot and Across the Country," U.S. Press Freedom Tracker, January 6, 2021; https://pressfreedomtracker.us/all -incidents/national-and-international-journalists-harassed-threatened -while-covering-riot-dc/.

452 *yelled one rioter:* United States of America v Sandra S. Weyer, a/k/a Sandra Suzanne Pomeroy, a/k/a Sandy Pomeroy Weyer, United States District Court, District of Columbia, filed June 24, 2021; https://www .justice.gov/usao-dc/case-multi-defendant/file/1407556/download.

452 *someone screamed:* Brittany Shammas, "Journalists Were Attacked, Threatened and Detained During Capitol Siege," *Washington Post*, January 9, 2021.

452 *threatened to shoot:* Katherine Jacobsen and Lucy Westcott, "'Three People Threatened to Shoot Me.' Journalists Describe Covering Mob Violence at the US Capitol," Committee to Protect Journalists, January 7, 2021.

452 *about ten rioters:* Angela Fu, "Reporters Covering the Capitol Attack Were Used to Harassment and Heckling. But Wednesday Was Different," Poynter, January 13, 2021.

455 *used the word "fight":* "Final Report, Select Committee to Investigate the January 6th Attack on the United States Capitol," 117th Congress, Second Session, House Report 117–663, December 22, 2022, 540.

456 *on live TV:* Ashley Parker, Josh Dawsey, and Philip Rucker, "Six Hours of Paralysis: Inside Trump's Failure to Act After a Mob Stormed the Capitol," *Washington Post*, January 11, 2021.

457 *famously told:* Bob Woodward and Robert Costa, "Transcript: Donald Trump Interview with Bob Woodward and Robert Costa," *Washington Post*, April 2, 2016.

459 *not legitimately elected:* Dan Balz, Scott Clement, and Emily Guskin, "Biden Wins Wide Approval for Handling of Transition, but Persistent GOP Skepticism on Issues Will Cloud the Opening of His Presidency, *Post*-ABC Poll Finds," *Washington Post*, January 17, 2021.

459 *election's legitimacy:* Ben Kamisar, "Two-Thirds of Republicans Still Don't Believe Biden Was Elected Legitimately," NBC News, October 25, 2022.

459 *eight of ten Americans:* David W. Moore, "Eight in Ten Americans to Accept Bush as 'Legitimate' President," Gallup, December 14, 2000.

Epilogue

461 *label my statement:* Dan Froomkin/PressWatchers.org (@froomkin), "OMG WaPo Actually Mounted This Atrocity on the Wall Near the National Desk, via @abeaujon . . . Hey WaPo'ers: You ARE at war, against liars and fabulists. And you're losing because you're not fighting hard enough for the truth," Twitter, August 25, 2021, 12:53 p.m.

463 *argued that objectivity:* Leonard Downie Jr. and Andrew Heyward, "Beyond Objectivity," Walter Cronkite School of Journalism and Mass Communication, Arizona State University, January 26, 2023; https://cronkitenewslab.com/wp-content/uploads/2023/01/Beyond-Objectivity-Report-2.pdf.

464 *deepening suspicions:* "Propaganda and the American Public," United

States Holocaust Memorial Museum; https://perspectives.ushmm.org /collection/propaganda-and-the-american-public.

466 *stepped into the office:* Benjamin Mullin, "How *The San Francisco Chronicle* Rebuilt Its Investigative Team," Poynter, December 5, 2016.

467 *left incomplete:* Lizzie Johnson, "An Alleged $500 Million Ponzi Scheme Preyed on Mormons, It Ended with FBI Gunfire," *Washington Post*, February 1, 2023.

468 *aptly put it:* "Dean Baquet to Lead Local Investigative Reporting Fellowship," *New York Times*, April 26, 2022.

469 *Subscriptions had fallen:* Sarah Ellison and Elahe Izadi, "*Washington Post* Lays Off 20 Newsroom Employees," *Washington Post*, January 24, 2023.

469 *report in* Axios: Mike Allen and Sara Fischer: "Exclusive: Bloomberg Eyes WSJ-Parent Dow Jones, *WaPo*," *Axios*, December 23, 2022.

470 *digital-only subscribers:* Ken Doctor, "The Newsonomics of *The New York Times'* Paywalls 2.0," Nieman Lab, November 21, 2013.

470 *competitive gap:* Claire Atkinson, "*The Washington Post* Still Plays Catch-Up, but Is Gaining on *The Times*," NBC News, December 28, 2017.

471 *then-CEO Mark Thompson said:* Sydney Ember, "New York Times Company Buys The Wirecutter," *New York Times*, October 24, 2016.

472 *devoting more "time and energy":* Email from Jeff Bezos to employees, Amazon, February 2, 2021; https://www.aboutamazon.com/news /company-news/email-from-jeff-bezos-to-employees.

473 *implicitly threatened:* Erik Wemple, "*Washington Examiner* Under Fire for Slam on *NYT* Reporter," *Washington Post*, March 4, 2022.

474 *accused Charlie:* Conn Carroll, "Charlie Savage Is the Reason No One Trusts Journalists," *Washington Examiner*, February 15, 2022.

475 *fine imposed:* Philip Bump, "A Judge Rebukes—and Punishes— Trump's False Russia Narrative," *Washington Post*, January 20, 2023.

475 *explaining the sanctions:* Donald J. Trump v. Hillary R. Clinton, et al., United States District Court, Southern District of Florida, Order on Sanctions, Donald M. Middlebrooks, January 19, 2023.

477 *defamation campaigns:* Dánae Vílchez, "'To persecute any critical voice': Jailed Guatemalan journalist Zamora's son on his father's arrest," Committee to Protect Journalists, October 12, 2022.

477 *Dada reflected:* "El Salvador: Speech of World Press Freedom Hero Carlos Dada at IPI WoCo," International Press Institute, September 16, 2022.

INDEX

ABOUT THE AUTHOR

Martin Baron is a longtime journalist and newspaper editor. He ran the newsrooms of *The Miami Herald* and *The Boston Globe* before being named executive editor of *The Washington Post* in 2013. His role in launching an investigation of the Catholic Church's cover-up of sexual abuse by clergy was portrayed in the Academy Award–winning movie *Spotlight*. Baron retired from daily journalism in early 2021 and now splits his time between western Massachusetts and New York City. *Collision of Power* is his first book.